ONE-ACT PLAYS
BY MODERN AUTHORS

EDITED BY
HELEN LOUISE COHEN
Author of "The Ballade"

WILDSIDE PRESS: MMIII

COPYRIGHT, 1921, BY
HARCOURT, BRACE AND COMPANY, INC.

Published by:

Wildside Press
P.O. Box 301
Holicong, PA 18928-0301
www.wildsidepress.com

To
M. S. S.

ACKNOWLEDGMENTS

Had not both authors and publishers acted with the greatest generosity, this collection could not have been made. Though the editor cannot adequately express her sense of obligation, she wishes at least to record explicitly her indebtedness to Mr. Harold Brighouse, Lord Dunsany, Mr. John Galsworthy, Lady Gregory, Mr. Percy MacKaye, Miss Jeannette Marks, Miss Josephine Preston Peabody, Professor Robert Emmons Rogers, Mr. Booth Tarkington, and Professor Stark Young. The editor also desires to thank Chatto & Windus, Duffield & Company, Gowans & Gray, Ltd., Harper & Brothers, Little, Brown & Company, John W. Luce & Company, G. P. Putnam's Sons, Charles Scribner's Sons, and The Sunwise Turn, for permissions granted ungrudgingly.

Through the courtesy of Mr. T. M. Cleland, director of the Beechwood Players, the pictures of the Beechwood Theatre appear. Miss Mary W. Carter, chairman of the Department of English in the High School in Montclair, New Jersey, contributed the photographs of the Garden Theatre. Other illustrations appear through the kindness of *Theatre Arts Magazine,* and of The Neighborhood Playhouse.

The editor is grateful to Mrs. John W. Alexander, Mr. B. Iden Payne, and Mrs. T. Bernstein for the privilege of personal conferences on the subject of the book. To Mr. Robert Edmond Jones, who has allowed three of his designs to be reproduced and who has read and corrected that part of the Introduction that deals with The New Art of the Theatre, the editor takes this opportunity of expressing her warm appreciation. Finally, the editor wishes to thank her friend, Helen Hopkins Crandell for her indefatigable work on the proofs of this book.

CONTENTS

	PAGE
INTRODUCTION	
The Workmanship of the One-Act Play	xiii
Theatres of To-day	
The Commercial Theatre and the Repertory Idea	xx
The Little Theatre	xxiii
The Irish National Theatre	xxvi
The New Art of the Theatre	xxix
Playmaking	xxxiv
The Theatre in the School	1
ROBERT EMMONS ROGERS	
THE BOY WILL	xxxviii
BOOTH TARKINGTON	
Introduction	3
BEAUTY AND THE JACOBIN	5
ERNEST DOWSON	
Introduction	53
THE PIERROT OF THE MINUTE	55
OLIPHANT DOWN	
Introduction	77
THE MAKER OF DREAMS	79
PERCY MACKAYE	
Introduction	97
GETTYSBURG	99
A. A. MILNE	
Introduction	113
WURZEL-FLUMMERY	115
HAROLD BRIGHOUSE	
Introduction	139
MAID OF FRANCE	141
LADY GREGORY	
Introduction	157
SPREADING THE NEWS	159
JEANNETTE MARKS	
Introduction	179
WELSH HONEYMOON	181

CONTENTS

	PAGE
JOHN MILLINGTON SYNGE	
Introduction	195
RIDERS TO THE SEA	198
LORD DUNSANY	
Introduction	211
A NIGHT AT AN INN	213
STARK YOUNG	
Introduction	226
THE TWILIGHT SAINT	227
LADY ALIX EGERTON	
Introduction	241
THE MASQUE OF THE TWO STRANGERS	244
MAURICE MAETERLINCK	
Introduction	265
THE INTRUDER	268
JOSEPHINE PRESTON PEABODY	
Introduction	287
FORTUNE AND MEN'S EYES	289
JOHN GALSWORTHY	
Introduction	323
THE LITTLE MAN	325

ILLUSTRATIONS

	PAGE
Twelfth Night on the stage of the Théâtre du Vieux Colombier in New York	xxiv
Design for *The Merchant of Venice* by Robert Edmond Jones	xxx
Design for *Good Gracious Annabelle* by Robert Edmond Jones	xxxii
Design for *The Seven Princesses* by Robert Edmond Jones	xxxiv
The Beechwood Theatre. Exterior and Interior	lviii
The Garden Theatre. The original site, and the theatre as it looks to-day	lx
Setting for *The Maker of Dreams* at The Neighborhood Playhouse designed by Aline Bernstein	79
Costumes for *The Masque of the Two Strangers* designed at the Washington Irving High School.	
Plate 1	240
Plate 2	253
Setting for *The Intruder* designed by Sam Hume	268

INTRODUCTION
THE WORKMANSHIP OF THE ONE-ACT PLAY

The one-act play is a new form of the drama and more emphatically a new form of literature. Its possibilities began to attract the attention of European and American writers in the last decade of the nineteenth century, those years when so many dramatic traditions lapsed and so many precedents were established. It is significant that the oldest play in the present collection is Maeterlinck's *The Intruder,* published in 1890.

The history of this new form is of necessity brief. Before its vogue became general, one-act plays were being presented in vaudeville houses in this country and were being used as curtain raisers in London theatres for the purpose of marking time until the late-dining audiences should arrive. With the exception of the famous Grand Guignol Theatre in Paris, where the entertainment for an evening might consist of several one-act plays, all of the hair-raising, blood-curdling variety, programs composed entirely of one-act plays were rare. Sir James Matthew Barrie is usually credited with being the first in England to write one-act plays intended to be grouped in a single production. A program of this character has been uncommon in the commercial theatre in America, but three of Barrie's one-act plays, constituting a single program, have met with enthusiastic response from American audiences.

There are two new developments in the history of the theatre that have encouraged and promoted the writing of one-act plays: the one is the Repertory Theatre abroad and the other is the Little Theatre movement on both sides of the Atlantic. The repertory of the Irish Players, for example, is composed largely of one-act plays, and American Little Theatres are given over almost exclusively to the one-act play.

The one-act play is in reality so new a phenomenon, in spite of the use that has been made of the form by playwrights like Pinero, Hauptmann, Chekov, Shaw, and others of the first rank, that it is still generally ignored in books on dramatic workmanship.[1] None the less, the status of the one-act play is established and a study of the plays of this length, which are rapidly increasing in number, discloses certain tendencies and laws which are exemplified in the form itself. Clayton Hamilton sums up the matter well when he says: "The one-act play is admirable in itself, as a medium of art. It shows the same relation to the full-length play as the short-story shows to the novel. It makes a virtue of economy of means. It aims to produce a single dramatic effect with the greatest economy of means that is consistent with the utmost emphasis. The method of the one-act play at its best is similar to the method employed by Browning in his dramatic monologues. The author must suggest the entire history of a soul by seizing it at some crisis of its career and forcing the spectator to look upon it from an unexpected and suggestive point of view. A one-act play in exhibiting the present should imply the past and intimate the future. The author has no leisure for laborious exposition; but his mere projection of a single situation should sum up in itself the accumulated results of many antecedent causes. . . . The form is complete, concise and self-sustaining; it requires an extraordinary force of imagination."[2]

To follow for a moment a train of thought suggested by Mr. Hamilton's timely and appreciative comment on the technique of the one-act play: All writers on the short-story agree that, to use Poe's phrase, "the vastly important artistic element, totality, or unity of effect" is indispensable to the successful short-story. This singleness of effect is an equally important consideration in the structure of the one-act play. A short-story is not a condensed novel any more than a one-act play is a condensed full-length play. There is no fixed length for the one-act play any more than there is for the short-story. The one-act play must have its "dominant incident" and "dominant character" like the short-story. The effect of the one-act play, as of the short-story, is measured by the way it makes its readers and spectators feel. Neither the short-story

[1] See, however, Clayton Hamilton, *Studies in Stagecraft*, New York, 1914, and B. Roland Lewis, *The Technique of the One-Act Play*, Boston, 1918.

[2] Clayton Hamilton, *Studies in Stagecraft*, New York, 1914, pp. 254-255.

nor the one-act play need necessarily "be founded on one of the passionate *cruces* of life, where duty and inclination come nobly to the grapple." One has but to consider the short-stories of Henry James or the one-act plays of Galsworthy or of Maeterlinck to be convinced that a *violent* struggle is not necessary to the art of either form.

This point is further illustrated in what Galsworthy himself says in general about drama in his famous essay, *Some Platitudes Concerning the Drama,* which should be read in connection with his satirical comedy, *The Little Man.* In that essay Galsworthy writes: "The plot! A good plot is that sure edifice which slowly rises out of the interplay of circumstance on temperament, and temperament on circumstance, within the enclosing atmosphere of an idea. A human being is the best plot there is. . . . Now true dramatic action is what characters do, at once contrary, as it were, to expectation, and yet because they have already done other things. . . . Good dialogue again is character, marshaled so as continually to stimulate interest or excitement." This commentary of Galsworthy's on dramatic technique offers to the student of *The Little Man* an unusual opportunity to verify a great critic's theory by a great playwright's practice. It is indeed the *character* of the Little Man that is the plot in this case; the plot may be said to begin when, according to stage direction, the hapless Baby wails, and to be well launched with the Little Man's deprecatory, "Herr Ober! Might I have a glass of beer?" These words distinguish him immediately from his bullying companions in the buffet. The highest point of interest, like the beginning of the plot, is to be found in the play of the Little Man's personality, at the point where he is left alone with the Baby, now a typhus suspect, and after an instant's wavering, bends all his puny energies to pacifying its uneasy cry. Again, the end of the plot comes with the tribute of the bewildered but adoring mother to the ineffably gentle Little Man.

But a one-act play that has any pretensions to literature must be looked upon as a law unto itself and should not be expected to conform to any set of arbitrary requirements. As a matter of fact, there are only a very few generalizations that can be made with regard to the structure or to the classification of the one-act play. Even this book contains plays that are not susceptible of any hard and fast classification. *The Intruder* and *Riders to the Sea* are indubitably tragedies, but *Fortune and Men's Eyes,* dealing, as it does, with the tragic theme of love's disillusionment, belongs not at all with the plays of Maeterlinck and Synge, shadowed, as they are, by death. And though the deaths are many and bloody in *A Night at an Inn,* the unreality of the romance is so strong that there is no such wrenching of the human sympathies as we associate with tragedy. *The Pierrot of the Minute* is superficially a Harlequinade, but Dowson's insistence on the theme of satiety brings it narrowly within the range of satire. *Beauty and the Jacobin* is rich in comedy; so is Lady Gregory's *Spreading the News,* and in both, the situations change imperceptibly from comedy to farce and from farce back to comedy.

The laws of the structure of the one-act play are in the nature of dramatic art no less flexible. It can be said that in order to secure that singleness of impression that is as essential to the one-act play as to the short-story, a single well sustained theme is necessary, a theme announced in some fashion early in the play. Indeed since the one-act play is a short dramatic form, it may be said in regard to the announcing of the theme that, " 'Twere well it were done quickly." In *Spreading the News,* the curtain is barely up before Mrs. Tarpey is telling the magistrate: " Business, is it? What business would the people here have but to be minding one another's business?" And at approximately the same moment in the action of *The Intruder,* the uncle, foreshadowing the theme of the mysterious coming of death, says: "When once illness has come into a house, it is as though a stranger had forced himself into the family circle."

The single dominant theme for its dramatic expression calls also for a single situation developing to a single climax. In the case of *Fortune and Men's Eyes,* it is the ballad-monger, who in crying his wares,

"Plays, Play not Fair,
Or how a *gentlewoman's* heart was took
By a player, that was King in a stage-play,"

gives us in the first few minutes of the play his ironical clue to the theme. And this theme is worked out in Mary Fytton's shallow intrigue with William Herbert, which culminates in the shattering of the Player's dream on that autumn day in South London at "The Bear and the Angel."

The single situation exemplifying the theme of *The Intruder* is found in the repeatedly expressed premonitions of the blind Grandfather, stationary in his armchair, whose heightened senses detect the presence of the Mysterious Stranger. The unity of effect secured in this play is only rivaled, not surpassed, by the wonderful totality of impression experienced by the reader of *The Fall of the House of Usher*. The unity of effect in *The Intruder* is secured also by Maeterlinck's description of the setting, which reminds the playgoer or the reader inevitably of Stevenson's familiar words: "Certain dark gardens cry aloud for murder; certain old houses demand to be haunted."

/ In general, as has been said, the plot of the one-act play, because of the time limitations, admits of no distracting incidents. For the same reason the characterization must be swift and direct. By Bartley Fallon's first speech in *Spreading the News*, Lady Gregory characterizes him completely. He needs but say: "Indeed it's a poor country and a scarce country to be living in. But I'm thinking if I went to America it's long ago the day I'd be dead," and the fundamental part of his character is fixed in the minds of the audience. From that moment it is just a question of filling in the picture with pantomime and further dialogue.

The characterization of the Player in *Fortune and Men's Eyes* begins at the moment that he enters the tavern, when Wat, the bear-ward, calls out:

> "I say, I've played. . . . There's not one man
> Of all the gang—save one. . . . Ay, there be one
> I grant you, now! . . . He used me in right sort;
> A man worth better trades."

Wat's verdict on the fair-mindedness of Master William Shakespeare of the Lord Chamberlain's company is borne out by the Player's own,

> "High fortune, man!
> Commend me to thy bear."
> [*Drinks and passes him the cup.*]

xviii   INTRODUCTION

The entrance of the ballad-monger gives Master Will an opening for a punning jest and, the action continuing, shows him sympathetic to the strayed lady-in-waiting, tender to the tavern boy, magnanimous to the false friend and falser love.

One method of characterization which the author allows herself to use in this play, no doubt to heighten the Elizabethan illusion, is rare in the contemporary drama: when this " dark lady of the sonnets " flees " The Bear and the Angel," the Player breaks forth into the self-revealing soliloquy, found so frequently in his own plays, and continuing as a dramatic convention until the last quarter of the nineteenth century.[1]

Characterization rests in part on pantomime. In *The Little Man,* the Dutch Youth is dumb throughout the play, but he is sufficiently characterized by his foolish demeanor and his recurrent laugh. The part of the Little Man himself is one long gesture of humility and dedication. In those one-act plays in which the old characters of the Harlequinade reappear, like *The Maker of Dreams* and *The Pierrot of the Minute,* pantomime transcends dialogue as a method of characterization. In the plays of the Irish dramatists, Synge, Yeats, and Lady Gregory, pantomime and dialogue contribute equally to the characterization, which is of a very high order, since all these dramatists were close observers of the Irish peasant characters of their plays.

Synge, especially, illustrates the following critical theory of Galsworthy: " The art of writing true dramatic dialogue is an austere art, denying itself all license, grudging every sentence devoted to the mere machinery of the play, suppressing all jokes and epigrams severed from character, relying for fun and pathos on the fun and tears of life. From start to finish good dialogue is hand-made, like good lace; clear, of fine texture, furthering with each thread the harmony and strength of a design to which all must be subordinated." A study of the dialogue of *Riders to the Sea* reveals just this harmony

[1] The Elizabethan platform stage survived until then in the shape of the long " apron," projecting in front of the proscenium. The characters were constantly stepping out of the frame of the picture; and while this visual convention maintained itself, there was nothing inconsistent or jarring in the auditory convention of the soliloquy. See William Archer, *Play-Making,* Boston, 1912, pp. 397-405.

between the dialogue and the inevitability of the plot, the dialogue and the simplicity of the characters.

The dialogue in *The Little Man* is the very idiom one would expect to issue from the mouth of the German colonel, the Englishman with the Oxford voice, or the intensely national American, as the case may be. The characters, though they have type names, are, as Mr. Galsworthy would probably be the first to explain, highly individualized. The author does not intend us to think that all Americans are like this loud-voiced traveler, or all Englishmen like the pharisaical gentleman who gives his wife the advertisements to read while he secures the news sheet for himself.

The function of dialogue is the same both in the long and in the short play. For, of course, both forms have many things in common. For instance, as in the full-length play it is necessary for the dramatist to carry forward the interest from act to act, to provide a " curtain " that will leave the audience in a state of suspense, so in the one-act play, the interest must be similarly relayed though the plot is confined to a single act. In *The Intruder*, every premonition expressed by the Grandfather grips the audience in such a way that they await from minute to minute the coming of the mysterious stranger. The tension is high in *A Night at an Inn* from the moment the curtain rises. In *Riders to the Sea*, the beginning of the suspense coincides with the opening of the play and lasts. " They're all gone now, and there isn't anything more the sea can do to me," says Maurya, and the audience experiences a rush of relief and a sense of release that the last words, " No man at all can be living for ever, and we must be satisfied," seem only to deepen.

A one-act play, then, has many structural features in common with the short-story; its plot must from beginning to end be dominated by a single theme; its crises may be crises of character as well as conflicts of will or physical conflicts; it must by a method of foreshadowing sustain the interest of the audience unflaggingly, but ultimately relieve their tension; it must achieve swift characterization by means of pantomime and dialogue; and its dialogue must achieve its effects by the same methods as the dialogue of longer plays, but by even greater economy of means. But when all is said and done, the success of a one-act play is judged not by its conformity to any set of hard and fast rules, but by its power to interest, enlighten, and hold an audience.

THEATRES OF TO-DAY

THE COMMERCIAL THEATRE AND THE REPERTORY IDEA

The term "Commercial Theatre" is rarely used without disparagement. The critic or the playwright who speaks of the Commercial Theatre usually does so either for the purpose of reflecting on the cheapness of the entertainment afforded, or in order to call attention to spectacular receipts.

In this country the Commercial Theatre stands for that form of big business in the theatrical world that produces dividends on the money invested comparable to those earned by the most prosperous of the large industries. This system has been, on the whole, a bad thing for the drama, because managers with their eye on attractions that should yield a return, let us say, of over ten per cent on the investment, have been unable to produce the superior play with an appeal to a definite, though perhaps limited audience, and have had to offer to the public the kind of play that would draw large audiences over a long period of time. The "longest run for the safest possible play" is thus conspicuously associated with the Commercial Theatre. As Clayton Hamilton says: "The trouble with the prevailing theatre system in America to-day is not that this system is commercial; for in any democratic country, it is not unreasonable to expect the public to defray the cost of the sort of drama that it wishes, and that, therefore, it deserves. The trouble is, rather, that our theatre system is devoted almost entirely to big business; and that in ignoring the small profits of small business it tends to exclude not only the uncommercial drama, but the non-commercial drama as well."[1] Here he makes a distinction between an "uncommercial" play, that is, a play that is a failure with all kinds of audiences, and the "non-commercial" play, which is capable of holding its own financially and yielding modest returns.

In the days before the pooling of theatrical interests in this

[1] Clayton Hamilton, *The Non-Commercial Drama. The Bookman*, May, 1915.

country there were indeed long runs, but in many of the large American cities "stock companies," composed of groups of actors and actresses all of about the same reputation and ability, were maintained that kept a number of plays, a "repertory," before the public in the course of a season and gave scope for experiment with various kinds of plays. But the "star system," which has now become common, has tended to drive out the "stock company" idea, with the result that the average company rests on the reputation of the "star" and dispenses with distinction in the "support." With the decay of the stock company, the repertory system, in the form in which it did once exist here in the Commercial Theatre, has also declined.

Both in Great Britain and in America the repertory system, long established on the Continent, has been reintroduced in order to combat the practices of the Commercial Theatre. For the most part the new repertory theatres have been endowed either by the State or by private individuals. "Absolute endowment for absolute freedom,"[1] has seemed to at least one American the only means of delivering the drama from commercial bondage. This phrase of Percy MacKaye's expresses his cherished belief that endowed civic theatres, which should encourage the participation of whole communities in a community form of drama, are what is needed in a democracy. John Masefield, in the following lines from the prologue written for the opening of the Liverpool Repertory Theatre, has found a poetic theme in this idea of an endowed theatre:

> "Men will not spend, it seems, on that one art
> Which is life's inmost soul and passionate heart;
> They count the theatre a place for fun,
> Where man can laugh at nights when work is done.
>
> If it were only that, 'twould be worth while
> To subsidize a thing which makes men smile;
> But it is more; it is that splendid thing,
> A place where man's soul shakes triumphant wing;
>
> A place of art made living, where men may see
> What human life is and has seemed to be
> To the world's greatest brains. . . .

[1] Percy MacKaye, *The Playhouse and the Play,* New York, 1909, p. 86.

INTRODUCTION

> O you who hark
> Fan to a flame through England this first spark,
> Till in this land there's none so poor of purse
> But he may see high deeds and hear high verse,
> And feel his folly lashed, and think him great
> In this world's tragedy of Life and Fate."[1]

In Great Britain repertory is associated with the interest and generosity of Miss A. E. F. Horniman, who will be mentioned in connection with the Irish National Theatre, and through whom, after some preliminary experiment, the Gaiety Theatre at Manchester was opened as the first repertory house in England, in the spring of 1908. Fifty-five different plays were produced in a little over two years—" twenty-eight new, seventeen revivals of modern English plays, five modern translations, and five classics."[2] In Miss Horniman's own words, her interest was in a Civilized Theatre. "A Civilized Theatre," she has written, "means that a city has something of cultivation in it, something to make literature grow; a real theatre, not a mere amusing toy. What we want is the opportunity for our men and women, our boys and girls to get a chance to see the works of the greatest dramatists of modern times, as well as the classics, for their pleasure as well as their cultivation. . . . Young dramatists should have a theatre where they can see the ripe works of the masters and see them well acted at a moderate price. There should be in every city a theatre where we can see the best drama worthily treated."[3] Owing to war conditions, the Manchester project has had to be abandoned, and so, for the most part, have other similar enterprises. They rarely became self-supporting, but depended on subsidy of one kind or another, which under new economic conditions is no longer forthcoming. The Birmingham Repertory Theatre continues, however, under the direction of John Drinkwater, and has become famous through its production of his *Abraham Lincoln.* " John Drinkwater, I see, has recently defined a Repertory Theatre," writes William Archer, in his latest article on the subject, " as one which ' puts plays into

---
[1] Quoted by Percy MacKaye in *The Civic Theatre*, New York, 1912, p. 114.
[2] P. P. Howe, *The Repertory Theatre*, New York, 1911, p. 59.
[3] A. E. F. Horniman, *The Manchester Players*, Poet Lore, Vol. XXV, No. 3, p. 212; p. 213.

stock which are good enough to stay there.' Enlarging this definition, I should call it a theatre which excluded the long unbroken run; which presents at least three different programs in each week (though a popular success may be performed three or even four times a week throughout a whole season); which can produce plays too good to be enormously popular; which makes a principle of keeping alive the great drama of the past, whether recent or remote; which has a company so large that it can, without overworking its actors, keep three or four plays ready for instant presentation; which possesses an ample stage equipped with the latest artistic and labor-saving appliances; and which offers such comfort in front of the house as to encourage an intelligent public to make it an habitual place of resort.

" That there exists in every great American city an intelligent public large enough to support one or more such playhouses is to my mind indisputable. But the theatre might have to be run at a loss for two or three opening seasons, until it had attracted and educated its habitual supporters. For even a public of high general intelligence needs a certain amount of special education in things of the theatre." This testimony is in a highly optimistic vein.

A talk with B. Iden Payne, once director of the Manchester Players, reveals the fact that in England at the present time the repertory idea is being taken over with more promise of success by the small groups that represent the Little Theatre movement in that country. The repertory theatre there did succeed in arousing in the locality in which, for the time being, it existed an interest in intelligent plays, but it was not equally successful in confirming a distaste for unintelligent plays. The study of these experiments will repay Americans who are interested in seeing the repertory idea fostered over here by endowment or otherwise.

THE LITTLE THEATRE

The year 1911 saw the beginning in the United States of the Little Theatre movement, which has grown with phenomenal rapidity and has spread in all directions. The first Little Theatres in this country were located in large cities; but in the course of time the idea has penetrated to small towns

INTRODUCTION

and rural communities all over the United States. Barns, wharves, saloons, and school assembly halls have been transformed into intimate little playhouses. There were European precedents for this idea. The Théâtre Libre, opened in Paris in 1887 by André Antoine as a protest against the kind of play then in favor, is generally called the first of this type. In the years from 1887 to 1911 Little Theatres were opened in Russia, in Belgium, in Germany, in Sweden, in Hungary, in England, in Ireland, and in France. In Europe these theatres came into being, generally speaking, in order to give freer play to the new arts of the theatre or for the purpose of encouraging a more intellectual type of drama than was being produced in the larger houses.

There are two conceptions of the Little Theatre current in the United States. According to one, it is a theatrical organization housed in a simple building, that makes its productions in the most economical way, does not pay its actors, does not charge admission, and uses scenery and properties that are cheaply manufactured at home.

The Little Theatre is, however, more commonly conceived of as a repertory theatre supported by the subscription system, producing its plays on a small stage in a small hall, selecting for production the kind of play not likely to be used by the Commercial Theatre, most frequently the one-act play, and committed to experiments in stage decoration, lighting, and the other stage arts. The Little Theatre and the one-act play have developed each other reciprocally, for the Little Theatre has encouraged the writing of one-act plays in Europe and in this country. The one-act play is the natural unit of production in the Little Theatre, both because it requires a less sustained performance from the actors, who have frequently been amateurs, and because it has offered in the same evening several opportunities to the various groups of artists collaborating in the productions of the Little Theatre. Though the movement has had the effect of stimulating community spirit and has been the means of solving grave community problems, the Little Theatre is not, in the technical sense, a community theatre; in the sense, that is, in which Percy MacKaye uses the word. It is not, in fact, so portentous an enterprise, because it does not enlist the participation of every member of a community. The community theatre is an example of civic co-

Twelfth Night on the stage of the Théâtre du Vieux Colombier, New York.

operation on a large scale; the Little Theatre, of the same kind of co-operation on a small scale.

Notably artistic results have been achieved by such Little Theatres as The Neighborhood Playhouse in New York, built in 1914 by the Misses Irene and Alice Lewisohn, in connection with the social settlement idea, to provide expression for the talents of a community that had been previously trained in dramatic classes for some years; by the Chicago Little Theatre, founded in 1911, now no longer in existence, but for a few years under the direction of Maurice Browne, a disciple of Gordon Craig's; by the Detroit Theatre of Arts and Crafts, once under the direction of Mr. Sam Hume, also a follower of Gordon Craig's; by the Washington Square Players, who during several seasons in New York gave a remarkable impetus to the writing of one-act plays in America; by the Provincetown Players, whose first productions were made on Cape Cod, who later opened a small playhouse in New York, and who gave the public an opportunity to know the plays of Eugene O'Neill; by the Portmanteau Theatre of Stuart Walker, that uses but one setting in its productions, but varies the effect with different colored lights, and as its name implies, is portable, one of the few of its kind in the world; by the 47 Workshop Theatre that has arisen as the result of the course in playwriting given at Harvard University by Professor George Pierce Baker, and the productions of which have served to introduce many new writers; and by the Théâtre du Vieux Colombier, that came to New York from Paris in 1917, and remained for two seasons to illustrate the best French practice. These theatres also enjoy the distinction of having experimented with repertory.

The Théâtre du Vieux Colombier was organized and is directed by Jacques Copeau. It is no casual amateur experiment. Its actors are professionals and its director is a scholar and an artist. In preparation for the original opening the company went into the country and established a little colony. "During five hours of each day they studied repertoire but they did far more. They performed exercises in physical culture and the dance: they read aloud and acted improvised dramatic scenes. They worked thus upon their bodies, their voices and their actions: made them subtle instruments in their command." They learned that in an artistic production every gesture, every word, every line, and every color counted. Naturally no group of amateurs or semi-professionals can approach the results of a company trained as M. Copeau's is. When he was over here, he was much interested in our Little Theatres. He said in one of his addresses: "All the *little theatres* which now swarm in America, ought to come to an understanding among themselves and unite, instead of trying to keep themselves apart and distinctive. The ideas which they possess in common have not even begun to be put into execution. They must be incorporated into life."[1]

The native Little Theatres, much simpler affairs than the Vieux Colombier, persist. They have made a place for themselves in American life, among the farms, in the suburbs, in the small towns, and in the cities. Sometimes, no doubt, they are like the one in Sinclair Lewis's Gopher Prairie; or they hardly outlast a season. But new ones spring up to replace those that have gone out of existence, and meanwhile the ends of wholesome community recreation are being served.

THE IRISH NATIONAL THEATRE

About 1890 began the movement which has since been known as the Celtic Renaissance, a movement that had for its object the lifting into literature of the songs, myths, romances, and legends treasured for countless generations in the hearts

[1] The kind of co-operation to which he looked forward is beginning. For instance, the New York Drama League announces a Little Theatre membership. "Its purpose is to serve the needs of the large and constantly growing public that is interested in the activities of the semi-professional and amateur community groups who read or produce plays. Under this new Membership there will be issued monthly, for ten issues a Play List of five pages, giving a concise but complete synopsis of new plays, both one-act and longer plays. It will show the number of characters required; the kind of audience to which the play would be likely to appeal; the royalty asked for production rights; the production necessities and other information of value to production groups or individuals. One page will be devoted to three or four standard older plays treated with the same detail of information. The Little Theatre Supplement . . . will continue to be issued each month, but will hereafter be a feature of the Little Theatre Membership only. It will contain the programs of the Little Theatres throughout the country; short accounts of what is going on among the various groups, and articles on Little Theatre problems, with hints on new, effective and economical methods of production."

of the Irish peasantry. In the same decade in Great Britain and on the Continent, tendencies were at work looking to the reform of the drama and its rescue from commercial formulas. The genesis of the Irish National Theatre, a pioneer in the field of repertory in Great Britain, and one of the first of the Little Theatres, is due to both of these influences.

Its first form was the Irish Literary Theatre, founded in 1899 by Edward Martyn, the author of *The Heather Field* and *Maeve,* George Moore, and William Butler Yeats. The first play produced by this organization was Yeats's *Countess Cathleen.* This enterprise employed only English actors, and did not assume to be purely national in scope. It came to an end in October, 1901. It was in October, 1902, that in *Samhain,* the organ of the Irish National Theatre, William Butler Yeats made the following announcement: " The Irish Literary Theatre has given place to a company of Irish actors." The nucleus of this new Irish National Theatre was certain companies of amateurs that W. G. Fay had assembled. These companies were composed of people who were unable to give full time to their interest in the drama, but who came from the office or the shop to rehearse at odd moments during the day and in the evening. The Irish National Theatre really developed from these amateur companies. It was strictly national in scope. The advisers, who were to include Synge, Lady Gregory, Padraic Colum, William Butler Yeats, and others, looked to the Irish National Theatre to bring the drama back to the people, to whom plays dealing with society life meant nothing. They intended also that their plays " should give them [the people] a quite natural pleasure, should either tell them of their own life, or of that life of poetry where every man can see his own magic, because there alone does human nature escape from arbitrary conditions." This program has been carried out with remarkable success.

October, 1902, is the date for the beginning of the Irish National Theatre. At first W. G. Fay, and his brother, Frank Fay, were in charge of the productions, the former as stage manager. Frank Fay had charge of training a company, in which the star system was unknown. He had studied French methods of stage diction and gesture, and the Irish Players are generally said to show the results of his familiarity with great French models. In 1913 a school of acting was organized in order to perpetuate the tradition created by the Fays.

Among the most famous playwrights who have written for the Irish National Theatre are Padraic Colum, John Millington Synge, William Butler Yeats, Lady Gregory, St. John G. Ervine, Æ (George W. Russell), and Lord Dunsany. At one time the theatre sent out, in a circular addressed to aspiring authors who showed promise, the following counsel: "A play to be suitable for performance at the Abbey should contain some criticism of life, founded on the experience or personal observation of the writer, or some vision of life, of Irish life by preference, important from its beauty or from some excellence of style, and this intellectual quality is not more necessary to tragedy than to the gayest comedy."[1]

In 1904 the Irish National Theatre was housed for the first time in its own playhouse, the Abbey Theatre. This change was made possible by the generosity of Miss A. E. F. Horniman, who saw the Irish Players when they first went to London in 1903. It was she who obtained the lease of the Mechanics' Institute in Dublin, increased its capacity, and rebuilt it, giving it rent free to the Players from 1904 to 1909, in addition to an annual subsidy which she allowed them. In 1910 the Abbey Theatre was bought from her by public subscription. The next year, the Irish Players paid their famous visit to the United States.

The Irish National Dramatic Company was organized as a protest against current theatrical practices. Its founders purposed to reform the various arts of the theatre. By encouraging native playwrights they hoped to do for the drama of Ireland what Ibsen and other writers had done for the drama in Scandinavian countries, where people go to the theatre to think as well as to feel. It was not intended in any sense that these new Irish players were to serve the purpose of propaganda; truth was not to be compromised in the service of a cause. Acting, too, was to be improved: redundant gesture was to be suppressed; repose was to be given its full value; speech was to be made more important than gesture. Yeats in particular had theories as to the way in which verse should be spoken on the stage; he advocated a cadenced chant,

---

[1] Lady Gregory, *Our Irish Theatre*, New York, 1913, p. 101.

monotonous but not sing-song, for the delivery of poetry. The simplification of costume and setting was also included in their scheme, for both were to be strictly accessory to the speech and movement of the characters.

They have been faithful to their ideals. The performances at the Abbey Theatre continue, although from time to time certain of the most eminent actors of the company have withdrawn, some to migrate to America. Among the plays produced in 1919 and 1920 by the National Theatre Society at the Abbey Theatre are W. B. Yeats's *The Land of Heart's Desire*, G. B. Shaw's *Androcles and the Lion*, Lady Gregory's *The Dragon*, and Lord Dunsany's *The Glittering Gate*.

THE NEW ART OF THE THEATRE

There are certain facts about the artistic transformation that the theatre is undergoing in the twentieth century with which students of the drama need to be familiar in order to picture for themselves how plays can be interpreted by means of design, color, and light. The transformation is definitely connected with a few famous names. In Europe two men, Edward Gordon Craig and Max Reinhardt, stand out as reformers in matters connected with the construction, the lighting, and the design of stage settings. In this country the artists of the theatre are, generally speaking, disciples of one or both of these great Europeans and their colleagues. The new stage artist studies the characterization and the situations in the play, the production of which he is directing, and tries to make his setting suggestive of the physical and emotional atmosphere in which the action of the drama moves.

Gordon Craig has written several books and many articles embodying his ideas on play production. In all his writings he emphasizes the importance of having one individual with complete authority and complete knowledge in charge of coordinating and subordinating the various arts that go to make the production of a play a symmetrical whole, his theory being that there is no one art that can be called to the exclusion of all others *the* Art of the Theatre: not the acting, not the play, not the setting, not the dance; but that all these properly harmonized through the personality of the director become the Art of the Theatre.

The kind of setting that has become identified in the popular mind with Gordon Craig is the simple monochrome background composed either of draperies or of screens. It is unfortunate that this popular idea should be so limited because, of course, the name of Gordon Craig should carry with it the suggestion of an infinite variety of ways of interpreting the play through design. His screens, built to stand alone, vary in number from one to four and sometimes have as many as ten leaves. They are either made of solid wood or are wooden frames covered with canvas. The screens with narrow leaves may be used to produce curved forms, and screens with broad leaves to enclose large rectangular spaces. The screens are one form of the setting composed of adjustable units, which can be adapted in an infinite variety of ways to the needs of the play.

The new ideas in European stagecraft began to be popularized in America in the year 1914-15, when under the auspices of the Stage Society, Sam Hume, now teaching the arts of the theatre at the University of California, and Kenneth Macgowan, the dramatic critic, arranged an exhibition that was shown in New York, Chicago, and other great centres, of new stage sets designed by Robert Edmond Jones, Sam Hume, and others who have since become famous. The models displayed on this occasion brought before the public for the first time the new method of lighting which, as much as anything else, differentiates the new theatre art from the old. It introduced the device of a concave back wall made of plaster, sometimes called by its German name " horizont," and a lighting equipment that would dye this plaster horizon with colors that melted into one another like the colors in the sky; a stage with " dimmers " for every circuit of lights, and sockets for high-power lamps at any spot from the stage.

In the same year that the Stage Society showed Robert Edmond Jones's models, he was given an opportunity to design the settings and costumes for Granville Barker's production of Anatole France's *The Man Who Married a Dumb Wife,* which may be said to have advertised the new practices in America more than any other single production.

Writing of his own work shortly after, Mr. Jones says: " While the scenery of a play is truly important, it should be so important that the audience should forget that it is present.

The Merchant of Venice. A room in Belmont. Design by Robert Edmond Jones. A great round window framed in the heavy molding of Mantegna and the pale clear sky of Northern Italy.

There should be fusion between the play and the scenery. Scenery isn't there to be looked at, it's really there to be forgotten. The drama is a fire, the scenery is the air that lifts the fire and makes it bright. . . . The audience that is always conscious of the back drop is paying a doubtful compliment to the painter. . . . Even costumes should be the handiwork of the scenic artist. Yes, and if possible, he should build the very furniture."[1] Robert Edmond Jones has not only designed settings and costumes for poetic and fantastic forms of drama, but he has also been called upon to plan the productions of realistic modern plays.

Three of his designs introducing three different aspects of his work have been here reproduced. The model for Maeterlinck's *The Seven Princesses* is an example of an attempt to present the essential significant structure of a setting in the simplest way conceivable and by so doing to stimulate the imagination of the spectator to create for itself the imaginative environment of the play. His design for a room in Belmont for *The Merchant of Venice* shows a great round window framed in the heavy molding of Mantegna and the pale, clear sky of Northern Italy. The scene for *Good Gracious Annabelle* is a corridor in an hotel. This scene is a typical example of a more or less abstract rendering of a literal scene. It was designed primarily with the idea of giving as many different exits and entrances as possible, in order that the action of the drama might be swift and varied.[2]

When Sam Hume was connected with the Detroit Theatre of Arts and Crafts, he used a symbolic and suggestive method for the setting of poetic plays the scene of which was laid in no definite locality. In this theatre he installed a permanent setting, including the following units: " Four pylons [square pillars], constructed of canvas on wooden frames, each of the three covered faces measuring two and one-half by eighteen feet; two canvas flats each three by eighteen feet; two sections of stairs three feet long, and one section eight feet long, of uniform eighteen-inch height; three platforms of the same height, respectively six, eight, and twelve feet long; dark green

---

[1] Robert Edmond Jones, *The Future Decorative Art of the Theatre, Theatre Magazine,* Vol. XXV, May, 1917, p. 266.
[2] Robert Edmond Jones himself has suggested the phrasing of these descriptions.

INTRODUCTION

hangings as long as the pylons; two folding screens for masking, covered with the same cloth as that used in the hangings, and as high as the pylons; and two irregular tree forms in silhouette.

"The pylons, flats, and stairs, and such added pieces as the arch and window, were painted in broken color . . . [1] so that the surfaces would take on any desired color under the proper lighting." [2] The economy of this method is illustrated by the fact that in one season nineteen plays were given in the Arts and Crafts Theatre at Detroit, and the settings for eleven of these were merely rearrangements of the permanent setting. This kind of setting is sometimes called "plastic"—a term which refers to the fact that the separate units are in the round, and not flat. The effect secured in settings representing outdoor scenes was made possible only by the use of a plaster horizon of the general type described in connection with the exhibition of the Stage Society.

Robert Edmond Jones and Sam Hume are two of an increasingly large number of artists in America, among whom should be mentioned Norman-bel Geddes, Maurice Browne, and Lee Simonson, who are experimenting with design, color, and light. Underlying the work of all of these is the belief that the whole production, the play, the acting, the lighting, and the setting, should be unified by some one dominating mood. In the work of these new artists, there is no place for the old-fashioned painted back drop, the use of which emphasizes the disparity between the painted and the actual perspective, though their backgrounds are by no means necessarily either screens or draperies. Another new style of background is the skeleton setting, a permanent structural foundation erected on the stage, which through the addition of draperies and movable properties, or the variation of lights, or the manipulation of screens, may serve for all the scenes of a play. A permanent structure of this sort, representing the Tower of London, was used by Robert Edmond Jones in a recent production of *Richard III* in New York, at the Plymouth Theatre. When Jacques Copeau conducted the Théâtre du Vieux Colombier in New York he had a permanent structure built on the stage of the Garrick Theatre,

[1] See p. xxxiii.
[2] Sheldon Cheney, *The Art Theatre*, New York, 1917, pp. 167-168.

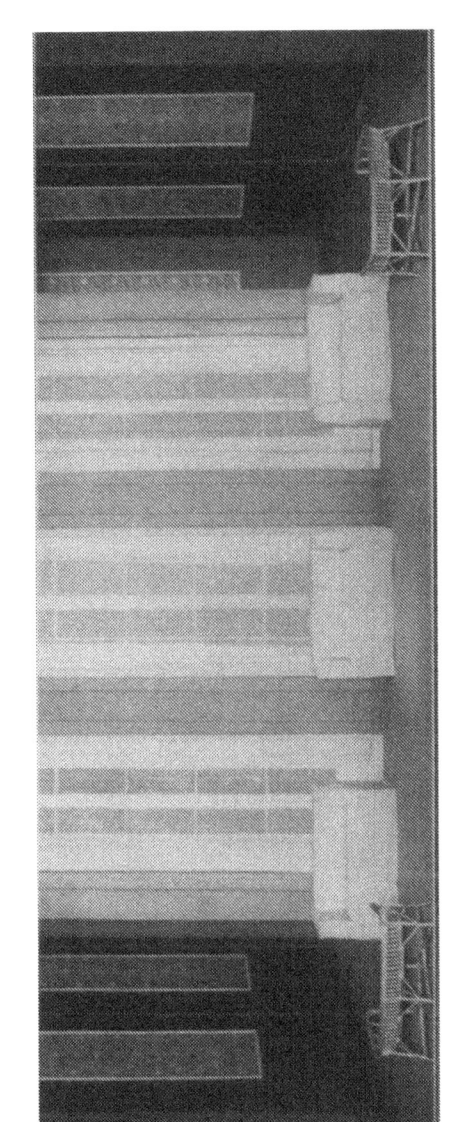

Good Gracious Annabelle. A corridor in a hotel. Design by Robert Edmond Jones. A typical example of a more or less abstract rendering of a literal scene. It was designed primarily with the idea of giving as many different exits and entrances as possible in order that the action of the drama might be swift and varied.

THE NEW ART OF THE THEATRE

that he used for all the plays he produced; at times the upper half of the stage was masked, at times the recess back of the two central columns was used. The aspect of the stage was often completely changed by the addition of tapestries, stairs, panels, screens, and furniture.

In the description of the equipment of the Detroit Theatre of Arts and Crafts, reference has been made to a method of painting the plastic units in broken color. This is so important a principle that it should be more generally understood by those who are interested in the theatre. The principle was put into operation by the Viennese designer, Joseph Urban. In practice it means that a canvas painted with red and with green spots upon which a red light is played, throws up only the red spots blended so as to produce a red surface, and that the same canvas under a green light shows a green surface; and, if both kinds of lights are used, then both the green and red spots are brought out, according to the proportion of the mixture of green and red in the light.

Color is being used now not only for decorative purposes, but also symbolically. The decorative use of color on the stage is, obviously, like the decorative use of color in the design of textiles, or stained glass, or posters. The symbolic use of color is less easy to interpret, but it is plain that in most people's minds red is connected with excitement and frenzy, and blues and grays, with an atmosphere of mystery. This is a very bald suggestion of some of the very subtle things that have been done with color on the modern stage.

The new methods of stage lighting make possible all kinds of color combinations and effects. The use of the plaster horizon (or of the cyclorama, a cheaper substitute, usually a straight semi-circular curtain enclosing the stage, made of either white or light blue cloth), combined with high-powered lights set at various angles on the stage, makes outdoor effects possible, the beauty of which is new to the theatre.[1] Nowadays footlights are not invariably discarded, but where they are used they are wired so that groups of them can be lighted when other sections are dimmed or darkened. When the setting shows an interior scene with a window, though the scene may be lighted from all sides, the window seems to be the

[1] For a description of modern lighting equipment for a Little Theatre compare the section on the Theatre in the School in this introduction.

source of all light. A good deal of the lighting on the stage is what is known in the interior decoration of houses as indirect lighting; colored lights are produced most simply by the interposition between the source of light and the stage of transparent colored slides, gelatine or glass.

In any production that is made under the influence of the new stagecraft, the costumes, like the setting of the play, are considered in connection with the resources of lighting. The costumes, whether historically correct or historically suggestive, whether of a period or conventionalized, are conceived in their three-fold relation to the characters of the play, the background, and the scheme of lights, by the designer or the director under whose general supervision the play is staged.

In general, American audiences are hardly conscious of the existence of these reforms. Here and there, it is true, the manager of a commercial theatre or an opera house has called in an artist to supervise his productions and has thus given publicity to the new way of making the arts of the theatre work together. Certain Little Theatres, also, have educated their followers in the significance of the new use of light and design to represent the mood of a play. The demands that the new method makes on craftsmanship have also commended it to students in schools and colleges interested in play production. Both the Little Theatres and the school theatres are doing a real service when they educate their communities in these new arts, for not only will this education increase the capacity of these particular audiences to enjoy the good things of the theatre, but the influence of these groups is bound in the long run to popularize the new stagecraft.

PLAYMAKING

Shortly before the death of William Dean Howells, he related the experience that he had had of being circularized by a correspondence school that offered to teach him the art of writing fiction in a phenomenally short time at a ridiculously low rate. In this instance, there was something wrong with the mailing list, but the fact remains that in universities successful courses in writing short-stories and plays are given and the best of these courses actually have turned out writers who achieve various degrees of success financially and artistically.

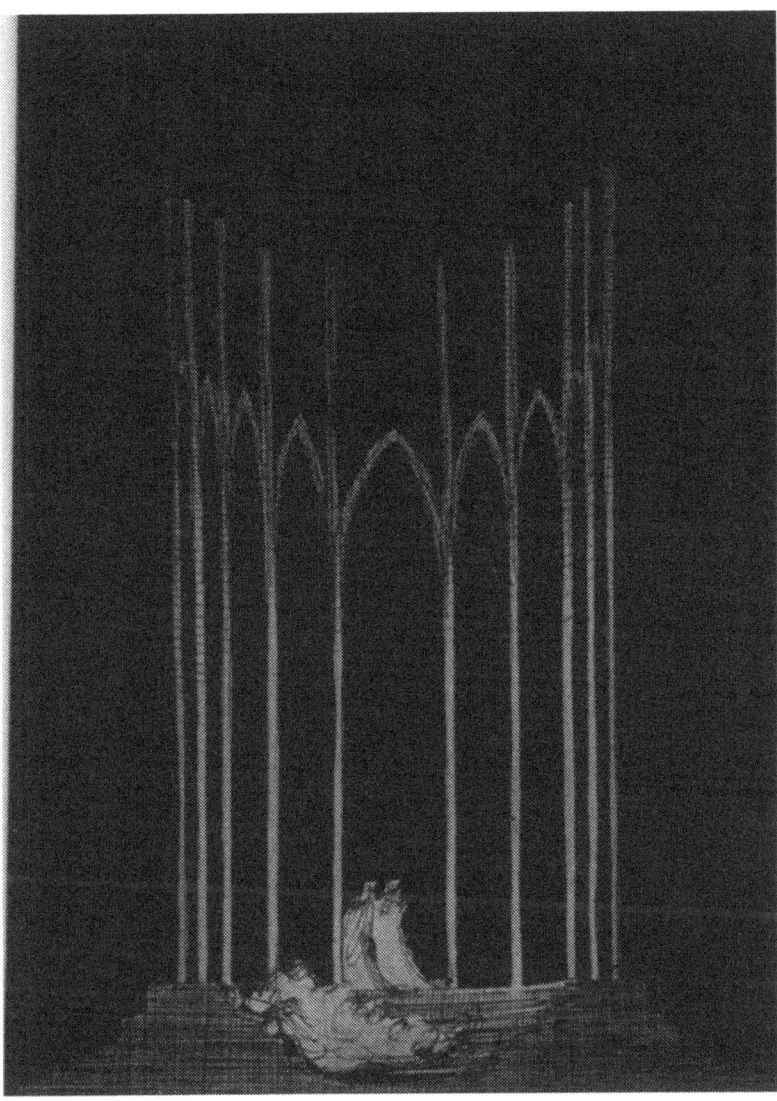

Courtesy of Theatre Arts Magazine

The Seven Princesses. Design by Robert Edmond Jones. An example of the attempt to present the essential significant structure of a setting in the simplest way conceivable and by so doing to stimulate the imagination of the spectator to create for itself the imaginative environment of the play.

It is plain that a brief treatise like the present one makes no such pretensions; it means merely to suggest some of the most obvious points of departure for students in the drama who wish to exercise themselves in the composition of the one-act play, much as a student of poetry will try his hand at a *ballade* or a sonnet without taking himself or his metrical exercises too seriously.

In the famous Perse School in Cambridge, England, the boys begin at the age of twelve to practise playmaking as an aid to the fuller understanding of Shakespeare's dramatic workmanship, and this work is developed throughout the rest of the course. The boys, having learned that Shakespeare himself used stories that he found ready to hand, discover in their own reading a story that will lend itself to dramatization. The story is told and retold from every angle. The class is then divided up into committees to every one of which is entrusted some part of the dramatization. One little committee busies itself with the setting, another with the structure, another with the comic characters, another with the songs that are interspersed and so on. These committees prepare rough notes to be presented in class. These notes may propose an outline of successive scenes, present the part of some principal character, or the "business" (illustrative action) of some minor part. Lessons of this sort are followed by composition rehearsals, where the dramatic and literary value of the proposed plot, characterization, pantomime, and dialogue are tested, and subjected to the criticism of teacher and boys. In the next lessons, the teacher brings to bear on the special problems on which the boys are working all the criticism that his wider range of reading and experience can suggest. In the light of his suggestions the various points are debated and the boys then proceed to careful fashioning, shaping, and writing. A rehearsal of the nearly finished product is held, followed by a final revision of the text. The work then goes forward to a public performance given with all due ceremony. In the higher classes playmaking is taught more especially in connection with writing and the boys are trained to imitate the style of various dramatists. Synge was used as a model at one time for, as one of the masters of the school explained: "The style of Synge is easy to copy because it is so largely composed of a certain phraseology. The same words, phrases, and turns of sentence occur again and again. Here are a few taken at random; the reader will find them in a context on almost any page of the plays: *It's myself—Is it me fight him?—I'm thinking—It's a poor (fine, great, hard, etc.) thing—A little path I have—Let you come—God help us all—Till Tuesday was a week—The end of time—The dawn of day—Let on—Kindly—Now,* as in *Walk out now—Surely—Maybe—Itself—At all—Afeard—Destroyed—It curse.* Synge is also mighty fond of the words *ditch* and *ewe*. And there are certain forms of rhythm about Synge's prose which are used with equal frequency, and are quick and easy to catch. So far from this imitation of style being an artificial method, the fact is that once a boy of sixteen or over has read a play or two of Synge's, if he has any power of style in him, it will be all but impossible to stop him writing like Synge for a few weeks." Learning playwriting from models recalls the method of Benjamin Franklin and Robert Louis Stevenson who in their youth wrote slavish imitations of the great masters in order to form their own prose style. Of course, it is not claimed that this work at the Perse School makes playwrights, only that it gives the boys a deeper appreciation of dramatic workmanship and furnishes a new kind of intellectual game to add to the joy of school life.

The one-act plays contained in this collection are, as has been suggested in what has been said about their construction, illustrative of various kinds of workmanship. Certain of them are excellent models for those who are experimenting with playwriting. The one-act play, not nearly so difficult a form as the full-length play, offers undergraduates in school and college and inexperienced writers generally unlimited scope for experiment.

The testimony of Lord Dunsany is to the effect that his play is made when he has discovered a motive. Asked whether he always began with a motive, "'Not always,' he said; 'I begin with anything or next to nothing. Then suddenly, I get started, and go through in a hurry. The main point is not to interrupt a mood. Writing is an easy thing when one is going strong and going fast; it becomes a hard thing only when the onward rush is impeded. Most of my short plays have been written in a sitting or two.'"[1] This passage is quoted because insight

[1] Clayton Hamilton, *Seen on the Stage*, New York, 1920, p. 239.

into the practice of professional writers is always helpful to amateurs. Dunsany uses "motive," it seems, as a convenient term for denoting the idea, the character, the incident or the mood that impels the dramatist to start writing a play. Such material is to be found everywhere. Many professional writers accumulate vast stores of such themes against the day when they may have the necessary leisure, energy, and insight to develop them.

It has been pointed out that there are only thirty-six possible dramatic situations in any case, and that no matter how the plot shapes itself, it is bound to classify itself somehow or other as one of the inescapable thirty-six. There is comfort also in the suggestion that Shakespeare drew practically all the dramatic material that he used so transcendently direct from the familiar and accessible narrative stores of his day. The young or inexperienced playwright need have no hesitation, then, in turning to such sources as the Greek myths for inspiration. Quite recently a highly successful one-act play of Phillip Moeller's proved that Helen of Troy is as eternally interesting as she is perenially beautiful. Maurice Baring draws on the old Greek stories, too, for several of his *Diminutive Dramas*. The Bible has proved dramatically suggestive to Lord Dunsany and to Stephen Phillips. The old ballads of *Fair Annie* and *The Wife of Usher's Well* have been found dramatically available. The myths of the old Norse Gods, used by Richard Wagner for his music dramas, contain much unmined dramatic gold. John Masefield and Sigurjónsson have converted Saga material to the uses of the drama. In old English literature, in *Widsith,* in the *Battle of Brunanburh,* the seeking dramatist may find. The romances of the Middle Ages, the fairy lore of all peoples, and the old Hindu animal fables are fertile in suggestion to the intending dramatist. What a wonderful one-act play, steeped in the mellow atmosphere of the Renaissance in Italy, might be made out of Browning's *My Last Duchess!* At least one new literary precedent has recently been created by the author who wrote a sequel to *Dombey and Son.* Certainly many famous novels and plays may be conceived as calling out for similar treatment at the hands of the experimental playwright. Famous literary and historic characters offer themselves as promising dramatic material. When Robert Emmons Rogers, author of the well-

xxxviii   INTRODUCTION

known play, *Behind a Watteau Picture,* was a sophomore at Harvard, he wrote the following charming little play on Shakespeare which is reprinted here, with the author's permission, as a pleasing example of a promising piece of apprentice work:[1]

THE BOY WILL

Within the White Luces Inn on a late afternoon in spring, 1582. The room is of heavy-beamed dark oak, stained by age and smoke, with a great, hooded fireplace on the left. At the back is a door with the upper half thrown back, and two wide windows through whose open lattices, overgrown with columbine, one can see the fresh country side in the setting sun. Under them are broad window seats. At the right, a door and a tall dresser filled with pewter plates and tankards. A couple of chairs, a stool and a low table stand about. ANNE, *a slim girl of sixteen, is mending the fire.* MASTER GEORGE PEELE, *a bold and comely young man, in worn riding dress and spattered boots, sprawls against the disordered table.* GILES, *a plump and peevish old rogue in tapster's cap and apron, stands by the door looking out.*

PEELE [*rousing himself*]. Giles! Gi-les!
GILES [*hurries to him*]. What more, zur? Wilt ha' the pastry or—?
PEELE. Another quart of sack.
GILES. Yus, zur! Anne, bist asleep? [*The girl rises slowly.*]
ANNE [*takes the tankard*]. He hath had three a'ready.
PEELE [*cheerfully*]. And shall have three more so I will. This player's life of mine is a weary one.
ANNE [*pertly*]. And a thirsty one, too, methinks.

[1] Robert Emmons Rogers, President of the Boston Drama League and Assistant Professor, specializing in modern literature and drama in the Massachusetts Institute of Technology, was born in Haddonfield, New Jersey, in 1888. He writes that his Anne Hathaway " was a particularly wild idealization based on Miss Adams as Peter Pan," and that even at eighteen he knew that his portrait of the girl, who was to be Shakespeare's wife, was not historically correct. Permission to perform the play must be secured from the author.

GILES [*scandalized*]. Come, wench! Ha' done gawking about, and haste! [ANNE *goes at right.*] 'Er be a forrard gel, zur, though hendy. I be glad 'er's none o' mine, but my brother's in Shottery. He canna say I love 'is way o' making wenches so saucy.

PEELE. A pox on you! The best-spirited maid I ha' seen in Warwickshire, I say. Forward? Man alive, wouldst have her like your blowsy wenches here, that lie i' the sun all day? I have seen no one so comely since I left London.

GILES [*feebly*]. But 'ere, zur, in Stratford—

PEELE [*hotly*]. Stratford? I doubt if God made Stratford! Another day here and I should die in torment. Your grass lanes, your rubbly houses, fat burgesses, old women, your young clouter-heads who have no care for a bravely acted stage-play. [*Bitingly.*] " Can any good come out of Stratford? "

GILES. Noa, Maister Peele! Others ha' spoke more fairly—

PEELE [*impatiently*]. My sack, man! Is the girl a-brewing it?

GILES. Anne! Anne! (I'll learn she to mess about.) Anne!

ANNE [*hurries in and serves* PEELE]. I heard you.

GILES. Then whoi cunst thee not bustle? Be I to lose my loongs over 'ee?

ANNE [*simply*]. Mistress Shakespeare called me to the butt'ry door. Will hath not been home all day, and she is fair anxious. She bade me send him home once I saw him.

PEELE [*drinking noisily*]. Who is it? [ANNE *is clearing the table.*]

GILES [*shortly*]. Poor John Shakespeare's son Will.

PEELE. A Stratford lad? A straw-headed beater of clods!

GILES. Nay, zur. A wild young un, as 'ull do noa honest work, but dreams the day long, or poaches the graät woods wi' young loons o' like stomach.

ANNE [*indignantly, dropping a dish*]. It's not true! He is no poacher.

PEELE [*grinning*]. What a touchy lass! No poacher, eh?

ANNE. Nay, sir, but the brightest lad in Stratford. He hath learning beyond the rest of us—and if he likes to wander i' the woods, 'tis for no ill—he loves the open air—and you should hear the little songs he makes!

PEELE. Do all the lads find in you such a defender, or

only—? [*She turns away.*] Nay, no offense! I should like to see this Will.

GILES [*grumpily*]. 'E 'ave noa will to help 'is father in these sorry times, but ever gawks at stage-plays. 'E 'ull come to noa good end. [*The player starts up.*]

PEELE. Stage-plays—no good end? Have a care, man!

GILES. Nay, zur—noa harm, zur! I—I—canna bide longer. [*Backs out.*]

ANNE [*at the window, wonderingly*]. He should be here. He hath never lingered till sunset before. [PEELE *comes up behind her.*]

PEELE. Troubled, lass?

ANNE. Nay, sir, but—but— [*Suddenly*] Listen!

PEELE [*blankly*]. To what? [*A faint singing without.*]

ANNE [*eagerly*]. Canst hear nothing—a lilt afar off?

PEELE [*nodding*]. Like a May-day catch? I hear it.

ANNE. 'Tis Will! Cousin, Will is coming. [GILES *comes back.*]

GILES [*peevishly*]. I canna help it. Byunt 'e later'n common?

A VOICE. [*The clear, boyish singing is coming very near.*]

> When springtime frights the winter cold, 5
> (Hark to the children singing!)
> The cowslip turns the fields to gold,
> The bird from 's nest is winging—

PEELE. Look you! There the boy comes.

ANNE [*leaning out the window*]. Isn't he coming here? Will! Will! [*He passes by the window singing the last words*

> Young hearts are gay, while yet 'tis May,
> Hark to the children singing!

and leaps in over the lower part of the door, a sturdy, ruddy boy, with merry face and a mop of brown hair. ANNE *greets him with outstretched hands.*]

ANNE [*reproachfully*]. Will! Thy mother was so anxious!

WILL. I did na' think. I ha' been in the woods all day and forgot everything till the sun set.

ANNE. All the day long? Thou must be weary.

WILL [*frankly*]. Nay, not very weary—but hungry.

ANNE. Poor boy. He shall have his supper now.

GILES [*protesting*]. 'E be allus eating 'ere, and I canna a-bear it. Let him sup at his own whoam.

WILL [*shaking his head*]. I dare na go home, for na doubt my father'll beat me rarely. I'll bide here till he be asleep. [*He places himself easily in the armchair by the fire.*]

GILES [*going sulkily*]. Thriftless young loon!

ANNE [*laying the table*]. Hast had a splendid day?

WILL [*absently*]. Aye. In the great park at Charlecote. There you can lie on your back in the grass under the high arches of the trees, where the sun rarely peeps in, and you can listen to the wind in the trees, and see it shake the blossoms about you, and watch the red deer and the rabbits and the birds—where everything is lovely and still. [*His voice trails off into silence.* ANNE *smiles knowingly.*]

ANNE. Thou'lt be making poetry before long, eh, Will?—Will? [*To* PEELE] The boy hath not heard a word I spoke.

PEELE [*coming forward*]. Would he hear me, I wonder! Boy!

WILL [*starting*]. Sir? [PEELE *looks down on him sternly.*]

PEELE. Dost know thou'rt in my chair?

WILL [*coolly*]. Thine? Indeed, 'tis very easy.

PEELE. Hark 'ee! Dost know my name?

WILL. I canna say I do.

PEELE [*distinctly*]. Master George Peele.

WILL. I thank thee, sir.

PEELE. Player in my Lord Admiral's Company.

WILL. [*His whole manner changes and he jumps up eagerly.*] A player? Oh—I did not know. Pray, take the seat.

PEELE [*amused*]. Dost think players are as lords? Most men have other views. [*Sits.* WILL *watches him, fascinated.*]

WILL. Nay, but—oh, I love to see stage-plays! Didst not play in Coventry three days agone, "The History of the Wicked King Richard"?

PEELE. Aye, aye. Behold in me the tyrant.

WILL. Thou? Rarely done! I mind me yet how the hump-backed king frowned and stamped about—thus [*imitating*]. Ha! Ha! 'Twas a brave play!

ANNE. Thy supper is ready, Will.

PEELE [*amused*]. The true player-instinct, on my soul!

WILL [*flattered*]. Dost truly think so? [ANNE *plucks his sleeve.*]

ANNE. Will, where are thy wits? Supper waits.

WILL [*apologetically*]. Oh—I—I—did na hear thee. [*He tries to eat, but his attention is ever distracted by the player's words.*]

PEELE. Is my reckoning ready, girl?

ANNE. Reckoning now, sir? Wilt thou—?

PEELE. Yes, yes, I go to-night. To-morrow Warwick, then the long road to Oxford, playing by the way—and London at last!

ANNE. And then? [WILL *listens intently.*]

PEELE. Then back to the old Blackfriars, where all the city will flock to our tragedies and chronicles—a long, merry life of it.

ANNE [*interested*]. And does the Queen ever come?

PEELE. Nay, child, we go to her. Last Christmas I played before her at court, in the great room at Whitehall, before the nobles and ambassadors and ladies—oh, a gay time—and the Queen said—

WILL [*starting up*]. What was the play?

ANNE. Eat thy supper, Will.

WILL [*impatiently*]. I want no more.

PEELE. So my young cockerel is awake again. Will, a boy of thy stamp is lost here in Stratford. Thou shouldst be in London with us. By cock and pie, I have a mind to steal thee for the company! [*Rises to pace the floor.*]

WILL [*breathlessly*]. To play in London?

ANNE. Nay, Will, he but jests. Thou'rt happier here than traipsing about wi' the players. [GILES *appears at back.*]

GILES. Nags be ready, zur, at sunset as thee'st bid. Shall I put the gear on?

PEELE [*sharply*]. Well fed and groomed? Nay, I will see them myself. [GILES *vanishes.* PEELE *turns at the door.*] Hark'ee, lass. Thy lad could do far worse than become a player. Good meat and drink, gold in 's pouch, favor at court, and true friends. I like the lad's spirit. [*He goes.* ANNE *drops into his chair by the fire. Twilight is coming on rapidly.* WILL *stands silent at the window looking after the player.*]

ANNE [*troubled*]. Will, what is it? Thou'rt very strange to-night.

THE BOY WILL

WILL [*wistfully*]. I—I—Oh, Anne, I want to go to London. I am a-weary of rusting in Stratford, where I can learn nothing new, save to grow old, following my father's trade.

ANNE. But in London?

WILL [*kindling*]. In London one can learn more marvels in a day than in a lifetime here; for there the streets are in a bustle all day long, and the whole world meets in them, soldiers and courtiers and men of war, from France and Spain and the new lands beyond the sea, all full of learning and pleasant tales of foreign wars and the wondrous things in the colonies. My schoolmaster told me of it. You can stand in St. Paul's and the whole world passes by, mad for knowledge and adventure. And then the stage-plays—!

ANNE. Oh, Will, why long for them?

WILL. Think how splendid they must be when the Queen herself loves to see 'em. If I were like this player-fellow, and acted with the Admiral's company! He laughed that he would take me with him—to be a player and perchance *write* plays, interludes, and noble tragedies! Think of it, Anne—to live in London and be one of all the rare company there, to write brave plays wi' sounding lines for all to wonder at, and have folk turn on the streets when I passed and whisper, " That be Will Shakespeare, the play-maker "—to act them even at court and gain the Queen's own thanks! Anne, London is so great and splendid! It beckons me wi' all its turmoil of affairs and its noble hearts ready to love a new comrade. [*Disconsolately*] And I must bide in Stratford?

ANNE [*gently*]. Come now, Will. No need to be so feverish. Sit down by me. What canst thou know of play-making? What canst thou do in London?

WILL [*he sits down by the hearth at her feet, looking into the firelight*]. I'll tell thee, Anne. Thy father and half the village call me a lazy oaf, that I stray i' the woods some days instead of helping my father. I canna help it. The fit comes on me, and I must be alone, out i' the great woods.

ANNE [*gladly*]. Then thou dost not poach?

WILL [*hastily*]. No, no—that is—sometimes I am with Hodge and Diccon and John a' Field, and 'tis hard not to chase the deer. Nay, look not so grave—I try to do no harm.

ANNE [*quietly*]. And when thou'rt alone?

WILL. Then I lie under the trees or wander through the

fields, and make plays to myself, as though I writ them in my mind, and cry the lines forth to the birds—they sound nobly, too—or make little songs and sing them i' the sunshine. They are but dreams, I know, but splendid ones—and the player looked wi' favor on me, and said I might make a good player, and he would take me with him.

ANNE. But he only jested.

WILL. No jest to me! I'll take him at his word and go with him to London. [*He starts up eagerly.*]

ANNE [*troubled*]. Will, Will! [PEELE *enters at the back.*]

PEELE. Hark 'ee, Giles, I go in half an hour!

WILL. Master Peele! [*Catches at his arm.*]

PEELE. Well, youngster?

WILL [*slowly*]. Thou—thou saidst I had a good spirit and would do well in London—in a stage company. Thou wert in jest, but—I will go with thee, if I may.

PEELE [*taken all aback*]. Go with me?

WILL [*earnestly*]. With the player's company—to London.

PEELE [*laughing*]. 'S wounds! Thou hast assurance! Dost think to become a great player at once?

WILL [*impatiently*]. Oh, I care not for the playing. Let me but be in London, to see the people there and be near the theatre. I'll be the players' servant, I'll hold the nobles' horses in the street—I'll do anything!

PEELE [*seriously*]. And go with us all over England on hard journeys to play to ignorant rustics?

WILL. Anywhere—I'll follow on to the world's end—only take me with you to London! [*As he speaks* GILES *and* MISTRESS SHAKESPEARE, *a kindly faced woman of middle age, dressed in housewife's cap and gown, appear at the door.*]

GILES. There 'e be, Mistress Shixpur.

MISTRESS S. [*as she enters*]. Oh, Will. [*He turns sharply.*]

WILL [*confusedly*]. Mother! I—I—did not know thou wert here.

MISTRESS S. Why didst not come home—and what dost thou want with this stranger?

ANNE. He would go to London with him.

MISTRESS S. [*aghast*]. To London. My Will?

WILL [*quietly*]. Thou knowest, mother, what I ha' told thee, things I told to no other, and now the good time has come that I can see more of England.

MISTRESS S. But I canna let thee go. Oh, Anne, I knew the boy was restless, but I did not think for it so soon. He is only a boy.

WILL [*coloring*]. In two years I shall be a man—I am a man now in spirit. I canna stay in Stratford. [MISTRESS SHAKESPEARE *sinks down in a chair.*]

MISTRESS S. What o' me? And, Will, 'twill break thy father's heart! [WILL *looks ashamed.*]

WILL. I know, he would not understand. 'Tis hard. He must not know till I be gone.

MISTRESS S. [*To* PEELE]. Oh, sir, how could you wish to lead the lad away? Hath not London enough a'ready?

PEELE [*who has been listening uncomfortably, faces her gravely*]. I but played with the lad at first, till I saw how earnest he was; then I would take him, for I loved his boldness. But, boy, I'll tell thee fairly, thou'lt do better here. Thou'st seen the brave side of it, the gay dresses, the good horses, the cheering crowds and the court-favor. But 'tis dark sometimes, too. The pouches often hang empty when the people turn away—the lords are as the clouded sun, now smiling, now cold—and there come the bitter days, when a man has no friends but the pot-mates of the moment, when every man's hand is against him for a vagabond and a rascal, when the prison-gates lay ever wide before him, and the fickle folk, crying after a *new* favorite, leave the old to starve.

ANNE. Will, canst not see? Thou'rt better here—

WILL [*bravely*]. I know—all this may wait me—but I must go.

MISTRESS S. [*alarmed*]. Must go, Will? [*He kneels by her side.*]

WILL [*tenderly*]. Hush, mother, I'll tell thee. 'Tis not entirely my longing, for this morning the keeper of old Lucy—

GILES. Ha, poaching again, young scamp!

WILL. Brought me before him—I was na poaching, I'll swear it, not so much as chasing the deer—but Sir Thomas had no patience, and bade me clear out, else he would seize me. I—I—dare na stay.

MISTRESS S. I feared it; thy father forbade thee in the great park. And now—Oh, Will, Will—I know well how thou'st longed to go from here—and now thou must—what shall I do, lacking thee?

PEELE [*frankly*]. Will, if thou must go, thou must. London is greater than Stratford, and there is much evil there, but thou'rt true-hearted, and—by my player's honor—I will stand by thee, till the hangman get me. But we must go soon. 'Tis a dark road to Warwick—I'll see to the horses. Is it a compact? [WILL *gives him his hands.*]

WILL [*huskily*]. A compact, sir—to the end. [PEELE *hurries out.*]

GILES. Look at 'e now, breaking 'is mother's heart, and mad wi' joy to revel in London. 'Tis little 'e recks of she.

WILL [*hotly*]. Thou liest. [*Bending over her*] Mother, 'tis not true. I do love thee and father, I love Stratford. I'll never forget it. But 'tis so little here, and I must get away to gain learning and do things i' the world, that I may bring home all I get; fame, if God grant it, money, if I gain it, all to those at home.

ANNE. Thou'rt over-confident.

WILL. Aye, because I'm young. God knows there is enough pain in London, and I'll get my share—but I'm *young!* Mother, thou'rt not angry?

MISTRESS S. I knew 'twas coming, and 'tis not so hard. We will always wait for thee at home, when thou'rt weary.

GILES [*at the door*]. The horses are waiting. 'Tis dark, Will.

WILL [*breaking down*]. Mother, mother!

MISTRESS S. The good God keep thee safe. Kiss me, Will. [*He bends over her, then stumbles to the door,* ANNE *following.*]

WILL [*turning*]. Anne—Anne—thou dost not despise me for deserting Stratford. I *must* go.

ANNE. Oh, I know. Thou'lt go to London and forget us all.

WILL. No, no, thou—I couldn't forget. I'll remember thee, Anne—I'll put thee in my plays; all my young maids and lovers shall be thee, as thou'rt now—and I'll bring thee rare gifts when I come home.

ANNE. I do na want them. Will—I—I—did na mean to be unkind. We were good friends, and I trust in thee, for the future, that thou'lt be great. Good-by—and do na forget the little playmate.

WILL. I will na forget [*kissing her*], and, Anne, be good to

my mother. [*She goes back to* MISTRESS SHAKESPEARE, *and he stands watching them in the dusk.*]
   PEELE [*at the window*]. Come, come, Will! We must go.
   WILL [*turning slowly*]. I—I'm coming, sir.

[THE CURTAIN.]

All the dramatic motives that have been enumerated so far have been more or less literary in origin, but " A play may start from almost anything: a detached thought that flashes through the mind; a theory of conduct or an act which one firmly believes or wishes only to examine; a bit of dialogue overheard or imagined; a setting, real or imagined, which creates emotion in the observer; a perfectly detached scene, the antecedents and consequences of which are as yet unknown; a figure glimpsed in a crowd which for some reason arrests the attention of the dramatist . . . a mere incident—heard in idle talk or observed; a story told only in barest outline or with the utmost detail." [1]

The great dramatic critic, William Archer, has said that " the only valid definition of the dramatic is: Any representation of imaginary personages which is capable of interesting an average audience assembled in a theater." For the purposes of the definition the Boy Will of Robert Emmons Rogers's little piece and Drinkwater's Abraham Lincoln are equally imaginary personages. In the case of the one-act play the theatre in question is more often than not a Little Theatre or a school theatre, the representation is more frequently at the moment by amateur than by professional actors and the audience, being small and close to the stage, is likely to assume a cooperative attitude towards the playwright, the actor, and the other immediate factors in the production. Since the success of a play depends on its adaptability to the requirements of actor, theatre, and audience, it is well for inexperienced playwrights to study the conditions under which one-act plays are likely to be produced.

One very practical consideration to hold in mind is that the one-act play has a shorter time in which to focus attention than

[1] George Pierce Baker, *Dramatic Technique,* Boston and New York, 1919, p. 47.

INTRODUCTION

the full-length play and so the indispensable preliminary exposition must be quickly disposed of and an urgent appeal to the emotional interest of the audience must be made at the beginning. As has been said, every artistic consideration that calls for singleness of impression in the short-story is of equal importance in determining the unified structure of the one-act play. For the reason that a one-act play is almost never given by itself, if for no other, its effect will be dissipated if plot, characterization, or atmosphere fails in unity.

The writer exercising himself in the art of play-making had best begin with the procedure common to many professional playwrights. This first step is the drawing up of a scenario, which is an outline showing the course of the story, identifying the characters, indicating the setting and atmosphere and explaining the nature of the play; that is, whether, for example, it is to be a fantasy like *The Pierrot of the Minute,* or a comedy of manners like *Wurzel-Flummery*.

Here for instance is such a scenario as might have been drawn up for *The Boy Will:*

THE BOY WILL (Historical fantasy)
Scenario for a one-act play, by
Robert Emmons Rogers

CHARACTERS
(in order of their appearance)

MASTER GEORGE PEELE, player of the Admiral's Company.
GILES, a plump and peevish old rogue, a tapster.
ANNE HATHAWAY, at sixteen a slim girl, niece to Giles.
WILL SHAKESPEARE, a sturdy, ruddy boy, Anne's playmate.
MISTRESS SHAKESPEARE, a kindly faced woman of middle age, Will's mother.

Within the White Luces Inn on a late afternoon in spring, 1582. (Here a description of the interior would follow.)

Peele is eating and drinking at the inn, waited on by Anne Hathaway.
Anne, scolded by Giles for her slowness, is commended as comely and spirited by Peele.
Peele abuses Stratford as a sleepy hole.
Anne explains her delay in fetching ale by the fact that Mistress Shakespeare has been at the back door inquiring for Will who has been gone all day.
Giles explains Will to Peele as a young poacher.

Anne indignantly denies the charge and praises Will as the brightest boy in Stratford.
Giles accuses him of gawking at plays and predicts a bad end for the boy.
Peele resents the implication.
Singing a May-day catch, Will enters. Afraid to go home because he has been wasting his day in Charlecote Park and fears father's scolding.
Goes off into a golden dream of his day in the woods.
Peele attracts his attention by announcing his profession.
Will shows his interest.
Is too distracted by Peele to eat.
Peele announces itinerary of his players and kindles Will's imagination with a mention of the Queen.
Threatens to carry Will off to London.
Anne discourages the plan.
Peele draws glowing pictures of actor's profession.
Will is all on fire for London in spite of Anne.
Tells Anne he's tired of being nagged.
Makes Peele promise to take him to London.
His mother comes for him and is aghast at the news, but finally consents to let Will go without his father's knowledge.
Peele then draws a picture of the actor as vagabond to discourage Will.
Anne holds out against his going.
Will tells how, though he has not been poaching, he has been warned by Sir Thomas Lucy to clear out.
His mother sees that he must go.
Will makes a compact with Peele.
Promises Anne rare gifts and kissing his mother goes.

The scenario drawn up, the next step is to develop the plot. The plot of a one-act play, to be effective, must be extraordinarily compact. The accepted laws of plot construction for all artistic narratives are the same. The climax must be carefully prepared for, as in Synge's *Riders to the Sea,* and the various devices used for heightening the suspense should be discovered and applied.

Characterization is more difficult for the tyro to manage than plot. Consistency of characterization is attained through discovering in the beginning a motive that will sufficiently account for the part taken by the character by means of speech and action, and through constantly testing the characterization by this motive. Such consistency of characterization is illustrated to perfection in Tarkington's *Beauty and the Jacobin.* The writer of the one-act play does not use many characters. " Examination of several hundred one-act plays has revealed that the average number of characters to a play is between three and four." [1]

Facility in writing dialogue is gained like facility in plot construction and in characterization only by the patient study of the work of experienced and successful playwrights. Dialogue that is witty, charming, ironical, or graceful is of dramatic value only as it is in character.

A little experience on the stage is a great help. Such experience teaches the value of skillfully planned exits and entrances for characters; helps the beginner to distinguish between action that should be related and action that should be seen; shows him how a scene must be devised to occupy the time it takes for a character to appear after he has telephoned that he is coming; and a variety of other practical considerations.

Stage directions are likely to be over-elaborated by the inexperienced. The best stage directions are those that deal only with matters of setting, lighting and essential pantomime or action. They should not, in general, be used for characterization.

But after all there can be no infallible recipes for dramatic writing. With the successful professional playwright, apprenticeship is often an unconscious stage. Plays succeed that break all the rules laid down by critics and professors of dramatic literature, but after all those rules were, to begin with, based on practices productive of success under other conditions. In any case some insight into the mechanics of dramatic art does make the reading of plays more interesting and does give an added zest to theatre going.

THE THEATRE IN THE SCHOOL

The giving of plays in schools is no new thing. One of the earliest English comedies, *Ralph Roister Doister,* was written in the middle of the sixteenth century by Nicholas Udall, a schoolmaster, probably to be performed at Westminister School at Christmas time. Many generations of boys in the English public schools have presented the plays of the Greek and Latin

---

[1] B. Roland Lewis, *The Technique of the One-Act Play,* Boston, 1918, p. 211.

THE THEATRE IN THE SCHOOL

dramatists; and schools and colleges in this country have also at times given performances of the classic drama. But until recently Shakespeare and the comedies of Sheridan and Goldsmith have been the chief dramatic fare both in the classroom and on the stage in American schools.

Modern plays are coming, however, to be more generally introduced into the course of study. The following significant list, prepared by Miss Anna H. Spaulding, is in use in the senior classes in English in the Brookline High School, at Brookline, Massachusetts:

Noah's Flood	Arms and the Man
Sacrifice of Isaac	Caesar and Cleopatra
Everyman	John Bull's Other Island
Everywoman	The Doctor's Dilemma
The Servant in the House	Strife
Ralph Roister Doister	Justice
Tales of the Mermaid Tavern	The Tragedy of Nan
Merchant of Venice	The Marrying of Ann Leete
Jew of Malta	Seven Short Plays
Tragedy of Shakespeare	The Land of Heart's Desire, or
Comedy of Shakespeare	The Countess Cathleen, or
The Rivals	Cathleen Ni Houlihan
The Good Natured Man	The Shadow of the Glen
She Stoops to Conquer	Riders to the Sea
Caste	The Birthright
The Lady of Lyons	The Truth
One Closet Drama	The Witching Hour, or
The Second Mrs. Tanqueray	As a Man Thinks
One Comedy of Pinero	The Scarecrow
The Silver King	The Piper
One Serious Play by Jones	Milestones
The Importance of Being Earnest	

Thirty-five of these plays are distinctly modern. Another list, in use as part of a course in contemporary literature given in the last half of the third year at the Washington Irving High School and including only modern plays, is reprinted below:

The Blue Bird	Pygmalion
The Melting Pot	The Piper
Milestones	Prunella
Justice, or	Sherwood
The Silver Box	The Land of Heart's Desire
	Spreading the News

INTRODUCTION

These plays are read and studied; that is to say, such topics as dramatic workmanship, theme, setting, characterization, dialogue, and diction are taken up in connection with each one and each one is made the starting point for a new interest in the drama of to-day.[1]

In another high school in New York, the Evander Childs, there is a four years' course of two periods a week in classroom study of the drama, old and new. All composition work is connected with this special interest.

Another kind of work based on contemporary drama was carried on by a group of first-year students in a certain high school who were much interested in a program of one-act plays to be presented in the school theatre. The teacher of English who had charge of this young class discussed the subject of the theatre audience with them both before and after the performance. The outcome of this analysis of the interests of the audience was an outline. These fourteen-year old girls said that the next time that they went to the theatre they would keep in mind the following considerations:

I. In regard to the play:
   A. Its title
   B. Classification
   C. Plot
   D. Characterization
   E. Dialogue
   F. Theme

II. In regard to the actors:
   A. Their intelligence
   B. Clearness of speech
   C. Ease of manner
   D. Facial expression (appropriateness of make-up)
   E. Pantomime or action
      1. Posture
      2. Gesture
      3. Repose

---

[1] Further interesting information on the reading and the study of modern plays in the schools may be found in the valuable article by F. G. Thompkins of the Central High School, Detroit, called *The Play Course in High School,* in *The English Journal* for November, 1920, and in the same issue, in the list of plays produced by St. Louis High Schools, prepared by Clarence Stratton, Chairman, National Council Committee on Plays.

THE THEATRE IN THE SCHOOL

F. Costumes
 1. Appropriateness as an index to character
 2. Color and design
 3. Harmony with the setting

III. In regard to the setting:
 A. The lighting
 B. Color and design
 C. Appropriateness as regards mood of play
 D. Suggestiveness
 E. Workmanship

One cannot help feeling that these young people were being effectively trained to enjoy the best drama in the best way.

Not only is modern drama being read and studied in the English classes, but the schools are becoming centres of Little Theatre movements and leading their communities in pageants and dramatic festivals. An editorial in *The New York Evening Post* in 1918 put it in this way: "As Froude states that in Tudor England there was acting everywhere from palace to inn-yard and village green, so, the prediction is made, future historians will record that in our America there was acting everywhere—in neighborhood theatres, portable theatres, church clubs, high schools and universities, settlements, open amphitheatres, and hotel ballrooms."

One reason that amateur dramatics have taken on a new lease of life in the schools is because other teachers besides teachers of English have become interested in the project of giving a play. Students in physics classes have planned and executed lighting systems for the school theatre, students in carpentering and manual arts have built the scenery from designs made in drawing classes, curtains have been stenciled, costumes made and cloths dyed in domestic art classes, programs printed by the school printing squad, music furnished by the school orchestra and dances taught by the physical training department. In most cases the line coaching and the general direction of the play have been part of the work in English.

A concrete example will illustrate this kind of co-operation. Several years ago the department of English at the Washington Irving High School gave two plays, *Three Pills in a Bottle,* a product of the 47 Workshop, by Rachel Lyman Field, and *The Goddess of the Woven Wind,* by Alice Rostetter. *The*

INTRODUCTION

Goddess of the Woven Wind had grown out of class-room work. The girls in an industrial course were studying the origin of the silk industry. A pamphlet stated that the wife of Hoangti, Si-Ling-Chi, was the first to prepare and weave silk. This legend offered suggestive dramatic material peculiarly appropriate for a girls' high school.

The work of obtaining the setting and the properties was divided between two committees, each working under the direction of a chairman. Since fifty dollars had been fixed as the limit of expenditure for the two plays, the problem was rather a difficult one. Fortunately, *Three Pills in a Bottle* calls for a small cast. The cast of *The Goddess of the Woven Wind,* however, included thirty-four girls, most of whom had to be orientally clad and equipped. The teacher who contemplates putting on a rather elaborate costume play in his or her high school will be interested to learn that the amount was so exactly fixed and the department so resourceful that fifty-one dollars and nine cents was the total sum spent on the two plays. Then, lest anyone think that there had been a miscalculation, let it be added that this sum included the money spent for hot chocolate to serve to the casts of the plays, between the afternoon and evening performances.

The problem of staging *Three Pills in a Bottle* was greatly simplified by the fact that the frontispiece of the play gives a simple, effective setting not difficult to copy. With the aid of some amateur carpentering, the regular interior set was easily transformed to suit the purpose. The problem of color was solved when the chairman of the committee found a patchwork quilt in the attic, during a visit to her mother's home; a conference with the janitress of her city apartment developed the fact that she possessed a freshly scrubbed wash-tub, which she was willing not only to donate to the cause, but to have painted green.

The task of staging *The Goddess of the Woven Wind* was difficult and interesting, because it was decidedly a costume play, and because it was a first production. Some of the difficulties that confronted the chairman of the committee for that play were amusing.

For instance, after some perplexed thought on the subject, she tacked the following list of costumes and properties on the Bulletin Board of the English office:

THE THEATRE IN THE SCHOOL

WANTED:

Mulberry tree
Gardener's spade
Teakwood stool
Chinese necklaces
Large, colorful abacus
Mandarin coats and hats
Sky-blue Chinese bowl
Chinese gong
Bamboo rod
Silk cocoons

She also advertised the need of these things and many others in all her classes. Within two weeks nearly everything had either appeared or been promised, except a Chinese gong with a proper "whang" to it, an unbreakable sky-blue bowl and the mulberry tree! A teacher in a neighboring school lent the company a splendid gong, sometimes used in their orchestra; a student transformed a wooden chopping bowl by means of clay and tempera into an exquisite piece of pottery, copied from a priceless bowl on exhibition at the Metropolitan Museum of Art.

The mulberry tree was still an unsolved problem, when Dugald Stuart Walker, the artist who has produced a number of plays at the Christadora House in New York, was consulted. He suggested that the tree be a conventionalized one of flat "drapes" of green and brown poplin, with cocoons sewn on in a simple border design.

The staging of the play then became a project for members of a third-year art class. During their English period they read the play, recited on the subject of the China of remote dynasties, constructed a miniature stage, and then, forming committees among themselves, worked out the practical details. One group purchased the necessary paint, another painted the vermilion sun. Her neighbor affixed it to a bamboo rod. To emphasize the Chinese setting, two girls made a frame with a dragon as head-piece and huge, colorful Chinese medallions to be sewn on the side drapery. The design for the medallions was obtained from a Chinese brass plate. Almost every girl in the class took part in the project. Interest was easily aroused, as a number of girls in this class took part in the play.

As for the costumes, for the thirty-four members of the

cast, only eight dollars' worth was hired. The rest were either borrowed or made by the girls. The most successful one, perhaps, that worn by the empress, was copied from an Edmund Dulac illustration of the Princess Badoura. The astrologers' costumes were obtained from photographs of *The Yellow Jacket,* lent by Mrs. Coburn. To complete the project, the girls wrote a composition explaining how to organize the staging of a costume play.

Meanwhile, the selection and coaching of the two casts was going on. Competition for the parts was open to the girls of the entire school. A great many girls were tried out before the two committees made a choice. In fact, every girl who was recommended by her English teacher was given an opportunity to read a part. In a number of cases two girls were assigned for one part and it was not known until almost the last moment who was to have the rôle or who was to understudy. Rehearsals were held at least three times a week, for three weeks, and a full-dress rehearsal was held two days before the final performance. It was thought advisable to allow a day to elapse between the last rehearsal and the real performance, in order to give the girls an opportunity to rest.

In coaching the plays, an effort was made to have a girl read the line properly without having it read to her. The members of the coaching committee would explain the mood or frame of mind to the speaker; the girl would then interpret the mood in her reading.

In addition to the coaching committee, several teachers sat at the back of the auditorium during rehearsals, to warn the speakers when they could not be heard.

The advertising campaign began soon after a choice of plays had been made. In compliance with the request of the Publicity Committee, one of the teachers of an art class and a teacher in the English Department assigned to their pupils the problem of making posters to advertise the plays. To the painter of the best one a prize was awarded.

Announcements of the play were posted by pupils in various parts of the building. Tiny brochures decorated with Chinese motives were prepared by students during an English period, and later were circulated among the faculty, and placed upon office bulletin boards, and in diaries. In writing these brochures the girls applied the knowledge they had gained in

THE THEATRE IN THE SCHOOL

studying the writing of advertisements. Two illustrated advertisements made in one class were displayed in other high schools; a number were sent in an envelope with tickets to patrons and distinguished friends of the schools. One class wrote letters to firms of wholesale silk merchants and importers, advertising *The Goddess of the Woven Wind,* the story of silk.

In order to increase the sale of tickets and to prepare an appreciative audience, various subjects were suggested to English teachers for projects in class work connected with the plays. In many classes every girl wrote and illustrated a paper on some topic pertaining to Chinese life, such as customs, costumes, religion, occupations, silk, China, umbrellas, fireworks, fans, position of women, objects of art. Oral compositions were devoted to phases of some of these subjects. In the oral work and in the written composition, accurate knowledge of authorities consulted was insisted upon. Chinese proverbs were studied. "A man knows, but a woman knows better," used by the author in her play, was one of the most popular ones. Translations, found in the *Literary Digest,* of Chinese poems of the sixteenth and of the eighteenth century were produced and read by the girls, many of whom brought to class all the Chinese articles they could find at home. Incense burners, fans, pitchers, embroideries, chop sticks, beads, shoes, vases, and even a Chinese newspaper, found their way to the class-room and were exhibited with pride. Interest in things Chinese was so great that clippings and prints continued coming in for almost two weeks after the play had been presented. Class visits were made to the Chinese exhibit at the Metropolitan Museum of Art and to importing houses in the neighborhood.

The kind of co-operation described has led in some schools to the establishment of workshops similar to those conducted in connection with certain university courses in playwriting and dramatics and with many of the Little Theatres. A paragraph that appeared recently in a calendar of the New York Drama League explains in a convincing way the necessity for a workshop in connection with all amateur producing. "One of the most vital problems that the amateur group has to solve," says the writer, " is that of securing a proper place for the preparing of a production. Not all organizations can hold rehearsals, paint scenery, experiment with lighting on costumes and scenery on

lviii   INTRODUCTION

the stage on which they are finally to play. Even where this is possible, it is costly. Much of the activity is now carried on in the homes of members so far as rehearsals go; in barns or garages as regards the painting of scenery and not at all so far as the lighting question is concerned. More often than not, a few hasty final rehearsals are relied upon to pull into shape some of the most important elements of a satisfactory performance.

" The remedy lies in the acquisition of a workshop. A large room with a very high ceiling will serve admirably. But you must be able to work recklessly in it, sawing wood, hammering nails, mussing things up generally with paint and riddling the walls and ceiling with hooks and screws to hang lighting apparatus and other properties. An old-fashioned barn can be converted into an ideal workshop, if provision is made for proper heating. All the activity should be concentrated in the workshop and there is no reason why all the experimentalists cannot be at work at once—the carpenters, the scene painters, the electricians, the property men, and even the actors with their director."

The use of miniature model stages is becoming more and more common in the schools, the preliminary model serving the workshop, until the background, lighting, properties, and costumes are completed. It is an excellent thing for schools to start a collection of models of famous theatres and notably successful stage-sets. The material for these exists in illustrated books and magazines and in the mass of descriptive material in regard to the stage that is now being published.[1]

Two school theatres designed especially for the purpose of

---

[1] There is a comprehensive list of books published by the Public Library of New York that is an indispensable guide to amateurs interested in Little Theatres and play production and in matters connected with lighting, scenery, costumes, and theatre building; it is W. B. Gamble, *The Development of Scenic Art and Stage Machinery*, New York, 1920. Cf. also the articles of Irving Pichel that have appeared from time to time in *The Theatre Arts Magazine*. The three following books are especially valuable for school theatres: Barrett H. Clark, *How to Produce Amateur Plays*, Boston, 1917; Constance D'Arcy Mackay, *Costumes and Scenery for Amateurs. A Practical Working Handbook*, New York, 1915 (the illustrations are especially valuable); and Evelyn Hilliard, Theodora McCormick, Kate Oglebay, *Amateur and Educational Dramatics*, New York, 1917.

Interior of the Beechwood Theatre.

Exterior of the Beechwood Theatre.

THE THEATRE IN THE SCHOOL   lix

fostering in the schools to which they are attached an interest in the drama are the Garden Theatre of the high school at Montclair, New Jersey, and the Beechwood Theatre in the private school at Scarborough-on-Hudson, New York, built by Frank A. Vanderlip. At Montclair the present high school building was completed in 1914. To the northeast of the building at that time was a ravine which afforded a natural amphitheatre. The site was perfect, and a gift from a public-spirited citizen, Mrs. Henry Lang, made it possible to create on this spot a very artistic and beautiful place for outdoor performances, either plays or pageants.

On the slope nearest the building are semi-circular rows of concrete seats accommodating about fifteen hundred people. A brook spanned by two arched bridges separates the audience from the stage. Back of the turf stage is a graveled stage slightly raised and reached by two flights of steps. The pergola and trees make a beautiful background. The house in the rear is a part of the plant and is used for dressing and make-up.

The Beechwood Theatre within the school has a proscenium opening of twenty-seven feet and a stage depth, back to the plaster horizon, of the same dimensions. There are two complete sets of drapery, one of coarse écru linen and one of blue velvet; there is also a stock drawing-room set of thirty pieces. Back of the stage are ten dressing-rooms. The lighting arrangements are extraordinarily complete: the theatre has a standard electrical equipment of footlights and borders and a switchboard of the best type to which has recently been added the latest lighting devices, consisting of an X-ray border, the end section of which is on a separate dimmer, a thousand-watt centre floodlight, six five-hundred watt-spotlights, each on separate dimmers, in the false proscenium or tormentor,[1] and a line of one-thousand-watt floodlights for lighting the plaster

[1] For the explanation of this and kindred technical terms, see Arthur Edwin Krows, *Play Production in America*, New York, 1916.
Cf. Maurice Browne, *The Temple of a Living Art. The Drama*, Chicago, 1913, No. 12, p. 168: "Nor is this just a question of stage jargon; that man or woman who would establish an Art Theatre that is an Art Theatre and not a pet rabbit fed by hand, must be able to design it, to ventilate it, to decorate it, to equip its stage, to light it (and to handle its lighting himself, or his electricians will not listen to him), to plan his costumes and scenery, aye, and at a shift, to make them with his own hand."

INTRODUCTION

sky. All of this recently added equipment is controlled from a separate portable switchboard.

Though this plant was built primarily for the school, it is used also by the Beechwood Players, a Little Theatre organization, and by other community clubs which comprise an orchestra, a chorus, a group interested in the fine arts, and a poetry circle. Mr. Vanderlip looks forward to the development of a school of the arts of the theatre from the nucleus of the Beechwood community clubs. With this idea in mind he has just built a workshop for the Beechwood Players in a separate building. It contains power woodworking machines, and rooms for painting scenery and for the costume department, the latter containing power sewing machines.

There is no doubt but that these two schools have unique facilities for developing an interest in the acted drama. But artistic results have often been secured in the school theatre with equipment falling far short of the ideal standards achieved at Montclair and at Scarborough. Other less fortunate schools are, moreover, at no particular disadvantage when it comes to the class-room study of the drama for which this book is primarily planned, this work being the first step in the direction of a more intelligent attitude toward modern plays and modern theatres. A class-room reading of modern plays without any accessories, as Shakespeare is often read from the seats and the aisles, is one of the most practical methods of speech and voice improvement. Louis Calvert, the eminent actor, speaking of this kind of training says: "After all it is one of the simplest things in the world to learn to speak correctly, to take thought and begin and end each word properly. . . . A little attention to one's everyday conversation will often work wonders. If one schools himself for a while to speak a little more slowly, and to give each syllable its due, it is surprising how naturally and rapidly his speech will clarify. If we take care of the consonants, the vowels will take care of themselves."

At the present time, then, the theatre in the schools means a variety of things. It means first and foremost, as suggested by the latest college entrance requirements, the study of modern plays, side by side with the classics. It means also the improvement of English speech, through the interpretation and the reading aloud of the text. It means a study of the new art of the theatre such as the present book suggests. It means often

Ravine where the Garden Theatre was built.

The Garden Theatre.

the presentation of plays before outside audiences and the consequent strengthening of the ties that should exist between the school and the community. It may mean the co-operation of several departments of the school in the production; and, in this case, it usually results in the establishment of some kind of a workshop. And finally, in certain favored schools, it means the erection of model Little Theatres. It seems fair to suppose that this newly aroused interest in modern drama and in modern methods of production in the schools will have far-reaching results.

BEAUTY AND THE JACOBIN

By
BOOTH TARKINGTON

Since the days of Edward Eggleston, Indiana has been accumulating literary traditions until at the present time it rivals New England in the variety of its literary associations. Newton Booth Tarkington, born in Indianapolis in 1869, and continuing to make his home there still in the old family house on North Pennsylvania Street, is one of the most distinguished of the Hoosier writers. As a lad of eleven he began his friendship with James Whitcomb Riley, then a neighbor. "He acknowledges (shaking his head in reflection at the depth of it) that the spirit of Riley has exercised over him a strong, if often unconsciously felt, influence all his life." The delicious stories of Penrod and of the William Sylvanus Baxter of *Seventeen* that Booth Tarkington has told for the unalloyed delight of old and young are said to reproduce quite accurately the author's recollection of his own boyhood pranks and associations in the Middle-Western city of his birth. Tarkington went first to Phillips Exeter Academy and later to Purdue University at Lafayette, Indiana, before he became a member of the class of '93 at Princeton. His popularity and his good fellowship are still cherished memories on the campus.

It seems that he was infallibly associated in the undergraduate mind with the singing of *Danny Deever;* so much so, that whenever he appeared on the steps at Nassau Hall there would be an immediate demand for his speciality, a demand that often caused him to retire as inconspicuously as possible from the crowd. These old days are commemorated in the following verses, a copy of which, framed, hangs on the walls of the Princeton Club in New York.

RONDEL

"The same old Tark—just watch him shy
  Like hunted thing, and hide, if let,
  Away behind his cigarette,
When 'Danny Deever' is the cry.

Keep up the call and by and by
We'll make him sing, and find he's yet
  The same old Tark.

No 'Author Leonid' we spy
In him, no cultured ladies' pet:
He just drops in, and so we get
The good old song, and gently guy
The same old Tark—just watch him shy!"

No biography of Booth Tarkington, no matter how brief, should omit to mention that he was elected to the Indiana State Legislature and sat for a time in that body, where he accumulated, no doubt, some data on the subject of Indiana politics that he may afterwards have put to literary use.

He has found the subject for most of his novels and plays [1] in contemporary American life, which he treats unsentimentally, spiritedly, and vigorously. *Beauty and the Jacobin*, like his famous and fascinating tale, *Monsieur Beaucaire,* is exceptional among his works in deserting the modern American scene for an Eighteenth Century situation. The story and the play are likely, for this reason, to be compared. The tone of *Monsieur Beaucaire* is more urbane, more whimsical, more romantic than the mood of *Beauty and the Jacobin* which " breaks with the pretty, pretty kind of thing. There is a new quality in the texture of the writing. . . . The plot here springs directly from character, and the action of the piece is inevitable. *Beauty and the Jacobin* gives evidence of being the first conscious and determined, as it is the first consistent, effort of the author to leave the surface and work from the inside of his characters out. . . . The whole of the little drama is scintillant with wit, delicate and at times brilliant and somewhat Shavian, which flashes out poignantly against the sombreness of its background." [2]

Beauty and the Jacobin was published in 1912 and has had at least one performance on the professional stage. On November 12, 1912, it was played by members of the company then acting in *Fanny's First Play,* at a matinée at the Comedy Theatre, in New York. It has always been a favorite with amateurs and quite recently was performed in St. Louis by one of the dramatic clubs of that city.

[1] For a bibliography of his works through the year 1913, see Asa Don Dickinson, *Booth Tarkington, a Gentleman from Indiana,* Garden City, no date.

[2] Robert Cortes Holliday, *Booth Tarkington,* Garden City and New York, 1918, pp. 155-156; p. 157.

BEAUTY AND THE JACOBIN

Our scene is in a rusty lodging-house of the Lower Town, Boulogne-sur-Mer, and the time, the early twilight of dark November in northern France. This particular November is dark indeed, for it is November of the year 1793, Frimaire of the Terror. The garret room disclosed to us, like the evening lowering outside its one window, and like the times, is mysterious, obscure, smoked with perplexing shadows; these flying and staggering to echo the shiftings of a young man writing at a desk by the light of a candle.

We are just under the eaves here; the dim ceiling slants; and there are two doors: that in the rear wall is closed; the other, upon our right, and evidently leading to an inner chamber, we find ajar. The furniture of this mean apartment is chipped, faded, insecure, yet still possessed of a haggard elegance; shamed odds and ends, cheaply acquired by the proprietor of the lodging-house, no doubt at an auction of the confiscated leavings of some emigrant noble. The single window, square and mustily curtained, is so small that it cannot be imagined to admit much light on the brightest of days; however, it might afford a lodger a limited view of the houses opposite and the street below. In fact, as our eyes grow accustomed to the obscurity we discover it serving this very purpose at the present moment, for a tall woman stands close by in the shadow, peering between the curtains with the distrustfulness of a picket thrown far out into an enemy's country. Her coarse blouse and skirt, new and as ill-fitting as sacks, her shopwoman's bonnet and cheap veil, and her rough shoes are naïvely denied by her sensitive, pale hands and the high-bred and in-bred face, long profoundly marked by loss and fear, and now very white, very watchful. She is not more than forty, but her hair, glimpsed beneath the clumsy bonnet, shows much grayer than need be at that age. This is ANNE DE LASEYNE.

*The intent young man at the desk, easily recognizable as her
brother, fair and of a singular physical delicacy, is a finely
completed product of his race; one would pronounce him
gentle in each sense of the word. His costume rivals his
sister's in the innocence of its attempt at disguise: he wears
a carefully soiled carter's frock, rough new gaiters, and
a pair of dangerously aristocratic shoes, which are not too
dusty to conceal the fact that they are of excellent make
and lately sported buckles. A tousled cap of rabbit-skin,
exhibiting a tricolor cockade, crowns these anomalies,
though not at present his thin, blond curls, for it has been
tossed upon a dressing-table which stands against the wall
to the left. He is younger than* MADAME DE LASEYNE,
*probably by more than ten years; and, though his features
so strikingly resemble hers, they are free from the permanent impress of pain which she bears like a mourning-
badge upon her own.*

*He is expending a feverish attention upon his task, but with
patently unsatisfactory results; for he whispers and mutters
to himself, bites the feather of his pen, shakes his head
forebodingly, and again and again crumples a written sheet
and throws it upon the floor. Whenever this happens*
ANNE DE LASEYNE *casts a white glance at him over her
shoulder—his desk is in the center of the room—her
anxiety is visibly increased, and the temptation to speak
less and less easily controlled, until at last she gives way
to it. Her voice is low and hurried.*

ANNE. Louis, it is growing dark very fast.

LOUIS. I had not observed it, my sister. [*He lights a
second candle from the first; then, pen in mouth, scratches at
his writing with a little knife.*]

ANNE. People are still crowding in front of the wine-shop
across the street.

LOUIS [*smiling with one side of his mouth*]. Naturally.
Reading the list of the proscribed that came at noon. Also
waiting, amiable vultures, for the next bulletin from Paris.
It will give the names of those guillotined day before yesterday.
For a good bet: our own names [*he nods toward the other
room*]—yes, hers, too—are all three in the former. As for
the latter—well, they can't get us in that now.

ANNE [*eagerly*]. Then you are certain that we are safe?
LOUIS. I am certain only that they cannot murder us day before yesterday. [*As he bends his head to his writing a woman comes in languidly through the open door, bearing an armful of garments, among which one catches the gleam of fine silk, glimpses of lace and rich furs—a disordered burden which she dumps pell-mell into a large portmanteau lying open upon a chair near the desk. This new-comer is of a startling gold-and-ivory beauty; a beauty quite literally striking, for at the very first glance the whole force of it hits the beholder like a snowball in the eye; a beauty so obvious, so completed, so rounded, that it is painful; a beauty to rivet the unenvious stare of women, but from the full blast of which either king or man-peasant would stagger away to the confessional. The egregious luster of it is not breathed upon even by its overspreading of sullen revolt, as its possessor carelessly arranges the garments in the portmanteau. She wears a dress all gray, of a coarse texture, but exquisitely fitted to her; nothing could possibly be plainer, or of a more revealing simplicity. She might be twenty-two; at least it is certain that she is not thirty. At her coming,* LOUIS *looks up with a sigh of poignant wistfulness, evidently a habit; for as he leans back to watch her he sighs again. She does not so much as glance at him, but speaks absently to* MADAME DE LASEYNE. *Her voice is superb, as it should be; deep and musical, with a faint, silvery huskiness.*]

ELOISE [*the new-comer*]. Is he still there?
ANNE. I lost sight of him in the crowd. I think he has gone. If only he does not come back!
LOUIS [*with grim conviction*]. He will.
ANNE. I am trying to hope not.
ELOISE. I have told you from the first that you overestimate his importance. Haven't I said it often enough?
ANNE [*under her breath*]. You have!
ELOISE [*coldly*]. He will not harm you.
ANNE [*looking out of the window*]. More people down there; they are running to the wine-shop.
LOUIS. Gentle idlers! [*The sound of triumphant shouting comes up from the street below.*] That means that the list of the guillotined has arrived from Paris.
ANNE [*shivering*]. They are posting it in the wine-shop win-

dow. [*The shouting increases suddenly to a roar of hilarity, in which the shrilling of women mingles.*]

LOUIS. Ah! One remarks that the list is a long one. The good people are well satisfied with it. [*To* ELOISE] My cousin, in this amiable populace which you champion, do you never scent something of—well, something of the graveyard scavenger? [*She offers the response of an unmoved glance in his direction, and slowly goes out by the door at which she entered.* LOUIS *sighs again and returns to his scribbling.*]

ANNE [*nervously*]. Haven't you finished, Louis?

LOUIS [*indicating the floor strewn with crumpled slips of paper*]. A dozen.

ANNE. Not good enough?

LOUIS [*with a rueful smile*]. I have lived to discover that among all the disadvantages of being a Peer of France the most dangerous is that one is so poor a forger. Truly, however, our parents are not to be blamed for neglecting to have me instructed in this art; evidently they perceived I had no talent for it. [*Lifting a sheet from the desk.*] Oh, vile! I am not even an amateur. [*He leans back, tapping the paper thoughtfully with his pen.*] Do you suppose the Fates took all the trouble to make the Revolution simply to teach me that I have no skill in forgery? Listen. [*He reads what he has written.*] " Committee of Public Safety. In the name of the Republic. To all Officers, Civil and Military: Permit the Citizen Balsage "—that's myself, remember—" and the Citizeness Virginie Balsage, his sister "—that's you, Anne—" and the Citizeness Marie Balsage, his second sister "—that is Eloise, you understand—" to embark in the vessel *Jeune Pierrette* from the port of Boulogne for Barcelona. Signed: Billaud Varennes. Carnot. Robespierre." Execrable! [*He tears up the paper, scattering the fragments on the floor.*] I am not even sure it is the proper form. Ah, that Dossonville!

ANNE. But Dossonville helped us—

LOUIS. At a price. Dossonville! An individual of marked attainment, not only in penmanship, but in the art of plausibility. Before I paid him he swore that the passports he forged for us would take us not only out of Paris, but out of the country.

ANNE. Are you sure we must have a separate permit to embark?

LOUIS. The captain of the *Jeune Pierrette* sent one of his sailors to tell me. There is a new Commissioner from the National Committee, he said, and a special order was issued this morning. They have an officer and a file of the National Guard on the quay to see that the order is obeyed.

ANNE. But we bought passports in Paris. Why can't we here?

LOUIS. Send out a street-crier for an accomplished forger? My poor Anne! We can only hope that the lieutenant on the quay may be drunk when he examines my dreadful " permit." Pray a great thirst upon him, my sister! [*He looks at a watch which he draws from beneath his frock.*] Four o'clock. At five the tide in the river is poised at its highest; then it must run out, and the *Jeune Pierrette* with it. We have an hour. I return to my crime. [*He takes a fresh sheet of paper and begins to write.*]

ANNE [*urgently*]. Hurry, Louis!

LOUIS. Watch for Master Spy.

ANNE. I cannot see him. [*There is silence for a time, broken only by the nervous scratching of* LOUIS'S *pen.*]

LOUIS [*at work*]. Still you don't see him?

ANNE. No. The people are dispersing. They seem in a good humor.

LOUIS. Ah, if they knew— [*He breaks off, examines his latest effort attentively, and finds it unsatisfactory, as is evinced by the noiseless whistle of disgust to which his lips form themselves. He discards the sheet and begins another, speaking rather absently as he does so.*] I suppose I have the distinction to be one of the most hated men in our country, now that all the decent people have left it—so many by a road something of the shortest! Yes, these merry gentlemen below there would be still merrier if they knew they had within their reach a forfeited " Emigrant." I wonder how long it would take them to climb the breakneck flights to our door. Lord, there'd be a race for it! Prize-money, too, I fancy, for the first with his bludgeon.

ANNE [*lamentably*]. Louis, Louis! Why didn't you lie safe in England?

LOUIS [*smiling*]. Anne, Anne! I had to come back for a good sister of mine.

ANNE. But I could have escaped alone.

LOUIS. That is it—" alone "! [*He lowers his voice as he glances toward the open door.*] For she would not have moved at all if I hadn't come to bully her into it. A fanatic, a fanatic!

ANNE [*brusquely*]. She is a fool. Therefore be patient with her.

LOUIS [*warningly*]. Hush.

ELOISE [*in a loud, careless tone from the other room*]. Oh, I heard you! What does it matter? [*She returns, carrying a handsome skirt and bodice of brocade and a woman's long mantle of light-green cloth, hooded and lined with fur. She drops them into the portmanteau and closes it.*] There! I've finished your packing for you.

LOUIS [*rising*]. My cousin, I regret that we could not provide servants for this flight. [*Bowing formally.*] I regret that we have been compelled to ask you to do a share of what is necessary.

ELOISE [*turning to go out again*]. That all?

LOUIS [*lifting the portmanteau*]. I fear—

ELOISE [*with assumed fatigue*]. Yes, you usually do. What now?

LOUIS [*flushing painfully*]. The portmanteau is too heavy. [*He returns to the desk, sits, and busies himself with his writing, keeping his grieved face from her view.*]

ELOISE. You mean you're too weak to carry it?

LOUIS. Suppose at the last moment it becomes necessary to hasten exceedingly—

ELOISE. You mean, suppose you had to run, you'd throw away the portmanteau. [*Contemptuously.*] Oh, I don't doubt you'd do it!

LOUIS [*forcing himself to look up at her cheerfully*]. I dislike to leave my baggage upon the field, but in case of a rout it might be a temptation—if it were an impediment.

ANNE [*peremptorily*]. Don't waste time. Lighten the portmanteau.

LOUIS. You may take out everything of mine.

ELOISE. There's nothing of yours in it except your cloak. You don't suppose—

ANNE. Take out that heavy brocade of mine.

ELOISE. Thank you for not wishing to take out my fur-lined cloak and freezing me at sea!

LOUIS [*gently*]. Take out both the cloak and the dress.

ELOISE [*astounded*]. What!
LOUIS. You shall have mine. It is as warm, but not so heavy.
ELOISE [*angrily*]. Oh, I am sick of your eternal packing and unpacking! I am sick of it!
ANNE. Watch at the window, then. [*She goes swiftly to the portmanteau, opens it, tosses out the green mantle and the brocaded skirt and bodice, and tests the weight of the portmanteau.*] I think it will be light enough now, Louis.
LOUIS. Do not leave those things in sight. If our landlord should come in—
ANNE. I'll hide them in the bed in the next room. Eloise! [*She points imperiously to the window.* ELOISE *goes to it slowly and for a moment makes a scornful pretense of being on watch there; but as soon as* MADAME DE LASEYNE *has left the room she turns, leaning against the wall and regarding* LOUIS *with languid amusement. He continues to struggle with his ill-omened " permit," but, by and by, becoming aware of her gaze, glances consciously over his shoulder and meets her half-veiled eyes. Coloring, he looks away, stares dreamily at nothing, sighs, and finally writes again, absently, like a man under a spell, which, indeed, he is. The pen drops from his hand with a faint click upon the floor. He makes the movement of a person suddenly awakened, and, holding his last writing near one of the candles, examines it critically. Then he breaks into low, bitter laughter.*]
ELOISE [*unwillingly curious*]. You find something amusing?
LOUIS. Myself. One of my mistakes, that is all.
ELOISE [*indifferently*]. Your mirth must be indefatigable if you can still laugh at those.
LOUIS. I agree. I am a history of error.
ELOISE. You should have made it a vocation; it is your one genius. And yet—truly because I am a fool I think, as Anne says—I let you hector me into a sillier mistake than any of yours.
LOUIS. When?
ELOISE [*flinging out her arms*]. Oh, when I consented to this absurd journey, this *tiresome* journey—with *you!* An " escape "? From nothing. In " disguise." Which doesn't disguise.

LOUIS [*his voice taut with the effort for self-command*]. My sister asked me to be patient with you, Eloise—

ELOISE. Because I am a fool, yes. Thanks. [*Shrewishly.*] And then, my worthy young man? [*He rises abruptly, smarting almost beyond endurance.*]

LOUIS [*breathing deeply*]. Have I not been patient with you?

ELOISE [*with a flash of energy*]. If *I* have asked you to be anything whatever—with me!—pray recall the petition to my memory.

LOUIS [*beginning to let himself go*]. Patient! Have I ever been anything but patient with you? Was I not patient with you five years ago when you first harangued us on your " Rights of Man " and your monstrous republicanism? Where you got hold of it all I don't know—

ELOISE [*kindling*]. Ideas, my friend. Naturally, incomprehensible to you. Books! Brains! Men!

LOUIS. " Books! Brains! Men! " Treason, poison, and mobs! Oh, I could laugh at you then: they were only beginning to kill us, and I was patient. Was I not patient with you when these Republicans of yours drove us from our homes, from our country, stole all we had, assassinated us in dozens, in hundreds, murdered our King? [*He walks the floor, gesticulating nervously.*] When I saw relative after relative of my own—aye, and of yours, too—dragged to the abattoir— even poor, harmless, kind André de Laseyne, whom they took simply because he was my brother-in-law—was I not patient? And when I came back to Paris for you and Anne, and had to lie hid in a stable, every hour in greater danger because you would not be persuaded to join us, was I not patient? And when you finally did consent, but protested every step of the way, pouting and—

ELOISE [*stung*]. " Pouting! "

LOUIS. And when that stranger came posting after us so obvious a spy—

ELOISE [*scornfully*]. Pooh! He is nothing.

LOUIS. Is there a league between here and Paris over which he has not dogged us? By diligence, on horseback, on foot, turning up at every posting-house, every roadside inn, the while you laughed at me because I read death in his face! These two days we have been here, is there an hour when you could look from that window except to see him grinning up from the wine-shop door down there?

ELOISE [*impatiently, but with a somewhat conscious expression*]. I tell you not to fear him. There is nothing in it.

LOUIS [*looking at her keenly*]. Be sure I understand why you do not think him a spy! You believe he has followed us because you—

ELOISE. I expected that! Oh, I knew it would come! [*Furiously.*] I never saw the man before in my life!

LOUIS [*pacing the floor*]. He is unmistakable; his trade is stamped on him; a hired trailer of your precious " Nation's."

ELOISE [*haughtily*]. The Nation is the People. You malign because you fear. The People is sacred!

LOUIS [*with increasing bitterness*]. Aren't you tired yet of the Palais Royal platitudes? I have been patient with your Mericourtisms for so long. Yes, always I was patient. Always there was time; there was danger, but there was a little time. [*He faces her, his voice becoming louder, his gestures more vehement.*] But now the *Jeune Pierrette* sails this hour, and if we are not out of here and on her deck when she leaves the quay, my head rolls in Samson's basket within the week, with Anne's and your own to follow! *Now*, I tell you, there is no more time, and *now*—

ELOISE [*suavely*]. Yes? Well? " Now? " [*He checks himself; his lifted hand falls to his side.*]

LOUIS [*in a gentle voice*]. I am still patient. [*He looks into her eyes, makes her a low and formal obeisance, and drops dejectedly into the chair at the desk.*]

ELOISE [*dangerously*]. Is the oration concluded?

LOUIS. Quite.

ELOISE [*suddenly volcanic*]. Then " *now* " you'll perhaps be " patient " enough to explain why I shouldn't leave you instantly. Understand fully that I have come thus far with you and Anne solely to protect you in case you were suspected. " *Now*," my little man, you are safe: you have only to go on board your vessel. Why should I go with you? Why do you insist on dragging me out of the country?

LOUIS [*wearily*]. Only to save your life; that is all.

ELOISE. My life! Tut! My life is safe with the People —my People! [*She draws herself up magnificently.*] The

Nation would protect me! I gave the people my whole fortune when they were starving. After that, who in France dare lay a finger upon the Citizeness Eloise d'Anville!

Louis. I have the idea sometimes, my cousin, that perhaps if you had not given them your property they would have taken it, anyway. [*Dryly.*] They did mine.

Eloise [*agitated*]. I do not expect you to comprehend what I felt—what I feel! [*She lifts her arms longingly.*] Oh, for a Man!—a Man who could understand me!

Louis [*sadly*]. That excludes me!

Eloise. Shall I spell it?

Louis. You are right. So far from understanding you, I understand nothing. The age is too modern for me. I do not understand why this rabble is permitted to rule France; I do not even understand why it is permitted to live.

Eloise [*with superiority*]. Because you belong to the class that thought itself made of porcelain and the rest of the world clay. It is simple: the mud-ball breaks the vase.

Louis. You belong to the same class, even to the same family.

Eloise. You are wrong. One circumstance proves me no aristocrat.

Louis. What circumstance?

Eloise. That I happened to be born with brains. I can account for it only by supposing some hushed-up ancestral scandal. [*Brusquely.*] Do you understand that?

Louis. I overlook it. [*He writes again.*]

Eloise. Quibbling was always a habit of yours. [*Snapping at him irritably.*] Oh, stop that writing! You can't do it, and you don't need it. You blame the people because they turn on you now, after you've whipped and beaten and ground them underfoot for centuries and centuries and—

Louis. Quite a career for a man of twenty-nine!

Eloise. I have said that quibbling was—

Louis [*despondently*]. Perhaps it is. To return to my other deficiencies, I do not understand why this spy who followed us from Paris has not arrested me long before now. I do not understand why you hate me. I do not understand the world in general. And in particular I do not understand the art of forgery. [*He throws down his pen.*]

Eloise. You talk of "patience"! How often have I explained that you would not need passports of any kind if you would let me throw off my incognito. If anyone questions you, it will be sufficient if I give my name. All France knows the Citizeness Eloise d'Anville. Do you suppose the officer on the quay would dare oppose—

LOUIS [*with a gesture of resignation*]. I know you think it.

ELOISE [*angrily*]. You tempt me not to prove it. But for Anne's sake—

LOUIS. Not for mine. That, at least, I understand. [*He rises.*] My dear cousin, I am going to be very serious—

ELOISE. O heaven! [*She flings away from him.*]

LOUIS [*plaintively*]. I shall not make another oration—

ELOISE. Make anything you choose. [*Drumming the floor with her foot.*] What does it matter?

LOUIS. I have a presentiment—I ask you to listen—

ELOISE [*in her irritation almost screaming*]. How can I *help* but listen? And Anne, too! [*With a short laugh.*] You know as well as I do that when that door is open everything you say in this room is heard in there. [*She points to the open doorway, where* MADAME DE LASEYNE *instantly makes her appearance, and after exchanging one fiery glance with* ELOISE *as swiftly withdraws, closing the door behind her with outraged emphasis.*]

ELOISE [*breaking into a laugh*]. Forward, soldiers!

LOUIS [*reprovingly*]. Eloise!

ELOISE. Well, *open* the door, then, if you want her to hear you make love to me! [*Coolly.*] That's what you're going to do, isn't it?

LOUIS [*with imperfect self-control*]. I wish to ask you for the last time—

ELOISE [*flouting*]. There are so many last times!

LOUIS. To ask you if you are sure that you know your own heart. You cared for me once, and—

ELOISE [*as if this were news indeed*]. I did? Who under heaven ever told you that?

LOUIS [*flushing*]. You allowed yourself to be betrothed to me, I believe.

ELOISE. "Allowed" is the word, precisely. I seem to recall changing all that the very day I became an orphan—and my own master! [*Satirically polite.*] Pray correct me if my memory errs. How long ago was it? Six years? Seven?

LOUIS [*with emotion*]. Eloise, Eloise, you did love me then! We were happy, both of us, so very happy—
ELOISE [*sourly*]. "Both!" My faith! But I must have been a brave little actress.
LOUIS. I do not believe it. You loved me. I— [*He hesitates.*]
ELOISE. Do get on with what you have to say.
LOUIS [*in a low voice*]. I have many forebodings, Eloise, but the strongest—and for me the saddest—is that this is the last chance you will ever have to tell—to tell me— [*He falters again.*]
ELOISE [*irritated beyond measure, shouting*]. To tell you what?
LOUIS [*swallowing*]. That your love for me still lingers.
ELOISE [*promptly*]. Well, it doesn't. So *that's* over!
LOUIS. Not quite yet. I—
ELOISE [*dropping into a chair*]. O Death!
LOUIS [*still gently*]. Listen. I have hope that you and Anne may be permitted to escape; but as for me, since the first moment I felt the eyes of that spy from Paris upon me I have had the premonition that I would be taken back—to the guillotine, Eloise. I am sure that he will arrest me when I attempt to leave this place to-night. [*With sorrowful earnestness.*] And it is with the certainty in my soul that this is our last hour together that I ask you if you cannot tell me that the old love has come back. Is there nothing in your heart for me?
ELOISE. Was there anything in *your* heart for the beggar who stood at your door in the old days?
LOUIS. Is there nothing for him who stands at yours now, begging for a word?
ELOISE [*frowning*]. I remember you had the name of a disciplinarian in your regiment. [*She rises to face him.*] Did you ever find anything in your heart for the soldiers you ordered tied up and flogged? Was there anything in your heart for the peasants who starved in your fields?
LOUIS [*quietly*]. No; it was too full of you.
ELOISE. Words! Pretty little words!
LOUIS. Thoughts. Pretty, because they are of you. All, always of you—always, my dear. I never really think of anything but you. The picture of you is always before the eyes of my soul; the very name of you is forever in my heart.

With a rueful smile.] And it is on the tips of my fingers, sometimes when it shouldn't be. See. [*He steps to the desk and shows her a scribbled sheet.*] This is what I laughed at a while ago. I tried to write, with you near me, and unconsciously I let your name creep into my very forgery! I wrote it as I wrote it in the sand when we were children; as I have traced it a thousand times on coated mirrors—on frosted windows. [*He reads the writing aloud.*] " Permit the Citizen Balsage and his sister, the Citizeness Virginie Balsage, and his second sister, the Citizeness Marie Balsage, and Eloise d'Anville "—so I wrote!—" to embark upon the vessel *Jeune Pierrette*—" You see? [*He lets the paper fall upon the desk.*] Even in this danger, that I feel closer and closer with every passing second, your name came in of itself. I am like that English Mary: if they will open my heart when I am dead, they shall find, not " Calais," but " Eloise "!

ELOISE [*going to the dressing-table*]. Louis, that doesn't interest me. [*She adds a delicate touch or two to her hair, studying it thoughtfully in the dressing-table mirror.*]

LOUIS [*somberly*]. I told you long ago—

ELOISE [*smiling at her reflection*]. So you did—often!

LOUIS [*breathing quickly*]. I have nothing new to offer. I understand. I bore you.

ELOISE. Louis, to be frank: I don't care what they find in your heart when they open it.

LOUIS [*with a hint of sternness*]. Have you never reflected that there might be something for me to forgive you?

ELOISE [*glancing at him over her shoulder in frowning surprise*]. What!

LOUIS. I wonder sometimes if you have ever found a flaw in your own character.

ELOISE [*astounded*]. So! [*Turning sharply upon him.*] You are assuming the right to criticize me, are you? Oho!

LOUIS [*agitated*]. I state merely—I have said—I think I forgive you a great deal—

ELOISE [*beginning to char*]. You do! You bestow your gracious pardon upon me, do you? [*Bursting into flame.*] Keep your forgiveness to yourself! When I want it I'll kneel at your feet and beg it of you! You can *kiss* me then, for then you will know that " the old love has come back "!

LOUIS [*miserably*]. When you kneel—

ELOISE. Can you picture it—*Marquis?* [*She hurls his title at him, and draws herself up in icy splendor.*] I am a woman of the Republic!
LOUIS. And the Republic has no need of love.
ELOISE. Its daughter has no need of yours!
LOUIS. Until you kneel to me. You have spoken. It is ended. [*Turning from her with a pathetic gesture of farewell and resignation, his attention is suddenly arrested by something invisible. He stands for a moment transfixed. When he speaks, it is in an altered tone, light and at the same time ominous.*] My cousin, suffer the final petition of a bore. Forgive my seriousness; forgive my stupidity, for I believe that what one hears now means that a number of things are indeed ended. Myself among them.
ELOISE [*not comprehending*]. "What one hears?"
LOUIS [*slowly*]. In the distance. [*Both stand motionless to listen, and the room is silent. Gradually a muffled, multitudinous sound, at first very faint, becomes audible.*]
ELOISE. What is it?
LOUIS [*with pale composure*]. Only a song! [*The distant sound becomes distinguishable as a singing from many unmusical throats and pitched in every key, a drum-beat booming underneath; a tumultuous rumble which grows slowly louder. The door of the inner room opens, and* MADAME DE LASEYNE *enters.*]
ANNE [*briskly, as she comes in*]. I have hidden the cloak and the dress beneath the mattress. Have you—
LOUIS [*lifting his hand*]. Listen! [*She halts, startled. The singing, the drums, and the tumult swell suddenly much louder, as if the noise-makers had turned a corner.*]
ANNE [*crying out*]. The "Marseillaise"!
LOUIS. The "Vultures' Chorus"!
ELOISE [*in a ringing voice*]. The Hymn of Liberty!
ANNE [*trembling violently*]. It grows louder.
LOUIS. *Nearer!*
ELOISE [*running to the window*]. They are coming this way!
ANNE [*rushing ahead of her*]. They have turned the corner of the street. Keep back, Louis!
ELOISE [*leaning out of the window, enthusiastically*]. *Vive la—* [*She finishes with an indignant gurgle as* ANNE DE

LASEYNE, *without comment, claps a prompt hand over her mouth and pushes her vigorously from the window.*]
ANNE. A mob—carrying torches and dancing. [*Her voice shaking wildly.*] They are following a troop of soldiers.
LOUIS. The National Guard.
ANNE. Keep back from the window! A man in a tricolor scarf marching in front.
LOUIS. A political, then—an official of their government.
ANNE. O Virgin, have mercy! [*She turns a stricken face upon her brother.*] It is that—
LOUIS [*biting his nails*]. Of course. Our spy. [*He takes a hesitating step toward the desk; but swings about, goes to the door at the rear, shoots the bolt back and forth, apparently unable to decide upon a course of action; finally leaves the door bolted and examines the hinges.* ANNE, *meanwhile, has hurried to the desk, and, seizing a candle there, begins to light others in a candelabrum on the dressing-table. The noise outside grows to an uproar; the "Marseillaise" changes to "Ça ira"; and a shaft of the glare from the torches below shoots through the window and becomes a staggering red patch on the ceiling.*]
ANNE [*feverishly*]. Lights! Light those candles in the sconce, Eloise! Light all the candles we have. [ELOISE, *resentful, does not move.*]
LOUIS. No, no! Put them out!
ANNE. Oh, fatal! [*She stops him as he rushes to obey his own command.*] If our window is lighted he will believe we have no thought of leaving, and pass by. [*She hastily lights the candles in a sconce upon the wall as she speaks; the shabby place is now brightly illuminated.*]
LOUIS. He will not pass by. [*The external tumult culminates in riotous yelling, as, with a final roll, the drums cease to beat.* MADAME DE LASEYNE *runs again to the window.*]
ELOISE [*sullenly*]. You are disturbing yourselves without reason. They will not stop here.
ANNE [*in a sickly whisper*]. They *have* stopped.
LOUIS. At the door of this house? [MADAME DE LASEYNE, *leaning against the wall, is unable to reply, save by a gesture. The noise from the street dwindles to a confused, expectant murmur.* LOUIS *takes a pistol from beneath his blouse, strides to the door, and listens.*]

ANNE [*faintly*]. He is in the house. The soldiers followed him.

LOUIS. They are on the lower stairs. [*He turns to the two women humbly.*] My sister and my cousin, my poor plans have only made everything worse for you. I cannot ask you to forgive me. We are caught.

ANNE [*vitalized with the energy of desperation*]. Not till the very last shred of hope is gone. [*She springs to the desk and begins to tear the discarded sheets into minute fragments.*] Is that door fastened?

LOUIS. They'll break it down, of course.

ANNE. Where is our passport from Paris?

LOUIS. Here. [*He gives it to her.*]

ANNE. Quick! Which of these " permits " is the best?

LOUIS. They're all hopeless— [*He fumbles among the sheets on the desk.*]

ANNE. Any of them. We can't stop to select. [*She thrusts the passport and a haphazard sheet from the desk into the bosom of her dress. An orderly tramping of heavy shoes and a clinking of metal become audible as the soldiers ascend the upper flight of stairs.*]

ELOISE. All this is childish. [*Haughtily.*] I shall merely announce—

ANNE [*uttering a half-choked scream of rage*]. You'll announce nothing! Out of here, both of you!

LOUIS. No, no!

ANNE [*with breathless rapidity, as the noise on the stairs grows louder*]. Let them break the door in if they will; only let them find me alone. [*She seizes her brother's arm imploringly as he pauses, uncertain.*] Give me the chance to make them think I am here alone.

LOUIS. I can't—

ANNE [*urging him to the inner door*]. Is there any other possible hope for us? Is there any other possible way to gain even a little time? Louis, I want your word of honor not to leave that room unless I summon you. I must have it! [*Overborne by her intensity, LOUIS nods despairingly, allowing her to force him toward the other room. The tramping of the soldiers, much louder and very close, comes to a sudden stop. There is a sharp word of command, and a dozen muskets ring on the floor just beyond the outer door.*]

ELOISE [*folding her arms*]. You needn't think I shall consent to hide myself. I shall tell them—
ANNE [*in a surcharged whisper*]. You will *not* ruin us! [*With furious determination, as a loud knock falls upon the door.*] In there, I tell you! [*Almost physically she sweeps both* ELOISE *and* LOUIS *out of the room, closes the door upon them, and leans against it, panting. The knocking is repeated. She braces herself to speak.*]
ANNE [*with a catch in her throat*]. Who is—there?
A SONOROUS VOICE. French Republic!
ANNE [*faltering*]. It is—it is difficult to hear. What do you—
THE VOICE. Open the door.
ANNE [*more firmly*]. That is impossible.
THE VOICE. Open the door.
ANNE. What is your name?
THE VOICE. Valsin, National Agent.
ANNE. I do not know you.
THE VOICE. Open!
ANNE. I am here alone. I am dressing. I can admit no one.
THE VOICE. For the last time: open!
ANNE. No!
THE VOICE. Break it down. [*A thunder of blows from the butts of muskets falls upon the door.*]
ANNE [*rushing toward it in a passion of protest*]. No, no, no! You shall not come in! I tell you I have not finished dressing. If you are men of honor— Ah! [*She recoils, gasping, as a panel breaks in, the stock of a musket following it; and then, weakened at rusty bolt and crazy hinge, the whole door gives way and falls crashing into the room. The narrow passage thus revealed is crowded with shabbily uniformed soldiers of the National Guard, under an officer armed with a saber. As the door falls a man wearing a tricolor scarf strides by them, and, standing beneath the dismantled lintel, his hands behind him, sweeps the room with a smiling eye.*
This personage is handsomely, almost dandiacally dressed in black; his ruffle is of lace, his stockings are of silk; the lapels of his waistcoat, overlapping those of his long coat, exhibit a rich embroidery of white and crimson. These and other details of elegance, such as his wearing powder upon his dark hair, indicate either insane daring or an importance quite over-

whelming. *A certain easy power in his unusually brilliant eyes favors the probability that, like Robespierre, he can wear what he pleases. Undeniably he has distinction. Equally undeniable is something in his air that is dapper and impish and lurking. His first glance over the room apparently affording him acute satisfaction, he steps lightly across the prostrate door,* MADAME DE LASEYNE *retreating before him but keeping herself between him and the inner door. He comes to an unexpected halt in a dancing-master's posture, removing his huge hat—which displays a tricolor plume of ostrich feathers—with a wide flourish, an intentional burlesque of the old-court manner.*

VALSIN. Permit me. [*He bows elaborately.*] Be gracious to a recent fellow-traveler. I introduce myself. At your service: Valsin, Agent of the National Committee of Public Safety. [*He faces about sharply.*] Soldiers! [*They stand at attention.*] To the street door. I will conduct the examination alone. My assistant will wait on this floor, at the top of the stair. Send the people away down below there, officer. Look to the courtyard. Clear the streets. [*The officer salutes, gives a word of command, and the soldiers shoulder their muskets, march off, and are heard clanking down the stairs.* VALSIN *tosses his hat upon the desk, and turns smilingly to the trembling but determined* MADAME DE LASEYNE.]

ANNE [*summoning her indignation*]. How dare you break down my door! How dare you force your—

VALSIN [*suavely*]. My compliments on the celerity with which the citizeness has completed her toilet. Marvelous. An example to her sex.

ANNE. You intend robbery, I suppose.

VALSIN [*with a curt laugh*]. Not precisely.

ANNE. What, then?

VALSIN. I have come principally for the returned Emigrant, Louis Valny-Cherault, formerly called Marquis de Valny-Cherault, formerly of the former regiment of Valny; also formerly—

ANNE [*cutting him off sharply*]. I do not know what you mean by all these names—and " formerlies "!

VALSIN. No? [*Persuasively.*] Citizeness, pray assert that I did not encounter you last week on your journey from Paris—

ANNE [*hastily*]. It is true I have been to Paris on business;

you may have seen me—I do not know. Is it a crime to return from Paris?

VALSIN [*in a tone of mock encouragement*]. It will amuse me to hear you declare that I did not see you traveling in company with Louis Valny-Cherault. Come! Say it.

ANNE [*stepping back defensively, closer to the inner door*]. I am alone, I tell you! I do not know what you mean. If you saw me speaking with people in the diligence, or at some posting-house, they were only traveling acquaintances. I did not know them. I am a widow—

VALSIN. My condolences. Poor, of course?

ANNE. Yes.

VALSIN. And lonely, of course? [*Apologetically.*] Loneliness is in the formula: I suggest it for fear you might forget.

ANNE [*doggedly*]. I am alone.

VALSIN. Quite right.

ANNE [*confusedly*]. I am a widow, I tell you—a widow, living here quietly with—

VALSIN [*taking her up quickly*]. Ah—"*with*"! Living here alone, and also "with"—whom? Not your late husband?

ANNE [*desperately*]. With my niece.

VALSIN [*affecting great surprise*]. Ah! A niece! And the niece, I take it, is in your other room yonder?

ANNE [*huskily*]. Yes.

VALSIN [*taking a step forward*]. Is she pretty? [ANNE *places her back against the closed door, facing him grimly. He assumes a tone of indulgence.*] Ah, one must not look: the niece, likewise, has not completed her toilet.

ANNE. She is—asleep.

VALSIN [*glancing toward the dismantled doorway*]. A sound napper! Why did you not say instead that she was—shaving? [*He advances, smiling.*]

ANNE [*between her teeth*]. You shall not go in! You cannot see her! She is—

VALSIN [*laughing*]. Allow me to prompt you. She is not only asleep; she is ill. She is starving. Also, I cannot go in because she is an orphan. Surely, she is an orphan? A lonely widow and her lonely orphan niece. Ah, touching—and sweet!

ANNE [*hotly*]. What authority have you to force your way into my apartment and insult—

VALSIN [*touching his scarf*]. I had the honor to mention the French Republic.

ANNE. So! Does the French Republic persecute widows and orphans?

VALSIN [*gravely*]. No. It is the making of them!

ANNE [*crying out*]. Ah, horrible!

VALSIN. I regret that its just severity was the cause of your own bereavement, Citizeness. When your unfortunate husband, André, formerly known as the Prince de Laseyne—

ANNE [*defiantly, though tears have sprung to her eyes*]. I tell you I do not know what you mean by these titles. My name is Balsage.

VALSIN. Bravo! The Widow Balsage, living here in calm obscurity with her niece. Widow Balsage, answer quickly, without stopping to think. [*Sharply.*] How long have you lived here?

ANNE. Two months. [*Faltering.*]—A year!

VALSIN [*laughing*]. Good. Two months and a year! No visitors? No strangers?

ANNE. No.

VALSIN [*wheeling quickly and picking up* LOUIS'S *cap from the dressing-table*]. This cap, then, belongs to your niece.

ANNE [*flustered, advancing toward him as if to take it*]. It was—it was left here this afternoon by our landlord.

VALSIN [*musingly*]. That is very, very puzzling. [*He leans against the dressing-table in a careless attitude, his back to her.*]

ANNE [*cavalierly*]. Why " puzzling "?

VALSIN. Because I sent him on an errand to Paris this morning. [*She flinches, but he does not turn to look at her, continuing in a tone of idle curiosity.*] I suppose your own excursion to Paris was quite an event for you, Widow Balsage. You do not take many journeys?

ANNE. I am too poor.

VALSIN. And you have not been contemplating another departure from Boulogne?

ANNE. No.

VALSIN [*still in the same careless attitude, his back toward her and the closed door*]. Good. It is as I thought: the portmanteau is for ornament.

ANNE [*choking*]. It belongs to my niece. She came only an hour ago. She has not unpacked.
VALSIN. Naturally. Too ill.
ANNE. She had traveled all night; she was exhausted. She went to sleep at once.
VALSIN. Is she a somnambulist?
ANNE [*taken aback*]. Why?
VALSIN [*indifferently*]. She has just opened the door of her room in order to overhear our conversation. [*Waving his hand to the dressing-table mirror, in which he had been gazing.*] Observe it, Citizeness Laseyne.
ANNE [*demoralized*]. I do not—I— [*Stamping her foot.*] How often shall I tell you my name is Balsage!
VALSIN [*turning to her apologetically*]. My wretched memory. Perhaps I might remember better if I saw it written: I beg a glance at your papers. Doubtless you have your certificate of citizenship—
ANNE [*trembling*]. I have papers, certainly.
VALSIN. The sight of them—
ANNE. I have my passport; you shall see. [*With wildly shaking hands she takes from her blouse the passport and the " permit," crumpled together.*] It is in proper form— [*She is nervously replacing the two papers in her bosom when with a sudden movement he takes them from her. She cries out incoherently, and attempts to recapture them.*]
VALSIN [*extending his left arm to fend her off*]. Yes, here you have your passport. And there you have others. [*He points to the littered floor under the desk.*] Many of them!
ANNE. Old letters! [*She clutches at the papers in his grasp.*]
VALSIN [*easily fending her off*]. Doubtless! [*He shakes the " permit " open.*] Oho! A permission to embark—and signed by three names of the highest celebrity. Alas, these unfortunate statesmen, Billaud Varennes, Carnot, and Robespierre! Each has lately suffered an injury to his right hand. What a misfortune for France! And what a coincidence! One has not heard the like since we closed the theatres.
ANNE [*furiously struggling to reach his hand*]. Give me my papers! Give me—
VALSIN [*holding them away from her*]. You see, these un-

lucky great men had their names signed for them by somebody else. And I should judge that this somebody else must have been writing quite recently—less than half an hour ago, from the freshness of the ink—and in considerable haste; perhaps suffering considerable anguish of mind, Widow Balsage! [MADAME DE LASEYNE, *overwhelmed, sinks into a chair. He comes close to her, his manner changing startlingly.*]

VALSIN [*bending over with sudden menace, his voice loud and harsh*]. Widow Balsage, if you intend no journey, why have you this forged permission to embark on the *Jeune Pierrette?* Widow Balsage, *who* is the Citizen Balsage?

ANNE [*faintly*]. My brother.

VALSIN [*straightening up*]. Your first truth. [*Resuming his gaiety.*] Of course he is not in that room yonder with your niece.

ANNE [*brokenly*]. No, no, no; he is not! He is not here.

VALSIN [*commiseratingly*]. Poor woman! You have not even the pleasure to perceive how droll you are.

ANNE. I perceive that I am a fool! [*She dashes the tears from her eyes and springs to her feet.*] I also perceive that you have denounced us before the authorities here—

VALSIN. Pardon. In Boulogne it happens that *I* am the authority. I introduce myself for the third time: Valsin, Commissioner of the National Committee of Public Safety. Tallien was sent to Bordeaux; Collot to Lyons; I to Boulogne. Citizeness, were all of the august names on your permit genuine, you could no more leave this port without my counter-signature than you could take wing and fly over the Channel!

ANNE [*with a shrill laugh of triumph*]. You have overreached yourself! You're an ordinary spy: you followed us from Paris—

VALSIN [*gaily*]. Oh, I intended you to notice that!

ANNE [*unheeding*]. You have claimed to be Commissioner of the highest power in France. We can prove that you are a common spy. You may go to the guillotine for that. Take care, Citizen! So! You have denounced us; we denounce you. I'll have you arrested by your own soldiers. I'll call them— [*She makes a feint of running to the window. He watches her coolly, in silence; and she halts, chagrined.*]

VALSIN [*pleasantly*]. I was sure you would not force me to

be premature. Remark it, Citizeness Laseyne: I am enjoying all this. I have waited a long time for it.

ANNE [*becoming hysterical*]. I am the Widow Balsage, I tell you! You do not know us—you followed us from Paris. [*Half sobbing.*] You're a spy—a hanger-on of the police. We will prove—

VALSIN [*stepping to the dismantled doorway*]. I left my assistant within hearing—a species of animal of mine. I may claim that he belongs to me. A worthy patriot, but skillful, who has had the honor of a slight acquaintance with you, I believe. [*Calling.*] Dossonville! [DOSSONVILLE, *a large man, flabby of flesh, loose-mouthed, grizzled, carelessly dressed, makes his appearance in the doorway. He has a harsh and reckless eye; and, obviously a flamboyant bully by temperament, his abject, doggish deference to* VALSIN *is instantly impressive, more than confirming the latter's remark that* DOSSONVILLE "*belongs*" *to him.* DOSSONVILLE, *apparently, is a chattel indeed, body and soul. At sight of him* MADAME DE LASEYNE *catches at the desk for support and stands speechless.*]

VALSIN [*easily*]. Dossonville, you may inform the Citizeness Laseyne what office I have the fortune to hold.

DOSSONVILLE [*coming in*]. Bright heaven! All the world knows that you are the representative of the Committee of Public Safety. Commissioner to Boulogne.

VALSIN. With what authority?

DOSSONVILLE. Absolute—unlimited! Naturally. What else would be useful?

VALSIN. You recall this woman, Dossonville?

DOSSONVILLE. She was present when I delivered the passport to the Emigrant Valny-Cherault, in Paris.

VALSIN. Did you forge that passport?

DOSSONVILLE. No. I told the Emigrant I had. Under orders. [*Grinning.*] It was genuine.

VALSIN. Where did you get it?

DOSSONVILLE. From you.

VALSIN [*suavely*]. Sit down, Dossonville. [*The latter, who is standing by a chair, obeys with a promptness more than military.* VALSIN *turns smilingly to* MADAME DE LASEYNE.] Dossonville's instructions, however, did not include a "permit" to sail on the *Jeune Pierrette*. All of which, I confess, Citizeness, has very much the appearance of a trap! [*He tosses the two*

papers upon the desk. Utterly dismayed, she makes no effort to secure them. He regards her with quizzical enjoyment.]
ANNE. Ah—you— [*She fails to speak coherently.*]
VALSIN. Dossonville has done very well. He procured your passport, brought your "disguises," planned your journey, even gave you directions how to find these lodgings in Boulogne. Indeed, I instructed him to omit nothing for your comfort. [*He pauses for a moment.*] If I am a spy, Citizeness Laseyne, at least I trust your gracious intelligence may not cling to the epithet "ordinary." My soul! but I appear to myself a most uncommon type of spy—a very intricate, complete, and unusual spy, in fact.
ANNE [*to herself, weeping*]. Ah, poor Louis!
VALSIN [*cheerfully*]. You are beginning to comprehend? That is well. Your niece's door is still ajar by the discreet width of a finger, so I assume that the Emigrant also begins to comprehend. Therefore I take my ease! [*He seats himself in the most comfortable chair in the room, crossing his legs in a leisurely attitude, and lightly drumming the tips of his fingers together, the while his peaceful gaze is fixed upon the ceiling. His tone, as he continues, is casual.*] You understand, my Dossonville, having long ago occupied this very apartment myself, I am serenely aware that the Emigrant can leave the other room only by the window; and as this is the fourth floor, and a proper number of bayonets in the courtyard below are arranged to receive any person active enough to descend by a rope of bed-clothes, one is confident that the said Emigrant will remain where he is. Let us make ourselves comfortable, for it is a delightful hour—an hour I have long promised myself. I am in a good humor. Let us all be happy. Citizeness Laseyne, enjoy yourself. Call me some bad names!
ANNE [*between her teeth*]. If I could find one evil enough!
VALSIN [*slapping his knee delightedly*]. There it is: the complete incompetence of your class. You poor aristocrats, you do not even know how to swear. Your ancestors knew how! They were fighters; they knew how to swear because they knew how to attack; you poor moderns have no profanity left in you, because, poisoned by idleness, you have forgotten even how to resist. And yet you thought yourselves on top, and so you were —but as foam is on top of the wave. You forgot that power, like genius, always comes from underneath, because it is pro-

duced only by turmoil. We have had to wring the neck of your feather-head court, because while the court was the nation the nation had its pockets picked. You were at the mercy of anybody with a pinch of brains: adventurers like Mazarin, like Fouquet, like Law, or that little commoner, the woman Fish, who called herself Pompadour and took France—France, merely!—from your King, and used it to her own pleasure. Then, at last, after the swindlers had well plucked you—at last, unfortunate creatures, the People got you! Citizeness, the People had starved: be assured they will eat you to the bone—and then eat the bone! You are helpless because you have learned nothing and forgotten everything. You have forgotten everything in this world except how to be fat!

DOSSONVILLE [*applauding with unction*]. Beautiful! It is beautiful, all that! A beautiful speech!

VALSIN. Ass!

DOSSONVILLE [*meekly*]. Perfectly, perfectly.

VALSIN [*crossly*]. That wasn't a speech; it was the truth. Citizeness Laseyne, so far as you are concerned, I am the People. [*He extends his hand negligently, with open palm.*] And I have got you. [*He clenches his fingers, like a cook's on the neck of a fowl.*] Like that! And I'm going to take you back to Paris, you and the Emigrant. [*She stands in an attitude eloquent of despair. His glance roves from her to the door of the other room, which is still slightly ajar; and, smiling at some fugitive thought, he continues, deliberately.*] I take you: you and your brother—and that rather pretty little person who traveled with you. [*There is a breathless exclamation from the other side of the door, which is flung open violently, as* ELOISE—*flushed, radiant with anger, and altogether magnificent—sweeps into the room to confront* VALSIN.]

ELOISE [*slamming the door behind her*]. Leave this Jack-in-Office to me, Anne!

DOSSONVILLE [*dazed by the vision*]. Lord! What glory! [*He rises, bowing profoundly, muttering hoarsely.*] Oh, eyes! Oh, hair! Look at her shape! Her chin! The divine—

VALSIN [*getting up and patting him reassuringly on the back*]. The lady perceives her effect, my Dossonville. It is no novelty. Sit down, my Dossonville. [*The still murmurous* DOSSONVILLE *obeys.* VALSIN *turns to* ELOISE, *a brilliant light in his eyes.*] Let me greet one of the nieces of Widow Balsage

—evidently not the sleepy one, and certainly not ill. Health so transcendent—

ELOISE [*placing her hand upon* MADAME DE LASEYNE'S *shoulder*]. This is a clown, Anne. You need have no fear of him whatever. His petty authority does not extend to us.

VALSIN [*deferentially*]. Will the niece of Widow Balsage explain why it does not?

ELOISE [*turning upon him fiercely*]. Because the patriot Citizeness Eloise d'Anville is here!

VALSIN [*assuming an air of thoughtfulness*]. Yes, she is here. That " permit " yonder even mentions her by name. It is curious. I shall have to go into that. Continue, niece.

ELOISE [*with supreme haughtiness*]. This lady is under her protection.

VALSIN [*growing red*]. Pardon. Under whose protection?

ELOISE [*sulphurously*]. Under the protection of Eloise d'Anville! [*This has a frightful effect upon* VALSIN; *his face becomes contorted; he clutches at his throat, apparently half strangled, staggers, and falls choking into the easy-chair he has formerly occupied.*]

VALSIN [*gasping, coughing, incoherent*]. Under the pro— the protection— [*He explodes into peal after peal of uproarious laughter.*] The protection of— Aha, ha, ha, ho, ho, ho! [*He rocks himself back and forth unappeasably.*]

ELOISE [*with a slight lift of the eyebrows*]. This man is an idiot.

VALSIN [*during an abatement of his attack*]. Oh, pardon! It is—too—much—too much for me! You say—these people are—

ELOISE [*stamping her foot*]. Under the protection of Eloise d'Anville, imbecile! You cannot touch them. She wills it! [*At this,* VALSIN *shouts as if pleading for mercy, and beats the air with his hands. He struggles to his feet and, pounding himself upon the chest, walks to and fro in the effort to control his convulsion.*]

ELOISE [*to* ANNE, *under cover of the noise he makes*]. I was wrong: he is not an idiot.

ANNE [*despairingly*]. He laughs at you.

ELOISE [*in a quick whisper*]. Out of bluster; because he is afraid. He is badly frightened. I know just what to do. Go into the other room with Louis.

ANNE [*protesting weakly*]. I can't hope—
ELOISE [*flashing from a cloud*]. You failed, didn't you?
[MADAME DE LASEYNE, *after a tearful perusal of the stern resourcefulness now written in the younger woman's eyes, succumbs with a piteous gesture of assent and goes out forlornly.* ELOISE *closes the door and stands with her back to it.*]
VALSIN [*paying no attention to them*]. Eloise d'Anville! [*Still pacing the room in the struggle to subdue his hilarity.*] This young citizeness speaks of the protection of Eloise d'Anville! [*Leaning feebly upon* DOSSONVILLE'S *shoulder.*] Do you hear, my Dossonville? It is an ecstasy. Ecstasize, then. Scream, Dossonville!
DOSSONVILLE [*puzzled, but evidently accustomed to being so, cackles instantly*]. Perfectly. Ha, ha! The citizeness is not only stirringly beautiful, she is also—
VALSIN. She is also a wit. Susceptible henchman, concentrate your thoughts upon domesticity. In this presence remember your wife!
ELOISE [*peremptorily*]. Dismiss that person. I have something to say to you.
VALSIN [*wiping his eyes*]. Dossonville, you are not required. We are going to be sentimental, and heaven knows you are not the moon. In fact, you are a fat old man. Exit, obesity! Go somewhere and think about your children. Flit, whale!
DOSSONVILLE [*rising*]. Perfectly, my chieftain. [*He goes to the broken door.*]
ELOISE [*tapping the floor with her shoe*]. Out of hearing!
VALSIN. The floor below.
DOSSONVILLE. Well understood. Perfectly, perfectly! [*He goes out through the hallway; disappears, chuckling grossly. There are some moments of silence within the room, while he is heard clumping down a flight of stairs; then* VALSIN *turns to* ELOISE *with burlesque ardor.*]
VALSIN. "Alone at last!"
ELOISE [*maintaining her composure*]. Rabbit!
VALSIN [*dropping into the chair at the desk, with mock dejection*]. Repulsed at the outset! Ah, Citizeness, there were moments on the journey from Paris when I thought I detected a certain kindness in your glances at the lonely stranger.
ELOISE [*folding her arms*]. You are to withdraw your sol-

diers, countersign the "permit," and allow my friends to embark at once.

VALSIN [*with solemnity*]. Do you give it as an order, Citizeness?

ELOISE. I do. You will receive suitable political advancement.

VALSIN [*in a choked voice*]. You mean as a—a reward?

ELOISE [*haughtily*]. *I* guarantee that you shall receive it! [*He looks at her strangely; then, with a low moan, presses his hand to his side, seeming upon the point of a dangerous seizure.*]

VALSIN [*managing to speak*]. I can only beg you to spare me. You have me at your mercy.

ELOISE [*swelling*]. It is well for you that you understand that!

VALSIN [*shaking his hand ruefully*]. Yes; you see I have a bad liver: it may become permanently enlarged. Laughter is my great danger.

ELOISE [*crying out with rage*]. *Oh!*

VALSIN [*dolorously*]. I have continually to remind myself that I am no longer in the first flush of youth.

ELOISE. Idiot! Do you not know who I am!

VALSIN. You? Oh yes— [*He checks himself abruptly; looks at her with brief intensity; turns his eyes away, half closing them in quick meditation; smiles, as upon some secret pleasantry, and proceeds briskly.*] Oh yes, yes, I know who you are.

ELOISE [*beginning haughtily*]. Then you—

VALSIN [*at once cutting her off*]. As to your name, I do not say. Names at best are details; and your own is a detail that could hardly be thought to matter. *What* you are is obvious: you joined Louis and his sister in Paris at the barriers, and traveled with them as "Marie Balsage," a sister. You might save us a little trouble by giving us your real name; you will probably refuse, and the police will have to look it up when I take you back to Paris. Frankly, you are of no importance to us, though of course we'll send you to the Tribunal. No doubt you are a poor relative of the Valny-Cheraults, or, perhaps, you may have been a governess in the Laseyne family, or—

ELOISE [*under her breath*]. Idiot! Idiot!

VALSIN [*with subterranean enjoyment, watching her side-*

long]. Or the good-looking wife of some faithful retainer of the Emigrant's, perhaps.

ELOISE [*with a shrill laugh*]. Does the Committee of Public Safety betray the same intelligence in the appointment of *all* its agents? [*Violently.*] Imbecile, I—

VALSIN [*quickly raising his voice to check her*]. You are of no importance, I tell you! [*Changing his tone.*] Of course I mean politically. [*With broad gallantry.*] Otherwise, I am the first to admit extreme susceptibility. I saw that you observed it on the way—at the taverns, in the diligence, at the posting-houses, at—

ELOISE [*with serenity*]. Yes. I am accustomed to oglers.

VALSIN. Alas, I believe you! My unfortunate sex is but too responsive.

ELOISE [*gasping*]. "Responsive"— Oh!

VALSIN [*indulgently*]. Let us return to the safer subject. Presently I shall arrest those people in the other room and, regretfully, you too. But first I pamper myself; I chat; I have an attractive woman to listen. In the matter of the arrest, I delay my fire; I do not flash in the pan, but I lengthen my fuse. Why? For the same reason that when I was a little boy and had something good to eat, I always first paid it the compliments of an epicure. I looked at it a long while. I played with it. Then—I devoured it! I am still like that. And Louis yonder is good to eat, because I happen not to love him. However, I should mention that I doubt if he could recall either myself or the circumstance which annoyed me; some episodes are sometimes so little to certain people and so significant to certain other people. [*He smiles, stretching himself luxuriously in his chair.*] Behold me, Citizeness! I am explained. I am indulging my humor: I play with my cake. Let us see into what curious little figures I can twist it.

ELOISE. Idiot!

VALSIN [*pleasantly*]. I have lost count, but I think that is the sixth idiot you have called me. Aha, it is only history, which one admires for repeating itself. Good! Let us march. I shall play— [*He picks up the "permit" from the desk, studies it absently, and looks whimsically at her over his shoulder, continuing:*] I shall play with—with all four of you.

ELOISE [*impulsively*]. Four?

VALSIN. I am not easy to deceive; there are four of you here.

ELOISE [*staring*]. So?

VALSIN. Louis brought you and his sister from Paris: a party of three. This "permit" which he forged is for four; the original three and the woman you mentioned a while ago, Eloise d'Anville. Hence she must have joined you here. The deduction is plain: there are three people in that room: the Emigrant, his sister, and this Eloise d'Anville. To the trained mind such reasoning is simple.

ELOISE [*elated*]. Perfectly!

VALSIN [*with an air of cunning*]. Nothing escapes me. You see that.

ELOISE. At first glance! I make you my most profound compliments. Sir, you are an eagle!

VALSIN [*smugly*]. Thanks. Now, then, pretty governess, you thought this d'Anville might be able to help you. What put that in your head?

ELOISE [*with severity*]. Do you pretend not to know what she is?

VALSIN. A heroine I have had the misfortune never to encounter. But I am informed of her character and history.

ELOISE [*sternly*]. Then you understand that even the Agent of the National Committee risks his head if he dares touch people she chooses to protect.

VALSIN [*extending his hand in plaintive appeal*]. Be generous to my opacity. How could *she* protect anybody?

ELOISE [*with condescension*]. She has earned the gratitude—

VALSIN. Of whom?

ELOISE [*superbly*]. Of the Nation!

VALSIN [*breaking out again*]. Ha, ha, ha! [*Clutching at his side.*] Pardon, oh, pardon, liver of mine. I must not die; my life is still useful.

ELOISE [*persisting stormily*]. Of the People, stupidity! Of the whole People, dolt! Of France, blockhead!

VALSIN [*with a violent effort, conquering his hilarity*]. There! I am saved. Let us be solemn, my child; it is better for my malady. You are still so young that one can instruct you that individuals are rarely grateful; "the People," never. What you call "the People" means folk who are not always sure of their next meal; therefore their great political and patriotic question is the cost of food. Their heroes are the champions who are going to make it cheaper; and when these champions fail them or cease to be useful to them, then they either forget these poor champions—or eat them. Let us hear what your Eloise d'Anville has done to earn the reward of being forgotten instead of eaten.

ELOISE [*her lips quivering*]. She surrendered her property voluntarily. She gave up all she owned to the Nation.

VALSIN [*genially*]. And immediately went to live with her relatives in great luxury.

ELOISE [*choking*]. The Republic will protect her. She gave her whole estate—

VALSIN. And the order for its confiscation was already written when she did it.

ELOISE [*passionately*]. Ah—*liar!*

VALSIN [*smiling*]. I have seen the order. [*She leans against the wall, breathing heavily. He goes on, smoothly.*] Yes, this martyr " gave " us her property; but one hears that she went to the opera just the same and wore more jewels than ever, and lived richly upon the Laseynes and Valny-Cheraults, until *they* were confiscated. Why, all the world knows about this woman; and let me tell you, to your credit, my governess, I think you have a charitable heart: you are the only person I ever heard speak kindly of her.

ELOISE [*setting her teeth*]. Venom!

VALSIN [*observing her slyly*]. It is with difficulty I am restraining my curiosity to see her—also to hear her!—when she learns of her proscription by a grateful Republic.

ELOISE [*with shrill mockery*]. Proscribed? Eloise d'Anville proscribed? Your inventions should be more plausible, Goodman Spy! I *knew* you were lying—

VALSIN [*smiling*]. You do not believe—

ELOISE [*proudly*]. Eloise d'Anville is a known Girondist. The Gironde is the real power in France.

VALSIN [*mildly*]. That party has fallen.

ELOISE [*with fire*]. Not far! It will revive.

VALSIN. Pardon, Citizeness, but you are behind the times, and they are very fast nowadays—the times. The Gironde is dead.

ELOISE [*ominously*]. It may survive *you,* my friend. Take care!

VALSIN [*unimpressed*]. The Gironde had a grand façade, and that was all. It was a party composed of amateurs and orators; and of course there were some noisy camp-followers and a few comic-opera vivandières, such as this d'Anville. In short, the Gironde looked enormous because it was hollow. It was like a pie that is all crust. We have tapped the crust—with a knife, Citizeness. There is nothing left.

ELOISE [*contemptuously*]. You say so. Nevertheless, the Rolands—

VALSIN [*gravely*]. Roland was found in a field yesterday; he had killed himself. His wife was guillotined the day after you left Paris. Every one of their political friends is proscribed.

ELOISE [*shaking as with bitter cold*]. It is a lie! Not Eloise d'Anville!

VALSIN [*rising*]. Would you like to see the warrant for her arrest? [*He takes a packet of documents from his breast pocket, selects one, and spreads it open before her.*] Let me read you her description: " Eloise d'Anville, aristocrat. Figure, comely. Complexion, blond. Eyes, dark blue. Nose, straight. Mouth, wide—"

ELOISE [*in a burst of passion, striking the warrant a violent blow with her clenched fist*]. Let them dare! [*Beside herself, she strikes again, tearing the paper from his grasp. She stamps upon it.*] Let them dare, I say!

VALSIN [*picking up the warrant*]. Dare to say her mouth is wide?

ELOISE [*cyclonic*]. Dare to arrest her!

VALSIN. It does seem a pity. [*He folds the warrant slowly and replaces it in his pocket.*] Yes, a great pity. She was the one amusing thing in all this somberness. She will be missed. The Revolution will lack its joke.

ELOISE [*recoiling, her passion exhausted*]. Ah, infamy! [*She turns from him, covering her face with her hands.*]

VALSIN [*with a soothing gesture*]. Being only her friend, you speak mildly. The d'Anville herself would call it blasphemy.

ELOISE [*with difficulty*]. She is—so vain—then?

VALSIN [*lightly*]. Oh, a type—an actress.

ELOISE [*her back to him*]. How do you know? You said—

VALSIN. That I had not encountered her. [*Glibly.*] One knows best the people one has never seen. Intimacy confuses judgment. I confess to that amount of hatred for the former Marquis de Valny-Cherault that I take as great an interest in all that concerns him as if I loved him. And the little d'Anville concerns him—yes, almost one would say, consumes him. The unfortunate man is said to be so blindly faithful that he can speak her name without laughing.

ELOISE [*stunned*]. Oh!

VALSIN [*going on, cheerily*]. No one else can do that, Citizeness. Jacobins, Cordeliers, Hébertists, even the shattered relics of the Gironde itself, all alike join in the colossal laughter at this Tricoteuse in Sèvres—this Jeanne d'Arc in rice-powder!

ELOISE [*tragically*]. They laugh—and proclaim her an outlaw!

VALSIN [*waving his hand carelessly*]. Oh, it is only that we are sweeping up the last remnants of aristocracy, and she goes with the rest—into the dust-heap. She should have remained a royalist; the final spectacle might have had dignity. As it is, she is not of her own class, not of ours: neither fish nor flesh nor—but yes, perhaps, after all, she is a fowl.

ELOISE [*brokenly*]. Alas! Homing—with wounded wing! [*She sinks into a chair with pathetic grace, her face in her hands.*]

VALSIN [*surreptitiously grinning*]. Not at all what I meant. [*Brutally.*] Peacocks don't fly.

ELOISE [*regaining her feet at a bound*]. You imitation dandy! You—

VALSIN [*with benevolence*]. My dear, your indignation for your friend is chivalrous. It is admirable; but she is not worth it. You do not understand her: you have probably seen her so much that you have never seen her as she is.

ELOISE [*witheringly*]. But you, august Zeus, having *never* seen her, will reveal her to me!

VALSIN [*smoothly urbane*]. If you have ears. You see, she is not altogether unique, but of a variety known to men who are wise enough to make a study of women.

ELOISE [*snapping out a short, loud laugh in his face*]. Pouff!

VALSIN [*unruffled*]. I profess myself an apprentice. The science itself is but in its infancy. Women themselves understand very well that they are to be classified, and they fear that we shall perceive it: they do not really wish to be known. Yet it is coming; some day our cyclopedists will have you sorted, classed, and defined with precision; but the d'Alembert of the future will not be a woman, because no woman so disloyal will ever be found. Men have to acquire loyalty to their sex: yours is an instinct. Citizen governess, I will give you a reading of the little d'Anville from this unwritten work. To begin—

ELOISE [*feverishly interested, but affecting languor*]. *Must* you?

VALSIN. To Eloise d'Anville the most interesting thing about a rose-bush has always been that Eloise d'Anville could smell it. Moonlight becomes important when it falls upon her face; sunset is worthy when she grows rosy in it. To her mind, the universe was set in motion to be the background for a decoration, and she is the decoration. She believes that the cathedral was built for the fresco. And when a dog interests her, it is because he would look well beside her in a painting. Such dogs have no minds. I refer you to all the dogs in the portraits of Beauties.

ELOISE [*not at all displeased; pretending carelessness*]. Ah, you have heard that she is beautiful?

VALSIN. Far worse: that she is a Beauty. Let nothing ever tempt *you*, my dear, into setting up in that line. For you are very well-appearing, I assure you; and if you had been surrounded with all the disadvantages of the d'Anville, who knows but that you might have become as famous a Beauty as she? What makes a Beauty is not the sumptuous sculpture alone, but a very peculiar arrogance—not in the least arrogance of mind, my little governess. In this, your d'Anville emerged from childhood full-panoplied indeed; and the feather-head court fell headlong at her feet. It was the fated creature's ruin.

ELOISE [*placidly*]. And it is because of her beauty that you drag her to the guillotine?

VALSIN. Bless you, I merely convey her!

ELOISE. Tell me, logician, was it not her beauty that inspired her to give her property to the Nation?

VALSIN. It was.

ELOISE. What perception! I am faint with admiration. And no doubt it was her beauty that made her a Republican?

VALSIN. What else?

ELOISE. Hail, oracle! [*She releases an arpeggio of satiric laughter.*]

VALSIN. That laugh is diaphanous. I see you through it, already convinced. [*She stops laughing immediately.*] Ha! we may proceed. Remark this, governess: a Beauty is the living evidence of man's immortality; the one plain proof that he has a soul.
ELOISE. It is not so bad then, after all?
VALSIN. It is utterly bad. But of all people a Beauty is most conscious of her duality. Her whole life is based upon her absolute knowledge that her Self and her body are two. She sacrifices all things to her beauty because her beauty feeds her Self with a dreadful food which it has made her unable to live without.
ELOISE. My little gentleman, you talk like a sentimental waiter. Your metaphors are all hot from the kitchen.
VALSIN [*nettled*]. It is natural; unlike your Eloise, I am *really* of " the People "—and starved much in my youth.
ELOISE. But, like her, you are still hungry.
VALSIN. A Beauty is a species of cannibal priestess, my dear. She will make burnt-offerings of her father and her mother, her sisters—her lovers—to her beauty, that it may in turn bring her the food she must have or perish.
ELOISE. *Boum!* [*She snaps her fingers.*] And of course she bathes in the blood of little children?
VALSIN [*grimly*]. Often.
ELOISE [*averting her gaze from his*]. This mysterious food—
VALSIN. Not at all mysterious. Sensation. There you have it. And that is why Eloise d'Anville is a renegade. You understand perfectly.
ELOISE. You are too polite. No.
VALSIN [*gaily*]. Behold, then! Many women who are not Beauties are beautiful, but in such women you do not always discover beauty at your first glance: it is disclosed with a subtle tardiness. It does not dazzle; it is reluctant; but it grows as you look again and again. You get a little here, a little there, like glimpses of children hiding in a garden. It is shy, and sometimes closed in from you altogether, and then, unexpectedly, this belated loveliness springs into bloom before your very eyes. It retains the capacity of surprise, the vital element of charm. But the Beauty lays all waste before her at a stroke: it is soon over. Thus your Eloise, brought to court, startled Versailles; the sensation was overwhelming. Then Versailles

got used to her, just as it had to its other prodigies: the fountains were there, the King was there, the d'Anville was there; and naturally, one had seen them; saw them every day—one talked of matters less accepted. That was horrible to Eloise. She had tasted; the appetite, once stirred, was insatiable. At any cost she must henceforth have always the sensation of being a sensation. She must be the pivot of a reeling world. So she went into politics. Ah, Citizeness, there was one man who understood Beauties—not Homer, who wrote of Helen! Romance is gallant by profession, and Homer lied like a poet. For the truth about the Trojan War is that the wise Ulysses made it, not because Paris stole Helen, but because the Trojans were threatening to bring her back.

ELOISE [*unwarily*]. Who was the man that understood Beauties?

VALSIN. Bluebeard. [*He crosses the room to the dressing-table, leans his back against it in an easy attitude, his elbows resting upon the top.*]

ELOISE [*slowly, a little tremulously*]. And so Eloise d'Anville should have her head cut off?

VALSIN. Well, she thought she was in politics, didn't she? [*Suavely.*] You may be sure she thoroughly enjoyed her hallucination that she was a great figure in the Revolution—which was cutting off the heads of so many of her relatives and old friends! Don't waste your pity, my dear.

ELOISE [*looking at him fixedly*]. Citizen, you must have thought a great deal about my unhappy friend. She might be flattered by so searching an interest.

VALSIN [*negligently*]. Not interest in her, governess, but in the Emigrant who cools his heels on the other side of that door, greatly to my enjoyment, waiting my pleasure to arrest him. The poor wretch is the one remaining lover of this girl: faithful because he let his passion for her become a habit; and he will never get over it until he has had possession. She has made him suffer frightfully, but I shall never forgive her for not having dealt him the final stroke. It would have saved me all the bother I have been put to in avenging the injury he did me.

ELOISE [*frowning*]. What "final stroke" could she have "dealt" him?

VALSIN [*with sudden vehement intensity*]. She could have

loved him! [*He strikes the table with his fist.*] I see it! I see it! Beauty's husband! [*Pounding the table with each exclamation, his voice rising in excitement.*] What a vision! This damned, proud, loving Louis, a pomade bearer! A buttoner! An errand-boy to the perfumer's, to the chemist's, to the milliner's! A groom of the powder-closet—

ELOISE [*snatching at the opportunity*]. How noisy you are!

VALSIN [*discomfited, apologetically*]. You see, it is only so lately that we of "the People" have dared even to whisper. Of course, now that we are free to shout, we overdo it. We let our voices out, we let our joys out, we let our hates out. We let everything out—except our prisoners! [*He smiles winningly.*]

ELOISE [*slowly*]. Do you guess what all this bluster—this tirade upon the wickedness of beauty—makes me think?

VALSIN. Certainly. Being a woman, you cannot imagine a bitterness which is not "personal."

ELOISE [*laughing*]. "Being a woman," I think that the person who has caused you the greatest suffering in your life must be very good-looking!

VALSIN [*calmly*]. Quite right. It was precisely this d'Anville. I will tell you. [*He sits on the arm of a chair near her, and continues briskly.*] I was not always a politician. Six years ago I was a soldier in the Valny regiment of cavalry. That was the old army, that droll army, that royal army; so ridiculous that it was truly majestic. In the Valny regiment we had some rouge-pots for officers—and for a colonel, who but our Emigrant yonder! Aha! we suffered in the ranks, let me tell you, when Eloise had been coy; and one morning it was my turn. You may have heard that she was betrothed first to Louis and later to several others? My martyrdom occurred the day after she had announced to the court her betrothal to the young Duc de Creil, whose father afterward interfered. Louis put us on drill in a hard rain: he had the habit of relieving his chagrin like that. My horse fell, and happened to shower our commander with mud. Louis let out all his rage upon me: it was an excuse, and, naturally, he disliked mud. But I was rolling in it, with my horse: I also disliked it—and I was indiscreet enough to attempt some small reply. That finished my soldiering, Citizeness. He had me tied to a post before the barracks for the rest of the day. I remember with remarkable distinctness that the valets of heaven had neglected to warm the rain for that bath; that it was February; and that Louis's orders had left me nothing to wear upon my back except an unfulsome descriptive placard and my modesty. Altogether it was a disadvantageous position, particularly for the exchange of repartee with such of my comrades as my youthful amiability had not endeared; I have seldom seen more cheerful indifference to bad weather. Inclement skies failed to injure the spectacle: it was truly the great performance of my career; some people would not even go home to eat, and peddlers did a good trade in cakes and wine. In the evening they whipped me conscientiously—my tailor has never since made me an entirely comfortable coat. Then they gave me the place of honor at the head of a procession by torchlight and drummed me out of camp with my placard upon my back. So I adopted another profession: I had a friend who was a doctor in the stables of d'Artois; and I knew horses. He made me his assistant.

ELOISE [*shuddering*]. You are a veterinarian!

VALSIN [*smiling*]. No; a horse-doctor. It was thus I " retired " from the army and became a politician. My friend was only a horse-doctor himself, but his name happened to be Marat.

ELOISE. Ah, frightful! [*For the first time she begins to feel genuine alarm.*]

VALSIN. The sequence is simple. If Eloise d'Anville hadn't coquetted with young Creil I shouldn't be Commissioner here to-day, settling my account with Louis. I am in his debt for more than the beating: I should tell you there was a woman in my case, a slender lace-maker with dark eyes—very pretty eyes. She had furnished me with a rival, a corporal; and he brought her for a stroll in the rain past our barracks that day when I was attracting so much unsought attention. They waited for the afterpiece, enjoyed a pasty and a bottle of Beaune, and went away laughing cozily together. I did not see my pretty lace-maker again, not for years—not until a month ago. Her corporal was still with her, and it was their turn to be undesirably conspicuous. They were part of a procession passing along the Rue St. Honoré on its way to the Place of the Revolution. They were standing up in the cart; the lace-maker had grown fat, and she was scolding her poor corporal bitterly. What a habit that must have been!—they were not five minutes from the guillotine. I own that a thrill

BEAUTY AND THE JACOBIN   43

of gratitude to Louis temporarily softened me toward him, though at the very moment I was following him through the crowd. At least he saved me from the lace-maker!

ELOISE [*shrinking from him*]. You are horrible!

VALSIN. To my regret you must find me more and more so.

ELOISE [*panting*]. You *are* going to take us back to Paris, then? To the Tribunal—and to the— [*She covers her eyes with her hands.*]

VALSIN [*gravely*]. I can give you no comfort, governess. You are involved with the Emigrant, and, to be frank, I am going to do as horrible things to Louis as I can invent—and I am an ingenious man. [*His manner becomes sinister.*] I am near the top. The cinders of Marat are in the Pantheon, but Robespierre still flames; and he claims me as his friend. I can do what I will. And I have much in store for Louis before he shall be so fortunate as to die!

ELOISE [*faintly*]. And—and Eloise—d'Anville? [*Her hands fall from her face: he sees large, beautiful tears upon her cheeks.*]

VALSIN [*coldly*]. Yes. [*She is crushed for the moment; then, recovering herself with a violent effort, lifts her head defiantly and stands erect, facing him.*]

ELOISE. You take her head because your officer punished you, six years ago, for a breach of military discipline!

VALSIN [*in a lighter tone*]. Oh no. I take it, just as she injured me—incidentally. In truth, Citizeness, it isn't I who take it: I only arrest her because the government has proscribed her.

ELOISE. And you've just finished telling me you were preparing tortures for her! I thought you an intelligent man. Pah! You're only a gymnast. [*She turns away from him haughtily and moves toward the door.*]

VALSIN [*touching his scarf of office*]. True. I climb. [*She halts suddenly, as if startled by this; she stands as she is, her back to him, for several moments, and does not change her attitude when she speaks.*]

ELOISE [*slowly*]. You climb alone.

VALSIN [*with a suspicious glance at her*]. Yes—alone.

ELOISE [*in a low voice*]. Why didn't you take the lace-maker with you? You might have been happier. [*Very slowly she turns and comes toward him, her eyes full upon his: she moves deliberately and with incomparable grace. He seems to be making an effort to look away, and failing: he cannot release his eyes from the glorious and starry glamour that holds them. She comes very close to him, so close that she almost touches him.*]

ELOISE [*in a half-whisper*]. You might have been happier with—a friend—to climb with you.

VALSIN [*demoralized*]. Citizeness—I am—I—

ELOISE [*in a voice of velvet*]. Yes, Say it. You are—

VALSIN [*desperately*]. I have told you that I am the most susceptible of men.

ELOISE [*impulsively putting her hand on his shoulder*]. Is it a crime? Come, my friend, you are a man who *does* climb: you will go over all. You believe in the Revolution because you have used it to lift you. But other things can help you, too. Don't you need them?

VALSIN [*understanding perfectly, gasping*]. Need what? [*She draws her hand from his shoulder, moves back from him slightly, and crosses her arms upon her bosom with a royal meekness.*]

ELOISE [*grandly*]. Do I seem so useless?

VALSIN [*in a distracted voice*]. Heaven help me! What do you want?

ELOISE. Let these people go. [*Hurriedly, leaning near him.*] I have promised to save them: give them their permit to embark, and I— [*She pauses, flushing beautifully, but does not take her eyes from him.*] I—I do not wish to leave France. My place is in Paris. You will go into the National Committee. You can be its ruler. You *will* rule it! I believe in you! [*Glowing like a rose of fire.*] I will go with you. I will help you! I will marry you!

VALSIN [*in a fascinated whisper*]. Good Lord! [*He stumbles back from her, a strange light in his eyes.*]

ELOISE. You are afraid—

VALSIN [*with sudden loudness*]. I am! Upon my soul, I am afraid!

ELOISE [*smiling gloriously upon him*]. Of what, my friend? Tell me of what?

VALSIN [*explosively*]. Of myself! I am afraid of myself because I am a prophet. This is precisely what I foretold to myself you would do! I knew it, yet I am aghast when it happens—aghast at my own cleverness!

ELOISE [*bewildered to blankness*]. What?

VALSIN [*half hysterical with outrageous vanity*]. I swear I knew it, and it fits so exactly that I am afraid of myself! *Aha,* Valsin, you rogue! I should hate to have you on *my* track! Citizen governess, you are a wonderful person, but not so wonderful as this devil of a Valsin!

ELOISE [*vaguely, in a dead voice*]. I cannot understand what you are talking about. Do you mean—

VALSIN. And what a spell was upon me! I was near calling Dossonville to preserve me.

ELOISE [*speaking with a strange naturalness, like a child's*]. You mean—you don't want me?

VALSIN. Ah, Heaven help me, I am going to laugh again! Oh, ho, ho! I am spent! [*He drops into a chair and gives way to another attack of uproarious hilarity.*] Ah, ha, ha, ha! Oh, my liver, ha, ha! No, Citizeness, I do not want you! Oh, ha, ha, ha!

ELOISE. *Oh!* [*She utters a choked scream and rushes at him.*] Swine!

VALSIN [*warding her off with outstretched hands*]. Spare me! Ha, ha, ha! I am helpless! Ho, ho, ho! Citizeness, it would not be worth your while to strangle a man who is already dying!

ELOISE [*beside herself*]. Do you dream that I *meant* it?

VALSIN [*feebly*]. Meant to strangle me?

ELOISE [*frantic*]. To give myself to you!

VALSIN. In short, to—to marry me! [*He splutters.*]

ELOISE [*furiously*]. It was a ruse—

VALSIN [*soothingly*]. Yes, yes, a trick. I saw that all along.

ELOISE [*even more infuriated*]. For their sake, beast! [*She points to the other room.*] To save *them!*

VALSIN [*wiping his eyes*]. Of course, of course. [*He rises, stepping quickly to the side of the chair away from her and watching her warily.*] *I* knew it was to save them. We'll put it like that.

ELOISE [*in an anger of exasperation*]. It *was* that!

VALSIN. Yes, yes. [*Keeping his distance.*] I saw it from the first. [*Suppressing symptoms of returning mirth.*] It was perfectly plain. You mustn't excite yourself—nothing could have been clearer! [*A giggle escapes him, and he steps hastily backward as she advances upon him.*]

ELOISE. Poodle! Valet! Scum of the alleys! Sheep of the prisons! Jailer! Hangman! Assassin! Brigand! Horse-doctor! [*She hurls the final epithet at him in a climax of ferocity which wholly exhausts her; and she sinks into the chair by the desk, with her arms upon the desk and her burning face hidden in her arms.* VALSIN, *morbidly chuckling, in spite of himself, at each of her insults, has retreated farther and farther, until he stands with his back against the door of the inner room, his right hand behind him, resting on the latch. As her furious eyes leave him he silently opens the door, letting it remain a few inches ajar and keeping his back to it. Then, satisfied that what he intends to say will be overheard by those within, he erases all expression from his face, and strides to the dismantled doorway in the passage.*]

VALSIN [*calling loudly*]. Dossonville! [*He returns, coming down briskly to* ELOISE. *His tone is crisp and soldier-like.*] Citizeness, I have had my great hour. I proceed with the arrests. I have given you four plenty of time to prepare yourselves. Time? Why, the Emigrant could have changed clothes with one of the women in there a dozen times if he had hoped to escape in that fashion—as historical prisoners *have* won clear, it is related. Fortunately, that is impossible just now; and he will not dare to attempt it.

DOSSONVILLE [*appearing in the hallway*]. Present, my chieftain!

VALSIN [*sharply*]. Attend, Dossonville. The returned Emigrant, Valny-Cherault, is forfeited; but because I cherish a special grievance against him, I have decided upon a special punishment for him. It does not please me that he should have the comfort and ministrations of loving women on his journey to the Tribunal. No, no; the presence of his old sweetheart would make even the scaffold sweet to him. Therefore I shall take him alone. I shall let these women go.

DOSSONVILLE. What refinement! Admirable! [ELOISE *slowly rises, staring incredulously at* VALSIN.]

VALSIN [*picking up the "permit" from the desk*]. "Permit the Citizen Balsage and his sister, the Citizeness Virginie Balsage, and his second sister, Marie Balsage, and Eloise d'Anville—" Ha! You see, Dossonville, since one of these

three women is here, there are two in the other room with the
Emigrant. They are to come out, leaving him there. First,
however, we shall disarm him. You and I have had sufficient
experience in arresting aristocrats to know that they are not
always so sensible as to give themselves up peaceably, and I
happened to see the outline of a pistol under the Emigrant's
frock the other day in the diligence. We may as well save one
of us from a detestable hole through the body. [*He steps
toward the door, speaking sharply.*] Emigrant, you have
heard. For your greater chagrin, these three devoted women
are to desert you. Being an aristocrat, you will pretend to
prefer this arrangement. They are to leave at once. Throw
your pistol into this room, and I will agree not to make the
arrest until they are in safety. They can reach your vessel in
five minutes. When they have gone, I give you my word not
to open this door for ten. [*A pistol is immediately thrown
out of the door, and falls at* VALSIN'S *feet. He picks it up, his
eyes alight with increasing excitement.*]
  VALSIN [*tossing the pistol to* DOSSONVILLE]. Call the lieutenant. [DOSSONVILLE *goes to the window, leans out, and
beckons.* VALSIN *writes hastily at the desk, not sitting down.*]
"Permit the three women Balsage to embark without delay
upon the *Jeune Pierrette*. Signed: Valsin." There, Citizeness,
is a "permit" which permits. [*He thrusts the paper into the
hand of* ELOISE, *swings toward the door of the inner room, and
raps loudly upon it.*] Come, my feminines! Your sailors await
you—brave, but no judges of millinery. There's a fair wind
for you; and a grand toilet is wasted at sea. Come, charmers;
come! [*The door is half opened, and* MADAME DE LASEYNE,
*white and trembling violently, enters quickly, shielding as much
as she can the inexpressibly awkward figure of her brother, behind whom she extends her hand, closing the door sharply. He
wears the brocaded skirt which* MADAME DE LASEYNE *has
taken from the portmanteau, and* ELOISE'S *long mantle, the
lifted hood and* MADAME DE LASEYNE'S *veil shrouding his head
and face.*]
  VALSIN [*in a stifled voice*]. At last! At last one beholds
the regal d'Anville! No Amazon—
  DOSSONVILLE [*aghast*]. It looks like—
  VALSIN [*shouting*]. It doesn't! [*He bows gallantly to*
LOUIS.] A cruel veil, but, oh, what queenly grace! [LOUIS

stumbles in the skirt. VALSIN *falls back, clutching at his side. But* ELOISE *rushes to* LOUIS *and throws herself upon her knees at his feet. She pulls his head down to hers and kisses him through the veil.*]
 VALSIN [*madly*]. Oh, touching devotion! Oh, sisters! Oh, love! Oh, honey! Oh, petticoats—
 DOSSONVILLE [*interrupting humbly*]. The lieutenant, Citizen Commissioner. [*He points to the hallway, where the officer appears, standing at attention.*]
 VALSIN [*wheeling*]. Officer, conduct these three persons to the quay. Place them on board the *Jeune Pierrette*. The captain will weigh anchor instantly. [*The officer salutes.*]
 ANNE [*hoarsely to* LOUIS, *who is lifting the weeping* ELOISE *to her feet*]. Quick! In the name of—
 VALSIN. Off with you! [MADAME DE LASEYNE *seizes the portmanteau and rushes to the broken doorway, half dragging the others with her. They go out in a tumultuous hurry, followed by the officer.* ELOISE *sends one last glance over her shoulder at* VALSIN *as she disappears, and one word of concentrated venom:* "Buffoon!" *In wild spirits he blows a kiss to her. The fugitives are heard clattering madly down the stairs.*]
 DOSSONVILLE [*excitedly*]. We can take the Emigrant now. [*Going to the inner door.*] Why wait—
 VALSIN. That room is empty.
 DOSSONVILLE. What!
 VALSIN [*shouting with laughter*]. He's gone! Not barebacked, but in petticoats: that's worse! He's gone, I tell you! The other was the d'Anville.
 DOSSONVILLE. Then you recog—
 VALSIN. Imbecile, she's as well known as the Louvre! They're off on their honeymoon! She'll take him now! She will! She will, on the soul of a prophet! [*He rushes to the window and leans far out, shouting at the top of his voice:*] Quits with you, Louis! Quits! Quits! [*He falls back from the window and relapses into a chair, cackling ecstatically.*]
 DOSSONVILLE [*hoarse with astonishment*]. You've let him go! You've let 'em *all* go!
 VALSIN [*weak with laughter*]. Well, *you're* not going to inform. [*With a sudden reversion to extreme seriousness, he levels a sinister forefinger at his companion.*] And, also, take

care of your health, friend; remember constantly that you have a weak throat, *and don't you ever mention this to my wife!* These are bad times, my Dossonville, and neither you nor I will see the end of them. Good Lord! Can't we have a little fun as we go along? [*A fresh convulsion seizes him, and he rocks himself pitiably in his chair.*]

[THE CURTAIN.]

THE PIERROT OF THE MINUTE
A DRAMATIC FANTASY IN ONE ACT

By
ERNEST DOWSON

Performance Free

Ernest Christopher Dowson, now generally known simply as Ernest Dowson, was born at the Grove, Belmont Hill, Lee, Kent, August 2, 1867, and died in London thirty-three years later. His schooling, because of his delicate health, was irregular, and he spent too short a time at Queen's College, Oxford, to take a degree. He lived abroad much, but during his sojourns in London in the 'nineties belonged to the Rhymer's Club [1] that met in an upper room of Johnson's own "Cheshire Cheese." His death from consumption brought to a close a life marred by waste and sordid associations.

The Pierrot of the Minute, Ernest Dowson's only dramatic attempt, is touched like the preceding play with the glamour of the old régime. Its charming artificiality suggests the pastoral games to which the ladies and gentlemen of Louis XV's circle may have turned for relief after the formalities and extravagances of their life at court.

Dowson's play, written in 1892, is mentioned in one of his letters, dated October twenty-fourth of that year: "I have been frightfully busy," he wrote, "having rashly undertaken to make a little Pierrot play in verse . . . which is to be played at Aldershot and afterwards at the Chelsea Town Hall: the article to be delivered in a fortnight. So until this period of mental agony is past, I can go nowhere." Anyone who has ever had to write something that had to be ready on a certain date will understand the quality of Dowson's emotion in this letter.

A recent critic who has studied the literary fashions of the group to which Dowson belonged and found that the members were addicted to the frequent use of the adjective, white, says: "Ernest Dowson was dominated by a sense of whiteness. . . . *The Pierrot of the Minute* is a veritable symphony in white. He calls for 'white music' and the Moon Maiden rides through

---

[1] Yeats has commemorated this club in the following lines in his poem, *The Grey Rock:*

"Poets with whom I learned my trade,
Companions of the Cheshire Cheese."

the skies 'drawn by a team of milk-white butterflies,' and farther on in the same poem we have a palace of many rooms:

> "'Within the fairest, clad in purity,
> Our mother dwelt immemorially:
> Moon-calm, moon-pale, with moon-stones on her gown,
> The floor she treads with little pearls is sown. . .'"

When the play was given in this country at the McCallum Theatre at Northampton, Massachusetts, it was "staged in black and white, the garden set having black walls on which fantastic white forms were stenciled. The bench, the statue, and Pierrot and his lady love were in white. To have tried to depict a real garden would have crowded the small stage, so a garden was suggested, and by suggestion caught the spirit of the piece."[1]

Granville Bantock, the English musician, composed *The Pierrot of the Minute. A Comedy Overture to a Dramatic Phantasy by Ernest Dowson,* which he conducted at the Worcester Festival in 1908. This music in whole or part may be used in connection with a production of Dowson's play.

---

[1] Constance D'Arcy Mackay, *The Little Theatre in the United States,* New York, 1917, p. 97.

THE PIERROT OF THE MINUTE

CHARACTERS

A Moon Maiden.
Pierrot.

SCENE.—A glade in the Parc du Petit Trianon. In the center a Doric temple with steps coming down the stage. On the left a little Cupid on a pedestal. Twilight.

Enter Pierrot *with his hands full of lilies. He is burdened with a little basket. He stands gazing at the Temple and the Statue.*

Pierrot.
  My journey's end! This surely is the glade
  Which I was promised: I have well obeyed!
  A clue of lilies was I bid to find,
  Where the green alleys most obscurely wind;
  Where tall oaks darkliest canopy o'erhead,
  And moss and violet make the softest bed;
  Where the path ends, and leagues behind me lie
  The gleaming courts and gardens of Versailles;
  The lilies streamed before me, green and white;
  I gathered, following: they led me right,
  To the bright temple and the sacred grove:
  This is, in truth, the very shrine of Love!
[*He gathers together his flowers and lays them at the foot of Cupid's statue; then he goes timidly up the first steps of the temple and stops.*]
  It is so solitary, I grow afraid.
  Is there no priest here, no devoted maid?
  Is there no oracle, no voice to speak,
  Interpreting to me the word I seek?
[*A very gentle music of lutes floats out from the temple.*
  Pierrot *starts back; he shows extreme surprise; then he*

returns to the foreground, and crouches down in rapt attention until the music ceases. His face grows puzzled and petulant.]
Too soon! too soon! in that enchanting strain,
Days yet unlived, I almost lived again:
It almost taught me that I most would know—
Why am I here, and why am I Pierrot?
[*Absently he picks up a lily which has fallen to the ground, and repeats.*]
Why came I here, and why am I Pierrot?
That music and this silence both affright;
Pierrot can never be a friend of night.
I never felt my solitude before—
Once safe at home, I will return no more.
Yet the commandment of the scroll was plain;
While the light lingers let me read again.
[*He takes a scroll from his bosom and reads.*]
" He loves to-night who never loved before;
Who ever loved, to-night shall love once more."
I never loved! I know not what love is.
I am so ignorant—but what is this?
           [*Reads.*]
"*Who would adventure to encounter Love
Must rest one night within this hallowed grove.
Cast down thy lilies, which have led thee on,
Before the tender feet of Cupidon.*"
Thus much is done, the night remains to me.
Well, Cupidon, be my security!
Here is more writing, but too faint to read.
[*He puzzles for a moment, then casts the scroll down.*]
Hence, vain old parchment. I have learnt thy rede!
[*He looks round uneasily, starts at his shadow; then discovers his basket with glee. He takes out a flask of wine, pours it into a glass, and drinks.*]
Courage, mon Ami! I shall never miss
Society with such a friend as this.
How merrily the rosy bubbles pass,
Across the amber crystal of the glass.
I had forgotten you. Methinks this quest
Can wake no sweeter echo in my breast.
     [*Looks round at the statue, and starts.*]

THE PIERROT OF THE MINUTE

Nay, little god! forgive. I did but jest.
[*He fills another glass, and pours it upon the statue.*]
    This libation, Cupid, take,
      With the lilies at thy feet;
    Cherish Pierrot for their sake,
      Send him visions strange and sweet,
    While he slumbers at thy feet.
    Only love kiss him awake!
    Only love kiss him awake!
[*Slowly falls the darkness, soft music plays, while* PIERROT *gathers together fern and foliage into a rough couch at the foot of the steps which lead to the Temple d'Amour. Then he lies down upon it, having made his prayer. It is night. He speaks softly.*]
Music, more music, far away and faint:
It is an echo of mine heart's complaint.
Why should I be so musical and sad?
I wonder why I used to be so glad?
In single glee I chased blue butterflies,
Half butterfly myself, but not so wise,
For they were twain, and I was only one.
Ah me! how pitiful to be alone.
My brown birds told me much, but in mine ear
They never whispered this—I learned it here:
The soft wood sounds, the rustlings in the breeze,
Are but the stealthy kisses of the trees.
Each flower and fern in this enchanted wood
Leans to her fellow, and is understood;
The eglantine, in loftier station set,
Stoops down to woo the maidly violet.
In gracile pairs the very lilies grow:
None is companionless except Pierrot.
Music, more music! how its echoes steal
Upon my senses with unlooked for weal.
Tired am I, tired, and far from this lone glade
Seems mine old joy in rout and masquerade.
Sleep cometh over me, now will I prove,
By Cupid's grace, what is this thing called love.
        [*Sleeps.*]
[*There is more music of lutes for an interval, during which*

a bright radiance, white and cold, streams from the temple upon the face of PIERROT. *Presently a* MOON MAIDEN *steps out of the temple; she descends and stands over the sleeper.*]

THE LADY.
  Who is this mortal
   Who ventures to-night
  To woo an immortal?
   Cold, cold the moon's light,
  For sleep at this portal,
   Bold lover of night.
  Fair is the mortal
   In soft, silken white,
  Who seeks an immortal.
   Ah, lover of night,
  Be warned at the portal,
   And save thee in flight!

[*She stoops over him:* PIERROT *stirs in his sleep.*]
PIERROT [*murmuring*].
Forget not, Cupid. Teach me all thy lore:
" *He loves to-night who never loved before.*"
THE LADY.
Unwitting boy! when, be it soon or late,
What Pierrot ever has escaped his fate?
What if I warned him! He might yet evade,
Through the long windings of this verdant glade;
Seek his companions in the blither way,
Which, else, must be as lost as yesterday.
So might he still pass some unheeding hours
In the sweet company of birds and flowers.
How fair he is, with red lips formed for joy,
As softly curved as those of Venus' boy.
Methinks his eyes, beneath their silver sheaves,
Rest tranquilly like lilies under leaves.
Arrayed in innocence, what touch of grace
Reveals the scion of a courtly race?
Well, I will warn him, though, I fear, too late—
What Pierrot ever has escaped his fate?
But, see, he stirs, new knowledge fires his brain,
And Cupid's vision bids him wake again.

Dione's Daughter! but how fair he is,
Would it be wrong to rouse him with a kiss?
[*She stoops down and kisses him, then withdraws into the shadow.*]
PIERROT [*rubbing his eyes*].
Celestial messenger! remain, remain;
Or, if a vision, visit me again!
What is this light, and whither am I come
To sleep beneath the stars so far from home?
[*Rises slowly to his feet.*]
Stay, I remember this is Venus' Grove,
And I am hither come to encounter ——
THE LADY [*coming forward, but veiled*].
              Love!
PIERROT [*in ecstasy, throwing himself at her feet*].
Then have I ventured and encountered Love?
THE LADY.
Not yet, rash boy! and, if thou wouldst be wise,
Return unknowing; he is safe who flies.
PIERROT.
Never, sweet lady, will I leave this place
Until I see the wonder of thy face.
Goddess or Naiad! lady of this Grove,
Made mortal for a night to teach me love,
Unveil thyself, although thy beauty be
Too luminous for my mortality.
THE LADY [*unveiling*].
Then, foolish boy, receive at length thy will:
Now knowest thou the greatness of thine ill.
PIERROT.
Now have I lost my heart, and gained my goal.
THE LADY.
Didst thou not read the warning on the scroll?
[*Picks up the parchment.*]
PIERROT.
I read it all, as on this quest I fared,
Save where it was illegible and hard.
THE LADY.
Alack! poor scholar, wast thou never taught
A little knowledge serveth less than naught?

Hadst thou perused —— but, stay, I will explain
What was the writing which thou didst disdain.
[*Reads.*]
" *Au Petit Trianon,* at night's full noon,
Mortal, beware the kisses of the moon!
Whoso seeks her she gathers like a flower—
He gives a life, and only gains an hour."
PIERROT [*laughing recklessly*].
Bear me away to thine enchanted bower,
All of my life I venture for an hour.
THE LADY.
Take up thy destiny of short delight;
I am thy lady for a summer's night.
Lift up your viols, maidens of my train,
And work such havoc on this mortal's brain
That for a moment he may touch and know
Immortal things, and be full Pierrot.
White music, Nymphs! Violet and Eglantine!
To stir his tired veins like magic wine.
What visitants across his spirit glance,
Lying on lilies, while he watch me dance?
Watch, and forget all weary things of earth,
All memories and cares, all joy and mirth,
While my dance woos him, light and rhythmical,
And weaves his heart into my coronal.
Music, more music for his soul's delight:
Love is his lady for a summer's night.
[PIERROT *reclines, and gazes at her while she dances. The dance finished, she beckons to him: he rises dreamily, and stands at her side.*]
PIERROT.
Whence came, dear Queen, such magic melody?
THE LADY.
Pan made it long ago in Arcady.
PIERROT.
I heard it long ago, I know not where,
As I knew thee, or ever I came here.
But I forget all things—my name and race
All that I ever knew except thy face.
Who art thou, lady? Breathe a name to me,
That I may tell it like a rosary.

THE PIERROT OF THE MINUTE

Thou, whom I sought, dear Dryad of the trees,
How art thou designate—art thou Heart's-Ease?
THE LADY.
Waste not the night in idle questioning,
Since Love departs at dawn's awakening.
PIERROT.
Nay, thou art right; what recks thy name or state,
Since thou art lovely and compassionate.
Play out thy will on me: I am thy lyre.
THE LADY.
I am to each the face of his desire.
PIERROT.
I am not Pierrot, but Venus' dove,
Who craves a refuge on the breast of love.
THE LADY.
What wouldst thou of the maiden of the moon?
Until the cock crow I may grant thy boon.
PIERROT.
Then, sweet Moon Maiden, in some magic car,
Wrought wondrously of many a homeless star—
Such must attend thy journeys through the skies,—
Drawn by a team of milk-white butterflies,
Whom, with soft voice and music of thy maids,
Thou urgest gently through the heavenly glades;
Mount me beside thee, bear me far away
From the low regions of the solar day;
Over the rainbow, up into the moon,
Where is thy palace and thine opal throne;
There on thy bosom ——
THE LADY.
                    Too ambitious boy!
I did but promise thee one hour of joy.
This tour thou plannest, with a heart so light,
Could hardly be completed in a night.
Hast thou no craving less remote than this?
PIERROT.
Would it be impudent to beg a kiss?
THE LADY.
I say not that: yet prithee have a care!
Often audacity has proved a snare.

How wan and pale do moon-kissed roses grow—
Dost thou not fear my kisses, Pierrot?
PIERROT.
As one who faints upon the Libyan plain
Fears the oasis which brings life again!
THE LADY.
Where far away green palm trees seem to stand
May be a mirage of the wreathing sand.
PIERROT.
Nay, dear enchantress, I consider naught,
Save mine own ignorance, which would be taught.
THE LADY.
Dost thou persist?
PIERROT.
    I do entreat this boon!
[*She bends forward, their lips meet: she withdraws with a petulant shiver. She utters a peal of clear laughter.*]
THE LADY.
Why art thou pale, fond lover of the moon?
PIERROT.
Cold are thy lips, more cold than I can tell;
Yet would I hang on them, thine icicle!
Cold is thy kiss, more cold than I could dream
Arctus sits, watching the Boreal stream:
But with its frost such sweetness did conspire
That all my veins are filled with running fire;
Never I knew that life contained such bliss
As the divine completeness of a kiss.
THE LADY.
Apt scholar! so love's lesson has been taught,
Warning, as usual, has gone for naught.
PIERROT.
Had all my schooling been of this soft kind,
To play the truant I were less inclined.
Teach me again! I am a sorry dunce—
I never knew a task by conning once.
THE LADY.
Then come with me! below this pleasant shrine
Of Venus we will presently recline,
Until birds' twitter beckon me away
To my own home, beyond the milky-way.

I will instruct thee, for I deem as yet
Of Love thou knowest but the alphabet.
PIERROT.
In its sweet grammar I shall grow most wise,
If all its rules be written in thine eyes.
[THE LADY *sits upon a step of the temple, and* PIERROT *leans upon his elbow at her feet, regarding her.*]
Sweet contemplation! how my senses yearn
To be thy scholar always, always learn.
Hold not so high from me thy radiant mouth,
Fragrant with all the spices of the South;
Nor turn, O sweet! thy golden face away,
For with it goes the light of all my day.
Let me peruse it, till I know by rote
Each line of it, like music, note by note;
Raise thy long lashes, Lady! smile again:
These studies profit me.
[*Takes her hand.*]
THE LADY.
Refrain, refrain!
PIERROT [*with passion*].
I am but studious, so do not stir;
Thou art my star, I thine astronomer!
Geometry was founded on thy lip.
[*Kisses her hand.*]
THE LADY.
This attitude becomes not scholarship!
Thy zeal I praise; but, prithee, not so fast,
Nor leave the rudiments until the last,
Science applied is good, but 'twere a schism
To study such before the catechism.
Bear thee more modestly, while I submit
Some easy problems to confirm thy wit.
PIERROT.
In all humility my mind I pit
Against her problems which would test my wit.
THE LADY [*questioning him from a little book bound deliciously in vellum*].
What is Love?
Is it a folly,

>   Is it mirth, or melancholy?
>   Joys above,
>   Are there many, or not any?
>   What is love?
>
> PIERROT [*answering in a very humble attitude of scholarship*].
>   If you please,
>   A most sweet folly!
>   Full of mirth and melancholy:
>   Both of these!
>   In its sadness worth all gladness,
>   If you please!
>
> THE LADY.
>   Prithee where,
>   Goes Love a-hiding?
>   Is he long in his abiding
>   Anywhere?
>   Can you bind him when you find him;
>   Prithee, where?
>
> PIERROT.
>   With spring days
>   Love comes and dallies:
>   Upon the mountains, through the valleys
>   Lie Love's ways.
>   Then he leaves you and deceives you
>   In spring days.
>
> THE LADY.
>   Thine answers please me: 'tis thy turn to ask.
>   To meet thy questioning be now my task.
>
> PIERROT.
>   Since I know thee, dear Immortal,
>   Is my heart become a blossom,
>   To be worn upon thy bosom.
>   When thou turn me from this portal,
>   Whither shall I, hapless mortal,
>   Seek love out and win again
>   Heart of me that thou retain?
>
> THE LADY.
>   In and out the woods and valleys,
>   Circling, soaring like a swallow,
>   Love shall flee and thou shalt follow:

Though he stops awhile and dallies,
Never shalt thou stay his malice!
Moon-kissed mortals seek in vain
To possess their hearts again!

PIERROT.
Tell me, Lady, shall I never
Rid me of this grievous burden?
Follow Love and find his guerdon
In no maiden whatsoever?
Wilt thou hold my heart for ever?
Rather would I thine forget,
In some earthly Pierrette!

THE LADY.
Thus thy fate, what'er thy will is!
Moon-struck child, go seek my traces
Vainly in all mortal faces!
In and out among the lilies,
Court each rural Amaryllis:
Seek the signet of Love's hand
In each courtly Corisande!

PIERROT.
Now, verily, sweet maid, of school I tire:
These answers are not such as I desire.

THE LADY.
Why art thou sad?

PIERROT.
     I dare not tell.

THE LADY [*caressingly*].
        Come, say!

PIERROT.
Is love all schooling, with no time to play?

THE LADY.
Though all love's lessons be a holiday,
Yet I will humor thee: what wouldst thou play?

PIERROT.
What are the games that small moon-maids enjoy,
Or is their time all spent in staid employ?

THE LADY.
Sedate they are, yet games they much enjoy:
They skip with stars, the rainbow is their toy.

PIERROT.
  That is too hard!
THE LADY.
                    For mortal's play.
PIERROT.
                              What then?
THE LADY.
  Teach me some pastime from the world of men.
PIERROT.
  I have it, maiden.
THE LADY.
                    Can it soon be taught?
PIERROT.
  A single game, I learnt it at the Court.
  I sit by thee.
THE LADY.
                    But, prithee, not so near.
PIERROT.
  That is essential, as will soon appear.
  Lay here thine hand, which cold night dews anoint,
  Washing its white ——
THE LADY.
                              Now is this to the point?
PIERROT.
  Prithee, forebear! Such is the game's design.
THE LADY.
  Here is my hand.
PIERROT.
                    I cover it with mine.
THE LADY.
  What must I next?
                    [*They play.*]
PIERROT.
                    Withdraw.
THE LADY.
                              It goes too fast.
[*They continue playing, until* PIERROT *catches her hand.*]
PIERROT [*laughing*].
  'Tis done. I win my forfeit at the last.
[*He tries to embrace her. She escapes; he chases her round the stage; she eludes him.*]

THE LADY.
  Thou art not quick enough. Who hopes to catch
  A moon-beam, must use twice as much despatch.
PIERROT [*sitting down sulkily*].
  I grow aweary, and my heart is sore.
  Thou dost not love me; I will play no more.
[*He buries his face in his hands.* THE LADY *stands over him.*]
THE LADY.
  What is this petulance?
PIERROT.
                         'Tis quick to tell—
  Thou hast but mocked me.
THE LADY.
                         Nay! I love thee well!
PIERROT.
  Repeat those words, for still within my breast
  A whisper warns me they are said in jest.
THE LADY.
  I jested not: at daybreak I must go,
  Yet loving thee far better than thou know.
PIERROT.
  Then, by this altar, and this sacred shrine,
  Take my sworn troth, and swear thee wholly mine!
  The gods have wedded mortals long ere this.
THE LADY.
  There was enough betrothal in my kiss.
  What need of further oaths?
PIERROT.
                         That bound not thee!
THE LADY.
  Peace! since I tell thee that it may not be.
  But sit beside me whilst I soothe thy bale
  With some moon fancy or celestial tale.
PIERROT.
  Tell me of thee, and that dim, happy place
  Where lies thine home, with maidens of thy race!
THE LADY [*seating herself*].
  Calm is it yonder, very calm; the air
  For mortals' breath is too refined and rare;
  Hard by a green lagoon our palace rears
  Its dome of agate through a myriad years.

A hundred chambers its bright walls enthrone,
Each one carved strangely from a precious stone.
Within the fairest, clad in purity,
Our mother dwelleth immemorially:
Moon-calm, moon-pale, with moon stones on her gown,
The floor she treads with little pearls is sown;
She sits upon a throne of amethysts,
And orders mortal fortunes as she lists;
I, and my sisters, all around her stand,
And, when she speaks, accomplish her demand.

PIERROT.
Methought grim Clotho and her sisters twain
With shriveled fingers spun this web of bane!

THE LADY.
Theirs and my mother's realm is far apart;
Hers is the lustrous kingdom of the heart,
And dreamers all, and all who sing and love,
Her power acknowledge, and her rule approve.

PIERROT.
Me, even me, she hath led into this grove.

THE LADY.
Yea, thou art one of hers! But, ere this night,
Often I watched my sisters take their flight
Down heaven's stairway of the clustered stars
To gaze on mortals through their lattice bars;
And some in sleep they woo with dreams of bliss
Too shadowy to tell, and some they kiss.
But all to whom they come, my sisters say,
Forthwith forget all joyance of the day,
Forget their laughter and forget their tears,
And dream away with singing all their years—
Moon-lovers always!
                    [*She sighs.*]
PIERROT.
                    Why art sad, sweet Moon?
                [*Laughs.*]
THE LADY.
For this, my story, grant me now a boon.

PIERROT.
I am thy servitor.

THE LADY.
          Would, then, I knew
  More of the earth, what men and women do.
PIERROT.
  I will explain.
THE LADY.
          Let brevity attend
  Thy wit, for night approaches to its end.
PIERROT.
  Once was I a page at Court, so trust in me:
  That's the first lesson of society.
THE LADY.
  Society?
PIERROT.
          I mean the very best.
  Pardy! thou wouldst not hear about the rest.
  I know it not, but am a *petit maître*
  At rout and festival and *bal champêtre*.
  But since example be instruction's ease,
  Let's play the thing.—Now, Madame, if you please!
[*He helps her to rise, and leads her forward: then he kisses her hand, bowing over it with a very courtly air.*]
THE LADY.
  What am I, then?
PIERROT.
          A most divine Marquise!
  Perhaps that attitude hath too much ease.
          [*Passes her.*]
  Ah, that is better! To complete the plan,
  Nothing is necessary save a fan.
THE LADY.
  Cool is the night, what needs it?
PIERROT.
          Madame, pray
  Reflect, it is essential to our play.
THE LADY [*taking a lily*].
  Here is my fan!
PIERROT.
          So, use it with intent:
  The deadliest arm in beauty's armament!

THE LADY.
What do we next?
PIERROT.
      We talk!
THE LADY.
         But what about?
PIERROT.
We quiz the company and praise the rout;
Are polished, petulant, malicious, sly,
Or what you will, so reputations die.
Observe the Duchess in Venetian lace,
With the red eminence.
THE LADY.
        A pretty face!
PIERROT.
For something tarter set thy wits to search—
" She loves the churchman better than the church."
THE LADY.
Her blush is charming; would it were her own!
PIERROT.
Madame is merciless!
THE LADY.
       Is that the tone?
PIERROT.
The very tone: I swear thou lackest naught.
Madame was evidently bred at Court.
THE LADY.
Thou speakest glibly: 'tis not of thine age.
PIERROT.
I listened much, as best becomes a page.
THE LADY.
I like thy Court but little ——
PIERROT.
         Hush! the Queen!
Bow, but not low—thou knowest what I mean.
THE LADY.
Nay, that I know not!
PIERROT.
       Though she wear a crown,
'Tis from La Pompadour one fears a frown.

THE LADY.
Thou art a child: thy malice is a game.
PIERROT.
A most sweet pastime—scandal is its name.
THE LADY.
Enough, it wearies me.
PIERROT.
                        Then, rare Marquise,
Desert the crowd to wander through the trees.
[*He bows low, and she curtsies; they move round the stage. When they pass before the Statue he seizes her hand and falls on his knee.*]
THE LADY.
What wouldst thou now?
PIERROT.
                        Ah, prithee, what, save thee!
THE LADY.
Was this included in thy comedy?
PIERROT.
Ah, mock me not! In vain with quirk and jest
I strive to quench the passion in my breast;
In vain thy blandishments would make me play:
Still I desire far more than I can say.
My knowledge halts, ah, sweet, be piteous,
Instruct me still, while time remains to us,
Be what thou wist, Goddess, moon-maid, *Marquise*,
So that I gather from thy lips heart's ease,
Nay, I implore thee, think thee how time flies!
THE LADY.
Hush! I beseech thee, even now night dies.
PIERROT.
Night, day, are one to me for thy soft sake.
[*He entreats her with imploring gestures, she hesitates: then puts her finger on her lip, hushing him.*]
THE LADY.
It is too late, for hark! the birds awake.
PIERROT.
The birds awake! It is the voice of day!
THE LADY.
Farewell, dear youth! They summon me away.
[*The light changes, it grows daylight: and music imitates the*

twitter of the birds. They stand gazing at the morning: then PIERROT *sinks back upon his bed, he covers his face in his hands.*]
THE LADY [*bending over him*].
Music, my maids! His weary senses steep
In soft untroubled and oblivious sleep,
With Mandragore anoint his tired eyes,
That they may open on mere memories,
Then shall a vision seem his lost delight,
With love, his lady for a summer's night.
Dream thou hast dreamt all this, when thou awake,
Yet still be sorrowful, for a dream's sake.
I leave thee, sleeper! Yea, I leave thee now,
Yet take my legacy upon thy brow:
Remember me, who was compassionate,
And opened for thee once, the ivory gate.
I come no more, thou shalt not see my face
When I am gone to mine exalted place:
Yet all thy days are mine, dreamer of dreams,
All silvered over with the moon's pale beams:
Go forth and seek in each fair face in vain,
To find the image of thy love again.
All maids are kind to thee, yet never one
Shall hold thy truant heart till day be done.
Whom once the moon has kissed, loves long and late,
Yet never finds the maid to be his mate.
Farewell, dear sleeper, follow out thy fate.
[*The* MOON MAIDEN *withdraws: a song is sung from behind: it is full day.*]

THE MOON MAIDEN'S SONG

Sleep! Cast thy canopy
 Over this sleeper's brain,
Dim grow his memory,
 When he awake again.

Love stays a summer night,
 Till lights of morning come;
Then takes her wingèd flight
 Back to her starry home.

Sleep! Yet thy days are mine;
    Love's seal is over thee:
Far though my ways from thine,
    Dim though thy memory.

Love stays a summer night,
    Till lights of morning come;
Then takes her wingèd flight
    Back to her starry home.

[*When the song is finished, the curtain falls upon* PIERROT *sleeping.*]

EPILOGUE

[*Spoken in the character of* PIERROT]

The sun is up, yet ere a body stirs,
A word with you, sweet ladies and dear sirs,
(Although on no account let any say
That PIERROT *finished Mr. Dowson's play).*

One night not long ago, at Baden Baden,—
The birthday of the Duke,—his pleasure garden
Was lighted gaily with feu d'artifice,
With candles, rockets, and a center-piece
Above the conversation house, on high,
Outlined in living fire against the sky,
A glittering Pierrot, *radiant, white,*
Whose heart beat fast, who danced with sheer delight,
Whose eyes were blue, whose lips were rosy red,
Whose pompons too were fire, while on his head
He wore a little cap, and I am told
That rockets covered him with showers of gold.
" Take our applause, you well deserve to win it,"
They cried: " Bravo! the Pierrot *of the minute!"*
What with applause and gold, one must confess
That Pierrot *had " arrived," achieved success,*
When, as it happened, presently, alas!
A terrible disaster came to pass.
His nose grew dim, the people gave a shout,

His red lips paled, both his blue eyes went out.
There rose a sullen sound of discontent,
The golden shower of rockets was all spent;
He left off dancing with a sudden jerk,
For he was nothing but a firework.
The garden darkened and the people in it
Cried, " He is dead,—the Pierrot *of the minute!"*

With every artist it is even so;
The artist, after all, is a Pierrot—
A Pierrot *of the minute,* naïf, *clever,*
But Art is back of him, She lives for ever!

Then pardon my Moon Maid and me, because
We craved the golden shower of your applause!
Pray shrive us both for having tried to win it,
And cry, " Bravo! The Pierrot *of the minute!"*

THE MAKER OF DREAMS
A FANTASY IN ONE ACT

By
OLIPHANT DOWN

The Maker of Dreams by the late Oliphant Down was first given at the Royalty Theatre in Glasgow, November 20, 1911. The design for the setting here reproduced was used when the play was acted in March, 1915, at The Neighborhood Playhouse in New York. The picture does not show how touches of red here and there in the scene, and the brilliant blue sky, visible through the quaint windows, enhanced the character of the black and white of the walls and of the flower pots. The back wall of the set was mounted on casters and, while Pierrette slept, moved silently off stage, to disclose to the audience a formal garden at the back, where a miniature Pierrot and a tiny Pierrette did a joyous little dance, thus suggesting to the spectators Pierrette's happy dream.

Pierrot, the hero of this and of the preceding play, has had an interesting stage history. To understand him fully we have to go back to the comedy of masks that had fully developed in Italy by the time of the Renascence. This comedy was a special kind of play, the scenario of which only was written, the dialogue being improvised by the individual players. Each player wore a costume and a mask that never changed, and these fixed his identity. Most of the parts had a strong local flavor, the pedant, for example, hailing from Bologna, the overly shrewd merchant, from Venice. Many of the characters have become fixed types and reappear under their old names in various forms of modern drama. Pantaloon, Harlequin, Columbine, Punch and Judy, and Pierrot are among those who live on in modern drama. There is an enchanting play by Granville Barker and Dion Clayton Calthrop called *The Harlequinade,* that describes in a popular way the devious and uncertain paths traveled by these stock characters down the ages.

Pierrot's ancestry is not so clearly Italian as the others. Pedrolino, a mischievous, intriguing buffoon, Pagliaccio, a madcap who wore a painted hat of white wool and a garment of white linen, whose face was covered with flour, and who wore a white mask, have both been cited as types that may have contributed to the figure of Pierrot, whose name makes its first appearance in Molière's play, *Don Juan ou le Festin de Pierre.*

Not that this dull servant of Molière's is in any sense the counterpart of the Pierrot of our day who is by turns languishing or vivacious, impish or poetic, but never doltish. From the seventeenth century, Pierrot, his costume borrowed from the Neapolitan mask, Pulcinella, became more and more prominent on both the Italian and the French stage. It was a certain French pantomime actor by the name of Deburau who died a few years before the middle of the nineteenth century, who gave Pierrot the prominence that he enjoys to-day and who dressed the character in the guise that he most often assumes on the modern stage. "The short woolen tunic, with its great buttons and its narrow sleeves, that overhung the hands, soon became an ample calico blouse with wide long sleeves like those of the Italian Pagliaccio. He suppressed the collar, which cast an upward shadow from the footlights on to his face, and interfered with the play of his countenance, and instead of the white skull-cap of his predecessor, he emphasized the pallor of his face by framing it in a cap of black velvet."[1] The Pierrot of our fancy[2] comes to us also through the pictures of Watteau and Pater and the designs of Aubrey Beardsley.

A one-act farce, *The Quod Wrangle*, is the only other published play of Oliphant Down's. Its plot, as outlined in *The London Times* of March 4, 1914, reminds one strongly of O. Henry's *The Cop and the Anthem*.

[1] Maurice Sand, *The History of the Harlequinade*, London, 1915, Vol. I, p. 219.
[2] *Mon Ami Pierrot. Songs and Fantasies*, compiled by Kendall Banning, Chicago, 1917. This book presents the Pierrot of modern poetry and drama.

The Maker of Dreams at The Neighborhood Playhouse, designed by Aline Bernstein.

THE MAKER OF DREAMS

CHARACTERS

PIERROT.
PIERRETTE.
THE MANUFACTURER.

Evening. A room in an old cottage, with walls of dark oak, lit only by the moonlight that peers through the long, low casement-window at the back, and the glow from the fire that is burning merrily on the spectator's left. A cobbled street can be seen outside, and a door to the right of the window opens directly on to it. Opposite the fire is a kitchen dresser with cups and plates twinkling in the firelight. A high-backed oak settle, as though afraid of the cold moonlight, has turned its back on the window and warms its old timbers at the fire. In the middle of the room stands a table with a red cover; there are chairs on either side of it. On the hob, a kettle is keeping itself warm; whilst overhead, on the hood of the chimney-piece, a small lamp is turned very low.

A figure flits past the window and, with a click of the latch, PIERRETTE *enters. She hangs up her cloak by the door, gives a little shiver and runs to warm herself for a moment. Then, having turned up the lamp, she places the kettle on the fire. Crossing the room, she takes a tablecloth from the dresser and proceeds to lay tea, setting out crockery for two. Once she goes to the window and, drawing aside the common red casement-curtains, looks out, but returns to her work, disappointed. She puts a spoonful of tea into the teapot, and another, and a third. Something outside attracts her attention; she listens, her face brightening. A voice is heard singing:*

> " Baby, don't wait for the moon,
>   She is caught in a tangle of boughs;
>   And mellow and musical June
>   Is saying ' Good-night ' to the cows."

[*The voice draws nearer and a conical white hat goes past the window.* PIERROT *enters.*]

PIERROT [*throwing his hat to* PIERRETTE]. Ugh! How cold it is. My feet are like ice.

PIERRETTE. Here are your slippers. I put them down to warm. [*She kneels beside him, as he sits before the fire and commences to slip off his shoes.*]

PIERROT [*singing:*]

> " Baby, don't wait for the moon,
>   She will put out her tongue and grimace;
>   And mellow and musical June
>   Is pinning the stars in their place."

Isn't tea ready yet?

PIERRETTE. Nearly. Only waiting for the kettle to boil.

PIERROT. How cold it was in the market-place to-day! I don't believe I sang at all well. I can't sing in the cold.

PIERRETTE. Ah, you're like the kettle. He can't sing when he's cold either. Hurry up, Mr. Kettle, if you please.

PIERROT. I wish it were in love with the sound of its own voice.

PIERRETTE. I believe it is. Now it's singing like a bird. We'll make the tea with the nightingale's tongue. [*She pours the boiling water into the teapot.*] Come along.

PIERROT [*looking into the fire*]. I wonder. She had beauty, she had form, but had she soul?

PIERRETTE [*cutting bread and butter at the table*]. Come and be cheerful, instead of grumbling there to the fire.

PIERROT. I was thinking.

PIERRETTE. Come and have tea. When you sit by the fire, thoughts only fly up the chimney.

PIERROT. The whole world's a chimney-piece. Give people a thing as worthless as paper, and it catches fire in them and makes a stir; but real thought, they let it go up with the smoke.

THE MAKER OF DREAMS

PIERRETTE. Cheer up, Pierrot. See how thick I've spread the butter.
PIERROT. You're always cheerful.
PIERRETTE. I try to be happy.
PIERROT. Ugh! [*He has moved to the table. There is a short silence, during which* PIERROT *sips his tea moodily.*]
PIERRETTE. Tea all right?
PIERROT. Middling.
PIERRETTE. Only middling! I'll pour you out some fresh.
PIERROT. Oh, it's all right! How you do worry a fellow!
PIERRETTE. Heigh-ho! Shall I chain up that big black dog?
PIERROT. I say, did you see that girl to-day?
PIERRETTE. Whereabouts?
PIERROT. Standing by the horse-trough. With a fine air, and a string of great beads.
PIERRETTE. I didn't see her.
PIERROT. I did, though. And she saw me. Watched me all the time I was singing, and clapped her hands like anything each time. I wonder if it is possible for a woman to have a soul as well as such beautiful coloring.
PIERRETTE. She was made up!
PIERROT. I'm sure she was not. And how do you know? You didn't see her.
PIERRETTE. Perhaps I *did* see her.
PIERROT. Now, look here, Pierrette, it's no good your being jealous. When you and I took on this show business, we arranged to be just partners and nothing more. If I see anyone I want to marry, I shall marry 'em. And if you see anyone who wants to marry you, *you* can marry 'em.
PIERRETTE. I'm not jealous! It's absurd!
PIERROT [*singing abstractedly*].

"Baby, don't wait for the moon,
  She has scratched her white chin on the gorse;
And mellow and musical June
  Is bringing the cuckoo remorse."

PIERRETTE. Did you see that girl after the show?
PIERROT. No. She had slipped away in the crowd. Here, I've had enough tea. I shall go out and try to find her.
PIERRETTE. Why don't you stay in by the fire? You could help me to darn the socks.

PIERROT. Don't try to chaff me. Darning, indeed! I hope life has got something better in it than darning.
PIERRETTE. I doubt it. It's pretty much the same all the world over. First we wear holes in our socks, and then we mend them. The wise ones are those who make the best of it, and darn as well as they can.
PIERROT. I say, that gives me an idea for a song.
PIERRETTE. Out with it, then.
PIERROT. Well, I haven't exactly formed it yet. This is what flashed through my mind as you spoke: [*He runs up on to the table, using it as a stage.*]

" Life's a ball of worsted,
Unwind it if you can,
You who oft have boasted

[*He pauses for a moment, then hurriedly, in order to gloss over the false accenting.*]

That you are a man."

Of course that's only a rough idea.
PIERRETTE. Are you going to sing it at the show?
PIERROT [*jumping down from the table*]. You're always so lukewarm. A man of artistic ideas is as sensitively skinned as a baby.
PIERRETTE. Do stay in, Pierrot. It's so cold outside.
PIERROT. You want me to listen to you grumbling, I suppose.
PIERRETTE. Just now you said I was always cheerful.
PIERROT. There you are; girding at me again.
PIERRETTE. I'm sorry, Pierrot. But the market-place is dreadfully wet, and your shoes are awfully thin.
PIERROT. I tell you I will not stop in. I'm going out to find that girl. How do I know she isn't the very woman of my dreams?
PIERRETTE. Why are you always trying to picture an ideal woman?
PIERROT. Don't *you ever* picture an ideal man?
PIERRETTE. No, I try to be practical.
PIERROT. Women are so unimaginative! They are such pathetic, motherly things, and when they feel extra motherly they say, " I'm in love." All that is so sordid and petty. I

want a woman I can set on a pedestal, and just look up at her and love her.

PIERRETTE [*speaking very fervently*].

"Pierrot, don't wait for the moon,
 There's a heart chilling cold in her rays;
And mellow and musical June
 Will only last thirty short days."

PIERROT. Oh, I should never make you understand! Well, I'm off. [*As he goes out, he sings, sidelong, over his shoulder in a mocking tone, "Baby, don't wait for the moon."* PIERRETTE *listens for a moment to his voice dying away in the distance. Then she moves to the fire-place, and begins to stir the fire. As she kneels there, the words of an old recitation form on her lips. Half unconsciously she recites it again to an audience of laughing flames and glowing, thoughtful coals.*]

"There lives a maid in the big, wide world,
 By the crowded town and mart,
And people sigh as they pass her by;
 They call her Hungry Heart.

For there trembles that on her red rose lip
 That never her tongue can say,
And her eyes are sad, and she is not glad
 In the beautiful calm of day.

Deep down in the waters of pure, clear thought,
 The mate of her fancy lies;
Sleeping, the night is made fair by his light
 Sweet kiss on her dreaming eyes.

Though a man was made in the wells of time
 Who could set her soul on fire,
Her life unwinds, and she never finds
 This love of her heart's desire.

If you meet this maid of a hopeless love,
 Play not a meddler's part.
Silence were best; let her keep in her breast
 The dream of her hungry heart."

[*Overcome by tears, she hides her face in her hands. A slow, treble knock comes on the door;* PIERRETTE *looks up wonderingly. Again the knock sounds.*]

PIERRETTE. Come in. [*The door swings slowly open, as though of its own accord, and without, on the threshold, is seen* THE MANUFACTURER, *standing full in the moonlight. He is a curious, though kindly-looking, old man, and yet, with all his years, he does not appear to be the least infirm. He is the sort of person that children take to instinctively. He wears a quaintly cut, bottle-green coat, with silver buttons and large side-pockets, which almost hide his knee-breeches. His shoes have large buckles and red heels. He is exceedingly unlike a prosperous manufacturer, and, but for the absence of a violin, would be mistaken for a village fiddler. Without a word he advances into the room, and, again of its own accord, the door closes noiselessly behind him.*]

PIERRETTE [*jumping up and moving towards him*]. Oh, I'm so sorry. I ought to have opened the door when you knocked.

MANUFACTURER. That's all right. I'm used to opening doors. And yours opens much more easily than some I come across. Would you believe it, some people positively nail their doors up, and it's no good knocking. But there, you're wondering who I am.

PIERRETTE. I was wondering if you were hungry.

MANUFACTURER. Ah, a woman's instinct. But, thank you, no. I am a small eater; I might say a very small eater. A smile or a squeeze of the hand keeps me going admirably.

PIERRETTE. At least you'll sit down and make yourself at home.

MANUFACTURER [*moving to the settle*]. Well, I have a habit of making myself at home everywhere. In fact, most people think you can't make a *home* without *me*. May I put my feet on the fender? It's an old habit of mine. I always do it.

PIERRETTE. They say round here:

"Without feet on the fender
Love is but slender."

MANUFACTURER. Quite right. It is the whole secret of the domestic fireside. Pierrette, you have been crying.

PIERRETTE. I believe I have.

THE MAKER OF DREAMS

MANUFACTURER. Bless you, I know all about it. It's Pierrot. And so you're in love with him, and he doesn't care a little bit about you, eh? What a strange old world it is! And you cry your eyes out over him.

PIERRETTE. Oh, no, I don't often cry. But to-night he seemed more grumpy than usual, and I tried so hard to cheer him up.

MANUFACTURER. Grumpy, is he?

PIERRETTE. He doesn't mean it, though. It's the cold weather, and the show hasn't been paying so well lately. Pierrot wants to write an article about us for the local paper by way of an advertisement. He thinks the editor may print it if he gives him free passes for his family.

MANUFACTURER. Do you think Pierrot is worth your tears?

PIERRETTE. Oh, yes!

MANUFACTURER. You know, tears are not to be wasted. We only have a certain amount of them given to us just for keeping the heart moist. And when we've used them all up and haven't any more, the heart dries up, too.

PIERRETTE. Pierrot is a splendid fellow. You don't know him as well as I do. It's true he's always discontented, but it's only because he's not in love with anyone. You know, love does make a tremendous difference in a man.

MANUFACTURER. That's true enough. And has it made a difference in you?

PIERRETTE. Oh, yes! I put Pierrot's slippers down to warm, and I make tea for him, and all the time I'm happy because I'm doing something for him. If I weren't in love, I should find it a drudgery.

MANUFACTURER. Are you sure it's real love?

PIERRETTE. Why, yes!

MANUFACTURER. Every time you think of Pierrot, do you hear the patter of little bare feet? And every time he speaks, do you feel little chubby hands on your breast and face?

PIERRETTE [*fervently*]. Yes! Oh, yes! That's just it!

MANUFACTURER. You've got it right enough. But why is it that Pierrot can wake up all this poetry in you?

PIERRETTE. Because—oh, because he's just Pierrot.

MANUFACTURER. " Because he's just Pierrot." The same old reason.

PIERRETTE. Of course, he is a bit dreamy. But that's his

soul. I am sure he could do great things if he tried. And have you noticed his smile? Isn't it lovely! Sometimes, when he's not looking, I want ever so much to try it on, just to see how I should look in it. [*Pensively.*] But I wish he'd smile at me a little more often, instead of at others.

MANUFACTURER. Ho! So he smiles at others, does he?

PIERRETTE. Hardly a day goes by but there's some fine lady at the show. There was one there to-day, a tall girl with red cheeks. He is gone to look for her now. And it is not their faults. The poor things can't help being in love with him. [*Proudly.*] I believe everyone is in love with Pierrot.

MANUFACTURER. But supposing one of these fine ladies were to marry him?

PIERRETTE. Oh, they'd never do that. A fine lady would never marry a poor singer. If Pierrot were to get married, I think I should just . . . fade away. . . . Oh, but I don't know why I talk to you like this. I feel as if I had known you for a long, long time. [THE MANUFACTURER *rises from the settle and moves across to* PIERRETTE, *who is now folding up the white table-cloth.*]

MANUFACTURER [*very slowly*]. Perhaps you *have* known me for a long, long time. [*His tone is so kindly and impressive that* PIERRETTE *forgets the table-cloth and looks up at him. For a moment or two he smiles back at her as she gazes, spellbound; then he turns away to the fire again, with the little chuckle that is never far from his lips.*]

PIERRETTE [*taking a small bow from his side-pocket*]. Oh, look at this.

MANUFACTURER [*in mock alarm*]. Oh, oh, I didn't mean you to see that. I'd forgotten it was sticking out of my pocket. I used to do a lot of archery at one time. I don't get much chance now. [*He takes it and puts it back in his pocket.*]

PIERROT [*singing in the distance*].

" Baby, don't wait for the moon,
    She is drawing the sea in her net;
And mellow and musical June
    Is teaching the rose to forget."

MANUFACTURER [*in a whisper as the voice draws nearer*]. Who is that?

PIERRETTE. Pierrot. [*Again the conical white hat flashes past the window and* PIERROT *enters.*]
PIERROT. I can't find her anywhere. [*Seeing* THE MANUFACTURER.] Hullo! Who are you?
MANUFACTURER. I am a stranger to you, but Pierrette knew me in a moment.
PIERROT. An old flame perhaps?
MANUFACTURER. True, I am an old flame. I've lighted up the world for a considerable time. Yet when you say "old," there are many people who think I'm wonderfully well preserved for my age. How long do you think I've been trotting about?
PIERROT [*testily, measuring a length with his hands*]. Oh, about that long.
MANUFACTURER. I suppose being funny all day *does* get on your nerves.
PIERRETTE. Pierrot, you needn't be rude.
MANUFACTURER [*anxious to be alone with* PIERROT]. Pierrette, have you got supper in?
PIERRETTE. Oh, I must fly! The shops will all be shut. Will you be here when I come back?
MANUFACTURER [*bustling her out*]. I can't promise, but I'll try, I'll try. [PIERRETTE *goes out. There is a silence, during which* THE MANUFACTURER *regards* PIERROT *with amusement.*]
MANUFACTURER. Well, friend Pierrot, so business is not very brisk.
PIERROT. Brisk! If laughter meant business, it would be brisk enough, but there's no money. However, I've done one good piece of work to-day. I've arranged with the editor to put an article in the paper. That will fetch 'em. [*Singing*]:

"Please come one day and see our house that's down among the trees,
But do not come at four o'clock for then we count the bees,
And bath the tadpoles and the frogs, who splash the clouds with gold,
And watch the new-cut cucum*bers* perspiring with the cold."

That's a song I'm writing.
MANUFACTURER. Pierrot, if you had all the money in the world you wouldn't be happy.

PIERROT. Wouldn't I? Give me all the money in the world and I'll risk it. To start with, I'd build schools to educate the people up to high-class things.

MANUFACTURER. You dream of fame and wealth and empty ideals, and you miss all the best things there are. You are discontented. Why? Because you don't know how to be happy.

PIERROT [*reciting*]:

> " Life's a running brooklet,
> Catch the fishes there,
> You who wrote a booklet
> On a woman's hair."

[*Explaining.*] That's another song I'm writing. It's the second verse. Things come to me all of a sudden like that. I must run out a third verse, just to wind it up.

MANUFACTURER. Why don't you write a song without any end, one that goes on for ever?

PIERROT. I say, that's rather silly, isn't it?

MANUFACTURER. It all depends. For a song of that sort the singer must be always happy.

PIERROT. That wants a bit of doing in my line.

MANUFACTURER. Shall you and I transact a little business?

PIERROT. By all means. What seats would you like? There are the front rows covered in velvet, one shilling; wooden benches behind, sixpence; and, right at the back, the twopenny part. But, of course, you'll have shilling ones. How many shall we say?

MANUFACTURER. You don't know who I am.

PIERROT. That makes no difference. All are welcome, and we thank you for your courteous attention.

MANUFACTURER. Pierrot, I am a maker of dreams.

PIERROT. A what?

MANUFACTURER. I make all the dreams that float about this musty world.

PIERROT. I say, you'd better have a rest for a bit. I expect you're a trifle done up.

MANUFACTURER. Pierrot, Pierrot, your superior mind can't tumble to my calling. A child or one of the " people " would in a moment. I am a maker of dreams, little things that glide

THE MAKER OF DREAMS

about into people's hearts and make them glad. Haven't you often wondered where the swallows go to in the autumn? They come to my workshop, and tell me who wants a dream, and what happened to the dreams they took with them in the spring.

PIERROT. Oh, I say, you can't expect me to believe that.

MANUFACTURER. When flowers fade, have you never wondered where their colors go to, or what becomes of all the butterflies in the winter? There isn't much winter about my workshop.

PIERROT. I had never thought of it before.

MANUFACTURER. It's a kind of lost property office, where every beautiful thing that the world has neglected finds its way. And there I make my celebrated dream, the dream that is called "love."

PIERROT. Ho! ho! Now we're talking.

MANUFACTURER. You don't believe in it?

PIERROT. Yes, in a way. But it doesn't last. It doesn't last. If there is form, there isn't soul, and, if there is soul, there isn't form. Oh, I've tried hard enough to believe it, but, after the first wash, the colors run.

MANUFACTURER. You only got hold of a substitute. Wait until you see the genuine article.

PIERROT. But how is one to tell it?

MANUFACTURER. There are heaps of signs. As soon as you get the real thing, your shoulder-blades begin to tingle. That's love's wings sprouting. And, next, you want to soar up among the stars and sit on the roof of heaven and sing to the moon. Of course, that's because I put such a lot of the moon into my dreams. I break bits off until it's nearly all gone, and then I let it grow big again. It grows very quickly, as I dare say you've noticed. After a fortnight it is ready for use once more.

PIERROT. This is most awfully fascinating. And do the swallows bring all the dreams?

MANUFACTURER. Not always; I have other messengers. Every night when the big clock strikes twelve, a day slips down from the calendar, and runs away to my workshop in the Land of Long Ago. I give him a touch of scarlet and a gleam of gold, and say, "Go back, little Yesterday, and be a memory in the world." But my best dreams I keep for to-day. I buy babies, and fit them up with a dream, and then send them complete and carriage paid . . . in the usual manner.

PIERROT. I've been dreaming all my life, but they've always been dreams I made myself. I suppose I don't mix 'em properly.

MANUFACTURER. You leave out the very essence of them. You must put in a little sorrow, just to take away the oversweetness. I found that out very soon, so I took a little of the fresh dew that made pearls in the early morning, and I sprinkled my dreams with the gift of tears.

PIERROT [*ecstatically*]. The gift of tears! How beautiful! You know, I should rather like to try a real one. Not one of my own making.

MANUFACTURER. Well, there are plenty about, if you only look for them.

PIERROT. That is all very well, but who's going to look about for stray dreams?

MANUFACTURER. I once made a dream that would just suit you. I slipped it inside a baby. That was twenty years ago, and the baby is now a full-grown woman, with great blue eyes and fair hair.

PIERROT. It's a lot of use merely telling me about her.

MANUFACTURER. I'll do more. When I shipped her to the world, I kept the bill of lading. Here it is. You shall have it.

PIERROT. Thanks, but what's the good of it?

MANUFACTURER. Why, the holder of that is able to claim the goods; you will notice it contains a complete description, too. I promise you, you're in luck.

PIERROT. Has she red cheeks and a string of great beads?

MANUFACTURER. No.

PIERROT. Ah, then it is not she. Where shall I find her?

MANUFACTURER. That's for you to discover. All you have to do is to search.

PIERROT. I'll start at once. [*He moves as if to go.*]

MANUFACTURER. I shouldn't start out to-night.

PIERROT. But I want to find her soon. Somebody else may find her before me.

MANUFACTURER. Pierrot, there was once a man who wanted to gather mushrooms.

PIERROT [*annoyed at the commonplace*]. Mushrooms!

MANUFACTURER. Fearing people would be up before him, he started out overnight. Morning came, and he found none, so he returned disconsolate to his house. As he came through the garden, he found a great mushroom had grown up in the night by his very door-step. Take the advice of one who knows, and wait a bit.
PIERROT. If that's your advice. . . . But tell me this, do you think I shall find her?
MANUFACTURER. I can't say for certain. Would you consider yourself a fool?
PIERROT. Ah . . . of course . . . when you ask me a direct thing like that, you make it . . . er . . . rather awkward for me. But, if I may say so, as man to ma . . . I mean as man to . . . [*he hesitates*].
MANUFACTURER [*waiving the point*]. Yes, yes.
PIERROT. Well, I flatter myself that . . .
MANUFACTURER. Exactly. And that's your principal danger. Whilst you are striding along gazing at the stars, you may be treading on a little glow-worm. Shall I give you a third verse for your song?

"Life's a woman calling,
  Do not stop your ears,
Lest, when night is falling,
  Darkness brings you tears."

[THE MANUFACTURER'S *kindly and impressive tone holds* PIERROT *as it had held* PIERRETTE *some moments before. Whilst the two are looking at each other, a little red cloak dances past the window, and* PIERRETTE *enters with her marketing.*]
PIERRETTE. Oh, I'm so glad you're still here.
MANUFACTURER. But I must be going now. I am a great traveler.
PIERRETTE [*standing against the door, so that he cannot pass*]. Oh, you mustn't go yet.
MANUFACTURER. Don't make me fly out of the window. I only do that under very unpleasant circumstances.
PIERROT [*gaily, with mock eloquence*]. Pierrette, regard our visitor. You little knew whom you were entertaining. You see before you the maker of the dreams that slip about

the world like little fish among the rushes of a stream. He has given me the bill of lading of his great masterpiece, and it only remains for me to find her. [*Dropping to the commonplace.*] I wish I knew where to look.

MANUFACTURER. Before I go, I will give you this little rhyme:
"Let every woman keep a school,
For every man is born a fool."

[*He bows, and goes out quickly and silently.*]

PIERRETTE [*running to the door, and looking out*]. Why, how quickly he has gone! He's out of sight.

PIERROT. At last I am about to attain my great ideal. There will be a grand wedding, and I shall wear my white coat with the silver braid, and carry a tall gold-topped stick. [*Singing:*]

"If we play any longer, I fear you will get
Such a cold in the head, for the grass is so wet.
But during the night, Margareta divine,
I will hang the wet grass up to dry on the line."

Pierrette, I feel that I am about to enter into a man's inheritance, a woman's love.

PIERRETTE. I wish you every happiness.

PIERROT [*singing teasingly:*]

"We shall meet in our dreams, that's a thing understood;
You dream of the river, I'll dream of the wood.
I am visiting you, if the river it be;
If we meet in the wood, you are visiting me."

PIERRETTE. We must make lots of money, so that you can give her all she wants. I'll dance and dance until I fall, and the people will exclaim, "Why, she has danced herself to death."

PIERROT. You're right. We must pull the show together. I'll do that article for the paper at once. [*He takes paper, ink, etc., from the dresser, and, seating himself at the table, commences to write.*] "There has lately come to this town a company of strolling players, who give a show that is at once musical and droll. The audience is enthralled by Pierrot's magnificent singing and dancing, and . . . er . . . very much entertained by Pierrette's homely dancing. Pierrette is a charming comedienne of twenty, with . . ." what color hair?

PIERRETTE. Fair, quite fair.

PIERROT. Funny how one can see a person every day and not know the color of their hair. "Fair hair and . . ." eyes?

PIERRETTE. Blue, Pierrot.

PIERROT. "Fair hair and blue eyes." Fair! Blue! Oh, of course it's nonsense, though.

PIERRETTE. What's nonsense?

PIERROT. Something I was thinking. Most girls have fair hair and blue eyes.

PIERRETTE. Yes, Pierrot, we can't all be ideals.

PIERROT. How musical your voice sounds! I can't make it out. Oh, but, of course, it *is* all nonsense! [*He takes the bill of lading from his pocket and reads it.*]

PIERRETTE. What's nonsense? . . . Pierrot, won't you tell me?

PIERROT. Pierrette, stand in the light.

PIERRETTE. Is anything the matter?

PIERROT. I almost believe that nothing matters. [*Reading and glancing at her.*] " Eyes that say ' I love you '; arms that say ' I want you '; lips that say ' Why don't you? ' " Pierrette, is it possible! I've never noticed before how beautiful you are. You don't seem a bit the same. I believe you have lost your real face, and have carved another out of a rose.

PIERRETTE. Oh, Pierrot, what is it?

PIERROT. Love! I've found it at last. Don't you understand it all?

" I am a fool
Who has learned wisdom in your school."

To think that I've seen you every day, and never dreamed . . . dreamed! Yes, ah yes, it's one of his beautiful dreams. That is why my heart seems full of the early morning.

PIERRETTE. Ah, Pierrot!

PIERROT. Oh, how my shoulders tingle! I want to soar up, up. Don't you want to fly up to the roof of heaven and sing among the stars?

PIERRETTE. I have been sitting on the moon ever so long, waiting for my lover. Pierrot, let me try on your smile. Give it to me in a kiss. [*With their hands outstretched behind them, they lean towards each other, till their lips meet in a long kiss.*]

PIERRETTE [*throwing back her head with a deep sigh of happiness.*] Oh, I am so happy. This might be the end of all things.

PIERROT. Pierrette, let us sit by the fire and put our feet on the fender, and live happily ever after. [*They have moved slowly to the settle. As they sit there,* PIERROT *sings softly:*]

" Baby, don't wait for the moon,
    The stairs of the sky are so steep;
And mellow and musical June
    Is waiting to kiss you to sleep."

[*The lamp on the hood of the chimney-piece has burned down, leaving only the red glow from the fire upon their faces, as the curtain whispers down to hide them.*]

GETTYSBURG
A WOOD-SHED COMMENTARY

By
PERCY MACKAYE

Percy MacKaye was born in New York, March 16, 1875, the son of Steele MacKaye, a well-known dramatist and theatrical inventor of his day. " My own early dramatic training," writes the son, " was in the theatre in relation with my father's work there as dramatist, actor, and director." In another place he says: " I have not sought to conceal, or to put aside, the grateful enthusiasm I feel, as a son and comrade of Steele MacKaye, for those examples of untiring devotion to the theatre and of constructive achievement in its art, by which his life has been an inspiration to my own, to follow—however haltingly and through different means—the trail of his large leadership." Percy MacKaye was graduated from Harvard in 1897 and later spent a year studying at the University of Leipzig. After travel abroad, he returned to New York in 1900 and taught there in a private school till 1904. He spent some time in the next five years lecturing on the Drama of Democracy and the Civic Theatre at various American universities. In 1904 he joined the colony of artists and men of letters at Cornish, New Hampshire, the home of Saint-Gaudens, Maxfield Parrish, Winston Churchill, and others. Since that date Percy MacKaye has devoted himself wholly to poetry and the drama, writing community masques, plays of various kinds, and operas.[1] It is interesting to note that one of the latest products of his pen, *Washington, the Man Who Made Us, A Ballad Play*, was translated into French and presented by M. Copeau's players, at the Théâtre du Vieux Colombier, during their second season in New York, and later acted in English by Walter Hampden, the scene designs being made by Robert Edmond Jones. In October, 1920, he was invited to Miami University, Oxford, Ohio, not to teach but to continue his own creative work, quite untrammeled, filling there the first fellowship in creative literature ever established in this country.

Yankee Fantasies, a collection of five one-act plays of which *Gettysburg* is one, is the expression of Percy MacKaye's belief that the American dramatist may find " north of Boston," or,

[1] A list of his works is given in the latest *Who's Who in America.*

in fact, in almost any rural neighborhood, material for " quaint and lovely interpretation of our native environment now ignored." These plays, published in 1912, testified also to his conviction that the time had come for the development of the one-act play in this country, not only because this form is distinctive and capable of expressing what the full-length play cannot, but also because a receptive audience was already organized. He found even then that amateurs in schools, colleges, and elsewhere were clamoring to perform one-act plays, to see them performed, and to read them. At that date Little Theatres were just beginning to be, but in the preface to *Yankee Fantasies,* the author advocated the establishment of Studio Theatres, in essence experimental, many of which have since come into existence under different names, wherein playwrights might practice the new craft of the one-act play as in a workshop. The one-act play may be said to have arrived in the nine years that have elapsed since *Gettysburg* was published.

The one-act play has shown no tendency, however, to rival the short-story in the matter of local color. Kentucky, California, Iowa, Louisiana, to name but a few of the favored states which have served as rich backgrounds for many finely flavored narratives of American life, have been neglected as sources of dramatic material. But though Percy MacKaye may perhaps be matched with Mary Wilkins, there is no writer who has made notable use in the one-act play of localities, associated, for example, with the art of George W. Cable, Bret Harte, James Lane Allen, or Hamlin Garland. One of the paths of glory for the American dramatist lies undoubtedly in this direction.

GETTYSBURG

CHARACTERS

LINK TADBOURNE, *ox-yoke maker.*
POLLY, *his grandniece.*

The Place is country New Hampshire, at the present time.

SCENE.—*A woodshed, in the ell of a farm house.*

The shed is open on both sides, front and back, the apertures being slightly arched at the top. [In bad weather, these presumably may be closed by big double doors, which stand open now—swung back outward beyond sight.] Thus the nearer opening is the proscenium arch of the scene, under which the spectator looks through the shed to the background—a grassy yard, a road with great trunks of soaring elms, and the glimpse of a green hillside. The ceiling runs up into a gable with large beams.

On the right, at back, a door opens into the shed from the house kitchen. Opposite it, a door leads from the shed into the barn. In the foreground, against the right wall, is a work-bench. On this are tools, a long, narrow, wooden box, and a small oil stove, with steaming kettle upon it.

Against the left wall, what remains of the year's wood supply is stacked, the uneven ridges sloping to a jumble of stovewood and kindlings mixed with small chips on the floor, which is piled deep with mounds of crumbling bark, chips and wood-dust.

Not far from this mounded pile, at right center of the scene, stands a wooden arm-chair, in which LINK TADBOURNE, *in his shirt-sleeves, sits drowsing. Silhouetted by the sunlight beyond, his sharp-drawn profile is that of an old man, with white hair cropped close, and gray mustache of a faded black hue at the outer edges. Between his knees is a stout thong of wood, whittled round by the drawshave which his sleeping hand still holds in his lap. Against the side of his chair rests a thick wooden yoke and collar. Near him is a chopping-block.*

In the woodshed there is no sound or motion except the hum and floating steam from the tea-kettle. Presently the old man murmurs in his sleep, clenching his hand. Slowly the hand relaxes again. From the door, right, comes POLLY— *a sweet-faced girl of seventeen, quietly mature for her age. She is dressed simply. In one hand, she carries a man's wide-brimmed felt hat; over the other arm, a blue coat. These she brings toward* LINK. *Seeing him asleep, she begins to tiptoe, lays the coat and hat on the chopping-block, goes to the bench and trims the wick of the oil-stove, under the kettle. Then she returns and stands near* LINK, *surveying the shed.*

On closer scrutiny, the jumbled woodpile has evidently a certain order in its chaos: some of the splittings have been piled in irregular ridges; in places, the deep layer of wood-dust and chips has been scooped, and the little mounds slope and rise like miniature valleys and hills.*

Taking up a hoe, POLLY—*with careful steps*—*moves among the hollows, placing and arranging sticks of kindling, scraping and smoothing the little mounds with the hoe.*

As she does so, from far away, a bugle sounds.

LINK [*snapping his eyes wide open, sits up*].
    Hello! Cat-nappin' was I, Polly?
POLLY.   Just
    a kitten-nap, I guess.
        [*Laying the hoe down, she approaches.*]
            The yoke done?

---

* A suggestion for the appropriate arrangement of these mounds may be found in the map of the battle-field annexed to the volume by Capt. R. K. Beecham, entitled *Gettysburg*, A. C. McClurg, 1911.

LINK [*giving a final whittle to the yoke-collar thong*].
            Thar!
   When he's ben steamed a spell, and bended snug,
   I guess this feller'll sarve t' say "Gee" to—
   [*Lifting the other yoke-collar from beside his chair, he
      holds the whittled thong next to it, comparing the
      two with expert eye.*]
   and "Haw" to him. Beech every time, Sir; beech
   or walnut. Hang me if I'd shake a whip
   at birch, for ox-yokes.—Polly, are ye thar?
POLLY.
   Yes, Uncle Link.
LINK.   What's that I used to sing ye?
       "Polly, put the kittle on,
        Polly, put the kittle on,
        Polly, put the kittle on—" [*Chuckling.*]
   We'll give this feller a dose of ox-yoke tea!
POLLY.
   The kettle's boilin'.
LINK.   Wall, then, steep him good.
   [POLLY *takes from* LINK *the collar-thong, carries it to the
      work-bench, shoves it into the narrow end of the box,
      which she then closes tight and connects—by a piece
      of hose—to the spout of the kettle. At the further
      end of the box, steam then emerges through a small
      hole.*]
POLLY.
   You're feelin' smart to-day.
LINK.   Smart!—Wall, if I
   could git a hull man to swap legs with me,
   mebbe I'd arn my keep. But this here settin'
   dead an' alive, without no legs, day in,
   day out, don't make an old hoss wuth his oats.
POLLY [*cheerfully*].
   I guess you'll soon be walkin' round.
LINK.   Not if
   that doctor feller has his say: He says
   I can't never go agin this side o' Jordan;
   and looks like he's 'bout right.—Nine months to-
      morrer,
   Polly, gal, sence I had that stroke.

POLLY [*pointing to the ox-yoke*].
                                    You're fitter
   sittin' than most folks standin'.
LINK [*briskly*].   Oh, they can't
   keep my two hands from makin' ox-yokes. That's
   my second natur' sence I was a boy.
   [*Again in the distance a bugle sounds.* LINK *starts.*]
   What's that?
POLLY.   Why, that's the army veterans
   down to the graveyard. This is Decoration
   mornin': you ain't forgot?
LINK.   So 'tis, so 'tis.
   Roger, your young man—ha! [*Chuckling.*] He come
      and axed me
   was I agoin' to the cemetery.
   "Me? Don't I look it?" says I. Ha! "Don't I look
      it?"
POLLY.
   He meant—to decorate the graves.
LINK.   O' course;
   but I must take my little laugh. I told him
   I guessed I wa'n't persent'ble anyhow,
   my mústache and my boots wa'n't blacked this mornin'.
   I don't jest like t' talk about my legs.—
   Be you a-goin' to take your young school folks,
   Polly?
POLLY.
              Dear no! I told my boys and girls
   to march up this way with the band. I said
   I'd be a-stayin' home and learnin' how
   to keep school in the woodpile here with you.
LINK [*looking up at her proudly*].
   Schoolma'am at seventeen! Some smart, I tell ye!
POLLY [*caressing him*].
   School-master, you, past seventy; that's smarter!
   I tell 'em I learn from you, so's I can teach
   my young folks what the study-books leave out.
LINK.
   Sure ye don't want to jine the celebratin'?

POLLY.
    No *Sir!* We're goin' to celebrate right here,
    and you're to teach me to keep school some more.
    [*She holds ready for him the blue coat and hat.*]
LINK [*looking up*].
    What's thar?
POLLY.   Your teachin' rig.
    [*She helps him on with it.*]
LINK.   The old blue coat!—
    My, but I'd like to see the boys: [*Gazing at the hat.*]
                            the Grand
    Old Army Boys! [*Dreamily.*] Yes, we was boys: jest
    boys!
    Polly, you tell your young folks, when they study
    the books, that we was nothin' else but boys
    jest fallin' in love, with best gals left t' home—
    the same as you; and when the shot was singin',
    we pulled their pictur's out, and prayed to them
    'most more 'n the Allmighty.
    [LINK *looks up suddenly—a strange light in his face.*
       Again, to a far strain of music, the bugle sounds.]
                      Thar she blows
    Agin!
POLLY.
        They're marchin' to the graves with flowers.
LINK.
    My Godfrey! 't ain't so much thinkin' o' flowers
    and the young folks, their faces, and the blue
    line of old fellers marchin'—it's the music!
    that old brass voice a-callin'! Seems as though,
    legs or no legs, I'd have to up and foller
    to God-knows-whar, and holler—holler back
    to guns roarin' in the dark. No; durn it, no!
    I jest can't stan' the music.
POLLY [*goes to the work-bench, where the box is steaming*].
                        Uncle Link,
    you want that I should steam this longer?
LINK [*absently*].
                           Oh,
    A kittleful, a kittleful.

POLLY [*coming over to him*].
> Now, then,
> I'm ready for school.—I hope I've drawed the map all right.

LINK.
> Map? Oh, the map!
> [*Surveying the woodpile reminiscently, he nods.*]
> > Yes, thar she be: old Gettysburg!

POLLY.
> I know the places—most.

LINK.
So, *do* ye? Good, now: whar's your marker?

POLLY [*taking up the hoe*].
> > > > Here.

LINK.
Willoughby Run: whar's that?

POLLY [*points with the hoe toward the left of the woodpile*].
> That's farthest over next the barn door.

LINK. My, how we fit the Johnnies thar, the fust mornin'! Jest behind them willers, acrost the Run, that's whar we captur'd Archer. My, my!

POLLY. Over there—that's Seminary Ridge.
[*She points to different heights and depressions, as* LINK *nods his approval.*]
Peach Orchard, Devil's Den, Round Top, the Wheatfield—

LINK.
Lord, Lord, the Wheatfield!

POLLY [*continuing*].
> Cemetery Hill, Little Round Top, Death Valley, and this here is Cemetery Ridge.

LINK [*pointing to the little flag*].
> And colors flyin'!
> We *kep* 'em flyin' thar, too, all three days, from start to finish.

POLLY. Have I learned 'em right?

LINK.
    A number One, chick! Wait a mite: Culp's Hill:
    I don't jest spy Culp's Hill.
POLLY.   There wa'n't enough
    kindlin's to spare for that. It ought to lay
    east there, towards the kitchen.
LINK.   Let it go!
    That's whar us Yanks left our back door ajar
    and Johnson stuck his foot in: kep it thar,
    too, till he got it squoze off by old Slocum.
    Let Culp's Hill lay for now.—Lend me your marker.
    [POLLY *hands him the hoe. From his chair, he reaches*
            with it and digs in the chips.]
    Death Valley needs some scoopin' deeper. So:
    smooth off them chips.
             [POLLY *does so with her foot.*]
                    You better guess 't was deep
    as hell, that second day, come sundown.—Here,
        [*He hands back the hoe to her.*]
    flat down the Wheatfield yonder.
                [POLLY *does so.*]
                         Goda'mighty!
    that Wheatfield: wall, we flatted it down flatter
    than any pancake what you ever cooked,
    Polly; and 't wan't no maple syrup neither
    was runnin', slipp'ry hot and slimy black
    all over it, that nightfall.
POLLY.   Here's the road
    to Emmetsburg.
LINK.   No, 'tain't: this here's the pike
    to Taneytown, where Sykes's boys come sweatin',
    after an all-night march, jest in the nick
    to save our second day. The Emmetsburg
    road's thar.—Whar was I, 'fore I fell cat-nappin'?
POLLY.
    At sunset, July second, Sixty-three.
LINK [*nodding, reminiscent*].
    The Bloody Sundown! God, that crazy sun:
    she set a dozen times that afternoon,
    red-yeller as a punkin jacko'lantern,
    rairin' and pitchin' through the roarin' smoke

till she clean busted, like the other bombs,
behind the hills.
POLLY. My! Wa'n't you never scart
and wished you'd stayed t' home?
LINK. Scart? Wall, I wonder!
Chick, look a-thar: them little stripes and stars.
I heerd a feller onct, down to the store,—
a dressy mister, span-new from the city—
layin' the law down: "All this *stars and stripes,*"
says he, "and *red and white and blue* is rubbish,
mere sentimental rot, spread-eagleism!"
"I wan't t' know!" says I. "In Sixty-three,
I knowed a lad, named Link. Onct, after sundown
I met him stumblin'—with two dead men's muskets
for crutches—towards a bucket, full of ink—
water, they called it. When he'd drunk a spell,
he tuk the rest to wash his bullet holes.—
Wall, sir, he had a piece o' splintered stick,
with *red and white and blue,* tore 'most t' tatters,
a-danglin' from it. "Be you color sergeant?"
says I. "Not me," says Link; "the sergeant's dead,
but when he fell, he handed me this bit
o' *rubbish*—red and white and blue." And Link
he laughed. "What be you laughin' for?" says I.
"Oh, nothin'. Ain't it lovely, though!" says Link.
POLLY.
What did the span-new mister say to that?
LINK.
I didn't stop to listen. Them as never
heerd dead men callin' for the colors don't
guess what they be. [*Sitting up and blinking hard.*]
But this ain't keepin' school!
POLLY [*quietly*].
I guess I'm learnin' somethin', Uncle Link.
LINK.
The second day, 'fore sunset.
[*He takes the hoe and points with it.*]
Yon's the Wheatfield.
Behind it thar lies Longstreet with his rebels.
Here be the Yanks, and Cemetery Ridge
behind 'em. Hancock—he's our general—

he's got to hold the Ridge, till reinforcements
from Taneytown. But lose the Wheatfield, lose
the Ridge, and lose the Ridge—lose God-and-all!—
Lee, the old fox, he'd nab up Washington,
Abe Lincoln and the White House in one bite!—
So the Union, Polly,—me and you and Roger,
your Uncle Link, and Uncle Sam—is all
thar—growin' in that Wheatfield.

POLLY [*smiling proudly*].
                                      And they're growin'
still!

LINK.
        Not the wheat, though. Over them stone walls,
thar comes the Johnnies, thick as grasshoppers:
gray legs a-jumpin' through the tall wheat tops.
And now thar ain't no tops, thar ain't no wheat,
thar ain't no lookin': jest blind feelin' round
in the black mud, and trampin' on boys' faces,
and grapplin' with hell-devils, and stink o' smoke,
and stingin' smother, and—up thar through the dark—
that crazy punkin sun, like an old moon
lopsided, crackin' her red shell with thunder!

[*In the distance, a bugle sounds, and the low martial music
of a brass band begins. Again* LINK'S *face twitches,
and he pauses, listening. From this moment on, the
sound and emotion of the brass music, slowly growing
louder, permeates the scene.*]

POLLY.
    Oh! What was God a-thinkin' of, t' allow
the created world to act that awful?

LINK.
                                           Now,
I wonder!—Cast your eye along this hoe:
[*He stirs the chips and wood-dirt round with the hoe-iron.*]
Thar in that poked up mess o' dirt, you see
yon weeny chip of ox-yoke?—That's the boy
I spoke on: Link, Link Tadbourne: "Chipmunk Link,"
they call him, 'cause his legs is spry 's a squirrel's.—
Wall, mebbe some good angel, with bright eyes
like yourn, stood lookin' down on him that day,
keepin' the Devil's hoe from crackin' him.
[*Patting her hand, which rests on his hoe.*]

If so, I reckon, Polly, it was you.
But mebbe jest Old Nick, as he sat hoein'
them hills, and haulin' in the little heaps
o' squirmin' critters, kind o' reco'nized
Link as his livin' image, and so kep him
to put in an airthly hell, whar thar ain't no legs,
and worn-out devils sit froze in high-backed chairs,
list'nin' to bugles—bugles—bugles—callin'.
[LINK *clutches the sides of his chair, staring. The music draws nearer.* POLLY *touches him soothingly.*]
POLLY.
Don't, dear; they'll soon quit playin'. Never mind 'em.
LINK [*relaxing under her touch*].
No, never mind; that's right. It's jest that onct—
onct we was boys, onct we was boys—with legs.
But never mind. An old boy ain't a bugle.
Onct, though, he was: and all God's life a-snortin'
outn his nostrils, and Hell's mischief laughin'
outn his eyes, and all the mornin' winds
ablowin' *Glory Hallelujahs,* like
brass music, from his mouth.—But never mind!
'T ain't nothin': boys in blue ain't bugles now.
Old brass gits rusty, and old underpinnin'
gits rotten, and trapped chipmunks lose their legs.
[*With smoldering fire.*]
But jest the same—
[*His face convulses and he cries out, terribly—straining in his chair to rise.*]
—for holy God, that band!
Why don't they stop that band!
POLLY [*going*].
I'll run and tell them.
Sit quiet, dear. I'll be right back.
[*Glancing back anxiously,* POLLY *disappears outside. The approaching band begins to play " John Brown's Body."* LINK *sits motionless, gripping his chair.*]
LINK. Set quiet!
Dead folks don't set, and livin' folks kin stand,
and Link—he kin set quiet.—Goda'mighty,
how *kin* he set, and them a-marchin' thar
with old John Brown? Lord God, you ain't forgot

the boys, have ye? the boys, how they come marchin'
home to ye, live and dead, behind old Brown,
a-singin' *Glory* to ye! Jest look down:
thar's Gettysburg, thar's Cemetery Ridge:
don't say ye disremember *them!* And thar's
the colors: Look, he's picked 'em up—the sergeant's
blood splotched 'em some—but thar they be, still flyin'!
Link done that: Link—the spry boy, what they call
Chipmunk: you ain't forgot his double-step,
have ye? [*Again he cries out, beseechingly.*]—
     My God, why do You keep on marchin'
and leave him settin' here?
[*To the music outside, the voices of children begin to
 sing the words of "John Brown's Body." At the
 sound,* LINK'S *face becomes transformed with emotion, his body shakes and his shoulders heave and
 straighten.*]
       No!—I—*won't*—set!
[*Wresting himself mightily, he rises from his chair, and
      stands.*]
Them are the boys that marched to Kingdom-Come
ahead of us, but we keep fallin' in line.
Them voices—Lord, I guess you've brought along
your Sunday choir of young angel folks
to help the boys out.
  [*Following the music with swaying arms.*]
       Glory!—Never mind
me singin': you kin drown me out. But I'm
goin' t' jine in, or bust!
[*Joining with the children's voices, he moves unconsciously
 along the edge of the woodpile. With stiff steps—his
 one hand leaning on the hoe, his other reached as to
 unseen hands, that draw him—he totters toward the
 sunlight and the green lawn, at back. As he does so,
 his thin, cracked voice takes up the battle-hymn where
 the children's are singing it:*]

  "—a-mold'rin' in the grave,
John Brown's body lies a-mold'rin' in the grave,
John Brown's body lies a-mold'rin' in the grave,
  But his soul goes—"

[*Suddenly he stops, aware that he is walking, and cries aloud, astounded:*]
Lord, Lord, my legs!
Whar did Ye git my legs?
[*Shaking with delight, he drops his hoe, seizes up the little flag from the woodpile, and waves it joyously.*]
I'm comin', boys!
Link's loose agin: Chipmunk has sprung his trap.
[*With tottering gait, he climbs the little mound in the woodpile.*]
Now, boys, three cheers for Cemetery Ridge!
Jine in, jine in!
[*Swinging the flag.*]
Hooray!—Hooray!—Hooray!
[*Outside, the music grows louder, and the voices of old men and children sing martially to the brass music. With his final cheer, LINK stumbles down from the mound, brandishes in one hand his hat, in the other the little flag, and stumps off toward the approaching procession into the sunlight, joining his old cracked voice, jubilant, with the singers:*]

"—ry hallelujah,
Glory, glory hallelujah,
His truth is marchin' on!"

[THE CURTAIN.]

WURZEL-FLUMMERY *
A COMEDY IN ONE ACT

By

A. A. MILNE

Alan Alexander Milne was born January 18, 1882. He was a student at Westminster School, the library of which is familiar ground to every reader of Irving's *Sketch Book*. From there he proceeded to Trinity College, Cambridge. On his graduation, he went into journalism in London. He was assistant editor of *Punch* from 1906 to 1914. During the War he was a lieutenant in the Fourth Royal Warwickshire Regiment. In the introduction to his volume of *First Plays*, in which *Wurzel-Flummery* appears, he gives the following whimsical account of his career as a dramatist: " These five plays [*The Lucky One, The Boy Comes Home, Belinda, The Red Feather, Wurzel-Flummery*] were written in the order in which they appear now, during the years 1916 and 1917. They would hardly have been written had it not been for the War, although only one of them is concerned with that subject. To his other responsibilities the Kaiser now adds this volume.

" For these plays were not the work of a professional writer, but the recreation of a (temporary) professional soldier. Playwriting is a luxury to a journalist, as insidious as golf and much more expensive in time and money. When an article is written, the financial reward (and we may as well live as not) is a matter of certainty. A novelist, too, even if he is not in ' the front rank '—but I never heard of one who wasn't—can at least be sure of publication. But when a play is written, there is no certainty of anything save disillusionment.

" To write a play, then, while I was a journalist seemed to me a depraved proceeding, almost as bad as going to Lord's in the morning. I thought I could write one (we all think we can), but I could not afford so unpromising a gamble. But once in the Army the case was altered. No duty now urged me to write. My job was soldiering, and my spare time was my own affair. Other subalterns played bridge and golf; that was one way of amusing oneself. Another way was—why not?—to write plays.

" So we began with *Wurzel-Flummery*. I say ' we,' because another is mixed up in this business even more seriously than the Kaiser. She wrote; I dictated. And if a particularly fine evening drew us out for a walk along the byways—where there was no saluting, and one could smoke a pipe without shocking the Duke of Cambridge—then it was to discuss the last scene and to wonder what would happen in the next. We did not estimate the money or publicity which might come from this new venture; there has never been any serious thought of making money by my bridge-playing, nor desire for publicity when I am trying to play golf. But secretly, of course, we hoped. It was that which made it so much more exciting than any other game.

"Our hopes were realized to the following extent:

"Wurzel-Flummery was produced by Mr. Dion Boucicault at the New Theatre in April, 1917. It was originally written in three acts, in which form it was shown to one or two managers. At the beginning of 1917 I was offered the chance of production in a triple bill if I cut it down into a two-act play. To cut even a line is painful, but to cut thirty pages of one's first comedy, slaughtering whole characters on the way, has at least a certain morbid fascination. It appeared, therefore, in two acts; and one kindly critic embarrassed us by saying that a lesser artist would have written it in three acts, and most of the other critics annoyed us by saying that a greater artist would have written it in one act. However, I amused myself some months later by slaying another character—the office-boy, no less—thereby getting it down to one act, and was surprised to find that the one-act version was, after all, the best. . . . At least, I think it is. . . . At any rate, that is the version I am printing here; but, as can be imagined, I am rather tired of the whole business by now, and I am beginning to wonder if anyone ever did take the name of Wurzel-Flummery at all. Possibly the whole thing is an invention."

Wurzel-Flummery was first produced in this country at the Arts and Crafts Theatre in Detroit; recently it was acted again by The Players of St. Louis.

WURZEL-FLUMMERY

CHARACTERS

ROBERT CRAWSHAW, M.P.
MARGARET CRAWSHAW (*his wife*).
VIOLA CRAWSHAW (*his daughter*).
RICHARD MERITON, M.P.
DENIS CLIFTON.

SCENE.—ROBERT CRAWSHAW'S *town house. Morning.*

It is a June day before the War in the morning-room of ROBERT CRAWSHAW'S *town house. Entering it with our friend the house-agent, our attention would first be called to the delightful club fender round the fireplace. On one side of this a Chesterfield sofa comes out at right angles. In a corner of the sofa* MISS VIOLA CRAWSHAW *is sitting, deep in "The Times." The house-agent would hesitate to catalogue her, but we notice for ourselves, before he points out the comfortable armchair opposite, that she is young and pretty. In the middle of the room and facing the fireplace is (observe) a solid knee-hole writing-table, covered with papers and books of reference, and supported by a chair at the middle and another at the side. The rest of the furniture, and the books and pictures round the walls, we must leave until another time, for at this moment the door behind the sofa opens and* RICHARD MERITON *comes in. He looks about thirty-five, has a clean-shaven intelligent face, and is dressed in a dark tweed suit. We withdraw hastily, as he comes behind* VIOLA *and puts his hands over her eyes.*

RICHARD. Three guesses who it is.
VIOLA [*putting her hands over his*]. The Archbishop of Canterbury.

RICHARD. No.
VIOLA. The Archbishop of York.
RICHARD. Fortunately that exhausts the archbishops. Now, then, your last guess.
VIOLA. Richard Meriton, M.P.
RICHARD. Wonderful! [*He kisses the top of her head lightly and goes round to the club fender, where he sits with his back to the fireplace.*] How did you know? [*He begins to fill a pipe.*]
VIOLA [*smiling*]. Well, it couldn't have been father.
RICHARD. N-no, I suppose not. Not just after breakfast anyway. Anything in the paper?
VIOLA. There's a letter from father pointing out that——
RICHARD. I never knew such a man as Robert for pointing out.
VIOLA. Anyhow, it's in big print.
RICHARD. It would be.
VIOLA. You are very cynical this morning, Dick.
RICHARD. The sausages were cold, dear.
VIOLA. Poor Dick! Oh, Dick, I wish you were on the same side as father.
RICHARD. But he's on the wrong side. Surely I've told you that before. . . . Viola, do you really think it would make a difference?
VIOLA. Well, you know what he said about you at Basingstoke the other day.
RICHARD. No, I don't, really.
VIOLA. He said that your intellectual arrogance was only equaled by your spiritual instability. I don't quite know what it means, but it doesn't sound the sort of thing you want in a son-in-law.
RICHARD. Still, it was friendly of him to go right away to Basingstoke to say it. Anyhow, you don't believe it.
VIOLA. Of course not.
RICHARD. And Robert doesn't really.
VIOLA. Then why does he say it?
RICHARD. Ah, now you're opening up very grave questions. The whole structure of the British Constitution rests upon Robert's right to say things like that at Basingstoke. . . . But really, darling, we're very good friends. He's always asking my advice about things——he doesn't take it, of course, but

still he asks it; and it was awfully good of him to insist on my staying here while my flat was being done up. [*Seriously.*] I bless him for that. If it hadn't been for the last week I should never have known you. You were just " Viola "— the girl I'd seen at odd times since she was a child; and now— oh, why won't you let me tell your father? I hate it like this.

VIOLA. Because I love you, Dick, and because I know father. He would, as they say in novels, show you the door. [*Smiling.*] And I want you this side of the door for a little bit longer.

RICHARD [*firmly*]. I shall tell him before I go.

VIOLA [*pleadingly*]. But not till then; that gives us two more days. You see, darling, it's going to take me all I know to get round him. You see, apart from politics you're so poor —and father hates poor people.

RICHARD [*viciously*]. Damn money!

VIOLA [*thoughtfully*]. I think that's what father means by spiritual instability.

RICHARD. Viola! [*He stands up and holds out his arms to her. She goes to him and—*] Oh, Lord, look out!

VIOLA [*reaching across to the mantelpiece*]. Matches?

RICHARD. Thanks very much. [*He lights his pipe as* ROBERT CRAWSHAW *comes in.* CRAWSHAW *is forty-five, but his closely-trimmed mustache and whiskers, his inclination to stoutness, and the loud old-gentlemanly style in trousers which he affects with his morning-coat, make him look older, and, what is more important, the Pillar of the State which he undoubtedly is.*]

CRAWSHAW. Good-morning, Richard. Down at last?

RICHARD. Good-morning. I did warn you, didn't I, that I was bad at breakfasts?

CRAWSHAW. Viola, where's your mother?

VIOLA [*making for the door*]. I don't know, father; do you want her?

CRAWSHAW. I wish to speak to her.

VIOLA. All right, I'll tell her. [*She goes out.* RICHARD *picks up " The Times" and sits down again.*]

CRAWSHAW [*sitting down in a business-like way at his desk*]. Richard, why don't you get something to do?

RICHARD. My dear fellow, I've only just finished breakfast.

CRAWSHAW. I mean generally. And apart, of course, from your—ah—work in the House.
RICHARD [*a trifle cool*]. I have something to do.
CRAWSHAW. Oh, reviewing. I mean something serious. You should get a directorship or something in the City.
RICHARD. I hate the City.
CRAWSHAW. Ah! there, my dear Richard, is that intellectual arrogance to which I had to call attention the other day at Basingstoke.
RICHARD [*dryly*]. Yes, so Viola was telling me.
CRAWSHAW. You understood, my dear fellow, that I meant nothing personal. [*Clearing his throat.*] It is justly one of the proudest boasts of the Englishman that his political enmities are not allowed to interfere with his private friendships.
RICHARD [*carelessly*]. Oh, I shall go to Basingstoke myself one day.

Enter MARGARET. MARGARET *has been in love with* ROBERT CRAWSHAW *for twenty-five years, the last twenty-four years from habit. She is small, comfortable, and rather foolish; you would certainly call her a dear, but you might sometimes call her a poor dear.*

MARGARET. Good-morning, Mr. Meriton. I do hope your breakfast was all right.
RICHARD. Excellent, thank you.
MARGARET. That's right. Did you want me, Robert?
CRAWSHAW [*obviously uncomfortable*]. Yes—er—h'r'm—Richard—er—what are your—er—plans?
RICHARD. Is he trying to get rid of me, Mrs. Crawshaw?
MARGARET. Of course not. [*To* ROBERT.] Are you, dear?
CRAWSHAW. Perhaps we had better come into my room, Margaret. We can leave Richard here with the paper.
RICHARD. No, no; I'm going.
CRAWSHAW [*going to the door with him*]. I have some particular business to discuss. If you aren't going out, I should like to consult you in the matter afterwards.
RICHARD. Right. [*He goes out.*]
CRAWSHAW. Sit down, Margaret. I have some extraordinary news for you.
MARGARET [*sitting down*]. Yes, Robert?

CRAWSHAW. This letter has just come by hand. [*He reads it.*] "199, Lincoln's Inn Fields. Dear Sir, I have the pleasure to inform you that under the will of the late Mr. Antony Clifton you are a beneficiary to the extent of £50,000."

MARGARET. Robert!

CRAWSHAW. Wait! "A trifling condition is attached—namely, that you should take the name of—Wurzel-Flummery."

MARGARET. Robert!

CRAWSHAW. "I have the honor to be, your obedient servant, Denis Clifton." [*He folds the letter up and puts it away.*]

MARGARET. Robert, whoever is he? I mean the one who's left you the money?

CRAWSHAW [*calmly*]. I have not the slightest idea, Margaret. Doubtless we shall find out before long. I have asked Mr. Denis Clifton to come and see me.

MARGARET. Leaving you fifty thousand pounds! Just fancy!

CRAWSHAW. Wurzel-Flummery!

MARGARET. We can have the second car now, dear, can't we? And what about moving? You know you always said you ought to be in a more central part. Mr. Robert Crawshaw, M.P., of Curzon Street sounds so much more—more Cabinety.

CRAWSHAW. Mr. Robert Wurzel-Flummery, M.P., of Curzon Street—I don't know what *that* sounds like.

MARGARET. I expect that's only a legal way of putting it, dear. They can't really expect us to change our name to—Wurzley-Fothergill.

CRAWSHAW. Wurzel-Flummery.

MARGARET. Yes, dear, didn't I say that? I am sure you could talk the solicitor round—this Mr. Denis Clifton. After all, it doesn't matter to *him* what we call ourselves. Write him one of your letters, dear.

CRAWSHAW. You don't seem to apprehend the situation, Margaret.

MARGARET. Yes, I do, dear. This Mr.—Mr.—

CRAWSHAW. Antony Clifton.

MARGARET. Yes, he's left you fifty thousand pounds, together with the name of Wurzley-Fothergill-

CRAWSHAW. Wurzel—oh, well, never mind.

MARGARET. Yes, well, you tell the solicitor that you will take the fifty thousand pounds, but you don't want the name. It's too absurd, when everybody knows of Robert Crawshaw, M.P., to expect you to call yourself Wurzley-Fothergill.

CRAWSHAW [*impatiently*]. Yes, yes. The point is that this Mr. Clifton has left me the money on *condition* that I change my name. If I don't take the name, I don't take the money.

MARGARET. But is that legal?

CRAWSHAW. Perfectly. It is often done. People change their names on succeeding to some property.

MARGARET. I thought it was only when your name was Moses and you changed it to Talbot.

CRAWSHAW [*to himself*]. Wurzel-Flummery!

MARGARET. I wonder why he left you the money at all. Of course it was very nice of him, but if you didn't know him— Why do you think he did, dear?

CRAWSHAW. I know no more than this letter. I suppose he had—ah—followed my career, and was—ah—interested in it, and being a man with no relations, felt that he could—ah—safely leave this money to me. No doubt Wurzel-Flummery was his mother's maiden name, or the name of some other friend even dearer to him; he wished the name—ah—perpetuated, perhaps even recorded not unworthily in the history of our country, and—ah—made this will accordingly. In a way it is a kind of—ah—sacred trust.

MARGARET. Then, of course, you'll accept it, dear?

CRAWSHAW. It requires some consideration. I have my career to think about, my duty to my country.

MARGARET. Of course, dear. Money is a great help in politics, isn't it?

CRAWSHAW. Money wisely spent is a help in any profession. The view of riches which socialists and suchlike people profess to take is entirely ill-considered. A rich man, who spends his money thoughtfully, is serving his country as nobly as anybody.

MARGARET. Yes, dear. Then you think we *could* have that second car and the house in Curzon Street?

CRAWSHAW. We must not be led away. Fifty thousand pounds, properly invested, is only two thousand a year. When you have deducted the income-tax—and the tax on unearned income is extremely high just now—

MARGARET. Oh, but surely if we have to call ourselves Wurzel-Flummery it would count as *earned* income.

CRAWSHAW. I fear not. Strictly speaking, all money is earned. Even if it is left to you by another, it is presumably left to you in recognition of certain outstanding qualities which you possess. But Parliament takes a different view. I do not for a moment say that fifty thousand pounds would not be welcome. Fifty thousand pounds is certainly not to be sneezed at—

MARGARET. I should think not, indeed!

CRAWSHAW [*unconsciously rising from his chair*]. And without this preposterous condition attached I should be pleased to accept this trust, and I would endeavor, Mr. Speaker— [*He sits down again suddenly.*] I would endeavor, Margaret, to carry it out to the best of my poor ability. But—Wurzel-Flummery!

MARGARET. You would soon get used to it, dear. I had to get used to the name of Crawshaw after I had been Debenham for twenty-five years. It is surprising how quickly it comes to you. I think I only signed my name Margaret Debenham once after I was married.

CRAWSHAW [*kindly*]. The cases are rather different, Margaret. Naturally a woman, who from her cradle looks forward to the day when she will change her name, cannot have this feeling for the—ah—honor of his name, which every man— ah—feels. Such a feeling is naturally more present in my own case since I have been privileged to make the name of Crawshaw in some degree—ah—well-known, I might almost say famous.

MARGARET [*wistfully*]. I used to be called " the beautiful Miss Debenham of Leamington." Everybody in Leamington knew of me. Of course, I am very proud to be Mrs. Robert Crawshaw.

CRAWSHAW [*getting up and walking over to the fireplace*]. In a way it would mean beginning all over again. It is half the battle in politics to get your name before the public. " Whoever is this man Wurzel-Flummery? " people will say.

MARGARET. Anyhow, dear, let us look on the bright side. Fifty thousand pounds is fifty thousand pounds.

CRAWSHAW. It is, Margaret. And no doubt it is my duty to accept it. But—well, all I say is that a *gentleman* would have left it without any conditions. Or at least he would merely have expressed his *wish* that I should take the name, without going so far as to enforce it. Then I could have looked at the matter all round in an impartial spirit.

MARGARET [*pursuing her thoughts*]. The linen is marked R. M. C. now. Of course, we should have to have that altered. Do you think R. M. F. would do, or would it have to be R. M. W. hyphen F.?

CRAWSHAW. What? Oh—yes, there will be a good deal of that to attend to. [*Going up to her.*] I think, Margaret, I had better talk to Richard about this. Of course, it would be absurd to refuse the money, but—well, I should like to have his opinion.

MARGARET [*getting up*]. Do you think he would be very sympathetic, dear? He makes jokes about serious things—like bishops and hunting—just as if they weren't at all serious.

CRAWSHAW. I wish to talk to him just to obtain a new—ah—point of view. I do not hold myself in the least bound to act on anything he says. I regard him as a constituent, Margaret.

MARGARET. Then I will send him to you.

CRAWSHAW [*putting his hands on her shoulders*]. Margaret, what do you really feel about it?

MARGARET. Just whatever *you* feel, Robert.

CRAWSHAW [*kissing her*]. Thank you, Margaret; you are a good wife to me. [*She goes out.* CRAWSHAW *goes to his desk and selects a " Who's Who" from a little pile of reference-books on it. He walks round to his chair, sits down in it and begins to turn the pages, murmuring names beginning with " C " to himself as he gets near the place. When he finds it, he murmurs " Clifton—that's funny," and closes the book. Evidently the publishers have failed him.*]

Enter RICHARD.

RICHARD. Well, what's the news? [*He goes to his old seat on the fender.*] Been left a fortune?

CRAWSHAW [*simply*]. Yes. . . . By a Mr. Antony Clifton. I never met him and I know nothing about him.

RICHARD [*surprised*]. Not really? Well, I congratulate you. [*He sighs.*] To them that hath— But what on earth do you want my advice about?

CRAWSHAW. There is a slight condition attached.
RICHARD. Oho!
CRAWSHAW. The condition is that with this money—fifty thousand pounds—I take the name of—ah—Wurzel-Flummery.
RICHARD [*jumping up*]. What!
CRAWSHAW [*sulkily*]. I said it quite distinctly—Wurzel-Flummery. [RICHARD *in an awed silence walks over to the desk and stands looking down at the unhappy* CRAWSHAW. *He throws out his left hand as if introducing him.*]
RICHARD [*reverently*]. Mr. Robert Wurzel-Flummery, M.P., one of the most prominent of our younger Parliamentarians. Oh, you . . . oh! . . . oh, how too heavenly! [*He goes back to his seat, looks up and catches* CRAWSHAW'S *eye, and breaks down altogether.*]
CRAWSHAW [*rising with dignity*]. Shall we discuss it seriously, or shall we leave it?
RICHARD. How can we discuss a name like Wurzel-Flummery seriously? " Mr. Wurzel-Flummery in a few well-chosen words seconded the motion." . . . " ' Sir,' went on Mr. Wurzel-Flummery "— Oh, poor Robert!
CRAWSHAW [*sitting down sulkily*]. You seem quite certain that I shall take the money.
RICHARD. I am quite certain.
CRAWSHAW. Would *you* take it?
RICHARD [*hesitating*]. Well—I wonder.
CRAWSHAW. After all, as William Shakespeare says, " What's in a name?"
RICHARD. I can tell you something else that Shakespeare—*William* Shakespeare—said. [*Dramatically rising.*] Who steals my purse with fifty thousand in it—steals trash. [*In his natural voice.*] Trash, Robert. [*Dramatically again.*] But he who filches from me my good name of Crawshaw [*lightly*] and substitutes the rotten one of Wurzel—
CRAWSHAW [*annoyed*]. As a matter of fact, Wurzel-Flummery is a very good old name. I seem to remember some —ah—Hampshire Wurzel-Flummeries. It is a very laudable spirit on the part of a dying man to wish to—ah—perpetuate these old English names. It all seems to me quite natural and straightforward. If I take this money I shall have nothing to be ashamed of.

RICHARD. I see. . . . Look here, may I ask you a few questions? I should like to know just how you feel about the whole business?

CRAWSHAW [*complacently folding his hands*]. Go ahead.

RICHARD. Suppose a stranger came up in the street to you and said, "My poor man, here's five pounds for you," what would you do? Tell him to go to the devil, I supppose, wouldn't you?

CRAWSHAW [*humorously*]. In more parliamentary language, perhaps, Richard. I should tell him I never took money from strangers.

RICHARD. Quite so; but that if it were ten thousand pounds, you would take it?

CRAWSHAW. I most certainly shouldn't.

RICHARD. But if he died and left it to you, *then* you would?

CRAWSHAW [*blandly*]. Ah, I thought you were leading up to that. That, of course, is entirely different.

RICHARD. Why?

CRAWSHAW. Well—ah—wouldn't *you* take ten thousand pounds if it were left to you by a stranger?

RICHARD. I daresay I should. But I should like to know why it would seem different.

CRAWSHAW [*professionally*]. Ha—hum! Well—in the first place, when a man is dead he wants his money no longer. You can therefore be certain that you are not taking anything from him which he cannot spare. And in the next place, it is the man's dying wish that you should have the money. To refuse would be to refuse the dead. To accept becomes almost a sacred duty.

RICHARD. It really comes to this, doesn't it? You won't take it from him when he's alive, because if you did, you couldn't decently refuse him a little gratitude; but you know that it doesn't matter a damn to him what happens to his money after he's dead, and therefore you can take it without feeling any gratitude at all.

CRAWSHAW. No, I shouldn't put it like that.

RICHARD [*smiling*]. I'm sure you wouldn't, Robert.

CRAWSHAW. No doubt you can twist it about so that—

RICHARD. All right, we'll leave that and go on to the next point. Suppose a perfect stranger offered you five pounds to part your hair down the middle, shave off your mustache, and wear only one whisker—if he met you suddenly in the street, seemed to dislike your appearance, took out a fiver and begged you to hurry off and alter yourself—of course you'd pocket the money and go straight to your barber's?

CRAWSHAW. Now you are merely being offensive.

RICHARD. I beg your pardon. I should have said that if he had left you five pounds in his will?—well, then twenty pounds?—a hundred pounds?—a thousand pounds?—fifty thousand pounds?— [*Jumping up excitedly.*] It's only a question of price—fifty thousand pounds, Robert—a pink tie with purple spots, hair parted across the back, trousers with a patch in the seat, call myself Wurzel-Flummery—any old thing you like, you can't insult me—anything you like, gentlemen, for fifty thousand pounds. [*Lowering his voice.*] Only you must leave it in your will, and then I can feel that it is a sacred duty— a sacred duty, my lords and gentlemen. [*He sinks back into the sofa and relights his pipe.*]

CRAWSHAW [*rising with dignity*]. It is evidently useless to prolong this conversation.

RICHARD [*waving him down again*]. No, no, Robert; I've finished. I just took the other side—and I got carried away. I ought to have been at the Bar.

CRAWSHAW. You take such extraordinary views of things. You must look facts in the face, Richard. This is a modern world, and we are modern people living in it. Take the matter-of-fact view. You may like or dislike the name of— ah—Wurzel-Flummery, but you can't get away from the fact that fifty thousand pounds is not to be sneezed at.

RICHARD [*wistfully*]. I don't know why people shouldn't sneeze at money sometimes. I should like to start a society for sneezing at fifty thousand pounds. We'd have to begin in a small way, of course; we'd begin by sneezing at five pounds— and work up. . . . The trouble is that we're all inoculated in our cradles against that kind of cold.

CRAWSHAW [*pleasantly*]. You will have your little joke. But you know as well as I do that it is only a joke. There can be no serious reason why I should not take this money. And I—ah—gather that you don't think it will affect my career?

RICHARD [*carelessly*]. Not a bit. It'll help it. It'll get you into all the comic papers.

MARGARET *comes in at this moment, to the relief of* CRAWSHAW, *who is not quite certain if he is being flattered or insulted again.*

MARGARET. Well, have you told him?
RICHARD [*making way for her on the sofa*]. I have heard the news, Mrs. Crawshaw. And I have told Robert my opinion that he should have no difficulty in making the name of Wurzel-Flummery as famous as he has already made that of Crawshaw. At any rate I hope he will.
MARGARET. How nice of you!
CRAWSHAW. Well, it's settled then. [*Looking at his watch.*] This solicitor fellow should be here soon. Perhaps, after all, we can manage something about— Ah, Viola, did you want your mother?

Enter VIOLA.

VIOLA. Sorry, do I interrupt a family meeting? There's Richard, so it can't be very serious.
RICHARD. What a reputation!
CRAWSHAW. Well, it's over now.
MARGARET. Viola had better know, hadn't she?
CRAWSHAW. She'll have to know some time, of course.
VIOLA [*sitting down firmly on the sofa*]. Of course she will. So you'd better tell her now. I knew there was something exciting going on this morning.
CRAWSHAW [*embarrassed*]. Hum—ha— [*To* MARGARET.] Perhaps you'd better tell her, dear.
MARGARET [*simply and naturally*]. Father has come into some property, Viola. It means changing our name unfortunately. But your father doesn't think it will matter.
VIOLA. How thrilling! What is the name, mother?
MARGARET. Your father says it is—dear me, I shall never remember it.
CRAWSHAW [*mumbling*]. Wurzel-Flummery.
VIOLA [*after a pause*]. Dick, *you* tell me, if nobody else will.
RICHARD. Robert said it just now.
VIOLA. That wasn't a name, was it? I thought it was just a—do say it again, father.
CRAWSHAW [*sulkily but plainly*]. Wurzel-Flummery.

VIOLA [*surprised*]. Do you spell it like that? I mean like a wurzel and like flummery?

RICHARD. Exactly, I believe.

VIOLA [*to herself*]. Miss Viola Wurzel-Flummery—I mean they'd have to look at you, wouldn't they? [*Bubbling over.*] Oh, Dick, what a heavenly name! Who had it first?

RICHARD. They are an old Hampshire family—that is so, isn't it, Robert?

CRAWSHAW [*annoyed*]. I said I thought that I remembered —Margaret, can you find Burke there? [*She finds it, and he buries himself in the families of the great.*]

MARGARET. Well, Viola, you haven't told us how you like being Miss Wurzel-Flummery.

VIOLA. I haven't realized myself yet, mummy. I shall have to stand in front of my glass and tell myself who I am.

RICHARD. It's all right for *you*. You know you'll change your name one day, and then it won't matter what you've been called before.

VIOLA [*secretly*]. H'sh! [*She smiles lovingly at him, and then says aloud.*] Oh, won't it? It's got to appear in the papers, "A marriage has been arranged between Miss Viola Wurzel-Flummery . . ." and everybody will say, "And about time too, poor girl."

MARGARET [*to* CRAWSHAW]. Have you found it, dear?

CRAWSHAW [*resentfully*]. This is the 1912 edition.

MARGARET. Still, dear, if it's a very old family, it ought to be in by then.

VIOLA. I don't mind how old it is; I think it's lovely. Oh, Dick, what fun it will be being announced! Just think of the footman throwing open the door and saying—

MAID [*announcing*]. Mr. Denis Clifton. [*There is a little natural confusion as* CLIFTON *enters jauntily in his summer suiting with a bundle of papers under his arm.* CRAWSHAW *goes towards him and shakes hands.*]

CRAWSHAW. How do you do, Mr. Clifton? Very good of you to come. [*Looking doubtfully at his clothes.*] Er—it is Mr. Denis Clifton, the solicitor?

CLIFTON [*cheerfully*]. It is. I must apologize for not looking the part more, but my clothes did not arrive from Clarkson's in time. Very careless of them when they had promised.

And my clerk dissuaded me from the side-whiskers which I keep by me for these occasions.

CRAWSHAW [*bewildered*]. Ah yes, quite so. But you have—ah—full legal authority to act in this matter?

CLIFTON. Oh, decidedly. Oh, there's no question of that.

CRAWSHAW [*introducing*]. My wife—and daughter. [CLIFTON *bows gracefully.*] My friend, Mr. Richard Meriton.

CLIFTON [*happily*]. Dear me! Mr. Meriton too! This is quite a situation, as we say in the profession.

RICHARD [*amused by him*]. In the legal profession?

CLIFTON. In the theatrical profession. [*Turning to* MARGARET.] I am a writer of plays, Mrs. Crawshaw. I am not giving away a professional secret when I tell you that most of the managers in London have thanked me for submitting my work to them.

CRAWSHAW [*firmly*]. I understood, Mr. Clifton, that you were the solicitor employed to wind up the affairs of the late Mr. Antony Clifton.

CLIFTON. Oh, certainly. Oh, there's no doubt about my being a solicitor. My clerk, a man of the utmost integrity, not to say probity, would give me a reference. I am in the books; I belong to the Law Society. But my heart turns elsewhere. Officially I have embraced the profession of a solicitor— [*Frankly, to* MRS. CRAWSHAW.] But you know what these official embraces are.

MARGARET. I'm afraid— [*She turns to her husband for assistance.*]

CLIFTON [*to* RICHARD]. Unofficially, Mr. Meriton, I am wedded to the Muses.

VIOLA. Dick, isn't he lovely?

CRAWSHAW. Quite so. But just for the moment, Mr. Clifton, I take it that we are concerned with legal business. Should I ever wish to produce a play, the case would be different.

CLIFTON. Admirably put. Pray regard me entirely as the solicitor for as long as you wish. [*He puts his hat down on a chair with the papers in it, and taking off his gloves, goes on dreamily.*] Mr. Denis Clifton was superb as a solicitor. In spite of an indifferent make-up, his manner of taking off his gloves and dropping them into his hat— [*He does so.*]

MARGARET [*to* CRAWSHAW]. I think, perhaps, Viola and I—
RICHARD [*making a move too*]. We'll leave you to your business, Robert.
CLIFTON [*holding up his hand*]. Just one moment if I may. I have a letter for you, Mr. Meriton.
RICHARD [*surprised*]. For me?
CLIFTON. Yes. My clerk, a man of the utmost integrity—oh, but I said that before—he took it round to your rooms this morning, but found only painters and decorators there. [*He is feeling in his pockets and now brings the letter out.*] I brought it along, hoping that Mr. Crawshaw—but of course I never expected anything so delightful as this. [*He hands over the letter with a bow.*]
RICHARD. Thanks. [*He puts it in his pocket.*]
CLIFTON. Oh, but do read it now, won't you? [*To* MRS. CRAWSHAW.] One so rarely has an opportunity of being present when one's own letters are read. I think the habit they have on the stage of reading letters aloud to each other is such a very delightful one. [RICHARD, *with a smile and a shrug, has opened his letter while* CLIFTON *is talking.*]
RICHARD. Good Lord!
VIOLA. Dick, what is it?
RICHARD [*reading*]. "199, Lincoln's Inn Fields. Dear Sir, I have the pleasure to inform you that under the will of the late Mr. Antony Clifton you are a beneficiary to the extent of £50,000."
VIOLA. Dick!
RICHARD. "A trifling condition is attached—namely, that you should take the name of—Wurzel-Flummery." [CLIFTON, *with his hand on his heart, bows gracefully from one to the other of them.*]
CRAWSHAW [*annoyed*]. Impossible! Why should he leave any money to *you?*
VIOLA. Dick! How wonderful!
MARGARET [*mildly*]. I don't remember ever having had a morning quite like this.
RICHARD [*angrily*]. Is this a joke, Mr. Clifton?
CLIFTON. Oh, the money is there all right. My clerk, a man of the utmost—
RICHARD. Then I refuse it. I'll have nothing to do with

it. I won't even argue about it. [*Tearing the letter into bits.*] That's what I think of your money. [*He stalks indignantly from the room.*]

VIOLA. Dick! Oh, but, mother, he mustn't. Oh, I must tell him— [*She hurries after him.*]

MARGARET [*with dignity*]. Really, Mr. Clifton, I'm surprised at you. [*She goes out too.*]

CLIFTON [*looking round the room*]. And now, Mr. Crawshaw, we are alone.

CRAWSHAW. Yes. Well, I think, Mr. Clifton, you have a good deal to explain—

CLIFTON. My dear sir, I'm longing to begin. I have been looking forward to this day for weeks. I spent over an hour this morning dressing for it. [*He takes papers from his hat and moves to the sofa.*] Perhaps I had better begin from the beginning.

CRAWSHAW [*interested, indicating the papers*]. The documents in the case?

CLIFTON. Oh dear, no—just something to carry in the hand. It makes one look more like a solicitor. [*Reading the title.*] " Watherston v. Towser—*in re* Great Missenden Canal Company." My clerk invents the titles; it keeps him busy. He is very fond of Towser; Towser is always coming in. [*Frankly.*] You see, Mr. Crawshaw, this is my first real case, and I only got it because Antony Clifton is my uncle. My efforts to introduce a little picturesqueness into the dull formalities of the law do not meet with that response that one would have expected.

CRAWSHAW [*looking at his watch*]. Yes. Well, I'm a busy man, and if you could tell me as shortly as possible why your uncle left this money to me, and apparently to Mr. Meriton too, under these extraordinary conditions, I shall be obliged to you.

CLIFTON. Say no more, Mr. Crawshaw; I look forward to being entirely frank with you. It will be a pleasure.

CRAWSHAW. You understand, of course, my position. I think I may say that I am not without reputation in the country; and proud as I am to accept this sacred trust, this money which the late Mr. Antony Clifton has seen fit—[*modestly*] one cannot say why—to bequeath to me, yet the use of the name Wurzel-Flummery would be excessively awkward.

CLIFTON [*cheerfully*]. Excessively.

CRAWSHAW. My object in seeing you was to inquire if it was absolutely essential that the name should go with the money.

CLIFTON. Well [*thoughtfully*], you may have the name *without* the money if you like. But you must have the name.

CRAWSHAW [*disappointed*]. Ah! [*Bravely.*] Of course, I have nothing against the name, a good old Hampshire name—

CLIFTON [*shocked*]. My dear Mr. Crawshaw, you didn't think—you didn't really think that anybody had been called Wurzel-Flummery before? Oh no, no. You and Mr. Meriton were to be the first, the founders of the clan, the designers of the Wurzel-Flummery sporran—

CRAWSHAW. What do you mean, sir? Are you telling me that it is not a real name at all?

CLIFTON. Oh, it's a name all right. I know it is because—er—*I* made it up.

CRAWSHAW [*outraged*]. And you have the impudence to propose, sir, that I should take a made-up name?

CLIFTON [*soothingly*]. Well, all names are made up some time or other. Somebody had to think of—Adam.

CRAWSHAW. I warn you, Mr. Clifton, that I do not allow this trifling with serious subjects.

CLIFTON. It's all so simple, really. . . . You see, my Uncle Antony was a rather unusual man. He despised money. He was not afraid to put it in its proper place. The place he put it in was—er—a little below golf and a little above classical concerts. If a man said to him, " Would you like to make fifty thousand this afternoon? " he would say—well, it would depend what he was doing. If he were going to have a round at Walton Heath—

CRAWSHAW. It's perfectly scandalous to talk of money in this way.

CLIFTON. Well, that's how he talked about it. But he didn't find many to agree with him. In fact, he used to say that there was nothing, however contemptible, that a man would not do for money. One day I suggested that if he left a legacy with a sufficiently foolish name attached to it, somebody might be found to refuse it. He laughed at the idea. That put me on my mettle. " Two people," I said; " leave the same silly name to two people, two well-known people, rival politicians, say, men whose own names are already public property. Surely they wouldn't both take it." That touched him. " Denis, my boy, you've got it," he said. " Upon what vile bodies shall we experiment? " We decided on you and Mr. Meriton. The next thing was to choose the name. I started on the wrong lines. I began by suggesting names like Porker, Tosh, Bugge, Spiffkins—the obvious sort. My uncle—

CRAWSHAW [*boiling with indignation*]. How *dare* you discuss me with your uncle, sir! How dare you decide in this cold-blooded way whether I am to be called—ah—Tosh—or—ah—Porker!

CLIFTON. My uncle wouldn't hear of Tosh or Porker. He wanted a humorous name—a name he could roll lovingly round his tongue—a name expressing a sort of humorous contempt—Wurzel-Flummery! I can see now the happy ruminating smile which came so often on my Uncle Antony's face in those latter months. He was thinking of his two Wurzel-Flummeries. I remember him saying once—it was at the Zoo—what a pity it was he hadn't enough to divide among the whole Cabinet. A whole bunch of Wurzel-Flummeries; it would have been rather jolly.

CRAWSHAW. You force me to say, sir, that if *that* was the way you and your uncle used to talk together at the Zoo, his death can only be described as a merciful intervention of Providence.

CLIFTON. Oh, but I think he must be enjoying all this somewhere, you know. I hope he is. He would have loved this morning. It was his one regret that from the necessities of the case he could not live to enjoy his own joke; but he had hopes that echoes of it would reach him wherever he might be. It was with some such idea, I fancy, that toward the end he became interested in spiritualism.

CRAWSHAW [*rising solemnly*]. Mr. Clifton, I have no interest in the present whereabouts of your uncle, nor in what means he has of overhearing a private conversation between you and myself. But if, as you irreverently suggest, he is listening to us, I should like him to hear this. That, in my opinion, you are not a qualified solicitor at all, that you never had an uncle, and that the whole story of the will and the ridiculous condition attached to it is just the tomfool joke of a man who, by his own admission, wastes most of his time writing unsuccessful farces. And I propose—

CLIFTON. Pardon my interrupting. But you said farces. Not farces, comedies—of a whimsical nature.

CRAWSHAW. Whatever they were, sir, I propose to report the whole matter to the Law Society. And you know your way out, sir.

CLIFTON. Then I am to understand that you refuse the legacy, Mr. Crawshaw?

CRAWSHAW [*startled*]. What's that?

CLIFTON. I am to understand that you refuse the fifty thousand pounds?

CRAWSHAW. If the money is really there, I most certainly do not refuse it.

CLIFTON. Oh, the money is most certainly there—and the name. Both waiting for you.

CRAWSHAW [*thumping the table*]. Then, sir, I accept them. I feel it my duty to accept them, as a public expression of confidence in the late Mr. Clifton's motives. I repudiate entirely the motives that you have suggested to him, and I consider it a sacred duty to show what I think of your story by accepting the trust which he has bequeathed to me. You will arrange further matters with my solicitor. Good-morning, sir.

CLIFTON [*to himself as he rises*]. Mr. Crawshaw here drank a glass of water. [*To* CRAWSHAW.] Mr. Wurzel-Flummery, farewell. May I express the parting wish that your future career will add fresh luster to—my name. [*To himself as he goes out.*] Exit Mr. Denis Clifton with dignity. [*But he has left his papers behind him.* CRAWSHAW, *walking indignantly back to the sofa, sees the papers and picks them up.*]

CRAWSHAW [*contemptuously*]. "Watherston v. Towser—in re Great Missenden Canal Company." Bah! [*He tears them up and throws them into the fire. He goes back to his writing-table and is seated there as* VIOLA, *followed by* MERITON, *comes in.*]

VIOLA. Father, Dick doesn't want to take the money, but I have told him that of course he must. He must, mustn't he?

RICHARD. We needn't drag Robert into it, Viola.

CRAWSHAW. If Richard has the very natural feeling that it would be awkward for me if there were two Wurzel-Flummeries in the House of Commons, I should be the last to interfere with his decision. In any case, I don't see what concern it is of yours, Viola.

VIOLA [*surprised*]. But how can we get married if he doesn't take the money?

CRAWSHAW [*hardly understanding*]. Married? What does this mean, Richard?

RICHARD. I'm sorry it has come out like this. We ought to have told you before, but anyhow we were going to have told you in a day or two. Viola and I want to get married.

CRAWSHAW. And what did you want to get married on?

RICHARD [*with a smile*]. Not very much, I'm afraid.

VIOLA. We're all right now, father, because we shall have fifty thousand pounds.

RICHARD [*sadly*]. Oh, Viola, Viola!

CRAWSHAW. But naturally this puts a very different complexion on matters.

VIOLA. So of course he must take it, mustn't he, father?

CRAWSHAW. I can hardly suppose, Richard, that you expect me to entrust my daughter to a man who is so little provident for himself that he throws away fifty thousand pounds because of some fanciful objection to the name which goes with it.

RICHARD [*in despair*]. You don't understand, Robert.

CRAWSHAW. I understand this, Richard. That if the name is good enough for me, it should be good enough for you. You don't mind asking Viola to take *your* name, but you consider it an insult if you are asked to take *my* name.

RICHARD [*miserably to* VIOLA]. Do you want to be Mrs. Wurzel-Flummery?

VIOLA. Well, I'm going to be Miss Wurzel-Flummery anyhow, darling.

RICHARD [*beaten*]. Heaven help me! you'll make me take it. But you'll never understand.

CRAWSHAW [*stopping to administer comfort to him on his way out*]. Come, come, Richard. [*Patting him on the shoulder.*] I understand perfectly. All that you were saying about money a little while ago—it's all perfectly true, it's all just what I feel myself. But in practice we have to make allowances sometimes. We have to sacrifice our ideals for—ah—others. I shall be very proud to have you for a son-in-law, and to feel that there will be the two of us in Parliament together upholding the honor of the—ah—name. And perhaps now that we are to be so closely related, you may come to feel some day that your views could be—ah—more adequately put forward from *my* side of the House.

RICHARD. Go on, Robert; I deserve it.

CRAWSHAW. Well, well! Margaret will be interested in our news. And you must send that solicitor a line—or perhaps a telephone message would be better. [*He goes to the door and turns round just as he is going out.*] Yes, I think the telephone, Richard; it would be safer. [*Exit.*]

RICHARD [*holding out his hands to* VIOLA]. Come here, Mrs. Wurzel-Flummery.

VIOLA. Not Mrs. Wurzel-Flummery; Mrs. Dick. And soon, please, darling. [*She comes to him.*]

RICHARD [*shaking his head sadly at her*]. I don't know what I've done, Viola. [*Suddenly.*] But you're worth it. [*He kisses her, and then says in a low voice.*] And God help me if I ever stop thinking so!

Enter MR. DENIS CLIFTON. *He sees them, and walks about very tactfully with his back towards them, humming to himself.*

RICHARD. Hullo!

CLIFTON [*to himself*]. Now where did I put those papers? [*He hums to himself again.*] Now where—oh, I beg your pardon! I left some papers behind.

VIOLA. Dick, you'll tell him. [*As she goes out, she says to* CLIFTON.] Good-by, Mr. Clifton, and thank you for writing such nice letters.

CLIFTON. Good-by, Miss Crawshaw.

VIOLA. Just say it to see how it sounds.

CLIFTON. Good-by, Miss Wurzel-Flummery.

VIOLA [*smiling happily*]. No, not Miss, *Mrs.* [*She goes out.*]

CLIFTON [*looking in surprise from her to him*]. You don't mean—

RICHARD. Yes; and I'm taking the money after all, Mr. Clifton.

CLIFTON. Dear me, what a situation! [*Thoughtfully to himself.*] I wonder how a rough scenario would strike the managers.

RICHARD. Poor Mr. Clifton!

CLIFTON. Why poor?
RICHARD. You missed all the best part. You didn't hear what I said to Crawshaw about money before you came.
CLIFTON [*thoughtfully*]. Oh! was it very— [*Brightening up.*] But I expect Uncle Antony heard. [*After a pause.*] Well, I must be getting on. I wonder if you've noticed any important papers lying about, in connection with the Great Missenden Canal Company—a most intricate case, in which my clerk and I— [*He has murmured himself across to the fireplace, and the fragments of his important case suddenly catch his eye. He picks up one of the fragments.*] Ah, yes. Well, I shall tell my clerk that we lost the case. He will be sorry. He had got quite fond of that canal. [*He turns to go, but first says to* MERITON.] So you're taking the money, Mr. Meriton?
RICHARD. Yes.
CLIFTON. And Mr. Crawshaw too?
RICHARD. Yes.
CLIFTON [*to himself as he goes out*]. They are both taking it. [*He stops and looks up to* UNCLE ANTONY *with a smile.*] Good old Uncle Antony—*he* knew—*he* knew! [MERITON *stands watching him as he goes.*]

[THE CURTAIN.]

MAID OF FRANCE

By
HAROLD BRIGHOUSE

Miss Horniman could hardly have foreseen the development of a Manchester school of dramatists as the outcome of her experiment with repertory at the Gaiety Theatre in Manchester, because her purpose was to produce good plays irrespective of geographical limitations. But the fact is that the project was a source of real inspiration to a group of young Lancashire writers among whom may be mentioned Allan Broome, Stanley Houghton, and Harold Brighouse. There is no plainer illustration of the relations between the audience and the play, or between the theatre and the play, or between the actor and the play than the dramatic activity that followed the establishment of the Abbey Theatre in Dublin and the setting up of Miss Horniman's experiment in Manchester.

Although in this collection, Brighouse is represented by *Maid of France,* a play with no local Lancashire coloring, first given on July 16, 1917, in London, not Manchester (it was later produced at the Greenwich Village Theatre in New York, beginning April 18, 1918), he has up to the present time written seven plays about Lancashire. He has been particularly successful in one-act drama; *Lonesome Like, The Price of Coal,* and *Spring in Bloomsbury* have been popular here and in England. B. Iden Payne, who directed productions at the Gaiety Theatre for some time, says: " In all Harold Brighouse's plays there is in the acting more laughter than one would expect from the reading." A number of Brighouse's plays have been published; in the introduction to the latest volume,[1] he writes: " In another age than ours play-books were a favorite, if not the only form of light reading. . . . The reader mentally producing a play from the book in his hand looks through a magic casement at what he gloriously will instead of through a proscenium arch at the handiwork of a mere human producer." This playwright's attitude toward the reading of plays, with its appeal to the imagination, is one justification for a collection like the present one.

[1] Harold Brighouse, *Three Lancashire Plays,* London and New York, 1920. There is a bibliographical note at the end.

Brighouse is himself a Manchester man, having been born in Eccles, a suburb, on July 26, 1882. He was educated at the Manchester Grammar School. Until 1913 he was engaged in business, carrying on his literary work at the same time, but in that year he gave himself up exclusively to writing. Besides plays, he has written fiction and criticism. During the Great War, he was attached to the Intelligence Staff of the Air Ministry.

MAID OF FRANCE

CHARACTERS

JEANNE D'ARC.
BLANCHE, *a flower-girl.*
PAUL, *a French Poilu.*
FRED, *an English Tommy.*
GERALD SOAMES, *an English lieutenant.*

THE SCENE *represents one side of a square in a French town on Christmas Eve, 1916. The buildings shown have suffered from German shells, except the church in the center which stands immune, protected, as it were, by the statue of Jeanne d'Arc which stands on a pedestal, surrounded by steps in front of it. The church is lighted up within for the midnight mass, but it is its side which presents itself to one's view, so that the ingoing worshipers are not seen. The statue is of the Maid in her armor. It is nearly midnight on Christmas Eve and the lighting, which should not be too realistically obscure, suggests faint moonlight.*

PAUL, *a French private in war-worn uniform, stands by the steps, gazing adoringly at the statue. He is a charmingly simple, credulous man, in peace a peasant. To him there enters from the right,* BLANCHE, *a flower-girl, in a cloak, with a basket of flowers. In face and figure,* BLANCHE *must resemble the statue. She is a pert, impudent, extremely self-possessed saleswoman, burning, however, with the fierce light of French patriotism which, almost in spite of herself, is apt to get the better of her. Ready as she is to trade upon* PAUL'S *mystic reverence for the Maid, familiarity with the statue has not bred contempt in her. She stops by* PAUL, *offering her flowers with a cajoling smile.*

BLANCHE. Will you buy a flower, monsieur?
PAUL. Flower, mademoiselle? You can sell flowers at this hour when it is nearly midnight?

BLANCHE. There is moonlight, and I have a smile, monsieur. It is my smile which sells the flowers. Does not monsieur agree that it is irresistible?

PAUL [*uneasily*]. Mademoiselle has charm.

BLANCHE. And I have charms for you. My flowers. Will you not buy a flower, monsieur, and I will pin it to your uniform where it will draw all the ladies' eyes to you when you promenade on the boulevard?

PAUL. I do not promenade. I stay here.

BLANCHE. Here in the Square where it is dull and lonely? But on the boulevards are lights, monsieur, and gaiety, and people promenade because to-night is Christmas Eve.

PAUL. Mademoiselle, you're kind. Will you be kind to me and tell me something?

BLANCHE. What can I tell?

PAUL. I am only a peasant and I do not know many things. But you live in the town and you must know. They say, mademoiselle, they have told me, that there are miracles on Christmas Eve.

BLANCHE. Did you believe them?

PAUL. I did not know. I only hoped.

BLANCHE. What did you hope?

PAUL [*very earnestly*]. I have been told that stone can speak on Christmas Eve. And I want, oh, mademoiselle, I want to hear the blessed voice of our glorious Maid.

BLANCHE. Monsieur has sentiment.

PAUL [*pleadingly*]. You think that she will speak to me?

BLANCHE [*dropping all banter*]. Monsieur, she speaks in stone to all of us. She stands erect, serene, like the unconquerable spirit of France and cries defiance at the Boche. They sent their shells like hail and ground our homes to powder and made a desolation of our streets, but they could not touch the statue of the Maid nor the church she guards.

PAUL. And she speaks! She speaks!

BLANCHE. She is the soul of France, monsieur, defying tyranny, invincible and unafraid. She is a message to each one of us. As the shells fell all around and could not harm her, so must we stand unshaken for the France we love. She speaks of freedom and deliverance.

PAUL. And she will speak to me?

BLANCHE [*pityingly as she sees how literally he has taken her*]. Perhaps.

PAUL. What must I do, mademoiselle, to hear her voice?

BLANCHE [*seeing in this too good an opportunity for selling a flower*]. Will you not buy a flower for the Maid? They come from far away, from the South where there is always sun, and so they are not cheap. But, for a franc, you may have one lily of Lorraine to put upon the statue of the Maid.

PAUL. A lily of Lorraine!

BLANCHE [*showing a flower, then taking it back tantalizingly*]. See, monsieur! How could she refuse to speak to you if you gave her that?

PAUL. It is the way to make her speak! [*Puts out hand for the flower and then draws back.*] But a franc! And I have nothing but one sou.

BLANCHE. One sou! When flowers are so dear, and have to come so far! Mon dieu, monsieur, but you have had a thirsty day if a sou is all that you have left from the wine-shops.

PAUL. I did not spend it there, mademoiselle. I gave it to the church, this church where is the statue of our Maid.

BLANCHE [*only half scoffing*]. Monsieur is devout.

PAUL. Not always, mademoiselle. But I was born at Domremy where she was born and I have always adored our sainted Maid who died for France. Perhaps because of that, perhaps without the flower, Jeanne will speak to me at midnight when they say the statues come to life.

BLANCHE [*touched*]. Monsieur, I do not know. Perhaps she will. But see, here is a lily of Lorraine which I give you for the Maid. Put it upon her statue and perhaps it will awaken her to speech.

PAUL. Mademoiselle! [*Taking the flower.*] How can I thank you?

BLANCHE. I also am a maid of France, monsieur. You are a soldier and you fight for France. But I must sell my flowers now. Perhaps, when I have sold them, I will come again to see if Jeanne has spoken.

PAUL. You think she will?

BLANCHE. Monsieur, have faith. All things are possible on Christmas Eve. [*She moves L.* PAUL *goes to the statue and puts the lily on its breast.*]

BLANCHE. Holy Virgin, the lies I've told! What simplicity! But Jeanne might. She might. [*Exit* BLANCHE *L.* PAUL *stands, watching. An English lieutenant,* GERALD SOAMES, *enters R., carrying a small wreath of evergreens. He is awkward and self-conscious and stops short when he sees* PAUL, *annoyed in the English way at being found out in an act of sentiment. By consequence, the little ceremony he had proposed falls short of the impressiveness he designed for it.*]

GERALD. O Lord, there's a fellow there. Er— [PAUL *salutes.*] Oh—er—c'est ici la statue de Jeanne d'Arc, n'est-ce pas?

PAUL. Mais oui, monsieur.

GERALD. And that's about as far as my French will go. I say, you're not on duty, are you? Vous n'êtes pas de garde?

PAUL. Non, monsieur.

GERALD. No, of course you're not. Damned silly question to ask. All the same, I wish he'd take a hint. I say. Lord, I've forgotten the French for "have a drink." Besides, he couldn't. It's too late. I'll just do what I came for and go. [*Puts back into pocket the coin he had taken out.*] After all, the fellow's as good a right to be here as I have. I'll have one more shot. N'avez-vous pas des affaires?

PAUL. Mais non, monsieur. Pas ce soir. Je suis en congé.

GERALD. Heaven knows what that means, except that he's a fixture. Oh well, I don't care if he does see me. He'll not know what to make of it, anyhow. [*Up to statue.*] Jeanne d'Arc, I'm putting this wreath on your statue. It's an English wreath and it came from England. It's English holly and English ivy and it's supposed to mean that England's sorry for the awful things she did to you and I hope you've forgiven us all. [*He has cap off. Now puts cap on.*] I think that's all. [*Places wreath at statue's feet. Stands erect, salutes, turns.*] Hang that French fellow. I suppose he'll think I'm mad. [GERALD *goes down steps and off R.* PAUL *salutes, then goes up steps to look at the wreath.* FRED COLLEDGE, *an English private, enters L. Without noticing* PAUL, *he sits on the steps and lights a cigarette. In the light of his match he sees* PAUL, *gives a little amused laugh and lies back making himself comfortable, turning up coat-collar, etc.* PAUL *sees him, and is shocked. Comes down steps.*]

PAUL. Monsieur!

MAID OF FRANCE

FRED. Hullo, cockey. How are you getting on?
PAUL. Monsieur! This place. These steps. One does not est upon these steps.
FRED. Ho yes, one does. I'm doing it, so I ought to now.
PAUL. But here, monsieur. Outside the church.
FRED. That's all right. The better the place the better the eat. It ain't a feather-bed in the old house at home, but I've ort of lost the feather-bed 'abit lately.
PAUL. One should not sit on these steps, monsieur.
FRED. You must like that tune, old son, the way you stick o it. And, if you ask me, one should not do a pile of things hat one's been doing over here. Take me, now. By rights, I ught to be eating roast beef and plum-pudding to-morrow in very Street. Third turn on the left below the Mile End 'avilion, but I suppose I'm the same way as you. Going back n the train at 2 A.M. to eat my Christmas dinner in the blooming trenches. That's you, ain't it? And it's me, too. So let's it down together and do an entente for an hour. Don't talk nd I'll race you to where the dreams come from. [*He pulls* 'AUL *down genially beside him.*]
PAUL [*sitting*]. I ought not to sit here.
FRED. Ain't these steps soft enough for you?
PAUL. Monsieur, you do not understand. I come from Domremy.
FRED. Do you? I'm Mile End myself. What about it?
PAUL. But Domremy.
FRED. Can't say I'm much the wiser.
PAUL. But here, monsieur. This statue. It is our glorious naid. C'est Jeanne d'Arc.
FRED. Ark, eh? Is that old Noah? [*Gets up to look at* tatue.]
PAUL [*rising*]. Jeanne d'Arc, monsieur. She—
FRED. Oh, it's a lady, is it? Dressed like that for riding, reckon. So that's old Noah's wife, is it? Well, the old cock ad a bit of taste.
PAUL. It is Jeanne d'Arc. You call her—what do you call er?—Joan of—
FRED. Not guilty. I ain't so forward with the ladies. I lon't call them in their Christian names till I've been introluced.

PAUL. You English call her Joan of Arc. The great Jeanne d'Arc. She—

FRED. Wait a bit. Now don't excite me for a moment. I'm thinking. I've heard that name before.

PAUL. But yes, monsieur. In history.

FRED. That's done it. I take you, cockey. I knew it was a way back. Well, she's nothing in my life. [*Returns to steps and sits.*]

PAUL. She is of my life. I come from Domremy.

FRED. So you said.

PAUL. It was her birthplace.

FRED [*clapping him on the shoulder*]. Cockey, I'm with you now. I know the feeling. Why, we'd a man born in our street that played center-forward for the Arsenal. Makes you proud of the place where you were born. Na pooed now, poor devil. Got his head blown off last month. He was a sergeant in our lot. 'Ave a woodbine?

PAUL. Not here, monsieur.

FRED. Please yourself. Smoke your own. Them black things are no use to me. It's a rum country yours, old son. Light beer and black tobacco. But you fight on it all right. Oh yes, you fight all right. 'Ere, 'ave a piece of chocolate to keep the cold out. My missus sent me that.

PAUL [*accepting*]. Merci. I hope madame is well.

FRED. Eh? Who's madame? Oh, you mean old Sally. She's all right. In bed. That's where she is. And I'm here. But I could do with a bit of a snooze myself. Come on, let's do a doss together.

PAUL. A doss?

FRED. Yus. Wait a bit. I speak French when I'm 'appy. Je vais dormir. Vous likewise dormir.

PAUL. I did not come to sleep, monsieur. I came to watch.

FRED. Watch? What do you want to watch for here? No Germans here.

PAUL. C'est la nuit de Noël, monsieur. They say the statues come to life on Christmas Eve, and I am watching here to see if Jeanne will breathe and move and speak to a piou-piou from Domremy.

FRED. You know, old son, you could have scared me once with a tale like that. But not to-day. I've been seeing life lately. If old Nelson got down off his perch, and I met him walking in Trafalgar Square, I'd just salute and think no more about it. You can't raise my hair now.

PAUL. Then you believe that she will speak?

FRED. You go to sleep, cockey, and there's no knowing what you'll hear. Come on, old sport. Je dormir and vous dormir, and we'll be a blooming dormitory. [PAUL *hesitates, looks at statue, then lies by* FRED.] That's right. Lie close. Two can keep warmer than one. Oh well, good-night all. Merry Christmas, and to hell with the Kaiser. [*They sleep. The statue is darkened, and the lay figure of the statue is replaced by the living* JEANNE. *Bells chime midnight. As they begin,* JEANNE *awakes. With the first chime, light shines dimly on the statue. By the last chime, the statue is in brilliant light and* JEANNE *stirs on the pedestal and bends to the wreath. She lifts it, wondering.*]

JEANNE. The wreath is here. I did not dream it, then. I saw him come and lay the wreath at my feet. I saw his uniform, and the uniform was not of France. I saw his face, and it was not a Frenchman's face. I heard his voice, and the voice was an English voice. I do not understand. Why should the English bring a wreath to me? I do not want their wreath. I want no favors from an Englishman. I am Jeanne d'Arc. I am your enemy, you English, whom I made to bite the dust at Orléans and vanquished at Patay. It was I who bore the standard into the cathedral at Rheims when we crowned my Dauphin the anointed King of France, and English Bedford trembled at my name. Burgundians took me at Compiègne. Your English money bought me from them, and your English hatred gave me up to mocking priests to try for sorcery. You called me " Heretic," " Relapsed," " Apostate," and " Idolater," and burnt me for a witch in Rouen market-place. And now do you lay a wreath at Jeanne's feet? And do you think she thanks you? I scorn your wreath. This wreath an English soldier set at Jeanne's feet. I tear it, and I trample on it. [FRED *and* PAUL *have awakened during this speech. Both are bewildered at first, like men who dream. But as* JEANNE *is about to tear the wreath* FRED *interposes.*]

FRED. I dunno if I'm awake or asleep, but that there wreath, lady—I say, don't tear it. I don't know nothing about it bar what you've just said, but if any of our blokes put it there, you can take it from me it was kindly meant.

JEANNE. You? Who are you? You're—You're English.

FRED [*apologetically*]. Yus. I'm English. I don't see that I can help it, though. I just happen to be English same as a dawg. I'm sorry if it upsets you, but I'm English all right. And—No. Blimey, I won't apologize for it. I'm English. I'm English, and proud of it. So there!

JEANNE. Why are the English here in France? Why do I see so many of them?

PAUL. Maid—Jeanne—

JEANNE. You! You are not English. You are a soldier of France.

PAUL. I am of France.

JEANNE. Then shame to you, soldier of France! Shame on a Frenchman who can forget his pride of race and make a comrade of an Englishman!

PAUL. Maid, you do not understand.

JEANNE. No. I do not understand. I do not understand treachery. I do not understand baseness, dishonor, and the perfidy of one who has forgotten he is French. The English are the foes of France, and you consort with them. You—

FRED. 'Ere, 'ere, 'alf a mo'. Steady on, lady. You've got to learn something. All that stuff you've just been talking about the Battle of Waterloo. It's a wash-out now. We've cut it out. This 'ere bloke you're grousing at 'e's a friend of mine, and I'll pipe up for a friend when 'e's being reprimanded undeserving.

JEANNE. It is for that I blame a son of France, that he makes friends with you.

FRED. Well, it's your mistake. That's the worst of coming out of history. You're out of date. If I took my great-grandmother on a motor-bus to a picture-show, she'd have the same sort of fit that you've got, only it's worse with you. You're further back. And I'll tell you something. That old French froggy business is dead and gorn. We've given it up. Time's passed when an Englishman thought he could lick two Frenchmen with one hand tied behind his back. It's a back number, lady. Carpentier put the lid on that. You ask Billy Wells. Us blokes and the French, we're feeding out of one another's hands to-day.

JEANNE. I have seen the English and the French together in the streets. They do not fight.

FRED. Lord bless you, no. Provost-marshal wouldn't let 'em, if they wanted a friendly scrap.

JEANNE. They fraternize. I have seen them walking arm-in-arm.

FRED. That's natural enough.

JEANNE. Natural, for French and English!

FRED. Yes, lady, natural. If you'd seen the Frenchies fighting, same as I have, you'd want to walk arm-in-arm with them yourself, and be proud to do it, too.

PAUL. The English are our brothers, Maid.

FRED. Gorlummy, we're more than that. I've known brothers do the dirty on each other. Us and the French, we're —why, we're *pals*. So that's all right, lady. Just let me put that wreath back where you got it from. I'm sure you'll 'urt someone's feelings if you trample on it. [*He tries to take wreath, she prevents him.*]

JEANNE. When you have shown me why I should accept an English wreath, perhaps I will. So far I've yet to learn why a soldier of France is friendly with an Englishman.

FRED. I can't show you more than this, can I? [*Links arms with* PAUL.]

JEANNE. That is not reason.

PAUL [*unlinking his arm*]. Perhaps I can show you reason. I who was born at Domremy.

JEANNE. You come from there! My home?

PAUL. Yes.

JEANNE. You know St. Remy's church and the Meuse and the beech-tree where they said the fairies used to dance. The tree. Is it still there?

PAUL. I do not know.

JEANNE. And the fields! The fields where I kept my father's sheep, and the wolves would not come near when I had charge of them, and the birds came to me and ate bread from my lap. You know those fields of Domremy?

PAUL. I knew them once.

JEANNE. You knew my church. It still is there?

PAUL. Who can say?

JEANNE. Cannot you, who were baptized in it?

PAUL. Jeanne, the Germans came to Domremy. I do not know if anything is left.

JEANNE. The Germans? But the Germans did not count when I lived there.

FRED. No, and they'll count a sight less before so long.

PAUL. They came like a thunderstorm, Jeanne. They swept our men away. They tore up treaties, and they came through Belgium and ravished it, and took us unawares. They blotted out our frontiers and came on like the tide till even Paris heard the sound of German guns. And then the English came, slowly at first, and just a little late, but not too late, then more and more and all the time more English came. They swept the Germans from the seas and drove their ships to hide. Shoulder to shoulder they have fought for France. They hurled the Germans back from Paris, and when their soldiers fell more came and more. Their plowmen and their clerks, their great lords and their scullions, all came to France to fight with us for la patrie. Their women make munitions and—

FRED. Yus. I daresay. Very fine. Only that'll do. We ain't done nothing to make a song about.

PAUL. Our children and our children's children will make songs of what the English did.

FRED. You let 'em. Leave it to 'em. Way I look at it is this, lady. There's a big swelled-headed bully, and he gets a little fellow down and starts kicking 'im. Well, it ain't manners, and we blokes comes along to teach 'im wot's wot. That's all there is to it.

PAUL. There's more than I could tell in a hundred years, Jeanne.

FRED. Then what's the good of trying?

JEANNE. He tried because he had to make me understand your friendship and all the noble thought and noble deed that lie behind this little wreath. [*She raises the wreath.*]

FRED [*interposing*]. Oh, I say now, lady, go easy with that wreath, won't you? I—I wouldn't trample it if I were you. Battle of Waterloo's a long time ago.

JEANNE. Don't be afraid.

FRED. Gave me a turn to see you pick it up like that.

JEANNE [*putting it on her head*]. The English wreath is in its right place now. Here, on the head of Jeanne d'Arc. I'll wear that wreath forever. Give me your hand, you English soldier.

FRED. I've not washed since morning, lady.

JEANNE. Your hand, that fights for France. [*She takes it.*] And yours, soldier of France.

PAUL. Jeanne! But you— [*Holding back timidly.*]

JEANNE. I am where I would always be—[*she has a hand of both*]—amongst my fighting men. They have set me on a pedestal and made a saint of me, but I am better here, between you two, both soldiers of France. They will not let me fight for France to-day. Save for this mystic hour on Christmas Eve I am a thing of stone. But Jeanne lives on. Her spirit fights for France to-day as Jeanne fought five hundred years ago. And, in this hour when I am granted speech, I say, " Fight on, fight on for France till France and Belgium are free and the invader pays the price of treachery. And you, you English who have come to France, and you in England who are making arms for France, I, who have hated you, I, whom you burnt, I, Jeanne d'Arc of Rheims and Orléans, I give you thanks. My people are your people, and my cause your cause. Vivent! Vivent les Anglais!" [*During this speech she drops the soldiers' hands. They resume gradually their sleeping attitudes.* JEANNE *mounts her pedestal, and gives the last words from it, then becomes stone again. The light fades to darkness, then becomes the moonlight of the opening.* BLANCHE *enters L. She goes to the steps, looks at the sleeping soldiers, and stands above them. Her basket is empty but for one flower.*

PAUL [*stirring and seeing her*]. Jeanne!

BLANCHE. My name is Blanche, monsieur.

PAUL. But I—you—[*he rises*]. Mademoiselle, you are very like—

BLANCHE. I am the flower-girl whom you saw before you went to sleep, and I am very like myself, monsieur.

PAUL. Was I asleep? [*Looks at statue.*] Yes. There is Jeanne.

BLANCHE. Where else should Jeanne be but on her pedestal?

FRED [*stirring*]. Revelley again before you've hardly closed your blooming eyes. [*Sits up sharply on seeing* BLANCHE.] Hullo! You're—you're— [*Turns to* PAUL.] Why, cockey, it wasn't a yarn. The statues do walk about in France. There's one of them doing it.

PAUL. You saw her too?

FRED. Saw her? Of course I seen her. She's there. Ain't

you and me been talking familiar with her for the last ten minutes?
PAUL. Yes, with Jeanne.
FRED. Took my 'and she did, and chanced the dirt.
BLANCHE. You have been dreaming, monsieur. C'était une rêverie.
FRED. Who's raving? Well, it may be raving, but we all raved together. You and me and 'im, and I'll eat my bayonet raw if you didn't stand there and take us by the hands and tell us you were that there Joan of Arc what used to tell old Bonaparte what to do when he was in an 'ole.
BLANCHE. It was not I. There is the statue, monsieur. [*Points to it.*]
FRED. Where? [*Looks.*] Well, that's queer. You're the dead spit and image of 'er, too. And 'ere, 'ere, cockey! [*Takes* PAUL'S *arm excitedly.*]
PAUL. Monsieur?
FRED. Look at the statue. Look at its head. Who put that wreath on it? Did you climb up there?
PAUL. No.
FRED. No. You know you didn't. We saw her put it on herself.
PAUL. But, monsieur, then you have dreamed the same dream as I.
FRED. I saw you all right, and you saw me?
PAUL. I saw you.
FRED. And we both saw 'er. It's a rum go, cockey, but I told you I'd given up being surprised. Our lot and yours we're going whacks in licking the Germans, ain't we? Yus, and now we're going whacks in the same dream, so that's that and chance it. Ententing again, only extra cordial. [*Scratches head.*] I don't quite see where she comes in, though, if she ain't the statue.
BLANCHE. I am a flower-girl, monsieur.
FRED. Not so many flowers about you, then.
BLANCHE. I have sold out, all but one flower, monsieur, and I came back to see if you [*to* PAUL] had got your wish.
PAUL. Yes, mademoiselle, I had my wish. The saints sent Jeanne to me in a dream.
BLANCHE. You happy man, to get your wish!
PAUL. I am happy, mademoiselle. I have spoken with Jeanne d'Arc.

FRED. And you and me will be speaking with our sergeants if we don't buck up and catch that blinking train. Come on, old son, back to the Big Stink for us.
BLANCHE. Messieurs return to fight?
FRED. Lord love you, no. It's only a rumor about the war. We're a Cook's excursion on a joy-ride seeing the sights of France. [FRED and PAUL move R. together.]
BLANCHE. Monsieur!
FRED [stopping]. Well?
BLANCHE. I kept one flower back. It is for you—for the brave English soldier who goes out to fight for France.
FRED. Don't make me homesick. Reminds me of the flower-pots on my kitchen window-sill. [Takes flower and produces chocolate.] 'Ere, miss, 'ave a bit of chocolate. Made in England, that was.
BLANCHE. Monsieur will need it for himself.
FRED. Go on. Take it. I'm all right. It's Christmas Day and extra rations. [Kisses her.]
BLANCHE. Merci, monsieur. Et bonne chance, mes braves, bonne chance.
FRED. Oh, we'll chance it all right. Merry Christmas, old dear. [FRED and PAUL go off together R. BLANCHE watches them go. Lights in the church go out. Girls enter L. as if coming from Mass, singing a carol.

GIRLS

Noël! Noël! thy babe that lies
Within the manger, Mother-Maid,
Is King of earth and Paradise,
O guard him well, Noël, Noël
Ye shepherds sing, be not afraid.

O little hills of France, awake,
For angel hosts are chanting high,
His heart is piercéd for our sake,
Noël, Noël, we guard him well,
He liveth though all else shall die.

[BLANCHE joins them, singing as they cross.]

[THE CURTAIN.]

SPREADING THE NEWS

By
AUGUSTA GREGORY

Isabella Augusta Persse, later Lady Gregory, was born at Roxborough, County Galway, Ireland, in 1859. One who saw her in the early years of her married life describes her thus: "She was then a young woman, very earnest, who divided her hair in the middle and wore it smooth on either side of a broad and handsome brow. Her eyes were always full of questions. . . . In her drawing-room were to be met men of assured reputation in literature and politics and there was always the best reading of the times upon her tables."

Two closely related interests have always divided Lady Gregory's attention. Her occupation with the Irish Players has been constant, and she has from the beginning been a director of the Abbey Theatre, where *Spreading the News* was first performed on December 27, 1904. This play was also included in the American repertory of the Players, whom Lady Gregory accompanied on their visit to the United States in 1911. The spirit that she puts into her work with them is well illustrated by those lines of Blake which she quoted in a speech made at a dinner given her by *The Outlook* when she was in New York. Her hard work having been commented on, she replied:

> "I will not cease from mental strife
> Or let the sword fall from my hand
> Till we have built Jerusalem
> In—Ireland's—fair and lovely land."

In her book on *Our Irish Theatre, A Chapter of Autobiography,* she relates the story of how one day when she assembled the company for rehearsal in Washington, D. C., she invited them to leave their work and come with her to Mount Vernon for a holiday and picnic. "I told them," she writes, " the holiday was not a precedent, for we might go to a great many countries before finding so great a man to honor." Washington, it seems, had been a friend of her grandfather's who had been in America with his regiment.

Her other great interest has been the folklore of Ireland.

She has been called the Irish Malory, because through her retelling of the Irish sagas, she has popularized and made accessible the great cycles of heroic legends. She has employed for the vernacular of these romances and folk tales what she calls Kiltartan English, Kiltartan being the village near her home, the dialect of which she has assimilated and utilized. Lady Gregory has also used her historical and legendary knowledge for the background of some of her plays.

It is said that the original impulse that influenced Lady Gregory to interest herself in these old Irish stories came from Yeats, her friend and associate in the project of the Irish National Theatre. It was his suggestion in the first place that led to her writing *Cuchulain of Muirthemne*. " He could not have been long at Coole," writes George Moore of Yeats, "before he began to draw her attention to the beauty of the literature that rises among the hills and bubbles irresponsibly, and set her going from cabin to cabin taking down stories, and encouraging her to learn the original language of the country, so that they might add to the Irish idiom which the peasant had already translated into English, making in this way a language for themselves." The influence continues, for her latest book, *Visions and Beliefs in the West of Ireland,* contains two essays and notes from the pen of Yeats.

The literary association of Yeats and Lady Gregory has been a fruitful one for Ireland. Not only has Yeats encouraged Lady Gregory's researches into the past, but she has been of the greatest assistance to him in his work. When he is at Coole, she writes from his dictation, arranges his manuscript, reads to him and serves him as literary counselor.

Lady Gregory's life touches the life of Ireland at many points. In addition to her literary occupations, she lectures and co-operates actively with a number of societies that have as their aim social or political betterment.

SPREADING THE NEWS

CHARACTERS

BARTLEY FALLON.
MRS. FALLON.
JACK SMITH.
SHAWN EARLY.
TIM CASEY.
JAMES RYAN.
MRS. TARPEY.
MRS. TULLY.
JO MULDOON, *a policeman.*
A REMOVABLE MAGISTRATE.

SCENE.—The outskirts of a Fair. An Apple Stall. MRS. TARPEY *sitting at it.* MAGISTRATE *and* POLICEMAN *enter.*

MAGISTRATE. So that is the Fair Green. Cattle and sheep and mud. No system. What a repulsive sight!

POLICEMAN. That is so, indeed.

MAGISTRATE. I suppose there is a good deal of disorder in this place?

POLICEMAN. There is.

MAGISTRATE. Common assault?

POLICEMAN. It's common enough.

MAGISTRATE. Agrarian crime, no doubt?

POLICEMAN. That is so.

MAGISTRATE. Boycotting? Maiming of cattle? Firing into houses?

POLICEMAN. There was one time, and there might be again.

MAGISTRATE. That is bad. Does it go any farther than that?

POLICEMAN. Far enough, indeed.

MAGISTRATE. Homicide, then! This district has been shamefully neglected! I will change all that. When I was in the Andaman Islands, my system never failed. Yes, yes, I will change all that. What has that woman on her stall?

POLICEMAN. Apples mostly—and sweets.

MAGISTRATE. Just see if there are any unlicensed goods underneath—spirits or the like. We had evasions of the salt tax in the Andaman Islands.

POLICEMAN [*sniffing cautiously and upsetting a heap of apples*]. I see no spirits here—or salt.

MAGISTRATE [*to* MRS. TARPEY]. Do you know this town well, my good woman?

MRS. TARPEY [*holding out some apples*]. A penny the half-dozen, your honor.

POLICEMAN [*shouting*]. The gentleman is asking do you know the town! He's the new magistrate!

MRS. TARPEY [*rising and ducking*]. Do I know the town? I do, to be sure.

MAGISTRATE [*shouting*]. What is its chief business?

MRS. TARPEY. Business, is it? What business would the people here have but to be minding one another's business?

MAGISTRATE. I mean what trade have they?

MRS. TARPEY. Not a trade. No trade at all but to be talking.

MAGISTRATE. I shall learn nothing here. [JAMES RYAN *comes in, pipe in mouth. Seeing* MAGISTRATE *he retreats quickly, taking pipe from mouth.*]

MAGISTRATE. The smoke from that man's pipe had a greenish look; he may be growing unlicensed tobacco at home. I wish I had brought my telescope to this district. Come to the post-office, I will telegraph for it. I found it very useful in the Andaman Islands. [MAGISTRATE *and* POLICEMAN *go out left.*]

MRS. TARPEY. Bad luck to Jo Muldoon, knocking my apples this way and that way. [*Begins arranging them.*] Showing off he was to the new magistrate. [*Enter* BARTLEY FALLON *and* MRS. FALLON.]

BARTLEY. Indeed it's a poor country and a scarce country to be living in. But I'm thinking if I went to America it's long ago the day I'd be dead!

MRS. FALLON. So you might, indeed. [*She puts her basket on a barrel and begins putting parcels in it, taking them from under her cloak.*]

BARTLEY. And it's a great expense for a poor man to be buried in America.

MRS. FALLON. Never fear, Bartley Fallon, but I'll give you a good burying the day you'll die.

BARTLEY. Maybe it's yourself will be buried in the graveyard of Cloonmara before me, Mary Fallon, and I myself that will be dying unbeknownst some night, and no one a-near me. And the cat itself may be gone straying through the country, and the mice squealing over the quilt.

MRS. FALLON. Leave off talking of dying. It might be twenty years you'll be living yet.

BARTLEY [*with a deep sigh*]. I'm thinking if I'll be living at the end of twenty years, it's a very old man I'll be then!

MRS. TARPEY [*turns and sees them*]. Good morrow, Bartley Fallon; good morrow, Mrs. Fallon. Well, Bartley, you'll find no cause for complaining to-day; they are all saying it was a good fair.

BARTLEY [*raising his voice*]. It was not a good fair, Mrs. Tarpey. It was a scattered sort of a fair. If we didn't expect more, we got less. That's the way with me always; whatever I have to sell goes down and whatever I have to buy goes up. If there's ever any misfortune coming to this world, it's on myself it pitches, like a flock of crows on seed potatoes.

MRS. FALLON. Leave off talking of misfortunes, and listen to Jack Smith that is coming the way, and he singing. [*Voice of* JACK SMITH *heard singing:*]

> I thought, my first love,
> There'd be but one house between you and me,
> And I thought I would find
> Yourself coaxing my child on your knee.
> Over the tide
> I would leap with the leap of a swan,
> Till I came to the side
> Of the wife of the red-haired man!

[JACK SMITH *comes in; he is a red-haired man, and is carrying a hayfork.*]

MRS. TARPEY. That should be a good song if I had my hearing.

MRS. FALLON [*shouting*]. It's " The Red-haired Man's Wife."

Mrs. Tarpey. I know it well. That's the song that has a skin on it! [*She turns her back to them and goes on arranging her apples.*]

Mrs. Fallon. Where's herself, Jack Smith?

Jack Smith. She was delayed with her washing; bleaching the clothes on the hedge she is, and she daren't leave them, with all the tinkers that do be passing to the fair. It isn't to the fair I came myself, but up to the Five Acre Meadow I'm going, where I have a contract for the hay. We'll get a share of it into tramps to-day. [*He lays down hayfork and lights his pipe.*]

Bartley. You will not get it into tramps to-day. The rain will be down on it by evening, and on myself too. It's seldom I ever started on a journey but the rain would come down on me before I'd find any place of shelter.

Jack Smith. If it didn't itself, Bartley, it is my belief you would carry a leaky pail on your head in place of a hat, the way you'd not be without some cause of complaining. [*A voice heard, " Go on, now, go on out o' that. Go on I say."*]

Jack Smith. Look at that young mare of Pat Ryan's that is backing into Shaughnessy's bullocks with the dint of the crowd! Don't be daunted, Pat, I'll give you a hand with her. [*He goes out, leaving his hayfork.*]

Mrs. Fallon. It's time for ourselves to be going home. I have all I bought put in the basket. Look at there, Jack Smith's hayfork he left after him! He'll be wanting it. [*Calls.*] Jack Smith! Jack Smith!— He's gone through the crowd—hurry after him, Bartley, he'll be wanting it.

Bartley. I'll do that. This is no safe place to be leaving it. [*He takes up fork awkwardly and upsets the basket.*] Look at that now! If there is any basket in the fair upset, it must be our own basket! [*He goes out to right.*]

Mrs. Fallon. Get out of that! It is your own fault, it is. Talk of misfortunes and misfortunes will come. Glory be! Look at my new egg-cups rolling in every part—and my two pound of sugar with the paper broke—

Mrs. Tarpey [*turning from stall*]. God help us, Mrs. Fallon, what happened your basket?

Mrs. Fallon. It's himself that knocked it down, bad manners to him. [*Putting things up.*] My grand sugar that's destroyed, and he'll not drink his tea without it. I had best

SPREADING THE NEWS

go back to the shop for more, much good may it do him!
[*Enter* TIM CASEY.]

TIM CASEY. Where is Bartley Fallon, Mrs. Fallon? I want a word with him before he'll leave the fair. I was afraid he might have gone home by this, for he's a temperate man.

MRS. FALLON. I wish he did go home! It'd be best for me if he went home straight from the fair green, or if he never came with me at all! Where is he, is it? He's gone up the road [*jerks elbow*] following Jack Smith with a hayfork. [*She goes out to left.*]

TIM CASEY. Following Jack Smith with a hayfork! Did ever anyone hear the like of that. [*Shouts.*] Did you hear that news, Mrs. Tarpey?

MRS. TARPEY. I heard no news at all.

TIM CASEY. Some dispute I suppose it was that rose between Jack Smith and Bartley Fallon, and it seems Jack made off, and Bartley is following him with a hayfork!

MRS. TARPEY. Is he now? Well, that was quick work! It's not ten minutes since the two of them were here, Bartley going home and Jack going to the Five Acre Meadow; and I had my apples to settle up, that Jo Muldoon of the police had scattered, and when I looked round again Jack Smith was gone, and Bartley Fallon was gone, and Mrs. Fallon's basket upset, and all in it strewed upon the ground—the tea here—the two pound of sugar there—the egg-cups there— Look, now, what a great hardship the deafness puts upon me, that I didn't hear the commencement of the fight! Wait till I tell James Ryan that I see below; he is a neighbor of Bartley's, it would be a pity if he wouldn't hear the news! [*She goes out. Enter* SHAWN EARLY *and* MRS. TULLY.]

TIM CASEY. Listen, Shawn Early! Listen, Mrs. Tully, to the news! Jack Smith and Bartley Fallon had a falling out, and Jack knocked Mrs. Fallon's basket into the road, and Bartley made an attack on him with a hayfork, and away with Jack, and Bartley after him. Look at the sugar here yet on the road!

SHAWN EARLY. Do you tell me so? Well, that's a queer thing, and Bartley Fallon so quiet a man!

MRS. TULLY. I wouldn't wonder at all. I would never think well of a man that would have that sort of a moldering look. It's likely he has overtaken Jack by this. [*Enter* JAMES RYAN *and* MRS. TARPEY.]

JAMES RYAN. That is great news Mrs. Tarpey was telling me! I suppose that's what brought the police and the magistrate up this way. I was wondering to see them in it a while ago.

SHAWN EARLY. The police after them? Bartley Fallon must have injured Jack so. They wouldn't meddle in a fight that was only for show!

MRS. TULLY. Why wouldn't he injure him? There was many a man killed with no more of a weapon than a hayfork.

JAMES RYAN. Wait till I run north as far as Kelly's bar to spread the news! [*He goes out.*]

TIM CASEY. I'll go tell Jack Smith's first cousin that is standing there south of the church after selling his lambs. [*Goes out.*]

MRS. TULLY. I'll go telling a few of the neighbors I see beyond to the west. [*Goes out.*]

SHAWN EARLY. I'll give word of it beyond at the east of the green. [*Is going out when* MRS. TARPEY *seizes hold of him.*]

MRS. TARPEY. Stop a minute, Shawn Early, and tell me did you see red Jack Smith's wife, Kitty Keary, in any place?

SHAWN EARLY. I did. At her own house she was, drying clothes on the hedge as I passed.

MRS. TARPEY. What did you say she was doing?

SHAWN EARLY [*breaking away.*] Laying out a sheet on the hedge. [*He goes.*]

MRS. TARPEY. Laying out a sheet for the dead! The Lord have mercy on us! Jack Smith dead, and his wife laying out a sheet for his burying! [*Calls out.*] Why didn't you tell me that before, Shawn Early? Isn't the deafness the great hardship? Half the world might be dead without me knowing of it or getting word of it at all! [*She sits down and rocks herself.*] Oh, my poor Jack Smith! To be going to his work so nice and so hearty, and to be left stretched on the ground in the full light of the day! [*Enter* TIM CASEY.]

TIM CASEY. What is it, Mrs. Tarpey? What happened since?

MRS. TARPEY. Oh, my poor Jack Smith!

TIM CASEY. Did Bartley overtake him?

MRS. TARPEY. Oh, the poor man!
TIM CASEY. Is it killed he is?
MRS. TARPEY. Stretched in the Five Acre Meadow!
TIM CASEY. The Lord have mercy on us! Is that a fact?
MRS. TARPEY. Without the rites of the Church or a ha'porth!
TIM CASEY. Who was telling you?
MRS. TARPEY. And the wife laying out a sheet for his corpse. [*Sits up and wipes her eyes.*] I suppose they'll wake him the same as another? [*Enter* MRS. TULLY, SHAWN EARLY, *and* JAMES RYAN.]
MRS. TULLY. There is great talk about this work in every quarter of the fair.
MRS. TARPEY. Ochone! cold and dead. And myself maybe the last he was speaking to!
JAMES RYAN. The Lord save us! Is it dead he is?
TIM CASEY. Dead surely, and the wife getting provision for the wake.
SHAWN EARLY. Well, now, hadn't Bartley Fallon great venom in him?
MRS. TULLY. You may be sure he had some cause. Why would he have made an end of him if he had not? [*To* MRS. TARPEY, *raising her voice.*] What was it rose the dispute at all, Mrs. Tarpey?
MRS. TARPEY. Not a one of me knows. The last I saw of them, Jack Smith was standing there, and Bartley Fallon was standing there, quiet and easy, and he listening to " The Red-haired Man's Wife."
MRS. TULLY. Do you hear that, Tim Casey? Do you hear that, Shawn Early and James Ryan? Bartley Fallon was here this morning listening to red Jack Smith's wife, Kitty Keary that was! Listening to her and whispering with her! It was she started the fight so!
SHAWN EARLY. She must have followed him from her own house. It is likely some person roused him.
TIM CASEY. I never knew, before, Bartley Fallon was great with Jack Smith's wife.
MRS. TULLY. How would you know it? Sure it's not in the streets they would be calling it. If Mrs. Fallon didn't know of it, and if I that have the next house to them didn't

know of it, and if Jack Smith himself didn't know of it, it is not likely you would know of it, Tim Casey.

SHAWN EARLY. Let Bartley Fallon take charge of her from this out so, and let him provide for her. It is little pity she will get from any person in this parish.

TIM CASEY. How can he take charge of her? Sure he has a wife of his own. Sure you don't think he'd turn souper and marry her in a Protestant church?

JAMES RYAN. It would be easy for him to marry her if he brought her to America.

SHAWN EARLY. With or without Kitty Keary, believe me it is for America he's making at this minute. I saw the new magistrate and Jo Muldoon of the police going into the post-office as I came up—there was hurry on them—you may be sure it was to telegraph they went, the way he'll be stopped in the docks at Queenstown!

MRS. TULLY. It's likely Kitty Keary is gone with him, and not minding a sheet or a wake at all. The poor man, to be deserted by his own wife, and the breath hardly gone out yet from his body that is lying bloody in the field! [*Enter* MRS. FALLON.]

MRS. FALLON. What is it the whole of the town is talking about? And what is it you yourselves are talking about? Is it about my man Bartley Fallon you are talking? Is it lies about him you are telling, saying that he went killing Jack Smith? My grief that ever he came into this place at all!

JAMES RYAN. Be easy now, Mrs. Fallon. Sure there is no one at all in the whole fair but is sorry for you!

MRS. FALLON. Sorry for me, is it? Why would anyone be sorry for me? Let you be sorry for yourselves, and that there may be shame on you forever and at the day of judgment, for the words you are saying and the lies you are telling to take away the character of my poor man, and to take the good name off of him, and to drive him to destruction! That is what you are doing!

SHAWN EARLY. Take comfort now, Mrs. Fallon. The police are not so smart as they think. Sure he might give them the slip yet, the same as Lynchehaun.

MRS. TULLY. If they do get him, and if they do put a rope around his neck, there is no one can say he does not deserve it!

MRS. FALLON. Is that what you are saying, Bridget Tully,

and is that what you think? I tell you it's too much talk you have, making yourself out to be such a great one, and to be running down every respectable person! A rope, is it? It isn't much of a rope was needed to tie up your own furniture the day you came into Martin Tully's house, and you never bringing as much as a blanket, or a penny, or a suit of clothes with you and I myself bringing seventy pounds and two feather beds. And now you are stiffer than a woman would have a hundred pounds! It is too much talk the whole of you have. A rope is it? I tell you the whole of this town is full of liars and schemers that would hang you up for half a glass of whisky. [*Turning to go.*] People they are you wouldn't believe as much as daylight from without you'd get up to have a look at it yourself. Killing Jack Smith indeed! Where are you at all, Bartley, till I bring you out of this? My nice quiet little man! My decent comrade! He that is as kind and as harmless as an innocent beast of the field! He'll be doing no harm at all if he'll shed the blood of some of you after this day's work! That much would be no harm at all. [*Calls out.*] Bartley! Bartley Fallon! Where are you? [*Going out.*] Did anyone see Bartley Fallon? [*All turn to look after her.*]

JAMES RYAN. It is hard for her to believe any such a thing, God help her! [*Enter* BARTLEY FALLON *from right, carrying hayfork.*]

BARTLEY. It is what I often said to myself, if there is ever any misfortune coming to this world it is on myself it is sure to come! [*All turn round and face him.*]

BARTLEY. To be going about with this fork and to find no one to take it, and no place to leave it down, and I wanting to be gone out of this— Is that you, Shawn Early? [*Holds out fork.*] It's well I met you. You have no call to be leaving the fair for a while the way I have, and how can I go till I'm rid of this fork? Will you take it and keep it until such time as Jack Smith—

SHAWN EARLY [*backing*]. I will not take it, Bartley Fallon, I'm very thankful to you!

BARTLEY [*turning to apple stall*]. Look at it now, Mrs. Tarpey, it was here I got it; let me thrust it in under the stall. It will lie there safe enough, and no one will take notice of it until such time as Jack Smith—

MRS. TARPEY. Take your fork out of that! Is it to put trouble on me and to destroy me you waht? putting it there for the police to be rooting it out maybe. [*Thrusts him back.*]

BARTLEY. That is a very unneighborly thing for you to do, Mrs. Tarpey. Hadn't I enough care on me with that fork before this, running up and down with it like the swinging of a clock, and afeard to lay it down in any place! I wish I never touched it or meddled with it at all!

JAMES RYAN. It is a pity, indeed, you ever did.

BARTLEY. Will you yourself take it, James Ryan? You were always a neighborly man.

JAMES RYAN [*backing*]. There is many a thing I would do for you, Bartley Fallon, but I won't do that!

SHAWN EARLY. I tell you there is no man will give you any help or any encouragement for this day's work. If it was something agrarian now—

BARTLEY. If no one at all will take it, maybe it's best to give it up to the police.

TIM CASEY. There'd be a welcome for it with them surely! [*Laughter.*]

MRS. TULLY. And it is to the police Kitty Keary herself will be brought.

MRS. TARPEY [*rocking to and fro*]. I wonder now who will take the expense of the wake for poor Jack Smith?

BARTLEY. The wake for Jack Smith!

TIM CASEY. Why wouldn't he get a wake as well as another? Would you begrudge him that much?

BARTLEY. Red Jack Smith dead! Who was telling you?

SHAWN EARLY. The whole town knows of it by this.

BARTLEY. Do they say what way did he die?

JAMES RYAN. You don't know that yourself, I suppose, Bartley Fallon? You don't know he was followed and that he was laid dead with the stab of a hayfork?

BARTLEY. The stab of a hayfork!

SHAWN EARLY. You don't know, I suppose, that the body was found in the Five Acre Meadow?

BARTLEY. The Five Acre Meadow!

TIM CASEY. It is likely you don't know that the police are after the man that did it?

BARTLEY. The man that did it!

MRS. TULLY. You don't know, maybe, that he was made away with for the sake of Kitty Keary, his wife?

BARTLEY. Kitty Keary, his wife! [*Sits down bewildered.*]

MRS. TULLY. And what have you to say now, Bartley Fallon?

BARTLEY [*crossing himself*]. I to bring that fork here, and to find that news before me! It is much if I can ever stir from this place at all, or reach as far as the road!

TIM CASEY. Look, boys, at the new magistrate, and Jo Muldoon along with him! It's best for us to quit this.

SHAWN EARLY. That is so. It is best not to be mixed in this business at all.

JAMES RYAN. Bad as he is, I wouldn't like to be an informer against any man. [*All hurry away except* MRS. TARPEY, *who remains behind her stall. Enter* MAGISTRATE *and* POLICEMAN.]

MAGISTRATE. I knew the district was in a bad state, but I did not expect to be confronted with a murder at the first fair I came to.

POLICEMAN. I am sure you did not, indeed.

MAGISTRATE. It was well I had not gone home. I caught a few words here and there that roused my suspicions.

POLICEMAN. So they would, too.

MAGISTRATE. You heard the same story from everyone you asked?

POLICEMAN. The same story—or if it was not altogether the same, anyway it was no less than the first story.

MAGISTRATE. What is that man doing? He is sitting alone with a hayfork. He has a guilty look. The murder was done with a hayfork!

POLICEMAN [*in a whisper*]. That's the very man they say did the act; Bartley Fallon himself!

MAGISTRATE. He must have found escape difficult—he is trying to brazen it out. A convict in the Andaman Islands tried the same game, but he could not escape my system! Stand aside— Don't go far—have the handcuffs ready. [*He walks up to* BARTLEY, *folds his arms, and stands before him.*] Here, my man, do you know anything of John Smith?

BARTLEY. Of John Smith! Who is he, now?

POLICEMAN. Jack Smith, sir—Red Jack Smith!

MAGISTRATE [*coming a step nearer and tapping him on the shoulder*]. Where is Jack Smith?

BARTLEY [*with a deep sigh, and shaking his head slowly*]. Where is he, indeed?

MAGISTRATE. What have you to tell?

BARTLEY. It is where he was this morning, standing in this spot, singing his share of songs—no, but lighting his pipe—scraping a match on the sole of his shoe—

MAGISTRATE. I ask you, for the third time, where is he?

BARTLEY. I wouldn't like to say that. It is a great mystery, and it is hard to say of any man, did he earn hatred or love.

MAGISTRATE. Tell me all you know.

BARTLEY. All that I know— Well, there are the three estates; there is Limbo, and there is Purgatory, and there is—

MAGISTRATE. Nonsense! This is trifling! Get to the point.

BARTLEY. Maybe you don't hold with the clergy so? That is the teaching of the clergy. Maybe you hold with the old people. It is what they do be saying, that the shadow goes wandering, and the soul is tired, and the body is taking a rest— The shadow! [*Starts up.*] I was nearly sure I saw Jack Smith not ten minutes ago at the corner of the forge, and I lost him again— Was it his ghost I saw, do you think?

MAGISTRATE [*to* POLICEMAN]. Conscience-struck! He will confess all now!

BARTLEY. His ghost to come before me! It is likely it was on account of the fork! I to have it and he to have no way to defend himself the time he met with his death!

MAGISTRATE [*to* POLICEMAN]. I must note down his words. [*Takes out notebook.*] [*To* BARTLEY.] I warn you that your words are being noted.

BARTLEY. If I had ha' run faster in the beginning, this terror would not be on me at the latter end! Maybe he will cast it up against me at the day of judgment— I wouldn't wonder at all at that.

MAGISTRATE [*writing*]. At the day of judgment—

BARTLEY. It was soon for his ghost to appear to me—is it coming after me always by day it will be, and stripping the clothes off in the night time?— I wouldn't wonder at all at that, being as I am an unfortunate man!

MAGISTRATE [*sternly*]. Tell me this truly. What was the motive of this crime?

BARTLEY. The motive, is it?

MAGISTRATE. Yes; the motive; the cause.

BARTLEY. I'd sooner not say that.

MAGISTRATE. You had better tell me truly. Was it money?

BARTLEY. Not at all! What did poor Jack Smith ever have in his pockets unless it might be his hands that would be in them?

MAGISTRATE. Any dispute about land?

BARTLEY [*indignantly*]. Not at all! He never was a grabber or grabbed from anyone!

MAGISTRATE. You will find it better for you if you tell me at once.

BARTLEY. I tell you I wouldn't for the whole world wish to say what it was—it is a thing I would not like to be talking about.

MAGISTRATE. There is no use in hiding it. It will be discovered in the end.

BARTLEY. Well, I suppose it will, seeing that mostly everybody knows it before. Whisper here now. I will tell no lie; where would be the use? [*Puts his hand to his mouth, and* MAGISTRATE *stoops.*] Don't be putting the blame on the parish, for such a thing was never done in the parish before—it was done for the sake of Kitty Keary, Jack Smith's wife.

MAGISTRATE [*to* POLICEMAN]. Put on the handcuffs. We have been saved some trouble. I knew he would confess if taken in the right way. [POLICEMAN *puts on handcuffs.*]

BARTLEY. Handcuffs now! Glory be! I always said, if there was ever any misfortune coming to this place it was on myself it would fall. I to be in handcuffs! There's no wonder at all in that. [*Enter* MRS. FALLON, *followed by the rest. She is looking back at them as she speaks.*]

MRS. FALLON. Telling lies the whole of the people of this town are; telling lies, telling lies as fast as a dog will trot! Speaking against my poor respectable man! Saying he made an end of Jack Smith! My decent comrade! There is no better man and no kinder man in the whole of the five parishes! It's little annoyance he ever gave to anyone! [*Turns and sees him.*] What in the earthly world do I see before me? Bartley

Fallon in charge of the police! Handcuffs on him! Oh, Bartley, what did you do at all at all?

BARTLEY. Oh, Mary, there has a great misfortune come upon me! It is what I always said, that if there is ever any misfortune—

MRS. FALLON. What did he do at all, or is it bewitched I am?

MAGISTRATE. This man has been arrested on a charge of murder.

MRS. FALLON. Whose charge is that? Don't believe them! They are all liars in this place! Give me back my man!

MAGISTRATE. It is natural you should take his part, but you have no cause of complaint against your neighbors. He has been arrested for the murder of John Smith, on his own confession.

MRS. FALLON. The saints of heaven protect us! And what did he want killing Jack Smith?

MAGISTRATE. It is best you should know all. He did it on account of a love affair with the murdered man's wife.

MRS. FALLON [*sitting down*]. With Jack Smith's wife! With Kitty Keary!—Ochone, the traitor!

THE CROWD. A great shame, indeed. He is a traitor, indeed.

MRS. TULLY. To America he was bringing her, Mrs. Fallon.

BARTLEY. What are you saying, Mary? I tell you—

MRS. FALLON. Don't say a word! I won't listen to any word you'll say! [*Stops her ears.*] Oh, isn't he the treacherous villain? Ohone go deo!

BARTLEY. Be quiet till I speak! Listen to what I say!

MRS. FALLON. Sitting beside me on the ass car coming to the town, so quiet and so respectable, and treachery like that in his heart!

BARTLEY. Is it your wits you have lost or is it I myself that have lost my wits?

MRS. FALLON. And it's hard I earned you, slaving, slaving—and you grumbling, and sighing, and coughing, and discontented, and the priest wore out anointing you, with all the times you threatened to die!

BARTLEY. Let you be quiet till I tell you!

Mrs. Fallon. You to bring such a disgrace into the parish. A thing that was never heard of before!

Bartley. Will you shut your mouth and hear me speaking?

Mrs. Fallon. And if it was for any sort of a fine handsome woman, but for a little fistful of a woman like Kitty Keary, that's not four feet high hardly, and not three teeth in her head unless she got new ones! May God reward you, Bartley Fallon, for the black treachery in your heart and the wickedness in your mind, and the red blood of poor Jack Smith that is wet upon your hand! [*Voice of* Jack Smith *heard singing.*]

> The sea shall be dry,
>   The earth under mourning and ban!
> Then loud shall he cry
>   For the wife of the red-haired man!

Bartley. It's Jack Smith's voice—I never knew a ghost to sing before— It is after myself and the fork he is coming! [*Goes back. Enter* Jack Smith.] Let one of you give him the fork and I will be clear of him now and for eternity!

Mrs. Tarpey. The Lord have mercy on us! Red Jack Smith! The man that was going to be waked!

James Ryan. Is it back from the grave you are come?

Shawn Early. Is it alive you are, or is it dead you are?

Tim Casey. Is it yourself at all that's in it?

Mrs. Tully. Is it letting on you were to be dead?

Mrs. Fallon. Dead or alive, let you stop Kitty Keary, your wife, from bringing my man away with her to America!

Jack Smith. It is what I think, the wits are gone astray on the whole of you. What would my wife want bringing Bartley Fallon to America?

Mrs. Fallon. To leave yourself, and to get quit of you she wants, Jack Smith, and to bring him away from myself. That's what the two of them had settled together.

Jack Smith. I'll break the head of any man that says that! Who is it says it? [*To* Tim Casey.] Was it you said it? [*To* Shawn Early.] Was it you?

All together [*backing and shaking their heads*]. It wasn't I said it!

Jack Smith. Tell me the name of any man that said it!

ALL TOGETHER [*pointing to* BARTLEY]. It was *him* that said it!

JACK SMITH. Let me at him till I break his head! [BARTLEY *backs in terror. Neighbors hold* JACK SMITH *back.*]

JACK SMITH [*trying to free himself*]. Let me at him! Isn't he the pleasant sort of a scarecrow for any woman to be crossing the ocean with! It's back from the docks of New York he'd be turned [*trying to rush at him again*], with a lie in his mouth and treachery in his heart, and another man's wife by his side, and he passing her off as his own! Let me at him, can't you. [*Makes another rush, but is held back.*]

MAGISTRATE [*pointing to* JACK SMITH]. Policeman, put the handcuffs on this man. I see it all now. A case of false impersonation, a conspiracy to defeat the ends of justice. There was a case in the Andaman Islands, a murderer of the Mopsa tribe, a religious enthusiast—

POLICEMAN. So he might be, too.

MAGISTRATE. We must take both these men to the scene of the murder. We must confront them with the body of the real Jack Smith.

JACK SMITH. I'll break the head of any man that will find my dead body!

MAGISTRATE. I'll call more help from the barracks. [*Blows* POLICEMAN'S *whistle.*]

BARTLEY. It is what I am thinking, if myself and Jack Smith are put together in the one cell for the night, the handcuffs will be taken off him, and his hands will be free, and murder will be done that time surely!

MAGISTRATE. Come on! [*They turn to the right.*]

[THE CURTAIN.]

SPREADING THE NEWS

MUSIC FOR THE SONG IN THE PLAY
THE RED-HAIRED MAN'S WIFE

Spreading the News.

I thought, my first love, there'd be but one house between you and me, And I thought I would find yourself coaxing my child on your knee. Over the tide I would leap with the leap of a swan, Till I came to the side of the wife of the red-haired man.

AUTHOR'S NOTE

The idea of this play first came to me as a tragedy. I kept seeing as in a picture people sitting by the roadside, and a girl passing to the market, gay and fearless. And then I saw her passing by the same place at evening, her head hanging, the heads of others turned from her, because of some sudden story that had risen out of a chance word, and had snatched away her good name.

But comedy and not tragedy was wanted at our theatre to put beside the high poetic work, *The King's Threshold, The Shadowy Waters, On Baile's Strand, The Well of the Saints;* and I let laughter have its way with the little play. I was delayed in beginning it for a while, because I could only think of Bartley Fallon as dull-witted or silly or ignorant, and the handcuffs seemed too harsh a punishment. But one day by the seat at Duras a melancholy man who was telling me of the crosses he had gone through at home said—"But I'm thinking if I went to America, it's long ago to-day I'd be dead. And it's a great expense for a poor man to be buried in America." Bartley was born at that moment, and, far from harshness, I felt I was providing him with a happy old age in giving him the lasting glory of that great and crowning day of misfortune.

It has been acted very often by other companies as well as our own, and the Boers have done me the honor of translating and pirating it.

WELSH HONEYMOON

By
JEANNETTE MARKS

Jeannette Marks, playwright, poet, essayist, and writer of short stories, was born in 1875 at Chattanooga, Tennessee. She grew up in Philadelphia, however, where her father was a member of the faculty of the University of Pennsylvania. Her education in this country was supplemented by a sojourn at a school in Dresden. She took her first degree at Wellesley College in 1900, and her master's degree there in 1903. Her graduate studies were pursued at the Bodleian Library and at the British Museum. Since 1901 she has taught English literature at Mount Holyoke.

The play here reprinted, *Welsh Honeymoon,* was one of the two—the other was her *The Merry, Merry Cuckoo*—that won the Welsh National Theatre First Prize for the best Welsh plays in November, 1911, the year after Josephine Preston Peabody had carried off the palm at Stratford-on-Avon.

She writes in her preface to *Three Welsh Plays,* the collection from which *Welsh Honeymoon* is drawn:

" ' Poetry ' and ' song ' are words which convey, better than any other two words could, the priceless gifts of the Welsh people to the world. With their love for music, for beauty, for the significance of their land and its folklore, their inherent romance in the difficult art of living, they have transformed ugliness into beauty, turned loneliness into speech, and ever recalled life to its only permanent possessions in wonder and romance.

" Curiously enough, the Welsh, rich in poetry and music, have been almost altogether devoid of plays. But no one who has read those first Welsh tales in the ' Mabinogion ' (c. 1260) could for an instant think the Cymru devoid of the dramatic instinct. The Welsh way of interpreting experience is essentially dramatic. *The Dream of Maxen Wledig, The Dream of Rhonabwy,* both from the ' Mabinogion,' are sharply dramatic, although then and later Welsh literature remained practically devoid of the play form. Experience dramatized is, too, that Pilgrim's Progress of Gwalia: ' Y Bardd Cwsg ' (1703).

" Every gift of the Welsh would seem to promise the realization some day of a great national drama, for they have not only the gift of poetry and the power to seize the symbol—short cut through experience—which can, even as the crutch of Ibsen's Little Eyolf, lift a play into greatness; they have, also, natures profoundly emotional and yet intellectually critical. They are, humanly speaking, perfect tools for the achievement of great drama. But it is a drab journey from those 'Mabinogion' days of wonder, coarse and crude as they were in many ways, yet intensely vital, through the 'Bardd Cwsg' to Twm o'r Nant (1739-1810) the so-called 'Welsh Shakespeare,' whose Interludes might, with sufficient worrying, afford delectation to the rock-ribbed Puritanism which has stood, as much as any other oppression, in the way of Gwalia's full development of her genius for beauty.

"It was, then, a significant moment when 'The Welsh National Theatre' came into existence with so powerful a patron as Lord Howard de Walden, lessee of the Haymarket, and Owen Rhoscomyl (Captain Owen Vaughan) and other gifted Welsh literati for its sponsors. And it did not seem an insignificant moment to one person, the playwright of *The Merry Merry Cuckoo* and *Welsh Honeymoon,* when she learned through her friendly agent, Curtis Brown of London, that she had received one of the Welsh National Theatre's first prizes (1911)."

Jeannette Marks's interest in Wales is the result of a number of holidays spent in wandering through its highways and byways. Books of hers like *Through Welsh Doorways* and *Gallant Little Wales* bespeak an affectionate intimacy with homes and inhabitants. In the last named, especially, the chapters called "Cambrian Cottages" and "Welsh Wales" contain material that is highly illuminating in connection with the interpretation of her plays. Edward Knobloch, the playwright, is said to have pointed out to the author the dramatic situations inherent in her short stories and sketches, a suggestion which bore fruit in *Three Welsh Plays.*

The first performance of *Welsh Honeymoon* was given by the American Drama Society in Boston in February, 1916. It has also been produced by the Boston Women's City Club, the Vagabond Players in Baltimore, the Hull House Players in Chicago, and the Prince Street Players in Rochester.

WELSH HONEYMOON [1]

CHARACTERS

VAVASOUR JONES.
CATHERINE JONES, *his wife*.
EILIR MORRIS, *nephew of Vavasour Jones*.
MRS. MORGAN, *the baker*.
HOWELL HOWELL, *the milliner*.

PLACE.—*Beddgelert, a little village in North Wales.*

A Welsh kitchen. At back, in center, a deep ingle, with two hobs and fire bars fixed between, on either side settles. On the left-hand side near the fire a church; on the right, in a pile, some peat ready for use. Above the fireplace is a mantel on which are set some brass candlesticks, a deep copper cheese bowl, and two pewter plates. Near the left settle is a three-legged table set with teapot, cups and saucers for two, a plate of bread and butter, a plate of jam, and a creamer. At the right and to the right of the door, is a tall, highly polished, oaken grandfather's clock, with a shining brass face; to the left of the door is a tridarn. The tridarn dresser is lined with bright blue paper and filled with luster china. The floor is of beaten

---

[1] PRONUNCIATION OF WELSH NAMES

1 *ch* has, roughly, the same sound as in German or in the Scotch *loch*.
2 *dd* = English *th*, roughly, in brea*th*e.
3 *e* has, roughly, the sound of *ai* in d*ai*ry.
4 *f* = English *v*.
5 *ff* = English sharp *f*.
6 *ll* represents a sound intermediate between *th* and *fl*.
7 *w* as a consonant is pronounced as in English; as a vowel = *oo*.
8 *y* is sometimes like *u* in b*u*t, but sometimes like *ee* in gr*ee*n.
NOTE: *The author will gladly answer questions about pronunciation, costuming, etc., etc.*

clay, whitewashed around the edges; from the rafters of the peaked ceiling hang flitches of bacon, hams, and bunches of onions and herbs. On the hearth is a copper kettle singing gaily; and on either side of the fireplace are latticed windows opening into the kitchen. Through the door to the right, when open, may be seen the flagstones and cottages of a Welsh village street; through latticed windows the twinkling of many village lights.

It is about half after eleven on Allhallows' Eve in the village of Beddgelert.

At rise of curtain, the windows of kitchen are closed; the fire is burning brightly, and two candles are lighted on the mantelpiece. VAVASOUR JONES, *about thirty-five years old, dressed in a striped vest, a short, heavy blue coat, cut away in front, and with swallowtails behind, and trimmed with brass buttons, and somewhat tight trousers down to his boot tops, is standing by the open door at the right, looking out anxiously on to the glittering, rain-wet flagstone street and calling after someone.*

VAVASOUR [1] [*calling*]. Kats, Kats, mind ye come home soon from Pally Hughes's!

CATHERINE [*from a distance*]. Aye, I'm no wantin' to go, but I must. Good-by!

VAVASOUR. Good-by! Kats, ye mind about comin' home? [*There is no reply, and* VAVASOUR *looks still further into the rain-wet street. He calls loudly and desperately.*] Kats, Kats darlin', I cannot let you go without tellin' ye that—Kats, do ye hear? [*There is still no reply and after one more searching of the street,* VAVASOUR *closes the door and sits down on the end of the nearest settle.*]

VAVASOUR. Dear, dear, she's gone, an' I may never see her again, an' I'm to blame, an' she didn't know whatever that in the night— [*Loud knocking on the closed door;* VAVASOUR *jumps and stands irresolute.*] The devil, it can't be comin' for her already? [*The knocking grows louder.*]

VOICE [*calling*]. Catherine, Vavasour, are ye in?

VAVASOUR [*opening the door*]. Aye, come in, whoever ye

---

[1] The *a*'s are broad throughout, i. e., Kats is pronounced Kaats; Vavasour is Vavasoor: *ou* is oo.

are. [Mrs. Morgan, *the Baker, dressed in a scarlet whittle and freshly starched white cap beneath her tall Welsh beaver hat, enters, shaking the rain from her cloak.*]

Mrs. Morgan. Where's Catherine?

Vavasour. She's gone, Mrs. Morgan.

Mrs. Morgan. Gone? Are ye no goin'? Not goin' to Pally Hughes's on Allhallows' Eve?

Vavasour [*shaking his head and looking very white*]. Nay, I'm no feelin' well.

Mrs. Morgan. Aye, I see ye're ill?

Vavasour. Well, I'm not ill, but I'm not well. Not well at all, Mrs. Morgan.

Mrs. Morgan. We'll miss ye, but I must hurryin' on whatever; I'm late now. Good-night!

Vavasour [*speaking drearily*]. Good-night! [*He closes the door and returns to the settle, where he sits down by the pile of peat and drops his head in his hand. Then he starts up nervously for no apparent cause and opens one of the lattice windows. With an exclamation of fear, he slams it to and throws his weight against the door. Calling and holding hard to the door.*] Ye've no cause to come here! Ye old death's head, get away! [*Outside there is loud pounding on the door and a voice shouting for admittance.* Vavasour *is obliged to fall back as the door is gradually forced open, and a head is thrust in, a white handkerchief tied over it.*]

Howell Howell [*seeing the terror-stricken face of* Vavasour]. Well, man, what ails ye; did ye think I was a ghost? [Howell Howell, *the Milliner, in highlows and a plum-colored coat, a handkerchief on his hat, enters, stamping off the rain and closing the door. He carefully wipes off his plum-colored sleeves and speaks indignantly.*] Well, man, are ye crazy, keepin' me out in the rain that way? Where's Catherine?

Vavasour [*stammering*]. She's at P-p-p-ally Hughes's.

Howell Howell. Are ye no goin'?

Vavasour. Nay, Howell Howell, I'm no goin'.

Howell Howell. An' dressed in your best? What's the matter? Have ye been drinkin' whatever?

Vavasour [*wrathfully*]. Drinkin'! I'd better be drinkin' when neighbors go walkin' round the village on Allhallows' Eve with their heads done up in white.

Howell Howell. Aye, well, I can't be spoilin' the new

hat I have, that I cannot. A finer beaver there has never been in my shop. [*He takes off the handkerchief, hangs it where the heat of the fire will dry it a bit, and then, removing the beaver, shows it to* VAVASOUR, *turning it this way and that.*]

VAVASOUR [*absent-mindedly*]. Aye, grand, grand, man!

HOWELL HOWELL. What are ye gazin' at the clock for?

VAVASOUR [*guiltily*]. I'm no lookin' at anything.

HOWELL HOWELL. Well, indeed, I must be goin', or I shall be late at Pally Hughes's. Good-night.

VAVASOUR. Good-night. [*He closes the door and stands before the clock, studying it. While he is studying its face the door opens slowly, and the tumbled, curly head of a lad about eighteen years of age peers in. The door continues slowly to open.* VAVASOUR *unconscious all the while.*] 'Tis ten now. Ten, eleven, twelve; that's three hours left, 'tis; nay, nay, 'tis only two hours left, after all, an' then—

EILIR MORRIS [*bounding in and shutting the door behind him with a bang*]. Boo! Whoo—o—o!

VAVASOUR [*his face blanched, dropping limply on to the settle*]. The devil!

EILIR MORRIS [*troubled*]. Uch, the pity, Uncle! I didn't think, an' ye're ill!

VAVASOUR. Tut, tut, 'tis no matter, an' I'm not ill—not ill at all, but Eilir, lad, ye're kin, an'—could ye promise never to tell?

EILIR MORRIS [*who thinks his uncle has been drinking, speaks to him as if he would humor his whim*]. Aye, Uncle, I'm kin, an' I promise. Tell on. What is it? Are ye sick?

VAVASOUR [*drearily*]. Uch, lad, I'm not sick!

EILIR MORRIS. Well, what ails ye?

VAVASOUR. 'Tis Allhallows' Eve an'—

EILIR MORRIS. Aren't ye goin' to Pally Hughes's?

VAVASOUR [*moaning and rising*]. Ow, the devil, goin' to Pally Hughes's while 'tis drawin' nearer an' nearer an'—Ow! 'Tis the night when Catherine must go.

EILIR MORRIS. When Aunt Kats must go! What do you mean?

VAVASOUR. She'll be dead to-night at twelve.

EILIR MORRIS [*bewildered*]. Dead at twelve? But she's at Pally Hughes's. Does she know it?

VAVASOUR. No, but I do, an' to think I've been unkind to

her! I've tried this year to make up for it, but 'tis no use, lad; one year'll never make up for ten of harsh words, whatever. Ow! [*Groaning,* VAVASOUR *collapses on to the settle and rocks to and fro, moaning aloud.*]

EILIR MORRIS [*mystified*]. Well, ye've not been good to her, Uncle, that's certain; but ye've been different the past year.

VAVASOUR [*sobbing*]. Aye, but a year'll not do any good, an' she'll be dyin' at twelve to-night. Ow! I've turned to the scriptures to see what it says about a man an' his wife, but it'll no do, no do, no do!

EILIR MORRIS. Have ye been drinkin', Uncle?

VAVASOUR [*hotly*]. Drinkin'!

EILIR MORRIS. Well, indeed, no harm, but, Uncle, I cannot understand why Aunt Kats's goin' an' where.

VAVASOUR [*rising suddenly from the settle and seizing* EILIR *by the coat lapel*]. She's goin' to leave me, lad; 'tis Allhallows' Eve whatever! An' she'll be dyin' at twelve. Aye, a year ago things were so bad between us, on Allhallows' Eve I went down to the church porch shortly before midnight to see whether the spirit of your Aunt Kats would be called an'—

EILIR MORRIS. Uncle, 'twas fair killin' her!

VAVASOUR. I wanted to see whether she would live the twelve months out. An' as I was leanin' against the church wall, hopin', aye, lad, prayin' to see her spirit there, an' know she'd die, I saw somethin' comin' 'round the corner with white over its head.

EILIR MORRIS [*wailing*]. Ow—w!

VAVASOUR. It drew nearer an' nearer, an' when it came in full view of the church porch, it paused, it whirled around like that, an' sped away with the shroud flappin' about its feet, an' the rain beatin' down on its white hood.

EILIR MORRIS [*wailing again*]. Ow—w!

VAVASOUR. But there was time to see that it was the spirit of Catherine, an' I was glad because my wicked prayer had been answered, an' because with Catherine dyin' the next Allhallows', we'd have to live together only the year out.

EILIR MORRIS [*raising his hand*]. Hush, what's that?

VAVASOUR. 'Tis voices whatever. [*Both listen,* EILIR *goes to the window,* VAVASOUR *to the door. The voices become louder.*]

EILIR MORRIS. They're singin' a song at Paliy Hughes's.
[*Voices are audibly singing:*]

> Ni awn adre bawb dan ganu,
>   Ar hyd y nos;
> Saif ein hiaith safo Cymru,
>   Ar hyd y nos;
> Bydded undeb a brawdgarwch
> Ini'n gwlwm diogelwch,
> Felly canwn er hyfrydwch,
>   Ar hyd y nos.
>
> Sweetly sang beside a fountain,
>   All through the night,
> Mona's maiden on that mountain,
>   All through the night.
> When wilt thou, from war returning,
> In whose breast true love is burning,
> Come and change to joy my mourning,
>   By day and night?

VAVASOUR. Aye, they're happy, an' Kats does not know. I went home that night, lad, thinkin' 'twas the last year we'd have to live together, an', considerin' as 'twas the last year, I might just as well try to be decent an' kind. An' when I reached home, Catherine was up waitin' for me an' spoke so pleasantly, an' we sat down an' had a long talk—just like the days when we were courtin'.

EILIR MORRIS. Did she know, Uncle?

VAVASOUR [*puzzled*]. Nay, how could she know. But she seems queer,—as if she felt the evil comin'. Well, indeed, each day was sweeter than the one before, an' we were man an' wife in love an' kindness at last, but all the while I was thinkin' of that figure by the churchyard. Lad, lad, ye'll be marryin' before long,—be good to her, lad, be good to her! [VAVASOUR *lets go the lapels of* EILIR'S *coat and sinks back on to the settle, half sobbing. Outside the roar of wind and rain growing louder can be heard.*]

VAVASOUR [*looking at the clock*]. An' here 'tis Allhallows' Eve again, an' the best year of my life is past, an' she must die in an hour an' a half. Ow, ow! It has all come from my own evil heart an' evil wish. Think, lad, prayin' for her callin'; aye, goin' there, hopin' ye'd see her spirit, an' countin' on her death!

EILIR MORRIS [*mournfully*]. Aye, Uncle, 'tis bad, an' I've no word to say to ye for comfort. I recollect well the story Granny used to tell about Christmas Pryce; 'twas somethin' the same whatever. An' there was Betty Williams was called a year ago, an' is dead now; an' there was Silvan Griffith, an' Geffery, his friend, an' Silvan had just time to dig Geffery's grave an' then his own, too, by its side, an' they was buried the same day an' hour.

VAVASOUR [*wailing*]. Ow—w—w! [*At that moment the door is blown violently open by the wind; both men jump and stare out into the dark where only the dimmed lights of the rain-swept street are to be seen, and the very bright windows of Pally Hughes's cottage.*]

EILIR MORRIS. Uch, she'll be taken there!

VAVASOUR. Aye, an', Eilir, she was loath to go to Pally's, but I could not tell her the truth.

EILIR MORRIS. Are ye not goin', Uncle?

VAVASOUR. Nay, lad, I cannot go. I'm fair crazy. I'll just be stayin' home, waitin' for them to bring her back. Ow—w—w!

EILIR MORRIS. Tut, tut, Uncle, I'm sorry. I'll just see for ye what they're doin'. [EILIR *steps out and is gone for an instant. He comes back excitedly.*]

VAVASOUR [*shouting after him*]. Can ye see her, lad?

EILIR MORRIS [*returning*]. Dear, they've a grand display, raisins an' buns, an' spices an' biscuits—

VAVASOUR. But your Aunt Kats?

EILIR MORRIS. Aye, an' a grand fire, an' a tub with apples in it an'—

VAVASOUR. But Catherine?

EILIR MORRIS. Aye, she was there near the fire, an' just as I turned, they blew the lights out.

VAVASOUR. Blew the lights out! Uch, she'll be taken there whatever!

EILIR MORRIS. They're tellin' stories in the dark.

VAVASOUR. Go back again an' tell what ye can see of your Aunt Kats, lad.

EILIR MORRIS. Aye.

VAVASOUR [*shouting after him*]. Find where she's sittin',
lad—make certain of that.
EILIR MORRIS [*running in breathless*]. They're throwin'
nuts on the fire—
VAVASOUR. Is she there?
EILIR MORRIS. I'm thinkin' she is, but old Pally Hughes
was just throwin' a nut on the fire an'—
VAVASOUR [*impatiently*]. 'Tis no matter about Pally
Hughes whatever, but your Aunt Kats, did—
EILIR MORRIS. There was only the light of the fire; I did
not see her, but I'll go again.
VAVASOUR. Watch for her nut an' see does it burn brightly.
EILIR MORRIS [*going out*]. Aye.
VAVASOUR [*calling after*]. Mind, I'm wantin' to know
what she's doin'. [*He has scarcely spoken the last word when
a great commotion is heard: a door across the street being
slammed to violently, and the sound of running feet.* VAVASOUR
straightens up, his eyes in terror on the door, which CATHERINE
JONES *throws open and bursts through.*]
VAVASOUR [*holding out his arms*]. Catherine, is it really
ye! [CATHERINE, *after a searching glance at him, draws herself up.* VAVASOUR *draws himself up, too, and then stoops to
pick up some peat which he puts on the fire, and crosses over to
left and sits down on the settle near the chimney, without having embraced her.* CATHERINE'S *face is flushed, her eyes wild
under the pretty white cap she wears, a black Welsh beaver
above it. She is dressed in a scarlet cloak, under this a tight
bodice and short, full skirt, bright stockings, and clogs with
brass tips. Her apron is of heavy linen, striped; over her breast
a kerchief is crossed, and from the elbows down to the wrist
are full white sleeves stiffly starched.*]
CATHERINE. Yiss, yiss, 'twas dull at Pally's—very dull.
My nut didn't burn very brightly, an'—an'—well, indeed, my
feet was wet, an' I feared takin' a cold.
VAVASOUR. Yiss, yiss, 'tis better for ye here, dearie. [*Then
there is silence between them.* CATHERINE *still breathes heavily
from the running, and* VAVASOUR *shuffles his feet. While they
are both sitting there, unable to say a word, the door opens
without a sound, and* EILIR'S *curly head is thrust in. A guttural exclamation from him makes them start and look towards
the door, but he closes it before they can see him.* CATHERINE

then takes off her beaver and looks at VAVASOUR. VAVASOUR *opens his mouth, shuts it, and opens it again.*]

VAVASOUR [*desperately*]. Did ye have a fine time at Pally's?

CATHERINE. Aye, 'twas gay an' fine an'—an'—yiss, yiss, so 'twas an' so 'twasn't.

VAVASOUR [*his eyes seeking the clock*]. A quarter past eleven, uch! Katy, do ye recall Pastor Evan's sermon, the one he preached last New Year?

CATHERINE [*also glancing at the clock*]. Sixteen minutes after eleven—yiss—yiss—

VAVASOUR [*catching* CATHERINE'S *glance at the clock*]. Well, Catherine, do—

CATHERINE. Yiss, yiss, I said I did whatever. 'Twas about inheritin' the grace of life together.

VAVASOUR. Kats, dear, wasn't he sayin' that love is eternal, an' that—a man—an'—an'—his wife was lovin' for—for—

CATHERINE [*glancing at the clock and meeting* VAVASOUR'S *eyes just glancing away from the clock*]. Aye, lad, for everlastin' life! Uch, what have I done?

VAVASOUR [*unheeding and doubling up as if from pain*]. Half after eleven! Yiss, yiss, dear, didn't he say that the Lord was mindful of us—of our difficulties, an' our temptations an' our mistakes?

CATHERINE [*tragically*]. Aye, an' our mistakes. Ow, ow, ow, but a half hour's left!

VAVASOUR. Do ye think, dearie, that if a man were to—to—uch!—be unkind to his wife—an' was sorry an' his wife—his wife dies, that he'd be—be—

CATHERINE [*tenderly*]. Aye, I'm thinkin' so. An', lad dear, do ye think if anythin' was to happen to ye to-night,—yiss, *this* night,—that ye'd take any grudge against me away with ye?

VAVASOUR [*stiffening*]. Happen to *me*, Catherine? [VAVASOUR *collapses, groaning.* CATHERINE *goes to his side on the settle.*]

CATHERINE [*in an agonized voice*]. Uch, dearie, what is it, what is it, what ails ye?

VAVASOUR [*slanting an eye at the clock*]. Nothin', nothin' at all. Ow, the devil, 'tis twenty minutes before twelve whatever!

CATHERINE. Lad, lad, what is it?

VAVASOUR. 'Tis nothin', nothin' at all—'tis—ow!—'tis just a little pain across me.
CATHERINE [*her face whitening as she steals a look at the clock and puts her arm around* VAVASOUR]. Vavasour, lad dear, is that the wind in the chimney? Put your arm about me an' hold fast.
VAVASOUR [*both hands across his stomach, his eyes on the clock*]. Ow—ten minutes!
CATHERINE [*shaking all over*]. Is that a step at the door?
VAVASOUR [*unheeding*]. 'Tis goin' to strike now in a minute.
CATHERINE [*her eyes in horror on the clock*]. Five minutes before twelve!
VAVASOUR [*almost crying, his eyes fixed on the clock's face*]. Uch, the toad, the serpent!
CATHERINE [*her face in her hands*]. Dear God, he's goin' now!
VAVASOUR [*covering his eyes*]. Uch, the devil! Uch, the gates of hell! [CATHERINE *cries out,* VAVASOUR *groans loudly. The clock is striking: One, Two, Three, Four, Five, Six, Seven, Eight, Nine, Ten, Eleven, Twelve! The last loud clang vibrates and subsides. Through a chink in her fingers* CATHERINE *is peering at* VAVASOUR. *Through a similar chink his agonized eyes are peering at her.*]
CATHERINE [*gulping*]. Uch!
VAVASOUR. The devil!
CATHERINE [*putting out her hand to touch him*]. Lad, dear! [*They embrace, they kiss, they dance madly about. Then they do it all over again. While they are doing this,* EILIR *opens the door again and thrusts in his head. He stares open-eyed, open-mouthed at them, and leans around the side of the door to see what time it is, saying audibly "five minutes past twelve," grunts his satisfaction, and closes the door.*]
VAVASOUR [*mad with joy*]. Kats, are ye here, really here?
CATHERINE [*surprised*]. Am *I* here? Tut, lad, are ye here?
VAVASOUR [*shrewdly*]. Yiss, that is are we *both* here?
CATHERINE [*perplexed*]. Did ye think I wasn't goin' to be?
VAVASOUR [*suppressed intelligent joy in his eyes*]. No—o, not that, only I thought, I thought ye was goin' to—to—faint, Kats. I thought ye looked like it, Kats.

CATHERINE [*the happiness on her face vanishing, sinks on to the nearest settle*]. Uch, I'm a bad, bad woman, aye, Vavasour Jones, a *bad* woman!

VAVASOUR [*puzzled, yet lightly*]. Nay, Kats, nay!

CATHERINE [*desperately and almost in tears*]. Ye cannot believe what I must tell ye. Lad, a year ago this night I went to the church porch, hopin', aye, prayin', ye'd be called, that I'd see your spirit walkin'.

VAVASOUR [*starting and recovering himself*]. Catherine, ye did that!

CATHERINE [*plunging on with her confession*]. Aye, lad, I did, I'd been so unhappy with the quarrelin' an' hard words. I could think of nothin' but gettin' rid of them.

VAVASOUR [*in a tone of condemnation and standing over her*]. That was bad, very bad indeed!

CATHERINE. An' then, lad, when I reached the church corner an' saw your spirit was really there, *really* called, an' I knew ye'd not live the year out, I was frightened, but uch! lad, I was glad, I was indeed.

VAVASOUR [*looking grave*]. Catherine, 'twas a terrible thing to do!

CATHERINE [*meekly*]. Yiss, I know it now, but I didn't then. I was hard-hearted, an' I was weak with longin' to escape from it all. An' when I ran home I was frightened, but uch! lad, I was glad, too, an' now it hurts me so to think of it. Can you no comfort me?

VAVASOUR [*grudgingly, but not touching* CATHERINE'S *outstretched hand*]. Aye, well, I could, but, Kats, 'twas such a terrible thing to do!

CATHERINE. Yiss, yiss, ye'll never be able to forgive me, I'm thinkin'. An' then when ye came in from the lodge, ye spoke so pleasantly to me that I was troubled. An' now the year through it has grown better an' better, an' I could think of nothin' but lovin' ye, an' wishing' ye to live, an' knowin' I was the cause of your bein' called. Uch, lad, *can* ye forgive me?

VAVASOUR [*slowly*]. Aye, I can, none of us is without sin; but, Catherine, it was wrong, aye, aye, 'twas a wicked thing for a woman to do.

CATHERINE [*still more meekly*]. An' then to-night, lad, I was expectin' ye to go, knowin' ye couldn't live after twelve, an' ye sittin' there so innocent an' mournful. An' when the time came, I wanted to die myself. Uch!

VAVASOUR [*sitting down beside her and putting an arm about her as he speaks in a superior tone of voice*]. No matter, dearie, now. It *was* wrong in ye, but we're still here, an' it's been a sweet year, yiss, better nor a honeymoon, an' all the years after we'll make better nor this. There, there, Kats, let's have a bit of a wassail to celebrate our Allhallows' honeymoon, shall we?

CATHERINE [*starting to fetch a bowl*]. Yiss, lad, 'twould be fine, but, Vavasour, can ye forgive me, think, lad, for hopin', aye, an' prayin' to see your spirit called, just wishin' that ye'd not live the year out?

VAVASOUR [*with condescension*]. Kats, I can, an' I'm not layin' it up against ye, though 'twas a wicked thing for ye to do—for anyone to do. Now, darlin', fetch the bowl.

CATHERINE [*starting for the bowl again but turning on him*]. Vavasour, how does it happen that the callin' is set aside, an' that ye're really here? Such a thing has not been in Beddgelert in the memory of man.

VAVASOUR [*with dignity*]. I'm not sayin' how it's happened, Kats, but I'm thinkin' 'tis modern times whatever, an' things have changed—aye, indeed, 'tis modern times.

CATHERINE [*sighing contentedly*]. Good! 'Tis lucky 'tis modern times whatever!

[THE CURTAIN.]

RIDERS TO THE SEA

By

JOHN MILLINGTON SYNGE

"He was of a dark type of Irishman, though not blackhaired. Something in his air gave one the fancy that his face was dark from gravity. Gravity filled the face and haunted it, as though the man behind were forever listening to life's case before passing judgment. . . . When someone spoke to him he answered with grave Irish courtesy. When the talk became general he was silent. . . . His manner was that of a man too much interested in the life about him to wish to be more than a spectator. His interest was in life, not in ideas." In these words, John Masefield gives his first impressions of John Millington Synge, whom he met at a friend's house, in London, in January, 1903.

Synge, born April 16, 1871, at Newton Little, near Dublin, and dying in Dublin, March 24, 1909, belongs to that group of "inheritors of unfulfilled renown" who died before the prime of life was reached. He left six plays, notable the *Riders to the Sea* and *Deirdre of the Sorrows,* that are among the greatest in our language. He was delicate from the beginning, and after some education in private schools in Dublin and Bray, left school when about fourteen and studied with a tutor. In 1892 he took his B.A. degree from Trinity College, Dublin, whose rolls contain a number of names famous in English literature. While at college, he studied music at the Royal Irish Academy of Music, where he won a scholarship. His first impulse was to make music his career, and he spent portions of the next four years in Germany, France, and Italy studying music and traveling. In May, 1898, he first went to the Aran Islands, later to be the scene of *Riders to the Sea*. Thereafter in Paris in 1899 he met Yeats, who advised him to go back to the Aran Islands to renew his contact with the simple folk there. For the next three years he divided his time between Paris and Ireland. It was in 1904 that his play, *Riders to the Sea*,[1] was first produced. He was at Dublin that same year for the opening of the Abbey Theatre, of which he was one of the advisers. Whenever the Irish Players visited England, he

[1] For a list of Synge's other plays, see E. A. Boyd, *The Contemporary Drama of Ireland*, Boston, 1917.

traveled with them. In 1909 came the operation that ended his life.

Synge's book, *The Aran Islands,* which is a record of his various visits to these three islands lying about thirty miles off the coast of County Galway, is full of material that throws light on the setting and characterization of *Riders to the Sea.* The central incident in this play was suggested to Synge while he was sojourning on Inishmaan, the middle island of the Aran group, by a tale that he heard of a man whose body had been washed up on a distant coast, and who had been identified as belonging to the Islands, because of his characteristic garments. When on Inishmaan, Synge himself lived in just such a cottage as that which is the background for the tragedy of Maurya's sons. He wrote of this cottage, " The kitchen itself, where I will spend most of my time, is full of beauty and distinction. The red dresses of the women who cluster round the fire on their stools give a glow of almost Eastern richness, and the walls have been toned by the surf-smoke to a soft brown that blends with the gray earth-color of the floor. Many sorts of fishing-tackle, and the nets and oilskins of the men, are hung up on the walls or among the open rafters." And the following passage from his *Aran Islands* is an eloquent description of the atmosphere there: " A week of smoking fog has passed over and given me a strange sense of exile and desolation. I walk round the island nearly every day, yet I can see nothing anywhere but a mass of wet rock, a strip of surf, and then a tumult of waves.

" The slaty limestone has grown black with the water that is dripping on it, and wherever I turn there is the same gray obsession twining and wreathing itself among the narrow fields, and the same wail from the wind that shrieks and whistles in the loose rubble of the walls."

Mr. Masefield, in his recollections of Synge, reports also the following conversation between himself and the Irish playwright: Synge saying, " They [the islanders] asked me to fiddle to them so that they might dance," and Mr. Masefield asking, " Do you play, then? " and Synge answering, " I fiddle a little. I try to learn something different for them every time. The last time I learned to do conjuring tricks. They'd get tired of me if I didn't bring something new. I'm thinking of learning the penny whistle before I go again."

A later visitor [1] to the Aran Islands, Miss B. N. Hedderman, a district nurse, gives further evidences of the simplicity of those people from whom the characters of *Riders to the Sea* were drawn. She tells of a man who owned a house with two comfortable rooms in it, one of which he leveled ruthlessly because he had dreamed that it hindered the passage of the " good people." The illustrations in her little book showing cottage interiors and peasant costumes will be found useful by groups who are planning to produce *Riders to the Sea*. But the best guide to the costumes and social life of the West of Ireland is J. B. Yeats.[2]

The *Drama Calendar* of December 13, 1920, offers the following suggestion for a musical setting for the play: " The attention of Little Theatre directors is called to a musical prelude to Synge's *Riders to the Sea,* arranged by Henry F. Gilbert from the Symphonic Prologue, which was played at the Worcester Musical Festival this fall. This original arrangement of the material is intended to build the mood which the play sustains, and is simply orchestrated for seven instruments. Every Little Theatre should be able to gather such an orchestra. Here is an opportunity to give continuity to a program of one-acts; music answers a question which is one of the hardest the director has to solve: how a mood which is to be created and sustained in the brief space of twenty minutes shall not be too fleeting."

[1] B. N. Hedderman, *Glimpses of My Life in Aran*, Bristol, 1917.
[2] J. B. Yeats, *Life in the West of Ireland*, Dublin and London, 1912. The color prints and line drawings in this book are very beautiful. Cf. also J. M. Synge, *The Aran Islands*. With drawings by Jack B. Yeats, Dublin and London, 1907.

RIDERS TO THE SEA

A PLAY IN ONE ACT

First performed at the Molesworth Hall, Dublin, February 25, 1904.

CHARACTERS

MAURYA, *an old woman.*
BARTLEY, *her son.*
CATHLEEN, *her daughter.*
NORA, *a younger daughter.*
MEN AND WOMEN.

SCENE.—*An Island off the West of Ireland.*

Cottage kitchen, with nets, oil-skins, spinning wheel, some new boards standing by the wall, etc. CATHLEEN, *a girl of about twenty, finishes kneading cake, and puts it down in the pot-oven by the fire; then wipes her hands, and begins to spin at the wheel.* NORA, *a young girl, puts her head in at the door.*

NORA [*in a low voice*]. Where is she?
CATHLEEN. She's lying down, God help her, and may be sleeping, if she's able. [NORA *comes in softly, and takes a bundle from under her shawl.*]
CATHLEEN [*spinning the wheel rapidly*]. What is it you have?
NORA. The young priest is after bringing them. It's a shirt and a plain stocking were got off a drowned man in Donegal. [CATHLEEN *stops her wheel with a sudden movement, and leans out to listen.*]
NORA. We're to find out if it's Michael's they are, some time herself will be down looking by the sea.

CATHLEEN. How would they be Michael's, Nora? How would he go the length of that way to the far north?

NORA. The young priest says he's known the like of it. "If it's Michael's they are," says he, "you can tell herself he's got a clean burial by the grace of God, and if they're not his, let no one say a word about them, for she'll be getting her death," says he, "with crying and lamenting." [*The door which* NORA *half closed is blown open by a gust of wind.*]

CATHLEEN [*looking out anxiously*]. Did you ask him would he stop Bartley going this day with the horses to the Galway fair?

NORA. "I won't stop him," says he, "but let you not be afraid. Herself does be saying prayers half through the night, and the Almighty God won't leave her destitute," says he, "with no son living."

CATHLEEN. Is the sea bad by the white rocks, Nora?

NORA. Middling bad, God help us. There's a great roaring in the west, and it's worse it'll be getting when the tide's turned to the wind. [*She goes over to the table with the bundle.*] Shall I open it now?

CATHLEEN. Maybe she'd wake up on us, and come in before we'd done. [*Coming to the table.*] It's a long time we'll be, and the two of us crying.

NORA [*goes to the inner door and listens*]. She's moving about on the bed. She'll be coming in a minute.

CATHLEEN. Give me the ladder, and I'll put them up in the turf-loft, the way she won't know of them at all, and maybe when the tide turns she'll be going down to see would he be floating from the east. [*They put the ladder against the gable of the chimney;* CATHLEEN *goes up a few steps and hides the bundle in the turf-loft.* MAURYA *comes from the inner room.*]

MAURYA [*looking up at* CATHLEEN *and speaking querulously.*] Isn't it turf enough you have for this day and evening?

CATHLEEN. There's a cake baking at the fire for a short space [*throwing down the turf*] and Bartley will want it when the tide turns if he goes to Connemara. [NORA *picks up the turf and puts it round the pot-oven.*]

MAURYA [*sitting down on a stool at the fire*]. He won't go this day with the wind rising from the south and west. He won't go this day, for the young priest will stop him surely.

NORA. He'll not stop him, mother, and I heard Eamon Simon and Stephen Pheety and Colum Shawn saying he would go.

MAURYA. Where is he itself?

NORA. He went down to see would there be another boat sailing in the week, and I'm thinking it won't be long till he's here now, for the tide's turning at the green head, and the hooker's tacking from the east.

CATHLEEN. I hear someone passing the big stones.

NORA [*looking out*]. He's coming now, and he in a hurry.

BARTLEY [*comes in and looks round the room. Speaking sadly and quietly*]. Where is the bit of new rope, Cathleen, was bought in Connemara?

CATHLEEN [*coming down*]. Give it to him, Nora; it's on a nail by the white boards. I hung it up this morning, for the pig with the black feet was eating it.

NORA [*giving him a rope*]. Is that it, Bartley?

MAURYA. You'd do right to leave that rope, Bartley, hanging by the boards. [BARTLEY *takes the rope.*] It will be wanting in this place, I'm telling you, if Michael is washed up to-morrow morning, or the next morning, or any morning in the week, for it's a deep grave we'll make him by the grace of God.

BARTLEY [*beginning to work with the rope*]. I've no halter the way I can ride down on the mare, and I must go now quickly. This is the one boat going for two weeks or beyond it, and the fair will be a good fair for horses I heard them saying below.

MAURYA. It's a hard thing they'll be saying below if the body is washed up and there's no man in it to make the coffin, and I after giving a big price for the finest white boards you'd find in Connemara. [*She looks round at the boards.*]

BARTLEY. How would it be washed up, and we after looking each day for nine days, and a strong wind blowing a while back from the west and south?

MAURYA. If it wasn't found itself, that wind is raising the sea, and there was a star up against the moon, and it rising in the night. If it was a hundred horses, or a thousand horses you had itself, what is the price of a thousand horses against a son where there is one son only?

BARTLEY [*working at the halter, to* CATHLEEN]. Let you

go down each day, and see the sheep aren't jumping in on the rye, and if the jobber comes you can sell the pig with the black feet if there is a good price going.

MAURYA. How would the like of her get a good price for a pig?

BARTLEY [*to* CATHLEEN]. If the west wind holds with the last bit of the moon let you and Nora get up weed enough for another cock for the kelp. It's hard set we'll be from this day with no one in it but one man to work.

MAURYA. It's hard set we'll be surely the day you're drownd'd with the rest. What way will I live and the girls with me, and I an old woman looking for the grave? [BARTLEY *lays down the halter, takes off his old coat, and puts on a newer one of the same flannel.*]

BARTLEY [*to* NORA]. Is she coming to the pier?

NORA [*looking out*]. She's passing the green head and letting fall her sails.

BARTLEY [*getting his purse and tobacco*]. I'll have half an hour to go down, and you'll see me coming again in two days, or in three days, or maybe in four days if the wind is bad.

MAURYA [*turning round to the fire, and putting her shawl over her head*]. Isn't it a hard and cruel man won't hear a word from an old woman, and she holding him from the sea?

CATHLEEN. It's the life of a young man to be going on the sea, and who would listen to an old woman with one thing and she saying it over?

BARTLEY [*taking the halter*]. I must go now quickly. I'll ride down on the red mare, and the gray pony'll run behind me. . . . The blessing of God on you. [*He goes out.*]

MAURYA [*crying out as he is in the door*]. He's gone now, God spare us, and we'll not see him again. He's gone now, and when the black night is falling I'll have no son left me in the world.

CATHLEEN. Why wouldn't you give him your blessing and he looking round in the door? Isn't it sorrow enough is on everyone in this house without your sending him out with an unlucky word behind him, and a hard word in his ear? [MAURYA *takes up the tongs and begins raking the fire aimlessly without looking round.*]

NORA [*turning towards her*]. You're taking away the turf from the cake.

CATHLEEN [*crying out*]. The Son of God forgive us, Nora, we're after forgetting his bit of bread. [*She comes over to the fire.*]

NORA. And it's destroyed he'll be going till dark night, and he after eating nothing since the sun went up.

CATHLEEN [*turning the cake out of the oven*]. It's destroyed he'll be, surely. There's no sense left on any person in a house where an old woman will be talking forever. [MAURYA *sways herself on her stool.*]

CATHLEEN [*cutting off some of the bread and rolling it in a cloth; to* MAURYA]. Let you go down now to the spring well and give him this and he passing. You'll see him then and the dark word will be broken, and you can say "God speed you," the way he'll be easy in his mind.

MAURYA [*taking the bread*]. Will I be in it as soon as himself?

CATHLEEN. If you go now quickly.

MAURYA [*standing up unsteadily*]. It's hard set I am to walk.

CATHLEEN [*looking at her anxiously*]. Give her the stick, Nora, or maybe she'll slip on the big stones.

NORA. What stick?

CATHLEEN. The stick Michael brought from Connemara.

MAURYA [*taking a stick* NORA *gives her*]. In the big world the old people do be leaving things after them for their sons and children, but in this place it is the young men do be leaving things behind for them that do be old. [*She goes out slowly.* NORA *goes over to the ladder.*]

CATHLEEN. Wait, Nora, maybe she'd turn back quickly. She's that sorry, God help her, you wouldn't know the thing she'd do.

NORA. Is she gone round by the bush?

CATHLEEN [*looking out*]. She's gone now. Throw it down quickly, for the Lord knows when she'll be out of it again.

NORA [*getting the bundle from the loft*]. The young priest said he'd be passing to-morrow, and we might go down and speak to him below if it's Michael's they are surely.

CATHLEEN [*taking the bundle*]. Did he say what way they were found?

NORA [*coming down*]. "There were two men," says he, "and they rowing round with poteen before the cocks crowed, and the oar of one of them caught the body, and they passing the black cliffs of the north."

CATHLEEN [*trying to open the bundle*]. Give me a knife, Nora, the string's perished with the salt water, and there's a black knot on it you wouldn't loosen in a week.

NORA [*giving her a knife*]. I've heard tell it was a long way to Donegal.

CATHLEEN [*cutting the string*]. It is surely. There was a man in here a while ago—the man sold us that knife—and he said if you set off walking from the rocks beyond, it would be seven days you'd be in Donegal.

NORA. And what time would a man take, and he floating?

[CATHLEEN *opens the bundle and takes out a bit of a stocking. They look at them eagerly.*]

CATHLEEN [*in a low voice*]. The Lord spare us, Nora! isn't it a queer hard thing to say if it's his they are surely?

NORA. I'll get his shirt off the hook the way we can put the one flannel on the other. [*She looks through some clothes hanging in the corner.*] It's not with them, Cathleen, and where will it be?

CATHLEEN. I'm thinking Bartley put it on him in the morning, for his own shirt was heavy with the salt in it. [*Pointing to the corner.*] There's a bit of a sleeve was of the same stuff. Give me that and it will do. [NORA *brings it to her and they compare the flannel.*]

CATHLEEN. It's the same stuff, Nora; but if it is itself aren't there great rolls of it in the shops of Galway, and isn't it many another man may have a shirt of it as well as Michael himself?

NORA [*who has taken up the stocking and counted the stitches, crying out*]. It's Michael, Cathleen, it's Michael; God spare his soul, and what will herself say when she hears this story, and Bartley on the sea?

CATHLEEN [*taking the stocking*]. It's a plain stocking.

NORA. It's the second one of the third pair I knitted, and I put up three score stitches, and I dropped four of them.

CATHLEEN [*counts the stitches*]. It's that number is in it. [*Crying out.*] Ah, Nora, isn't it a bitter thing to think of him floating that way to the far north, and no one to keen him but the black hags that do be flying on the sea?

NORA [*swinging herself round, and throwing out her arms*

on the clothes]. And isn't it a pitiful thing when there is nothing left of a man who was a great rower and fisher, but a bit of an old shirt and a plain stocking?

CATHLEEN [*after an instant*]. Tell me is herself coming, Nora? I hear a little sound on the path.

NORA [*looking out*]. She is, Cathleen. She's coming up to the door.

CATHLEEN. Put these things away before she'll come in. Maybe it's easier she'll be after giving her blessing to Bartley, and we won't let on we've heard anything the time he's on the sea.

NORA [*helping* CATHLEEN *to close the bundle*]. We'll put them here in the corner. [*They put them into a hole in the chimney corner.* CATHLEEN *goes back to the spinning-wheel.*]

NORA. Will she see it was crying I was?

CATHLEEN. Keep your back to the door the way the light'll not be on you. [NORA *sits down at the chimney corner, with her back to the door.* MAURYA *comes in very slowly, without looking at the girls, and goes over to her stool at the other side of the fire. The cloth with the bread is still in her hand. The girls look at each other, and* NORA *points to the bundle of bread.*]

CATHLEEN [*after spinning for a moment*]. You didn't give him his bit of bread? [MAURYA *begins to keen softly, without turning round.*]

CATHLEEN. Did you see him riding down? [MAURYA *goes on keening.*]

CATHLEEN [*a little impatiently*]. God forgive you; isn't it a better thing to raise your voice and tell what you seen, than to be making lamentation for a thing that's done? Did you see Bartley, I'm saying to you.

MAURYA [*with a weak voice*]. My heart's broken from this day.

CATHLEEN [*as before*]. Did you see Bartley?

MAURYA. I seen the fearfulest thing.

CATHLEEN [*leaves her wheel and looks out*]. God forgive you; he's riding the mare now over the green head, and the gray pony behind him.

MAURYA [*starts, so that her shawl falls back from her head and shows her white tossed hair. With a frightened voice*]. The gray pony behind him.

CATHLEEN [*coming to the fire*]. What is it ails you, at all?
MAURYA [*speaking very slowly*]. I've seen the fearfulest thing any person has seen, since the day Bride Dara seen the dead man with the child in his arms.
CATHLEEN AND NORA. Uah. [*They crouch down in front of the old woman at the fire.*]
NORA. Tell us what it is you seen.
MAURYA. I went down to the spring well, and I stood there saying a prayer to myself. Then Bartley came along, and he riding on the red mare with the gray pony behind him. [*She puts up her hands, as if to hide something from her eyes.*] The Son of God spare us, Nora!
CATHLEEN. What is it you seen?
MAURYA. I seen Michael himself.
CATHLEEN [*speaking softly*]. You did not, mother; it wasn't Michael you seen, for his body is after being found in the far north, and he's got a clean burial by the grace of God.
MAURYA [*a little defiantly*]. I'm after seeing him this day, and he riding and galloping. Bartley came first on the red mare; and I tried to say "God speed you," but something choked the words in my throat. He went by quickly; and "The blessing of God on you," says he, and I could say nothing. I looked up then, and I crying, at the gray pony, and there was Michael upon it—with fine clothes on him, and new shoes on his feet.
CATHLEEN [*begins to keen*]. It's destroyed we are from this day. It's destroyed, surely.
NORA. Didn't the young priest say the Almighty God wouldn't leave her destitute with no son living?
MAURYA [*in a low voice, but clearly*]. It's little the like of him knows of the sea. . . . Bartley will be lost now, and let you call in Eamon and make me a good coffin out of the white boards, for I won't live after them. I've had a husband, and a husband's father, and six sons in this house—six fine men, though it was a hard birth I had with every one of them and they coming to the world—and some of them were found and some of them were not found, but they're gone now the lot of them. . . . There were Stephen, and Shawn, were lost in the great wind, and found after in the Bay of Gregory of the Golden Mouth, and carried up the two of them on the one plank, and in by that door. [*She pauses for a moment, the*

girls start as if they heard something through the door that is half open behind them.]

NORA [*in a whisper*]. Did you hear that, Cathleen? Did you hear a noise in the north-east?

CATHLEEN [*in a whisper*]. There's someone after crying out by the seashore.

MAURYA [*continues without hearing anything*]. There was Sheamus and his father, and his own father again, were lost in a dark night, and not a stick or sign was seen of them when the sun went up. There was Patch after was drowned out of a curagh that turned over. I was sitting here with Bartley, and he a baby, lying on my two knees, and I seen two women, and three women, and four women coming in, and they crossing themselves, and not saying a word. I looked out then, and there were men coming after them, and they holding a thing in the half of a red sail, and water dripping out of it— it was a dry day, Nora—and leaving a track to the door.

[*She pauses again with her hand stretched out towards the door. It opens softly and old women begin to come in, crossing themselves on the threshold, and kneeling down in front of the stage with red petticoats over their heads.*]

MAURYA [*half in a dream, to* CATHLEEN]. Is it Patch, or Michael, or what is it at all?

CATHLEEN. Michael is after being found in the far north, and when he is found there how could he be here in this place?

MAURYA. There does be a power of young men floating round in the sea, and what way would they know if it was Michael they had, or another man like him, for when a man is nine days in the sea, and the wind blowing, it's hard set his own mother would be to say what man was it.

CATHLEEN. It's Michael, God spare him, for they're after sending us a bit of his clothes from the far north. [*She reaches out and hands* MAURYA *the clothes that belonged to* MICHAEL. MAURYA *stands up slowly, and takes them in her hands.* NORA *looks out.*]

NORA. They're carrying a thing among them and there's water dripping out of it and leaving a track by the big stones.

CATHLEEN [*in a whisper to the women who have come in*]. Is it Bartley it is?

ONE OF THE WOMEN. It is surely, God rest his soul. [*Two younger women come in and pull out the table. Then* men carry in the body of BARTLEY, *laid on a plank, with a bit of a sail over it, and lay it on the table.*]

CATHLEEN [*to the women, as they are doing so*]. What way was he drowned?

ONE OF THE WOMEN. The gray pony knocked him into the sea, and he was washed out where there is a great surf on the white rocks. [MAURYA *has gone over and knelt down at the head of the table. The women are keening softly and swaying themselves with a slow movement.* CATHLEEN *and* NORA *kneel at the other end of the table. The men kneel near the door.*]

MAURYA [*raising her head and speaking as if she did not see the people around her*]. They're all gone now, and there isn't anything more the sea can do to me. . . . I'll have no call now to be up crying and praying when the wind breaks from the south, and you can hear the surf is in the east, and the surf is in the west, making a great stir with the two noises, and they hitting one on the other. I'll have no call now to be going down and getting Holy Water in the dark nights after Samhain, and I won't care what way the sea is when the other women will be keening. [*To* NORA.] Give me the Holy Water, Nora, there's a small sup still on the dresser. [NORA *gives it to her.*]

MAURYA [*drops* MICHAEL'S *clothes across* BARTLEY'S *feet, and sprinkles the Holy Water over him*]. It isn't that I haven't prayed for you, Bartley, to the Almighty God. It isn't that I haven't said prayers in the dark night till you wouldn't know what I'ld be saying; but it's a great rest I'll have now, and it's time surely. It's a great rest I'll have now, and great sleeping in the long nights after Samhain, if it's only a bit of wet flour we do have to eat, and maybe a fish that would be stinking. [*She kneels down again, crossing herself, and saying prayers under her breath.*]

CATHLEEN [*to an old man*]. Maybe yourself and Eamon would make a coffin when the sun rises. We have fine white boards herself bought, God help her, thinking Michael would be found, and I have a new cake you can eat while you'll be working.

THE OLD MAN [*looking at the boards*]. Are there nails with them?

CATHLEEN. There are not, Colum; we didn't think of the nails.

ANOTHER MAN. It's a great wonder she wouldn't think of the nails, and all the coffins she's seen made already.

CATHLEEN. It's getting old she is, and broken. [MAURYA *stands up again very slowly and spreads out the pieces of* MICHAEL'S *clothes beside the body, sprinkling them with the last of the Holy Water.*]

NORA [*in a whisper to* CATHLEEN]. She's quiet now and easy; but the day Michael was drowned you could hear her crying out from this to the spring well. It's fonder she was of Michael, and would anyone have thought that?

CATHLEEN [*slowly and clearly*]. An old woman will be soon tired with anything she will do, and isn't it nine days herself is after crying and keening, and making great sorrow in the house?

MAURYA [*puts the empty cup mouth downwards on the table, and lays her hands together on* BARTLEY'S *feet*]. They're all together this time, and the end is come. May the Almighty God have mercy on Bartley's soul, and on Michael's soul, and on the souls of Sheamus and Patch, and Stephen and Shawn [*bending her head*]; and may He have mercy on my soul, Nora, and on the soul of everyone is left living in the world. [*She pauses, and the keen rises a little more loudly from the women, then sinks away.*]

MAURYA [*continuing*]. Michael has a clean burial in the far north, by the grace of the Almighty God. Bartley will have a fine coffin out of the white boards, and a deep grave surely. What more can we want than that? No man at all can be living forever, and we must be satisfied. [*She kneels down again and the curtain falls slowly.*]

A NIGHT AT AN INN
A PLAY IN ONE ACT

By
LORD DUNSANY

Edward John Moreton Drax Plunkett, eighteenth baron Dunsany, was born in 1878, a lord of the British Empire, heir to an ancient barony, created by Henry VI in the middle of the fifteenth century. He went from Eton to Sandhurst, the English military college, held a lieutenancy in a famous regiment, the Coldstream Guards, saw active service in the South African War and served in the Great War as an officer in the Royal Inniskilling Fusiliers. He turned aside from his career as a soldier in 1906 to stand for West Wiltshire as the Conservative candidate, but he was defeated. He writes enthusiastically always of his interest in sport; he has gone to the ends of the earth to shoot big game. His first book, *The Gods of Pegana,* was published in 1905. He has since written sketches, fantastic tales, and plays,[1] and latterly introductions to the poems of Francis Ledwidge, the Irish peasant poet, who fell in battle in 1917. Dunsany's early plays were put on at the Abbey Theatre where Yeats produced *The Glittering Gate* in 1909.

The initial American productions were also made in Little Theatres, under the auspices of the Stage Society of Philadelphia and at The Neighborhood Playhouse in New York, where the first performance on any stage of *A Night at an Inn* was given on April 22, 1916. It was an immediate success and aroused great general interest in Dunsany's other plays. It was remarked at the time that its scene on an English moor was far from "his own Oriental Never Never Land," and that it recalled in its substance *The Moonstone* by Wilkie Collins and *The Mystery of Cloomber* by A. Conan Doyle. Dunsany, unlike the other playwrights associated with the Irish National Theatre, has borrowed the glamour of the Orient rather than that of Celtic lore, to heighten his dramatic effects. There is, in fact, much that is Biblical in his mood and in his diction.

When, at a later date, Lord Dunsany saw the production of

[1] For bibliography see E. A. Boyd, *The Contemporary Drama of Ireland,* Boston, 1917.

A Night at an Inn at The Neighborhood Playhouse, the effect of the play "exceeded his own expectations, and he was surprised to note the thrill which it communicated to his audience. 'It's a very simple thing,' he said,—'merely a story of some sailors who have stolen something and know that they are followed. Possibly it is effective because nearly everybody, at some time or other, has done something he was sorry for, has been afraid of retribution, and has felt the hot breath of a pursuing vengeance on the back of his neck. . . . *A Night at an Inn* was written between tea and dinner in a single sitting. That was very easy.'"[1]

A Night at an Inn is one of Dunsany's contributions to the revival of romance in our generation. In an article published ten years ago, called *Romance and the Modern Stage,* he wrote: "Romance is so inseparable from life that all we need, to obtain romantic drama, is for the dramatist to find any age or any country where life is not too thickly veiled and cloaked with puzzles and conventions, in fact to find a people that is not in the agonies of self-consciousness. For myself, I think it is simpler to imagine such a people, as it saves the trouble of reading to find a romantic age, or the trouble of making a journey to lands where there is no press. . . . The kind of drama that we most need to-day seems to me to be the kind that will build new worlds for the fancy; for the spirit, as much as the body, needs sometimes a change of scene."

[1] Clayton Hamilton, *Seen on the Stage,* New York, 1920, p. 238; p. 239.

A NIGHT AT AN INN

CHARACTERS

A. E. Scott-Fortesque (The Toff), *a dilapidated gentleman.*
William Jones (Bill)
Albert Thomas   } *merchant sailors.*
Jacob Smith (Sniggers)
First Priest of Klesh.
Second Priest of Klesh.
Third Priest of Klesh.
Klesh.

The curtain rises on a room in an inn. Sniggers *and* Bill *are talking,* The Toff *is reading a paper.* Albert *sits a little apart.*

Sniggers. What's his idea, I wonder?
Bill. I don't know.
Sniggers. And how much longer will he keep us here?
Bill. We've been here three days.
Sniggers. And 'aven't seen a soul.
Bill. And a pretty penny it cost us when he rented the pub.
Sniggers. 'Ow long did 'e rent the pub for?
Bill. You never know with him.
Sniggers. It's lonely enough.
Bill. 'Ow long did you rent the pub for, Toffy? [The Toff *continues to read a sporting paper; he takes no notice of what is said.*]
Sniggers. 'E's *such* a toff.
Bill. Yet 'e's clever, no mistake.
Sniggers. Those clever ones are the beggars to make a muddle. Their plans are clever enough, but they don't work, and then they make a mess of things much worse than you or me.
Bill. Ah!
Sniggers. I don't like this place.

BILL. Why not?

SNIGGERS. I don't like the looks of it.

BILL. He's keeping us here because here those niggers can't find us. The three heathen priests what was looking for us so. But we want to go and sell our ruby soon.

ALBERT. There's no sense in it.

BILL. Why not, Albert?

ALBERT. Because I gave those black devils the slip in Hull.

BILL. You give 'em the slip, Albert?

ALBERT. The slip, all three of them. The fellows with the gold spots on their foreheads. I had the ruby then and I give them the slip in Hull.

BILL. How did you do it, Albert?

ALBERT. I had the ruby and they were following me. . . .

BILL. Who told them you had the ruby? You didn't show it.

ALBERT. No. . . . But they kind of know.

SNIGGERS. They kind of know, Albert?

ALBERT. Yes, they know if you've got it. Well, they sort of mouched after me, and I tells a policeman and he says, O, they were only three poor niggers and they wouldn't hurt me. Ugh! When I thought of what they did in Malta to poor old Jim.

BILL. Yes, and to George in Bombay before we started.

SNIGGERS. Ugh!

BILL. Why didn't you give 'em in charge?

ALBERT. What about the ruby, Bill?

BILL. Ah!

ALBERT. Well, I did better than that. I walks up and down through Hull. I walks slow enough. And then I turns a corner and I runs. I never sees a corner but I turns it. But sometimes I let a corner pass just to fool them. I twists about like a hare. Then I sits down and waits. No priests.

SNIGGERS. What?

ALBERT. No heathen black devils with gold spots on their face. I give 'em the slip.

BILL. Well done, Albert!

SNIGGERS [*after a sigh of content*]. Why didn't you tell us?

ALBERT. 'Cause 'e won't let you speak. 'E's got 'is plans and 'e thinks we're silly folk. Things must be done 'is way. And all the time I've give 'em the slip. Might 'ave 'ad one

o' them crooked knives in him before now but for me who give 'em the slip in Hull.
  BILL. Well done, Albert! Do you hear that, Toffy? Albert has give 'em the slip.
  THE TOFF. Yes, I hear.
  SNIGGERS. Well, what do you say to that?
  THE TOFF. O. . . . Well done, Albert!
  ALBERT. And what a' you going to do?
  THE TOFF. Going to wait.
  ALBERT. Don't seem to know what 'e's waiting for.
  SNIGGERS. It's a nasty place.
  ALBERT. It's getting silly, Bill. Our money's gone and we want to sell the ruby. Let's get on to a town.
  BILL. But 'e won't come.
  ALBERT. Then we'll leave him.
  SNIGGERS. We'll be all right if we keep away from Hull.
  ALBERT. We'll go to London.
  BILL. But 'e must 'ave 'is share.
  SNIGGERS. All right. Only let's go. [*To* THE TOFF.] We're going, do you hear? Give us the ruby.
  THE TOFF. Certainly. [*He gives them a ruby from his waistcoat pocket; it is the size of a small hen's egg. He goes on reading his paper.*]
  ALBERT. Come on, Sniggers. [*Exeunt* ALBERT *and* SNIGGERS.]
  BILL. Good-by, old man. We'll give you your fair share, but there's nothing to do here—no girls, no halls, and we must sell the ruby.
  THE TOFF. I'm not a fool, Bill.
  BILL. No, no, of course not. Of course you ain't, and you've helped us a lot. Good-by. You'll say good-by?
  THE TOFF. Oh, yes. Good-by. [*Still reads his paper. Exit* BILL. THE TOFF *puts a revolver on the table beside him and goes on with his papers. After a moment the three men come rushing in again, frightened.*]
  SNIGGERS [*out of breath*]. We've come back, Toffy.
  THE TOFF. So you have.
  ALBERT. Toffy. . . . How did they get here?
  THE TOFF. They walked, of course.
  ALBERT. But it's eighty miles.
  SNIGGERS. Did you know they were here, Toffy?

The Toff. Expected them about now.
Albert. Eighty miles!
Bill. Toffy, old man . . . what are we to do?
The Toff. Ask Albert.
Bill. If they can do things like this, there's no one can save us but you, Toffy. . . . I always knew you were a clever one. We won't be fools any more. We'll obey you, Toffy.
The Toff. You're brave enough and strong enough. There isn't many that would steal a ruby eye out of an idol's head, and such an idol as that was to look at, and on such a night. You're brave enough, Bill. But you're all three of you fools. Jim would have none of my plans, and where's Jim? And George. What did they do to him?
Sniggers. Don't, Toffy!
The Toff. Well, then, your strength is no use to you. You want cleverness; or they'll have you the way they had George and Jim.
All. Ugh!
The Toff. Those black priests would follow you round the world in circles. Year after year, till they got the idol's eye. And if we died with it, they'd follow our grandchildren. That fool thinks he can escape from men like that by running round three streets in the town of Hull.
Albert. God's truth, *you* 'aven't escaped them, because they're 'ere.
The Toff. So I supposed.
Albert. You *supposed!*
The Toff. Yes, I believe there's no announcement in the Society papers. But I took this country seat especially to receive them. There's plenty of room if you dig, it is pleasantly situated, and, what is more important, it is in a very quiet neighborhood. So I am at home to them this afternoon.
Bill. Well, *you're* a deep one.
The Toff. And remember, you've only my wits between you and death, and don't put your futile plans against those of an educated gentleman.
Albert. If you're a gentleman, why don't you go about among gentlemen instead of the likes of us?
The Toff. Because I was too clever for them as I am too clever for you.
Albert. Too clever for them?

A NIGHT AT AN INN

THE TOFF. I never lost a game of cards in my life.
BILL. You never lost a game?
THE TOFF. Not when there was money in it.
BILL. Well, well!
THE TOFF. Have a game of poker?
ALL. No, thanks.
THE TOFF. Then do as you're told.
BILL. All right, Toffy.
SNIGGERS. I saw something just then. Hadn't we better draw the curtains?
THE TOFF. No.
SNIGGERS. What?
THE TOFF. Don't draw the curtains.
SNIGGERS. O, all right.
BILL. But, Toffy, they can see us. One doesn't let the enemy do that. I don't see why. . . .
THE TOFF. No, of course you don't.
BILL. O, all right, Toffy. [*All begin to pull out revolvers.*]
THE TOFF [*putting his own away*]. No revolvers, please.
ALBERT. Why not?
THE TOFF. Because I don't want any noise at my party. We might get guests that hadn't been invited. *Knives* are a different matter. [*All draw knives.* THE TOFF *signs to them not to draw them yet.* TOFFY *has already taken back his ruby.*]
BILL. I think they're coming, Toffy.
THE TOFF. Not yet.
ALBERT. When will they come?
THE TOFF. When I am quite ready to receive them. Not before.
SNIGGERS. I should like to get this over.
THE TOFF. Should you? Then we'll have them now.
SNIGGERS. Now?
THE TOFF. Yes. Listen to me. You shall do as you see me do. You will all pretend to go out. I'll show you how. I've got the ruby. When they see me alone they will come for their idol's eye.
BILL. How can they tell like this which of us has it?
THE TOFF. I confess I don't know, but they seem to.
SNIGGERS. What will you do when they come in?
THE TOFF. I shall do nothing.

SNIGGERS. What?

THE TOFF. They will creep up behind me. Then, my friends, Sniggers and Bill and Albert, who gave them the slip, will do what they can.

BILL. All right, Toffy. Trust us.

THE TOFF. If you're a little slow, you will see enacted the cheerful spectacle that accompanied the demise of Jim.

SNIGGERS. Don't, Toffy. We'll be there, all right.

THE TOFF. Very well. Now watch me. [*He goes past the windows to the inner door R. He opens it inwards, then under cover of the open door, he slips down on his knee and closes it, remaining on the inside, appearing to have gone out. He signs to the others, who understand. Then he appears to re-enter in the same manner.*]

THE TOFF. Now, I shall sit with my back to the door. You go out one by one, so far as our friends can make out. Crouch very low to be on the safe side. They mustn't see you through the window. [BILL *makes his sham exit.*]

THE TOFF. Remember, no revolvers. The police are, I believe, proverbially inquisitive. [*The other two follow* BILL. *All three are now crouching inside the door R.* THE TOFF *puts the ruby beside him on the table. He lights a cigarette. The door at the back opens so slowly that you can hardly say at what moment it began.* THE TOFF *picks up his paper. A native of India wriggles along the floor ever so slowly, seeking cover from chairs. He moves L. where* THE TOFF *is. The three sailors are R.* SNIGGERS *and* ALBERT *lean forward.* BILL'S *arm keeps them back. An arm-chair had better conceal them from the Indian. The black Priest nears* THE TOFF. BILL *watches to see if any more are coming. Then he leaps forward alone—he has taken his boots off—and knifes the Priest. The Priest tries to shout but* BILL'S *left hand is over his mouth.* THE TOFF *continues to read his sporting paper. He never looks around.*]

BILL [*sotto voce*]. There's only one, Toffy. What shall we do?

THE TOFF [*without turning his head*]. Only one?

BILL. Yes.

THE TOFF. Wait a moment. Let me think. [*Still apparently absorbed in his paper.*] Ah, yes. You go back, Bill. We must attract another guest. . . . Now, are you ready?

A NIGHT AT AN INN

BILL. Yes.

THE TOFF. All right. You shall now see my demise at my Yorkshire residence. You must receive guests for me. [*He leaps up in full view of the window, flings up both arms and falls to the floor near the dead Priest.*] Now, be ready. [*His eyes close. There is a long pause. Again the door opens, very, very slowly. Another priest creeps in. He has three golden spots upon his forehead. He looks round, then he creeps up to his companion and turns him over and looks inside of his clenched hands. Then he looks at the recumbent* TOFF. *Then he creeps toward him.* BILL *slips after him and knifes him like the other with his left hand over his mouth.*]

BILL [*sotto voce*]. We've only got two, Toffy.

THE TOFF. Still another.

BILL. What'll we do?

THE TOFF [*sitting up*]. Hum.

BILL. This is the best way, much.

THE TOFF. Out of the question. Never play the same game twice.

BILL. Why not, Toffy?

THE TOFF. Doesn't work if you do.

BILL. Well?

THE TOFF. I have it, Albert. You will now walk into the room. I showed you how to do it.

ALBERT. Yes.

THE TOFF. Just run over here and have a fight at this window with these two men.

ALBERT. But they're . . .

THE TOFF. Yes, they're dead, my perspicuous Albert. But Bill and I are going to resuscitate them. . . . Come on. [BILL *picks up a body under the arms.*]

THE TOFF. That's right, Bill. [*Does the same.*] Come and help us, Sniggers. . . . [SNIGGERS *comes.*] Keep low, keep low. Wave their arms about, Sniggers. Don't show yourself. Now, Albert, over you go. Our Albert is slain. Back you get, Bill. Back, Sniggers. Still, Albert. Mustn't move when he comes. Not a muscle. [*A face appears at the window and stays for some time. Then the door opens and, looking craftily round, the third Priest enters. He looks at his companions' bodies and turns round. He suspects something. He takes up one of the knives and with a knife in each hand he puts his back to the wall. He looks to the left and right.*]

THE TOFF. Come on, Bill. [*The Priest rushes to the door.* THE TOFF *knifes the last Priest from behind.*]

THE TOFF. A good day's work, my friends.

BILL. Well done, Toffy. Oh, you are a deep one!

ALBERT. A deep one if ever there was one.

SNIGGERS. There ain't any more, Bill, are there?

THE TOFF. No more in the world, my friend.

BILL. Aye, that's all there are. There were only three in the temple. Three priests and their beastly idol.

ALBERT. What is it worth, Toffy? Is it worth a thousand pounds?

THE TOFF. It's worth all they've got in the shop. Worth just whatever we like to ask for it.

ALBERT. Then we're millionaires now.

THE TOFF. Yes, and, what is more important, we no longer have any heirs.

BILL. We'll have to sell it now.

ALBERT. That won't be easy. It's a pity it isn't small and we had half a dozen. Hadn't the idol any other on him?

BILL. No, he was green jade all over and only had this one eye. He had it in the middle of his forehead and was a long sight uglier than anything else in the world.

SNIGGERS. I'm sure we ought all to be very grateful to Toffy.

BILL. And, indeed, we ought.

ALBERT. If it hadn't been for him. . . .

BILL. Yes, if it hadn't been for old Toffy. . . .

SNIGGERS. He's a deep one.

THE TOFF. Well, you see I just have a knack of foreseeing things.

SNIGGERS. I should think you did.

BILL. Why, I don't suppose anything happens that our Toff doesn't foresee. Does it, Toffy?

THE TOFF. Well, I don't think it does, Bill. I don't think it often does.

BILL. Life is no more than just a game of cards to our old Toff.

THE TOFF. Well, we've taken these fellows' trick.

SNIGGERS [*going to window*]. It wouldn't do for anyone to see them.

THE TOFF. Oh, nobody will come this way. We're all alone on a moor.

BILL. Where will we put them?

THE TOFF. Bury them in the cellar, but there's no hurry.

BILL. And what then, Toffy?

THE TOFF. Why, then we'll go to London and upset the ruby business. We have really come through this job very nicely.

BILL. I think the first thing that we ought to do is to give a little supper to old Toffy. We'll bury these fellows to-night.

ALBERT. Yes, let's.

SNIGGERS. The very thing!

BILL. And we'll all drink his health.

ALBERT. Good old Toffy!

SNIGGERS. He ought to have been a general or a premier. [*They get bottles from cupboard, etc.*]

THE TOFF. Well, we've earned our bit of a supper. [*They sit down.*]

BILL [*glass in hand*]. Here's to old Toffy, who guessed everything!

ALBERT *and* SNIGGERS. Good old Toffy!

BILL. Toffy, who saved our lives and made our fortunes.

ALBERT *and* SNIGGERS. Hear! Hear!

THE TOFF. And here's to Bill, who saved me twice to-night.

BILL. Couldn't have done it but for your cleverness, Toffy.

SNIGGERS. Hear, hear! Hear! Hear!

ALBERT. He foresees everything.

BILL. A speech, Toffy. A speech from our general.

ALL. Yes, a speech.

SNIGGERS. A speech.

THE TOFF. Well, get me some water. This whisky's too much for my head, and I must keep it clear till our friends are safe in the cellar.

BILL. Water? Yes, of course. Get him some water, Sniggers.

SNIGGERS. We don't use water here. Where shall I get it?

BILL. Outside in the garden. [*Exit* SNIGGERS.]

ALBERT. Here's to future!

BILL. Here's to Albert Thomas, Esquire.

ALBERT. And William Jones, Esquire. [*Re-enter* SNIGGERS, *terrified.*]

THE TOFF. Hullo, here's Jacob Smith, Esquire, J. P., alias Sniggers, back again.

SNIGGERS. Toffy, I've been thinking about my share in that ruby. I don't want it, Toffy; I don't want it.

THE TOFF. Nonsense, Sniggers. Nonsense.

SNIGGERS. You shall have it, Toffy, you shall have it yourself, only say Sniggers has no share in this 'ere ruby. Say it, Toffy, say it!

BILL. Want to turn informer, Sniggers?

SNIGGERS. No, no. Only I don't want the ruby, Toffy. . . .

THE TOFF. No more nonsense, Sniggers. We're all in together in this. If one hangs, we all hang; but they won't outwit me. Besides, it's not a hanging affair, they had their knives.

SNIGGERS. Toffy, Toffy, I always treated you fair, Toffy. I was always one to say, Give Toffy a chance. Take back my share, Toffy.

THE TOFF. What's the matter? What are you driving at?

SNIGGERS. Take it back, Toffy.

THE TOFF. Answer me, what are you up to?

SNIGGERS. I don't want my share any more.

BILL. Have you seen the police? [ALBERT *pulls out his knife.*]

THE TOFF. No, no knives, Albert.

ALBERT. What then?

THE TOFF. The honest truth in open court, barring the ruby. We were attacked.

SNIGGERS. There's no police.

THE TOFF. Well, then, what's the matter?

BILL. Out with it.

SNIGGERS. I swear to God. . . .

ALBERT. Well?

THE TOFF. Don't interrupt.

SNIGGERS. I swear I saw something *what I didn't like.*

THE TOFF. What you didn't like?

SNIGGERS [*in tears*]. O Toffy, Toffy, take it back. Take my share. Say you take it.

THE TOFF. What has he seen? [*Dead silence, only broken by* SNIGGERS'S *sobs. Then steps are heard. Enter a hideous idol. It is blind and gropes its way. It gropes its way to the ruby and picks it up and screws it into a socket in the forehead.*

SNIGGERS *still weeps softly, the rest stare in horror. The idol steps out, not groping. Its steps move off, then stop.*]
THE TOFF. O, great heavens!
ALBERT [*in a childish, plaintive voice*]. What is it, Toffy?
BILL. Albert, it is that obscene idol [*in a whisper*] come from India.
ALBERT. It is gone.
BILL. It has taken its eye.
SNIGGERS. We are saved.
A VOICE OFF [*with outlandish accent*]. Meestaire William Jones, Able Seaman. [THE TOFF *has never spoken, never moved. He only gazes stupidly in horror.*]
BILL. Albert, Albert, what is this? [*He rises and walks out. One moan is heard.* SNIGGERS *goes to the window. He falls back sickly.*]
ALBERT [*in a whisper*]. What has happened?
SNIGGERS. I have seen it. I have seen it. O, I have seen it! [*He returns to table.*]
THE TOFF [*laying his hand very gently on* SNIGGERS'S *arm, speaking softly and winningly.*] What was it, Sniggers?
SNIGGERS. I have seen it.
ALBERT. What?
SNIGGERS. O!
VOICE. Meestaire Albert Thomas, Able Seaman.
ALBERT. Must I go, Toffy? Toffy, must I go?
SNIGGERS [*clutching him*]. Don't move.
ALBERT [*going*]. Toffy, Toffy. [*Exit.*]
VOICE. Meestaire Jacob Smith, Able Seaman.
SNIGGERS. I can't go, Toffy. I can't go. I can't do it. [*He goes.*]
VOICE. Meestaire Arnold Everett Scott-Fortescue, late Esquire, Able Seaman.
THE TOFF. I did not foresee it. [*Exit.*]

[THE CURTAIN.]

THE TWILIGHT SAINT

By

STARK YOUNG

Stark Young, dramatist and critic, the author of *The Twilight Saint,* was born in Como, Mississippi, on October 11, 1881. He was graduated from the university of his native state and a year later took his master's degree at Columbia University. From 1907 to 1915 he taught at the University of Texas, and from 1915 to 1921 he was professor of English at Amherst College. His travels have taken him to Greece, and to Spain, and to Italy where he has lingered, making a special study of the native drama.

The text of *The Twilight Saint* has undergone revision by the author since its first appearance. It was acted in 1918 with *Madretta,* another of the author's plays, at the dramatic school of the Carnegie Institute of Technology in Pittsburgh, under the direction of Thomas Wood Stevens. The author writes: " The only instruction I should like to propose is that the actor of St. Francis keep him very simple, not get him moralizing and long-faced. In Egan's book on St. Francis [1] there is a picture of the preaching to the birds in which Boutet de Monvel shows a Tuscan type that is my idea of the man simplified." The play itself suggests charming by-ways of literature that lead in one direction perhaps to Hewlett's *Earthwork Out of Tuscany* and Josephine Preston Peabody's *The Wolf of Gubbio,* and in another possibly to the Saint's own *Little Flowers,* and *Canticle to the Sun.*

[1] Maurice F. Egan, *Everybody's St. Francis,* with pictures by M. Boutet de Monvel, New York, 1912.

THE TWILIGHT SAINT

CHARACTERS

GUIDO, *the husband, a young poet.*
LISETTA, *his wife.*
PIA, *a neighbor woman.*
ST. FRANCIS OF ASSISI.

In the year 1215 A.D.

A room in GUIDO'S *house, on a hillside near Bevagna. It is a poor apartment, clumsily kept. On your left near the front is a bed; on the floor by the bed lie scattered pages of manuscript. A table littered with manuscripts and crockery stands against the back wall of the room to the right. On the right hand wall is a big fireplace with copper vessels and brass. A bench sits by the fireplace and several stools about the room. On the stone flags two sheepskins are spread.*

Through the open door in the middle of the back wall rises the slope of a hill, green with spring and starred with flowers. A stream is visible through the grass and the drowsy sound of the water fills the air. The late yellow sunlight falls through a window over the bed like gilding and floods the hill without.

LISETTA *lies on the bed, still, her eyes closed.* PIA *sits on the ingle bench, halfway in the great fireplace, shelling peas. She is a little peasant woman with a kerchief on her head and a wrinkled face as brown as a nut.*
GUIDO *sits at the table, his face to the wall, his chin on his palm.*
PIA.
    Guido, Guido, thou hast not spoke this hour,
    Nor read one word nor written aught. Dear Lord,

    The lion on the palace at Assisi
    Sits not more still in stone! Guido, look thou!
GUIDO [*turning round without looking at her*].
    Yes, old Pia, good neighbor.
PIA.
    Yes, old Pia! Guido, grieve not so much,
    Lisetta will be well before the spring
    Comes round again.
GUIDO.
    Yes, Lisetta will be well perhaps. God grant!
PIA.
    Well, what then?
GUIDO.
    'Tis not only of her I think, Pia, here am I
    Shut in this house from month to month a nurse;
    Here lies she sick, this child, and may not stir;
    And I, lacking due means to hire, must serve
    The house; while my best self, my soul, my art,
    Rust. My soul is scorched with holy thirst,
    My temples throb, my veins run fire; but yet,
    For all my dim distress and vague desire,
    No word, no single song, no verse, has come—
    O Blessed God!—stifled with creature needs,
    And with necessity about my throat!
PIA.
    Thy corner is too hot, the glaring sun
    Is yet on the wall.
GUIDO.
    'Tis not that sun that maddens me, O Pia!
    Can you not see me shrunk? Have you not heard
    That other Guido of Perugia
    How he is grown? How lately at the feast
    That Ugolino, the great cardinal,
    Spread at Assisi Easter night, Guido
    Read certain of his verses and declaimed
    Pages of cursed sonnets to the guests.
PIA.
    Young Guido of Perugia, thy friend?
GUIDO.
    Yea. And when he ended, came the Duke
    Down from the dais to kiss that Guido's hand

THE TWILIGHT SAINT

    Humbly, and said that poesy was king.
PIA.
    Madonna, kissed by the Duke!
GUIDO.
    And I, O God, I might have honor too
    Could I but break this prison where I drudge!
PIA.
    Speak low, her sleep is light. Her road is hard
    As well as thine. For all this year, since thou
    Didst bring her to Rieto here to us,
    Hath she lain on her bed, broken with pain,
    This child that is thy wife and loveth thee.
GUIDO.
    Aye, yes, 'tis true, she loveth me, she loveth me,
    And I love her. 'Tis worse—add grief to care,
    And Poesy fares worse.
PIA.
    And she is grown most pale and still of late.
GUIDO.
    Look, Pia, how she lieth there like death,
    That far-off patience on her face. Now, now,
    Surely I needs must make a song! And yet
    I may not; ashes and floor-sweeping clog
    My soul within me!
PIA.
    Nay, let thy dreams pass. Look thou, how pale!
    Dear Lord, how blue her little veins do shine!
GUIDO.
    Thou art most kind, good neighbor, to come here
    Helping our house. And it is very strange
    That when we are so kind we cannot know
    The heart also. For in my soul I hear
    A bell summoning me always—
PIA.
    If I should stew in milk the peas, maybe—
    Do you think the child would eat it?
GUIDO.
    For thy world is not my world, kind old friend.
PIA.
    Why do you not walk, Guido, for a while,
    I have an hour yet.

GUIDO.
  Then I will go, Pia. But not for long,
  I will come back soon enough to my chores, be sure;
  Mine is a short tether.
[*He goes out.* LISETTA *on the bed opens her eyes.*]
LISETTA.
  Pia.
PIA.
  Yes, dear child.
LISETTA.
  Pia, turn my pillow, I am stifled.
PIA.
  There! Thou hast slept well?
LISETTA.
  I have not slept.
PIA.
  Holy Virgin, thou hast not slept!
LISETTA.
  Pia, think you I did not know? This month
  I scarce have slept for thinking on his lot.
  I read his fighting soul. Where are his songs,
  The great renown that waited him? Down, down,
  Struck by the self-same hand that shattered me.
  I listen night on night and hear him moan
  In his sleep—
PIA.
  It is his love for thee, Lisetta.
LISETTA.
  The padre from the village hemmed and said
  That God had sent me and my sickness here
  For Guido's cross to bear, his scourge. They thought
  I slept—
PIA.
  Thou hast dreamed this, he loveth thee, Lisetta.
LISETTA.
  Yea, loveth me somewhat but glory more.
  And I would have it so. O Mother of God,
  When wilt thou send me death? O Blessed Mother,
  I have lain so still!
PIA.
  Beware, Lisetta, tempt not God!

THE TWILIGHT SAINT

LISETTA.
Death is the sister of all them that weep, Pia.
PIA.
Child, child, try thou to sleep.
LISETTA.
For thy sake will I try.
PIA.
Aye, sleep now. I will smooth thy bed.
[PIA *begins to draw up the covers smooth. She stops suddenly to listen.*]
Hist!
LISETTA.
What, good Pia?
PIA.
Footsteps. Look, it is a monk.
[FRANCIS OF ASSISI *comes to the door.*]
FRANCIS.
I have not eaten food this day. Hast thou
Somewhat that I may eat?
PIA.
Alas, poor brother, sit thee here; there's bread
And cheese and lentils, eat thy store. Poor 'tis,
But given in His name.
FRANCIS.
I will eat then and bless thee.
PIA.
He taketh but a crust!
FRANCIS.
It is enough. He that hath eaten long
The bread of the heart hath little hunger in him.
PIA.
Sit thou and rest, poor soul.
FRANCIS.
Nay, I must go on. My daughter, child,
Thou sleepest not for all thy lowered lids.
Tears quiver on thy lashes, hast thou pain?
LISETTA.
The tears of women even in dreams may fall,
Good brother. Wilt thou not bide?
FRANCIS.
I must fare on.

LISETTA.
　　Aye, aye, the world lies open to thy hand,
　　But unto me this twelvemonth is a death.
　　The flesh is dead, and dying lies my soul,
　　Shrunk like a flower in my fevered hand.
FRANCIS [*he goes over and stands beside the bed*].
　　My dear.
LISETTA.
　　I may not see the stars rise on the hills,
　　Nor tend the flocks at even, nor rise to do
　　Aught of the small sweet round of duties owed
　　To him I love; but lie a burden to him,
　　Calling on death who heareth not.
FRANCIS.
　　My life hath given me words for thee to hear.
LISETTA.
　　Surely thy life is peace.
FRANCIS.
　　There is a life larger than life, that dwells
　　Invisible from all; whose lack alone
　　Is death. There in thy soul the stars may rise,
　　And at the even the gentle thoughts return
　　To flock the quiet pastures of the mind;
　　And in the large heart love is all thou owest
　　For service unto God and thy Beloved.
LISETTA.
　　Little Brother!
FRANCIS.
　　May you have God's peace, dear friends. Farewell.
[*He goes out.* PIA *stands a moment wiping her eyes, then returns to shelling the peas. There is a silence for a while.*]
PIA.
　　Why dost thou look so long upon the door?
LISETTA.
　　Pia, the spring smiles on the tender grass,
　　Surely the sun is brighter where he stood.
PIA.
　　'Tis a glaring sun for twilight.
LISETTA.
　　Pia, 'twill be the gentlest of all eves.

THE TWILIGHT SAINT

Surely God sent the brother for my need,
To give His peace.
PIA.
Aye, and my old heart ripens at his words
Like apples in the sun. 'Tis a sweet monk.
LISETTA.
Who is he, think you?
PIA.
One of the Little Poor Men, by his brown.
They are too thin, these brothers, and do lack
Stomach for life. [*She returns to the peas.*] Mark, oh,
   'tis merry now
To see the little beggars from their pods
Popping like schoolboys from their shoes in spring!
The season hath been so fine and dry this year
My peas are smaller and must have more work.
Well, well, labor is good, and things made scarce
Are better loved.
LISETTA.
Pia, thou art a good woman.
PIA.
Child, do not make me cry. 'Tis thy pure heart
Deceives thee. Stubborn I am and full of sloth,
And a wicked old thing.
LISETTA.
I would not grieve thee. Pia, 'twas my love
That sees thy goodness better than thyself.
PIA [*hanging the kettle of peas over the coals*].
Lisetta, I see the sky at the chimney top.
[PIA *begins to sing in her sweet, old, cracked voice, as she stirs the pot:*]

> *Firefly, firefly, come from the shadows,*
> *Twilight is falling over the meadows,*
> *Burn, little garden lamps, flicker and shimmer,*
> *Shine, little meadow stars, twinkle and glimmer,*
> *Firefly, firefly, shine, shine!*

LISETTA.
   Pia.
PIA.
   Yes.

LISETTA.
   Pia, come near me here. [PIA *kneels by the bed.*] Can
      you not see
   How much I love? If I could only speak
   To him or he to me, Guido, my love!
PIA.
   Surely he is beside thee often.
LISETTA.
   His hand is near, but not his heart.
PIA.
   Nay, child, 'tis Guido's way. He speaks but little.
   When I speak to him look what he says,
   " Yes, good Pia," 'tis not much.
LISETTA.
   Aye, tell me not. On winter nights I lay
   Hearing the tree limbs rattle there like hail,
   And from the corner eaves the dropping rain
   Like big dogs lapping all about—and he
   Spoke not to me. He sat beside his taper
   But never a line wrote down. Once I had words,
   Bright dreams, that shone through him, the same fire shone
   Through both, his songs were mine!
PIA.
   Yes, thine—rest thee, rest thee!
LISETTA.
   But more his, Pia, more his!
PIA.
   Aye, his. Wilt thou not eat the broth?
LISETTA.
   Not now, good Pia, 'tis not for food I die.
   'Tis not for food.
PIA.
   Yet thou must eat.
LISETTA.
   Wilt thou not read one song of these to me?
PIA.
   Close then thine eyes and rest.

[LISETTA *closes her eyes. A shepherd's pipe far-off and faint
   begins to play; from this on to the end of the play you
   can hear the shepherd's pipe.* PIA *takes up at random a*

sheet of the manuscripts. *She sighs a great sigh, and begins to mimic* LISETTA'S *voice.*]
  THE BALLAD OF THE RUNNING WATER
   O music locked amid the stones,
    Beside the—amid the—
LISETTA.
Read on—and thou hast told me day by day
Thou couldst not read.
PIA.
I read from hearing thee from day to day
Repeat the verses.
LISETTA.
Fie! Give them to me here.
[*She takes the paper and holds it in her hands on her breast, and reads without looking at it.*]
   O music locked amid the stones,
    My love hath spoken like to thee,
Pia, think you—Pia, do you not hear
The mowers and the reapers in the fields
Singing the evening song, and the twilight pipes?
The twilight is the hour when hearts break!
How many lonely twilights will there be
Ere God will spare me?
PIA [*kneeling*].
Hush, child, hush, darling!
[LISETTA *turns her face to the window by the bed.* PIA *strokes her hand and sings softly:*]
   Firefly, firefly, come from the shadows—
There!—he is coming now, I hear his steps
Upon the gravel road. Good-night, sweet child,
I'll get me home.
LISETTA.
Pia, good-night once more.
[PIA *slips away.* GUIDO *enters softly. The twilight is gone and the moon falls through the window over the bed. The hill outside is bright with moonlight.*]
GUIDO [*softly*].
Asleep, Lisetta?
LISETTA.
Guido! Ah, I have need of naught, Guido.
Thou needst not leave yet the pleasant air.

GUIDO.
  Lisetta, my love, I have been long from thee.
LISETTA.
  Let not that trouble thee, my needs are few,
  And Pia is most kind.
GUIDO.
  So little I may do.
LISETTA.
  Thou hast already served to weariness.

[*He kneels beside her bed.*]

GUIDO.
  My love, I have been long from thee, but now
  I will not leave thee any more. Oh, God,
  Let these kisses tell my heart to her.
LISETTA.
  Guido, my love, perhaps I dream of thee!
  Perhaps God sends a dream to solace me.
GUIDO.
  Along the stream I went and where it crossed
  Bevagna road—where the chestnut grows, thou knowest—
  Lisetta, I saw him.
LISETTA.
  Yes, yes, I know, whom sawest thou?
GUIDO.
  The brother, Francis of Assisi.
LISETTA.
  Guido, sawest thou him?
GUIDO.
  Aye, him. There had he stopped to rest, being spent;
  And round him came the birds, beating their wings
  Upon his cloak and lighting on his arm.
  I saw him smile on them and heard him speak!
  "My brother birds, little brothers, ye should love God
  Who gave you your wings and your bright songs and spread
  The soft air for you." He stroked their necks
  And blessed them. And then I saw his eyes.
  "Father," I cried, "speak thou to me, I faint
  Beside my way!"
LISETTA.
  Aye, and he said? Guido, what said he?

GUIDO.
"Thou art as one that lieth at the gate
Of Paradise and entereth not. For God
Hath given thee thy soul for its own life,
And not for glory among men."
LISETTA.
Guido!
GUIDO.
Lisetta, from his kind eyes I drank, and knew
How God had magnified my soul through him,
And sent me peace. And I returned to thee;
For here in thee have I my glory.
LISETTA.
Guido, the old spring comes back again. And now
I may speak. Guido, look through my window vines there
Where the stars rise. O Love, I have not slept
For lacking thee. And often have I seen
The moonlight lie like sleep upon the hill,
And in the garden of the sky the moon
Drift like a blown rose, Guido, and yet
I might not speak.
GUIDO.
Thou art my saint and shrine!
LISETTA.
Now shall my dream become thy song again,
And the long twilight be more sweet, Guido!
GUIDO.
I pray thee rest thee now and sleep. Good-night.
My full heart breaks in song; and I will sit
Hearing the blessed saints within my soul,
And will not stir from thee lest thou shouldst wake
When I might not be near to serve thy need.
[*The shepherd pipe far-off and faint is heard playing.*]

[THE CURTAIN.]

THE MASQUE OF THE TWO STRANGERS

By

LADY ALIX EGERTON

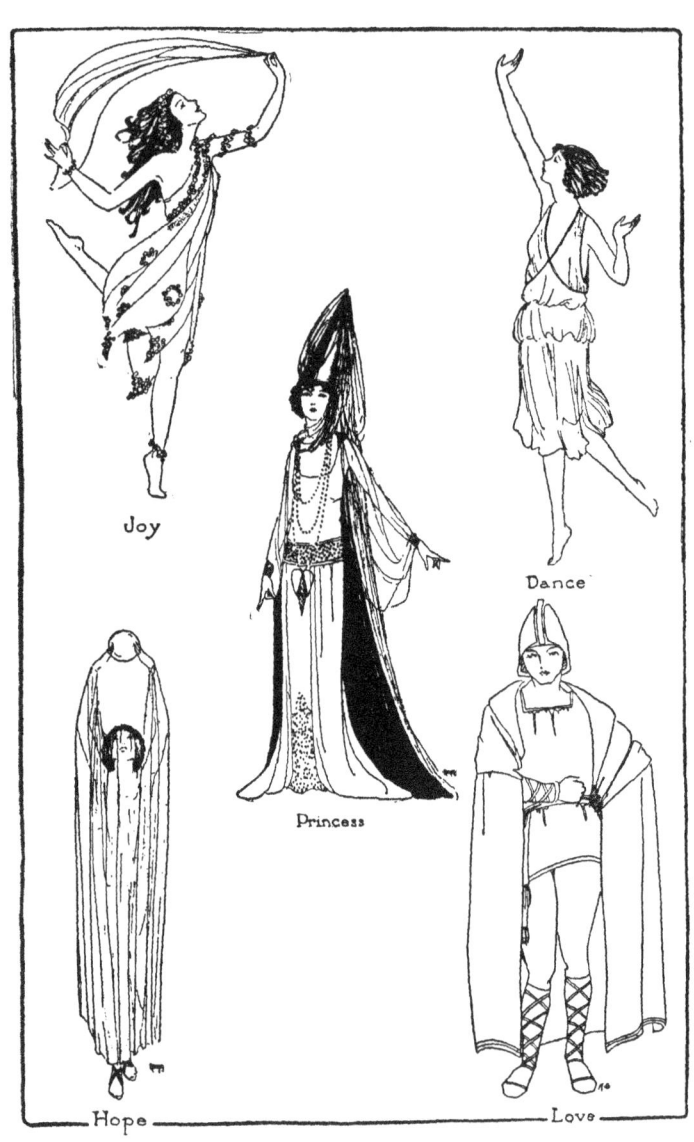

Costumes for *The Masque of the Two Strangers* designed at the Washington Irving High School.

Between the Lady Alice Egerton, who acted in the masque of *Comus,* which Milton composed for presentation before John, earl of Bridgewater, then President of Wales, and the Lady Alix Egerton, author of *The Masque of the Two Strangers,* lie three hundred years; but throughout these centuries the descendants of the first earl of Bridgewater have cherished consistently the great traditions of English literature. The family has owned for many generations the Ellesmere Chaucer and the Bridgewater manuscript of *Comus,* both of which have recently been edited by the twentieth century Lady Alix Egerton.

Her *The Masque of the Two Strangers* here reprinted was given at the Washington Irving High School in March, 1921. The designs for the costumes used in this production are here illustrated. The following notes will help the reader to reconstruct the costumes from the pictures:

I. *The Princess*
   White soft material.
   Spangled trimming.
   Mantle of blue.
   Veil of blue net.
   Hennin (head dress) in silver.

II. *Hope*
   Glass ball.
   Lavender under slip.
   Veil of rose pink.

III. *Joy*
   Draping of orange yellow.
   Flowers of various colors.
   Vermilion scarf.

IV. *Love*
   Long, full cape of deep purple;
      cowl falling back.
   Cerise costume.
   Silver surcoat and helmet.

V. *Laughter*
   Yellow and black.
   Trimming of bells.

VI. *Poetry*
   Light green with silver;
      paper design on border.

VII. *Song*
   Robe dyed in rainbow hues.
   Silver wings.
VIII. *Dance*
   Vermilion.
IX. *Power*
   Bright blue.
   Gems.
   Gilt headpiece jeweled.
   Mantle and sash of purple.
X. *Fame*
   Robe of deep green.
   Gold border.
   Laurel leaves on gold crown.
XI. *Riches*
   Knight's close-fitting short coat of henna.
   (Flannel dyed to represent felt or leather.)
   Gold lacings; gold paper design on coat;
      gold and henna helmet.
XII. *Service*
   Soft yellow shaded to brown at bottom
      of skirt and sleeves.
   Front panel of dark green forming part
      of head drapery.
XIII. *Sorrow*
   Gray.
XIV. *Herald*
   Dark red and gold.

PROLOGUE
[*Enter a* JESTER.]

Good people, of your gentle courtesy,
I pray your patience now, and list to me.
Before you I will here present to-day
A story told in the medieval way.
Now sad—now merry—here and there a song,
While through it all a meaning runs along.
On this side is the Court of Youth where dwells
A Princess who is held by magic spells.
On that is the vast Otherworld from whence
The great Immortals come for her defense.
Betwixt the greater and the lesser Power,
That duel that goes on from hour to hour
Throughout the ages, I would have you see
Depicted in this passing phantasy.
   [*Music of Masque begins.*]
The players come and I had best away;
I'll come back afterwards and end my say.

THE MASQUE OF THE TWO STRANGERS *

CHARACTERS

Joy.	A Herald.
Laughter.	Princess Douce-Cœur.
Song.	Sorrow.
Dance.	Fame.
Service.	Riches.
Poetry.	Power.
Hope.	Love.

Joy *and* Laughter *run in laughing, chase each other round the stage and pelt each other with flowers.*

Laughter [*flinging herself on the ground, breathless*].
   Ah, it is good to run and laugh again.
   I am so weary of these somber days.
Joy.
   And I of sitting silent in the house.
   We used before to have such merry games,
   Now Douce-cœur will not even smile.
Laughter [*mysteriously*].
   She says that she will never laugh again.
Joy.
   And when I called to her to come and play
   At hide-and-seek down in the rose-garden,
   She said her playing days were over now.
Laughter.
   It seems so strange. Only a while ago
   We played at ball across the laurel hedge,
   And when the ball fell in the fountain-court
   And rolled into the water, floating out

---

* I am indebted to Miss Italia Conti for the original scenario of the Masque, and to former Editors of *Vanity Fair* and *The Crown* for permission to reprint the two songs which were published in their journals.—Alix Egerton.

THE MASQUE OF THE TWO STRANGERS

To where the lilies lay half closed in sleep,
'Twas she who went in barefoot, with her dress
Kilted above her knees, and laughed to feel
The flicking of the golden fishes' tails.
She said her pink toes looked like coral shells,
And splashed the water just to see it shine
Like diamonds in the sun upon my hair.
A while ago she was a child with us.

JOY [*sighs*].
Laughter, I like not living at the Court. [*Starting.*]
Someone is coming.

[*They run and hide behind a seat.* SONG *enters, humming to herself and twisting flowers into a garland.* JOY *and* LAUGHTER *spring out upon her and catch hold of her hands one on each side.*]

LAUGHTER.   Why, 'tis only Song.
For three days now we have not heard thy voice.

SONG.
No, Douce-cœur says life is too sad for songs.
Yet music is a gift of the high gods
And like the birds I sing or I must die.

JOY [*coaxingly*].
Sing us a ballad while we are alone.
Old Service is asleep beside the well
And will not hear thee.

SONG [*sitting on the seat*].
Well, what shall I sing?
How would you like " All on an April Day? "

JOY [*clapping her hands*].
About the knight who rode to Amiens Town?

LAUGHTER.
Then will we sing the refrain, Joy and I.

SONG [*begins very softly, and, forgetting, sings louder to the end*].

> *A lover rode to Amiens town*
>   (*All on an April day*);
> *He looked not up, he looked not down*
> *But fixed his gaze on Amiens town*
>   (*Sing hey!—the Lover's Way*).

The cuckoo sang above his head
      (All on an April day);
The blossoming trees were white and red,
Yet still he never turned his head
      (Sing hey!—the Lover's Way).

The dappled grass with daisies strewn
      (All on an April day)
Was trodden by his horse's shoon;
He heeded not those daisies strewn
      (Sing hey!—the Lover's Way).

He wore a ragged surcoat green
      (All on an April day)
But no device thereon was seen,
Nor blazon on that surcoat green
      (Sing hey!—the Lover's Way).

He rode in by the Eastern Gate
      (All on an April day);
Though poor and mean was his estate
Kings have gone through that Eastern Gate
      (Sing hey!—the Lover's Way).

He stood by the Cathedral door
      (All on an April day)
And watched of ladies fair a score
Pass in through the Cathedral door
      (Sing hey!—the Lover's Way).

A knot of ribbon at his feet
      (All on an April day)
And one swift smile, such radiance sweet
Fell with the ribbon at his feet
      (Sing hey!—the Lover's Way).

He hid the token in his breast
      (All on an April day)
Yet to his lips full oft he prest
The ribbon hidden in his breast
      (Sing hey!—the Lover's Way).

A lover rode to Amiens town
      (All on an April day),

THE MASQUE OF THE TWO STRANGERS

A beggar wore a starry crown
And a King rode out of Amiens town
(Sing hey!—the Lover's Way).

[*After the 4th verse enter* DANCE, *who dances through the remaining verses.*]

[*Enter* SERVICE *hurriedly.*]

SERVICE. How now, what noise is this? Thou knowest, Song, thy voice may not be heard at all, and ye children too, ye will get sent away. Sure, that ye will. Here am I sent packing off to seek for the Wise Woman Poetry. The heralds too are up and down the land with proclamations. Go in, go in; Douce-cœur is wandering with the Gray Stranger in the garden, and when she comes, may want your company.

[*Enter* POETRY.]

POETRY.
  I am the mouthpiece of the Eternal Gods,
  And in my voice, that down the ages rings,
  Men hear the ceaseless heart-beats of the world.
  Without me all that has been would have died
  And lain forgotten in a silent grave.
  The present echoes what I once have sung,
  The future holds the secrets I have read.

SERVICE. Hail, and well met! I was but starting forth to seek thee. Thou who hast the wisdom of all time mayst help us in our hour of need; an evil spell has been cast about the Princess, and how it is to be broken, none of us know.

POETRY.
  Good Service, tell me all; for I presume,
  Despite the tender care which through her life
  Has shielded Douce-cœur like a ring of steel,
  That to her side some foe has won his way
  And dimmed the peaceful mirror of her soul.

SERVICE. Yea, truly, one evening as the sun was setting a woman clad in long gray robes entered the Palace gates and meeting the Princess on the terrace walk led her down among the cypresses. They sat long together in the twilight and ever since Douce-cœur is changed. No smile curves her lips, the sunlight is gone from her face, and she goes always with veiled head, and sad unseeing eyes. I heard but now her companions are to be sent away. Joy, Laughter, Song and Dance, all to be banished. This is the Gray Woman's doing, but why, no man can say.

POETRY.
  The stranger in gray robes of whom ye speak
  Is Sorrow's self, whose other name is Pain.
  She comes, and when she comes none may resist.
  Against her none have power to bar their gates.
  Ye who have always cherishèd Douce-cœur
  And guarded her from knowledge of the World,
  Have left her ignorance a prey to pain.
  Thus night has fallen on a tender heart
  That never saw the shadows for the sun.
  Queen Sorrow, who can hide the stars of heaven,
  Has torn the golden veil from top to hem,
  And in the outer darkness Douce-cœur stands,
  Seeing no rift to tell of light eclipsed,
  Knowing no key to all the mystery.

SERVICE. The King, her father, has sent proclamations forth that whoso can bring back the smiles to Douce-cœur's lips, the sunshine to her face, whoso can win her from the Gray Woman's side, on him shall half the kingdom be bestowed and Douce-cœur's hand in marriage. The Heralds have gone crying this abroad, and we have word three suitors are traveling here post-haste.

POETRY.
  I know not who these suitors chance to be
  But not by them may Sorrow be cast out.
  One only holds a mightier spell than hers,
  And I will send my constant messenger
  To seek him to the ends of all the Earth.
  Come to me, Child, who holdst Eternal Youth.

      [*Enter* HOPE.]

HOPE. Didst call me, Poetry?
POETRY.   Yea, child of my Heart,
  Go out into the wilderness for me.
  Find me the Stranger in a Pilgrim's garb
  Around whose head the song birds pipe their lays,
  Beneath whose feet the withered flowers revive.

Say, "In the Court of Youth Queen Sorrow reigns
And shadows lie like night on Douce-cœur's heart."
HOPE.
In the great Court of Youth, Queen Sorrow reigns
And shadows lie like night on Douce-cœur's heart.
POETRY.
Bid him come hither. Haste thee on thy way.

[*Exit* HOPE. *Trumpet music. Herald heard off.* "*Oyez! Oyez! Oyez!*"]

SERVICE. Here comes the Herald!

[*Enter* HERALD *repeating* "*Oyez! Oyez! Oyez!*"]

HERALD [*facing audience*]. Know all whom it may concern throughout this realm, that as One has come and brought darkness on the Land, to all good people is this Proclamation made. Whoso can drive the Gray Woman forth, whoso can free the Princess Douce-cœur from her spell, whoso can bring back the sunshine to the Land, unto him will be given the half of the kingdom, and the Hand of the Princess Douce-cœur in marriage. Given on this day of June. Oyez! Oyez! Oyez!"

[*Exit* HERALD. "*Oyez! Oyez! Oyez!*" *dies away in the distance.*]

[*Music. Enter* JOY, LAUGHTER, SONG *and* DANCE, *followed by* PRINCESS DOUCE-CŒUR *and* SORROW.]

SORROW.
Ye children of the Court, your hour has struck.
Your doom of banishment has been pronounced,
For where I am there can ye never be.
SONG.
Douce-cœur, I pray thee hear me. Let me sing
One of the old songs that we loved—may be
The memory of those happy days will rise
And lift the weight of sadness from thy face.
POETRY.
Douce-cœur, I charge thee, listen. All the past
Of Childhood calls thee in the voice of Song.
DOUCE-CŒUR.
Sing if thou wilt. Those days were long ago.

Song.

> I stood beside the lilac bush
>   While all its blossoms rained on me,
> I watched the white wraith of a moon
>   Turn to pale gold above the sea.
>
> I held a wand of almond bough
>   And waved it three times circlewise,
> I whispered words of faery lore
>   With beating heart and close shut eyes.
>
> I oped them on a forest scene
>   Of summer-land; the open glade
> Lay shining like a tourmaline
>   Set in a ring of duller jade.
>
> I saw three queens with shining crowns
>   Go riding by on palfreys gray;
> I saw three knights that followed close,
>   And dreams were in their eyes that day.
>
> I saw a minstrel with his harp,
>   His cloak was green and patched and torn;
> I saw a hunter with his bow,
>   I heard the winding of his horn.
>
> I saw a bush of lavender
>   With clouds of fluttering butterflies,
> Then I looked backward to the earth
>   And broke my faery spell with sighs.

Douce-cœur.
 I cannot bear thy music. In my heart
No answering chords respond. The past is dead.
I hear the tears of thousands in thy voice.
 When Sorrow speaks—I hear no tones but hers.
Sorrow.
 No, thou art mine, Princess. I hold thee fast.
Poetry.
 Douce-cœur, I bid thee raise thy heavy eyes.
Dance is the eldest daughter of my heart.
Born when the rhythm of the stars was voiced,
The past and future meet alike in her.
Let her bring back the sunshine to thy face.

DANCE.
    With flying feet we chased the hours away.
    I used to make thee clap thy hands in glee
    And thought to go with thee along the years.
DOUCE-CŒUR.
    My feet are lead, but dance on if thou wilt,
    What can the future hold for me and thee?
      [*As the Dance ends, she cries:*]
    Ah, Sorrow, bid them cease and drive them hence.
    Send Joy and Laughter, Song and Dance away.
    Call Silence here who is thy foster-child.
    I am afraid of all this mocking world
    And fain would live alone, alone with thee.
SORROW.
    Go forth, go forth into the wilderness. Here is no room for ye.
    Go forth into the void that lies beyond. Here I in majesty
    Henceforth shall reign, veiling the sun and stars to all eternity.
    Go forth. Let wide-eyed Silence take the place ye occupied before
    Where flowers ye scattered he henceforth shall strew ashes upon the floor.
    Twilight shall fall upon this Court of Youth now and for evermore.
      [*Exeunt* SONG, DANCE, JOY, *and* LAUGHTER.]
POETRY.
    Douce-cœur, thine eyes are bound. Thou dost but see
    With vision warped by her who holds thy hand.
    I, who have watched the web of Life unfold
    And hold the secrets of a million lives,
    Can tell thee from the heights whereon I dwell,
    It is not thus that thou wilt help the world.
    Thou canst not right the wrong with further wrong.
    But now thine ears are dulled; thou wilt not hear
    What I might teach thee.

[*During this speech enter* HERALD *who speaks to* SERVICE. *Exit* HERALD.]

SERVICE. Three suitors, Fame, Riches, and Power are at the gate, Princess, and claim an audience. They have banished the Gray Woman from the side of others and seek to do this for thee. With them they bring charms that have before broken the spells of Sorrow; these are beyond price but each asks in exchange thy hand in marriage as promised in the proclamation cried by the heralds.

DOUCE-CŒUR [*turning to* SORROW].
 What must I do?
SORROW. Bid them approach, my child;
 It may be their rich gifts will pleasure thee.

[*Enter* HERALD *followed by* FAME.]

HERALD.
 Fame, Lord of the Marches of the East, salutes thee.

[*Exit* HERALD.]

FAME.
 Fame am I called, Princess. I bring thee this
 Crown of Unfading Leaves for which men pray
 And toil throughout their lives—unsatisfied.
 It shall be thine unsought. Grant me thy hand,
 And thou shalt live in glamour of high destiny.
 Thy name shall sound in honor through the world;
 Thy words shall set the hearts of men aflame.
 Let me but place the wreath about thy head,
 Thus shalt thou strike this lyre with deathless notes
 Which shall, vibrating through the fields of space,
 Ring on, and on, nor ever find a goal.
SORROW.
 Deaf are the ears on which thy phrases fall.
 With one so young what are thy spells to mine?
DOUCE-CŒUR.
 I see thy wreath of leaves, entwined with asps
 Whose forked tongues whisper "jealousy and hate."
 Thy harp is out of tune with Sorrow's voice.
POETRY.
 She is too tender for thine upward way.
 The solitude of those who follow thee
 Is not for her. Pass on, my lord, pass on.

[*Enter* HERALD, *followed by* RICHES.]

THE MASQUE OF THE TWO STRANGERS

Costumes for *The Masque of the Two Strangers* designed at the Washington Irving High School.

HERALD.
Riches, Lord of the Marches of the West, salutes thee.

[*Exit* HERALD.]

RICHES.
My name is Riches, and I offer thee
A store of wealth exhaustless as the sand.
This is the symbol of my opulence,
A casket in whose depths gold never fails.
Grant me thy hand, and thou, Princess, shalt gain
All that the world contains of happiness.
Thy palace shall be built of precious stones,
And thou shalt walk on rose-leaves every day.
Sorrow shall be forgotten in my arms,
Nothing shall be denied thee wealth can buy.
All things—all men yield to the touch of gold.

SORROW.
Blind are the eyes on which thy visions rise.
My spells have turned thy glories into dust.

DOUCE-CŒUR.
The gold thou offerest me is stained with blood;
Thy precious stones were won with tears and toil;
The sum of all thy wealth could not reflower
The arid wastes that Sorrow has laid bare.

POETRY.
She is too simple for thy promises;
To one who knows not Sister Poverty
Thy lures, my lord, appear as idle words.

[*Enter* HERALD, *followed by* POWER.]

HERALD.
Power, Lord of the Marches North and South, salutes thee

[*Exit* HERALD.]

POWER.
My name, Princess, is Power and this my gift.
My brothers brought thee fair renown and gold
With freedom from the spells that Sorrow weaves.
All these I offer thee. If thou accept,
Together we will sway men's destinies,
Together we may rule their hearts—their souls—

Together turn the very universe.
Our throne shall rise a monument of might,
Its steps shall mount from the green land of earth,
Its canopy shall scrape the stars of Heaven.
SORROW.
I have set that about her like a net
Thou canst not deal with. Never yet, O Power,
Hast thou been known to cut through cords of fear.
DOUCE-CŒUR.
I would not wield thy scepter for an hour.
The burden of its weight would bear me down.
POETRY.
She is too young, too gentle for the heights
Where thou wouldst raise her. Be content, my lords;
What ye have done is well, but One alone
Can break the spell, and he is at the gates.
Already Hope returns. He comes, he comes.

[*Enter* HOPE *running.*]

HOPE.
The stranger comes; he whom I went to seek.
FAME.
The Stranger comes whose music fills the world.
RICHES.
The Stranger comes, whose treasure gilds the world.
POWER.
The Stranger comes, whose scepter rules the world.
POETRY [*to* SORROW].
Now shall thy spell be broken. Dost thou hear
The measured footsteps of approaching Fate?
The one who comes clad in a Pilgrim's garb
Has ever proved thy silent conqueror.
SORROW.
I yield to him who is the greatest here,
But those who have not met me by the way
Can never know him as he may be known.
They only who have trod the dark abyss
May dare to stand upon the topmost height.
For they whose eyes were blindfold for awhile
Alone can bear that blaze of brilliant light.
Thus have I brought thee more than all thy Court.

Learn from his lips to see the world anew.
I drew that gray veil all about thy head
Thinking perchance to keep thee for my own,
But thou wert made for sunlight, not for gloom.
Thus do I leave thee. Fare thee well, Princess!

[*Enter* Love.]

Douce-cœur [*starts up and tries to hold* Sorrow *back*].
Ah, stay with me, thou art my only friend!

[Love *and* Sorrow *look at each other, she draws her veil across her face and exit.*]

Douce-cœur.
Who art thou, Stranger, in a pilgrim's guise
Who comest unattended, unannounced?
Love.
I may not tell thee that. Thou first must learn
Out of thine own heart to recall my name.
Douce-cœur.
Fame, Power, and Riches brought me costly gifts
Which I refused.
Love.   I come with empty hands.
Douce-cœur.
Thy coming caused Queen Sorrow to depart;
What right hast thou to drive my friends from me?
Love.
I came to bring thee swift deliverance,
She laid a spell upon thee which in time
Had turned thy heart to unresponsive stone.
Douce-cœur.
She brought me peace and sure oblivion
Of all this dark and weary world around.
Love.
Art thou so sure, Princess, the world is dark?
Douce-cœur.
So sure? Have I not heard the children weep?
Is not my heart torn with their piteous cries?
We live, and round us lies their sea of tears,
A mighty sea that could engulf a realm.
Love.
I met a Child outside thy Palace once.

His dress was ragged, but he smiled at me,
And in his hand he held a purple flower.
I knew it for the magic flower of Dream.
I asked him "Art thou happy?" and he said
"I'm mostly hungry; sometimes I am cold;
And there are stones and thorns that hurt my feet,
But while my Flower lives I am quite content.
And I have friends too, in the Palace there;
Laughter and Dance they come and play with me.
I met that Child to-day, Princess. His face
Was white and pinched, and down his baby cheeks
The tears were running, "See, my Flower has died,
And Dance and Laughter have been sent away.
Joy too is gone. Queen Sorrow reigns at Court."
Even the children now can play no more.
He never knew before the world was dark.
Art thou so sure, Princess, the Child was wrong?
DOUCE-CŒUR.
Have I not heard bereavèd mothers weep?
LOVE.
There thou dost touch a chord in ignorance.
Thou canst not guess the strength of Motherhood,
The hopes, the joys, the passionate regrets.
She who has borne her child close to her heart
Has lit a star in Heaven that lights her way.
I kneel by them in their Gethsemane
And teach them how to weave immortal wreaths
Out of the sweetest flowers of Memory;
For them the sun still shines behind the clouds,
Art thou so sure the world is wholly dark?
DOUCE-CŒUR.
There echo in my ears the groans of Toil,
Of those who labor on from year to year
Until they sink beneath their weary lot.
LOVE.
Toil is the destiny of man, Princess,
And none may question the Supreme Decree.
Perchance through toil alone man may redeem
A past that is forgotten. Who can tell?
And there is still some aftermath of joy
In labor well achieved, some dignity

In toil accomplished. If the way is hard
And seeming endless, those who seek for me
Will often find me singing at their side.
Mine is the Brotherhood of Sympathy.
But thou hast banished Song, in silence now
The toilers have to go upon their way.
Art thou so sure, it was all dark before?

DOUCE-CŒUR.
What light is there for those who strive and fail?

LOVE.
One only fails. He whom some term Success,
He who gives heart and soul and youth and strength
To an unworthy cause. Failure is he
Who sacrifices me before the world,
Who prostitutes the God in him for what
Will turn to dust and ashes in his hand.
'Tis he alone is outcast though he thinks
Himself the sun of all the universe.
To those, Princess, who striving seem to fail,
It is not failure, for none see the end,
And they who sigh are only those who seek
An earlier consummation than is just;
If they cling fast to me they still behold
The white star-flowers Hope plants about the world.
Who knows to what fair land rough seas may lead?

DOUCE-CŒUR.
Lo! over all I see the cruel hand
Of Death outstretched, certain and pitiless.

LOVE.
The hand of Death is full of tenderness.
He leads men through that dark mysterious gate—
That all must pass into another life—
To other lives that through the cycles bring
The souls of men upward from step to step,
Uniting those for ever who are one.
Death hushes them like children on his breast.
Setting his own smile on their silent lips—
That tender smile of strange triumphant peace.
Death is my Brother, and I say to thee,
Learn to know me, thou wilt not fear his hand.

DOUCE-CŒUR.
  Another hand is knocking at my heart
  Whose touch I know not, and I feel afraid—
  Afraid to listen. Yet I long to hear.
  Stranger, who art thou? Let me see thy face.
LOVE.
  Learn to know me and thou shalt nothing fear.
DOUCE-CŒUR.
  Who art thou? Let me look into thine eyes.
LOVE.
  Learn to know me and thou wilt find the Light.
DOUCE-CŒUR.
  Pilgrim, who art thou? Let me know thy name.
LOVE.
  Dost thou not know me, Douce-cœur?
DOUCE-CŒUR [*slowly*].
  Thou art Love!
LOVE.
  And dost thou know the meaning of my name?
  Tell me thou art not fearful any more.
DOUCE-CŒUR.
  The darkness that was bound about mine eyes
  Is falling from me. In the growing light
  The answer to Life's riddle is made clear.
  I seem to stand upon a height, caught up
  In ecstasy of rapture near the sun.
  The day is dawning; far before my eyes
  I see the earth spread out there like a map.
  Shadow and sunshine traveling on the road
  O'ertake each other, mingle—and are one.
FAME.
  O Love, all hail! What is my crown to thine?
  Thy music is the song of all the stars
  Which rings through every heart attune to thine.
RICHES.
  O Love, all hail! What is my wealth to thine?
  Thy treasures are the moons of happiness,
  Thy boundless gold the sunshine of the world.
POWER.
  O Love, all hail! Thine is the greater rule,

The force predominating. Thou alone
Art the unvanquished King who conquers all.
POETRY.
O Love, whose face is sought by all the world,
Bid her go forth out of her Palace gates
Into her kingdom that lies all around,
Teach her what means to use to right the wrong
And ease the burden man has laid on man.
My voice that once could rouse men's sleeping souls
Grows weary, and men often heed me not,
Turning deaf ears that will not hear my words;
'Tis thou alone canst wind that mystic horn
Which wakes alike the sleeping and the dead.
DOUCE-CŒUR.
O Love, I pray thee call the children back,
I am ashamed to think I drove them forth,
I erred in ignorance. Forgive me, lord.

[*Enter* JOY, LAUGHTER, SONG *and* DANCE.]

LOVE.
All ye who came to battle Sorrow's spell,
Be with her now. And ye who hold in fee
Her happy days, go with her through the years.
I all unseen will guide her destiny.
And when, Princess, I come again to thee,
A worshiper will follow in my train.
From other lips than mine thou then shalt learn
The sweetest and the tenderest tale of all.
MUSIC.
Now let us join with Song. In merry mirth
Draw to a fitting close our Interlude.
SONG.
Sorrow reigned her little day
Love has driven her far away
Brought the sunshine back to Court
Thus we end in merry sport.

[*Exeunt* ALL.]

EPILOGUE

[*Enter* JESTER.]

The Tale is over and their parts are done,
And Love again has proved the strongest one.
I wonder has it pleased you now to see
The oldest tale told thus in phantasy.
And let your answer be whate'er it may,
Whether your thumbs be up or down to-day
Will hurt not me. I did not write the play.

[THE CURTAIN.]

THE INTRUDER

By
MAURICE MAETERLINCK

Maurice Polydore Marie Bernard Maeterlinck, to give him his full baptismal name, was born in Ghent on August 29, 1862. He was sent to the Jesuit College de Sainte-Barbe, the institution which another great Belgian, Emile Verhaeren, also attended. In 1885, Maeterlinck entered the University of Ghent to study law, but his practice of this profession was confined to a scant year or two. Maeterlinck's chief interest in his college years seems to have been the modern movement in Belgian literature. But the frequency of his visits to Paris increased in the years between 1886 and 1896, and finally in the latter year he settled there.

The following word picture supplements the photographs of Maeterlinck that are so frequently reproduced in our magazines and newspapers: " Maeterlinck is easily described: a man of about five feet nine in height, inclined to be stout; silver hair lends distinction to the large round head and boyish fresh complexion; blue-gray eyes, now thoughtful, now merry, and an unaffected off-hand manner. The features are not cut, left rather ' in the rough,' as sculptors say, even the heavy jaw and chin are drowned in fat; the forehead bulges and the eyes lose color in the light and seem hard; still, an interesting and attractive personality."

Maeterlinck's fame rests on his poetry and his essays no less than on his plays. *L'Intruse, The Intruder,* reprinted here, belongs to the early years of his activity as a playwright. It was printed in 1890 in a Belgian periodical, *La Wallonie,* and was acted for the first time a year later at Paul Fort's Théâtre d'Art in Paris, at a performance given for the benefit of the poet, Paul Verlaine, and the painter, Paul Gauguin. Maeterlinck, though publishing volumes of essays from time to time, continues to write for the theatre.[1] In 1908 *The Blue Bird,* dramatizing the quest for Truth, one of the most popular of modern plays, was given for the first time in Moscow, to be followed ten years later by the première in New York of a

[1] For bibliography, see Jethro Bithell, *Life and Writings of Maurice Maeterlinck,* London and New York, 1913.

sequel, *The Betrothal,* similarly dramatizing the search for Beauty. In 1910 came his translation of *Macbeth* into French. A year later he was awarded the Nobel prize for literature.

The Intruder, the theme of which is the mysterious coming of death, is an illustration of one of Maeterlinck's pet theories in regard to the subject matter of the drama. He expresses it in this way in his famous essay on *The Tragic in Daily Life:* " An old man, seated in his armchair, waiting patiently with his lamp beside him—submitting with bent head to the presence of his soul and his destiny—motionless as he is, does yet live in reality a deeper, more human, more universal life than . . . the captain who conquers in battle." To plays based on this theory has been given the name " static drama." *The Intruder* illustrates also Maeterlinck's use of symbols. The Grandfather in the play is blind, for instance; blind characters in Maeterlinck's plays are symbols of the spiritual blindness of the human race; the gardener sharpening his scythe stands for death; the mysterious quenching of the lamp—it may have gone out because there was no oil in it—signifies the going out of life.

The problem in the staging of this play is the " creation of a mood or atmosphere, rather than the unfolding of an action." One of the settings used in this country is here reproduced. It was designed for the Arts & Crafts Theatre of Detroit. Sheldon Cheney, whose description of Sam Hume's plastic units for the stage of this Little Theatre is given in the Introduction on page xxxi, has described the rearrangement of this equipment and the additions that can be made to it for the production of this play as follows: " For Maeterlinck's *The Intruder,* which demanded a room in an old château, one important addition was made, a flat with a door. At the left was the arch, then a pylon and curtain, and then the Gothic window with practicable casements added. The rest of the back wall was made up of the new door-piece flanked by curtains, while the third wall consisted of two pylons and curtains. Stairs and platforms were utilized before the window and under the arch. A small two-stair unit was added, leading to the new door. This arrangement afforded exactly that suggestion of spaciousness and mystery for which the play calls." When the play was given at the Independent Theatre in London in 1895, it was played behind a blue gauze curtain.

On one of Maeterlinck's visits to London, he was taken by

Alfred Sutro, the dramatist, to call on Barrie in his flat at the Adelphi. Maeterlinck was asked to write his name on the whitewashed wall of Barrie's studio. He did so and added above the signature: *"Au père de Peter Pan, et au grandpère de L'Oiseau Bleu."*

THE INTRUDER

CHARACTERS

THE THREE DAUGHTERS.
THE GRANDFATHER.
THE FATHER.
THE UNCLE.
THE SERVANT.

A dimly lighted room in an old country-house. A door on the right, a door on the left, and a small concealed door in a corner. At the back, stained-glass windows, in which the color green predominates, and a glass door opening on to a terrace. A Dutch clock in one corner. A lamp lighted.

THE THREE DAUGHTERS. Come here, grandfather. Sit down under the lamp.

THE GRANDFATHER. There does not seem to me to be much light here.

THE FATHER. Shall we go on to the terrace, or stay in this room?

THE UNCLE. Would it not be better to stay here? It has rained the whole week, and the nights are damp and cold.

THE ELDEST DAUGHTER. Still the stars are shining.

THE UNCLE. Ah! stars—that's nothing.

THE GRANDFATHER. We had better stay here. One never knows what may happen.

THE FATHER. There is no longer any cause for anxiety. The danger is past, and she is saved. . . .

THE GRANDFATHER. I fancy she is not going on well. . . .

THE FATHER. Why do you say that?

THE GRANDFATHER. I have heard her speak.

THE FATHER. But the doctors assure us we may be easy. . . .

THE UNCLE. You know quite well that your father-in-law likes to alarm us needlessly.

Courtesy of Theatre Arts Magazine

Setting for *The Intruder* composed of plastic units designed by Sam Hume.

THE INTRUDER

THE GRANDFATHER. I don't look at these things as you others do.

THE UNCLE. You ought to rely on us, then, who can see. She looked very well this afternoon. She is sleeping quietly now; and we are not going to spoil, without any reason, the first comfortable evening that luck has thrown in our way. . . . It seems to me we have a perfect right to be easy, and even to laugh a little, this evening, without apprehension.

THE FATHER. That's true; this is the first time I have felt at home with my family since this terrible confinement.

THE UNCLE. When once illness has come into a house, it is as though a stranger had forced himself into the family circle.

THE FATHER. And then you understood, too, that you should count on no one outside the family.

THE UNCLE. You are quite right.

THE GRANDFATHER. Why could I not see my poor daughter to-day?

THE UNCLE. You know quite well—the doctor forbade it.

THE GRANDFATHER. I do not know what to think. . . .

THE UNCLE. It is absurd to worry.

THE GRANDFATHER [*pointing to the door on the left*]. She cannot hear us?

THE FATHER. We shall not talk too loud; besides, the door is very thick, and the Sister of Mercy is with her, and she is sure to warn us if we are making too much noise.

THE GRANDFATHER [*pointing to the door on the right*]. He cannot hear us?

THE FATHER. No, no.

THE GRANDFATHER. He is asleep?

THE FATHER. I suppose so.

THE GRANDFATHER. Someone had better go and see.

THE UNCLE. The little one would cause *me* more anxiety than your wife. It is now several weeks since he was born, and he has scarcely stirred. He has not cried once all the time! He is like a wax doll.

THE GRANDFATHER. I think he will be deaf—dumb too, perhaps—the usual result of a marriage between cousins. . . . [*A reproving silence.*]

THE FATHER. I could almost wish him ill for the suffering he has caused his mother.

THE UNCLE. Do be reasonable; it is not the poor little thing's fault. He is quite alone in the room?

THE FATHER. Yes; the doctor does not wish him to stay in his mother's room any longer.

THE UNCLE. But the nurse is with him?

THE FATHER. No; she has gone to rest a little; she has well deserved it these last few days. Ursula, just go and see if he is asleep.

THE ELDEST DAUGHTER. Yes, father. [THE THREE SISTERS *get up, and go into the room on the right, hand in hand.*]

THE FATHER. When will your sister come?

THE UNCLE. I think she will come about nine.

THE FATHER. It is past nine. I hope she will come this evening, my wife is so anxious to see her.

THE UNCLE. She is certain to come. This will be the first time she has been here?

THE FATHER. She has never been into the house.

THE UNCLE. It is very difficult for her to leave her convent.

THE FATHER. Will she be alone?

THE UNCLE. I expect one of the nuns will come with her. They are not allowed to go out alone.

THE FATHER. But she is the Superior.

THE UNCLE. The rule is the same for all.

THE GRANDFATHER. Do you not feel anxious?

THE UNCLE. Why should we feel anxious? What's the good of harping on that? There is nothing more to fear.

THE GRANDFATHER. Your sister is older than you?

THE UNCLE. She is the eldest of us all.

THE GRANDFATHER. I do not know what ails me; I feel uneasy. I wish your sister were here.

THE UNCLE. She will come; she promised to.

THE GRANDFATHER. I wish this evening were over! [THE THREE DAUGHTERS *come in again.*]

THE FATHER. He is asleep?

THE ELDEST DAUGHTER. Yes, father; very sound.

THE UNCLE. What shall we do while we are waiting?

THE GRANDFATHER. Waiting for what?

THE UNCLE. Waiting for our sister.

THE FATHER. You see nothing coming, Ursula?

THE ELDEST DAUGHTER [*at the window*]. Nothing, father.

THE FATHER. Not in the avenue? Can you see the avenue?
THE DAUGHTER. Yes, father; it is moonlight, and I can see the avenue as far as the cypress wood.
THE GRANDFATHER. And you do not see anyone?
THE DAUGHTER. No one, grandfather.
THE UNCLE. What sort of a night is it?
THE DAUGHTER. Very fine. Do you hear the nightingales?
THE UNCLE. Yes, yes.
THE DAUGHTER. A little wind is rising in the avenue.
THE GRANDFATHER. A little wind in the avenue?
THE DAUGHTER. Yes; the trees are trembling a little.
THE UNCLE. I am surprised that my sister is not here yet.
THE GRANDFATHER. I cannot hear the nightingales any longer.
THE DAUGHTER. I think someone has come into the garden, grandfather.
THE GRANDFATHER. Who is it?
THE DAUGHTER. I do not know; I can see no one.
THE UNCLE. Because there is no one there.
THE DAUGHTER. There must be someone in the garden; the nightingales have suddenly ceased singing.
THE GRANDFATHER. But I do not hear anyone coming.
THE DAUGHTER. Someone must be passing by the pond, because the swans are scared.
ANOTHER DAUGHTER. All the fishes in the pond are diving suddenly.
THE FATHER. You cannot see anyone?
THE DAUGHTER. No one, father.
THE FATHER. But the pond lies in the moonlight. . . .
THE DAUGHTER. Yes; I can see that the swans are scared.
THE UNCLE. I am sure it is my sister who is scaring them. She must have come in by the little gate.
THE FATHER. I cannot understand why the dogs do not bark.
THE DAUGHTER. I can see the watch-dog right at the back of his kennel. The swans are crossing to the other bank! . . .
THE UNCLE. They are afraid of my sister. I will go and see. [*He calls.*] Sister! sister! Is that you? . . . There is no one there.

THE DAUGHTER. I am sure that someone has come into the garden. You will see.

THE UNCLE. But she would answer me!

THE GRANDFATHER. Are not the nightingales beginning to sing again, Ursula?

THE DAUGHTER. I cannot hear one anywhere.

THE GRANDFATHER. And yet there is no noise.

THE FATHER. There is a silence of the grave.

THE GRANDFATHER. It must be some stranger that scares them, for if it were one of the family they would not be silent.

THE UNCLE. How much longer are you going to discuss these nightingales.

THE GRANDFATHER. Are all the windows open, Ursula?

THE DAUGHTER. The glass door is open, grandfather.

THE GRANDFATHER. It seems to me that the cold is penetrating into the room.

THE DAUGHTER. There is a little wind in the garden, grandfather, and the rose-leaves are falling.

THE FATHER. Well, shut the door. It is late.

THE DAUGHTER. Yes, father. . . . I cannot shut the door.

THE TWO OTHER DAUGHTERS. We cannot shut the door.

THE GRANDFATHER. Why, what is the matter with the door, my children?

THE UNCLE. You need not say that in such an extraordinary voice. I will go and help them.

THE ELDEST DAUGHTER. We cannot manage to shut it quite.

THE UNCLE. It is because of the damp. Let us all push together. There must be something in the way.

THE FATHER. The carpenter will set it right to-morrow.

THE GRANDFATHER. Is the carpenter coming to-morrow?

THE DAUGHTER. Yes, grandfather; he is coming to do some work in the cellar.

THE GRANDFATHER. He will make a noise in the house.

THE DAUGHTER. I will tell him to work quietly. [*Suddenly the sound of a scythe being sharpened is heard outside.*]

THE GRANDFATHER [*with a shudder*]. Oh!

THE UNCLE. What is that?

THE DAUGHTER. I don't quite know; I think it is the gardener. I cannot quite see; he is in the shadow of the house.

THE FATHER. It is the gardener going to mow.
THE UNCLE. He mows by night?
THE FATHER. Is not to-morrow Sunday?—Yes.—I noticed that the grass was very long round the house.
THE GRANDFATHER. It seems to me that his scythe makes as much noise . . .
THE DAUGHTER. He is mowing near the house.
THE GRANDFATHER. Can you see him, Ursula?
THE DAUGHTER. No, grandfather. He stands in the dark.
THE GRANDFATHER. I am afraid he will wake my daughter.
THE UNCLE. We can scarcely hear him.
THE GRANDFATHER. It sounds to me as if he were mowing inside the house.
THE UNCLE. The invalid will not hear it; there is no danger.
THE FATHER. It seems to me that the lamp is not burning well this evening.
THE UNCLE. It wants filling.
THE FATHER. I saw it filled this morning. It has burnt badly since the window was shut.
THE UNCLE. I fancy the chimney is dirty.
THE FATHER. It will burn better presently.
THE DAUGHTER. Grandfather is asleep. He has not slept for three nights.
THE FATHER. He has been so much worried.
THE UNCLE. He always worries too much. At times he will not listen to reason.
THE FATHER. It is quite excusable at his age.
THE UNCLE. God knows what we shall be like at his age!
THE FATHER. He is nearly eighty.
THE UNCLE. Then he has a right to be strange.
THE FATHER. He is like all blind people.
THE UNCLE. They think too much.
THE FATHER. They have too much time to spare.
THE UNCLE. They have nothing else to do.
THE FATHER. And, besides, they have no distractions.
THE UNCLE. That must be terrible.
THE FATHER. Apparently one gets used to it.
THE UNCLE. I cannot imagine it.
THE FATHER. They are certainly to be pitied.
THE UNCLE. Not to know where one is, not to know where

one has come from, not to know whither one is going, not to be able to distinguish midday from midnight, or summer from winter—and always darkness, darkness! I would rather not live. Is it absolutely incurable?

THE FATHER. Apparently so.

THE UNCLE. But he is not absolutely blind?

THE FATHER. He can perceive a strong light.

THE UNCLE. Let us take care of our poor eyes.

THE FATHER. He often has strange ideas.

THE UNCLE. At times he is not at all amusing.

THE FATHER. He says absolutely everything he thinks.

THE UNCLE. But he was not always like this?

THE FATHER. No; once he was as rational as we are; he never said anything extraordinary. I am afraid Ursula encourages him a little too much; she answers all his questions. . . .

THE UNCLE. It would be better not to answer them. It's a mistaken kindness to him. [*Ten o'clock strikes.*]

THE GRANDFATHER [*waking up*]. Am I facing the glass door?

THE DAUGHTER. You have had a nice sleep, grandfather?

THE GRANDFATHER. Am I facing the glass door?

THE DAUGHTER. Yes, grandfather.

THE GRANDFATHER. There is nobody at the glass door?

THE DAUGHTER. No, grandfather; I do not see anyone.

THE GRANDFATHER. I thought someone was waiting. No one has come?

THE DAUGHTER. No one, grandfather.

THE GRANDFATHER [*to the* UNCLE *and* FATHER]. And your sister has not come?

THE UNCLE. It is too late; she will not come now. It is not nice of her.

THE FATHER. I'm beginning to be anxious about her. [*A noise, as of someone coming into the house.*]

THE UNCLE. She is here! Did you hear?

THE FATHER. Yes; someone has come in at the basement.

THE UNCLE. It must be our sister. I recognized her step.

THE GRANDFATHER. I heard slow footsteps.

THE FATHER. She came in very quietly.

THE UNCLE. She knows there is an invalid.

THE GRANDFATHER. I hear nothing now.

THE UNCLE. She will come up directly; they will tell her we are here.
THE FATHER. I am glad she has come.
THE UNCLE. I was sure she would come this evening.
THE GRANDFATHER. She is a very long time coming up.
THE UNCLE. However, it must be she.
THE FATHER. We are not expecting any other visitors.
THE GRANDFATHER. I cannot hear any noise in the basement.
THE FATHER. I will call the servant. We shall know how things stand. [*He pulls a bell-rope.*]
THE GRANDFATHER. I can hear a noise on the stairs already.
THE FATHER. It is the servant coming up.
THE GRANDFATHER. It sounds to me as if she were not alone.
THE FATHER. She is coming up slowly. . . .
THE GRANDFATHER. I hear your sister's step!
THE FATHER. I can only hear the servant.
THE GRANDFATHER. It is your sister! It is your sister! [*There is a knock at the little door.*]
THE UNCLE. She is knocking at the door of the back stairs.
THE FATHER. I will go and open myself. [*He partly opens the little door;* THE SERVANT *remains outside in the opening.*] Where are you?
THE SERVANT. Here, sir.
THE GRANDFATHER. Your sister is at the door?
THE UNCLE. I can only see the servant.
THE FATHER. It is only the servant. [*To* THE SERVANT.] Who was that, that came into the house?
THE SERVANT. Came into the house?
THE FATHER. Yes; someone came in just now?
THE SERVANT. No one came in, sir.
THE GRANDFATHER. Who is it sighing like that?
THE UNCLE. It is the servant; she is out of breath.
THE GRANDFATHER. Is she crying?
THE UNCLE. No; why should she be crying?
THE FATHER [*to* THE SERVANT]. No one came in just now?
THE SERVANT. No, sir.
THE FATHER. But we heard someone open the door!
THE SERVANT. It was I shutting the door.

THE FATHER. It was open?
THE SERVANT. Yes, sir.
THE FATHER. Why was it open at this time of night?
THE SERVANT. I do not know, sir. I had shut it myself.
THE FATHER. Then who was it that opened it?
THE SERVANT. I do not know, sir. Someone must have gone out after me, sir. . . .
THE FATHER. You must be careful.—Don't push the door; you know what a noise it makes!
THE SERVANT. But, sir, I am not touching the door.
THE FATHER. But you are. You are pushing as if you were trying to get into the room.
THE SERVANT. But, sir, I am three yards away from the door.
THE FATHER. Don't talk so loud. . . .
THE GRANDFATHER. Are they putting out the light?
THE ELDEST DAUGHTER. No, grandfather.
THE GRANDFATHER. It seems to me it has grown pitch dark all at once.
THE FATHER [*to* THE SERVANT]. You can go down again now; but do not make so much noise on the stairs.
THE SERVANT. I did not make any noise on the stairs.
THE FATHER. I tell you that you did make a noise. Go down quietly; you will wake your mistress. And if anyone comes now, say that we are not at home.
THE UNCLE. Yes; say that we are not at home.
THE GRANDFATHER [*shuddering*]. You must not say that!
THE FATHER. . . . Except to my sister and the doctor.
THE UNCLE. When will the doctor come?
THE FATHER. He will not be able to come before midnight. [*He shuts the door. A clock is heard striking eleven.*]
THE GRANDFATHER. She has come in?
THE FATHER. Who?
THE GRANDFATHER. The servant.
THE FATHER. No, she has gone downstairs.
THE GRANDFATHER. I thought that she was sitting at the table.
THE UNCLE. The servant?
THE GRANDFATHER. Yes.
THE UNCLE. That would complete one's happiness!

THE GRANDFATHER. No one has come into the room?
THE FATHER. No; no one has come in.
THE GRANDFATHER. And your sister is not here?
THE UNCLE. Our sister has not come.
THE GRANDFATHER. You want to deceive me.
THE UNCLE. Deceive you?
THE GRANDFATHER. Ursula, tell me the truth, for the love of God!
THE ELDEST DAUGHTER. Grandfather! Grandfather! what is the matter with you?
THE GRANDFATHER. Something has happened! I am sure my daughter is worse! . . .
THE UNCLE. Are you dreaming?
THE GRANDFATHER. You do not want to tell me! . . . I can see quite well there is something. . . .
THE UNCLE. In that case you can see better than we can.
THE GRANDFATHER. Ursula, tell me the truth!
THE DAUGHTER. But we have told you the truth, grandfather!
THE GRANDFATHER. You do not speak in your ordinary voice.
THE FATHER. That is because you frighten her.
THE GRANDFATHER. Your voice is changed too.
THE FATHER. You are going mad! [*He and* THE UNCLE *make signs to each other to signify* THE GRANDFATHER *has lost his reason.*]
THE GRANDFATHER. I can hear quite well that you are afraid.
THE FATHER. But what should we be afraid of?
THE GRANDFATHER. Why do you want to deceive me?
THE UNCLE. Who is thinking of deceiving you?
THE GRANDFATHER. Why have you put out the light?
THE UNCLE. But the light has not been put out; there is as much light as there was before.
THE DAUGHTER. It seems to me that the lamp has gone down.
THE FATHER. I see as well now as ever.
THE GRANDFATHER. I have millstones on my eyes! Tell me, girls, what is going on here! Tell me, for the love of God, you who can see! I am here, all alone, in darkness with-

out end! I do not know who seats himself beside me! I do not know what is happening a yard from me! . . . Why were you talking under your breath just now?

THE FATHER. No one was talking under his breath.

THE GRANDFATHER. You did talk in a low voice at the door.

THE FATHER. You heard all I said.

THE GRANDFATHER. You brought someone into the room! . . .

THE FATHER. But I tell you no one has come in!

THE GRANDFATHER. Is it your sister or a priest?—You should not try to deceive me.—Ursula, who was it that came in?

THE DAUGHTER. No one, grandfather.

THE GRANDFATHER. You must not try to deceive me; I know what I know.—How many of us are there here?

THE DAUGHTER. There are six of us round the table, grandfather.

THE GRANDFATHER. You are all round the table?

THE DAUGHTER. Yes, grandfather.

THE GRANDFATHER. You are there, Paul?

THE FATHER. Yes.

THE GRANDFATHER. You are there, Oliver?

THE UNCLE. Yes, of course I am here, in my usual place. That's not alarming, is it?

THE GRANDFATHER. You are there, Geneviève?

ONE OF THE DAUGHTERS. Yes, grandfather.

THE GRANDFATHER. You are there, Gertrude?

ANOTHER DAUGHTER. Yes, grandfather.

THE GRANDFATHER. You are here, Ursula?

THE ELDEST DAUGHTER. Yes, grandfather; next to you.

THE GRANDFATHER. And who is that sitting there?

THE DAUGHTER. Where do you mean, grandfather?—There is no one.

THE GRANDFATHER. There, there—in the midst of us!

THE DAUGHTER. But there is no one, grandfather!

THE FATHER. We tell you there is no one!

THE GRANDFATHER. But you cannot see—any of you!

THE UNCLE. Pshaw! You are joking?

THE GRANDFATHER. I do not feel inclined for joking, I can assure you.

THE UNCLE. Then believe those who can see.
THE GRANDFATHER [*undecidedly*]. I thought there was someone. . . . I believe I shall not live long. . . .
THE UNCLE. Why should we deceive you? What use would there be in that?
THE FATHER. It would be our duty to tell you the truth. . . .
THE UNCLE. What would be the good of deceiving each other?
THE FATHER. You could not live in error long.
THE GRANDFATHER [*trying to rise*]. I should like to pierce this darkness! . . .
THE FATHER. Where do you want to go?
THE GRANDFATHER. Over there. . . .
THE FATHER. Don't be so anxious. . . .
THE UNCLE. You are strange this evening.
THE GRANDFATHER. It is all of you who seem to me to be strange!
THE FATHER. Do you want anything? . . .
THE GRANDFATHER. I do not know what ails me.
THE ELDEST DAUGHTER. Grandfather! grandfather! What do you want, grandfather?
THE GRANDFATHER. Give me your little hands, my children.
THE THREE DAUGHTERS. Yes, grandfather.
THE GRANDFATHER. Why are you all three trembling, girls?
THE ELDEST DAUGHTER. We are scarcely trembling at all, grandfather.
THE GRANDFATHER. I fancy you are all three pale.
THE ELDEST DAUGHTER. It is late, grandfather, and we are tired.
THE FATHER. You must go to bed, and grandfather himself would do well to take a little rest.
THE GRANDFATHER. I could not sleep to-night!
THE UNCLE. We will wait for the doctor.
THE GRANDFATHER. Prepare me for the truth.
THE UNCLE. But there is no truth!
THE GRANDFATHER. Then I do not know what there is!
THE UNCLE. I tell you there is nothing at all!
THE GRANDFATHER. I wish I could see my poor daughter!

THE FATHER. But you know quite well it is impossible; she must not be awaked unnecessarily.

THE UNCLE. You will see her to-morrow.

THE GRANDFATHER. There is no sound in her room.

THE UNCLE. I should be uneasy if I heard any sound.

THE GRANDFATHER. It is a very long time since I saw my daughter! . . . I took her hands yesterday evening, but I could not see her! . . . I do not know what has become of her! . . . I do not know how she is. . . . I do not know what her face is like now. . . . She must have changed these weeks! . . . I felt the little bones of her cheeks under my hands. . . . There is nothing but the darkness between her and me, and the rest of you! . . . I cannot go on living like this . . . this is not living. . . . You sit there, all of you, looking with open eyes at my dead eyes, and not one of you has pity on me! . . . I do not know what ails me. . . . No one tells me what ought to be told me. . . . And everything is terrifying when one's dreams dwell upon it. . . . But why are you not speaking?

THE UNCLE. What should we say, since you will not believe us?

THE GRANDFATHER. You are afraid of betraying yourselves!

THE FATHER. Come now, be rational!

THE GRANDFATHER. You have been hiding something from me for a long time! . . . Something has happened in the house. . . . But I am beginning to understand now. . . . You have been deceiving me too long!—You fancy that I shall never know anything?—There are moments when I am less blind than you, you know! . . . Do you think I have not heard you whispering—for days and days—as if you were in the house of someone who had been hanged—I dare not say what I know this evening. . . . But I shall know the truth! . . . I shall wait for you to tell me the truth; but I have known it for a long time, in spite of you!—And now, I feel that you are all paler than the dead!

THE THREE DAUGHTERS. Grandfather! grandfather! What is the matter, grandfather?

THE GRANDFATHER. It is not you that I am speaking of, girls. No, it is not you that I am speaking of. . . . I know quite well you would tell me the truth—if they were not by!

. . . And besides, I feel sure that they are deceiving you as well. . . . You will see, children—you will see! . . . Do not I hear you all sobbing?

THE FATHER. Is my wife really so ill?

THE GRANDFATHER. It is no good trying to deceive me any longer; it is too late now, and I know the truth better than you! . . .

THE UNCLE. But *we* are not blind; we are not.

THE FATHER. Would you like to go into your daughter's room? This misunderstanding must be put an end to.— Would you?

THE GRANDFATHER [*becoming suddenly undecided*]. No, no, not now—not yet.

THE UNCLE. You see, you are not reasonable.

THE GRANDFATHER. One never knows how much a man has been unable to express in his life! . . . Who made that noise?

THE ELDEST DAUGHTER. It is the lamp flickering, grandfather.

THE GRANDFATHER. It seems to me to be very unsteady— very!

THE DAUGHTER. It is the cold wind troubling it. . . .

THE UNCLE. There is no cold wind, the windows are shut.

THE DAUGHTER. I think it is going out.

THE FATHER. There is no more oil.

THE DAUGHTER. It has gone right out.

THE FATHER. We cannot stay like this in the dark.

THE UNCLE. Why not?—I am quite accustomed to it.

THE FATHER. There is a light in my wife's room.

THE UNCLE. We will take it from there presently, when the doctor has been.

THE FATHER. Well, we can see enough here; there is the light from outside.

THE GRANDFATHER. Is it light outside?

THE FATHER. Lighter than here.

THE UNCLE. For my part, I would as soon talk in the dark.

THE FATHER. So would I. [*Silence.*]

THE GRANDFATHER. It seems to me the clock makes a great deal of noise. . . .

THE ELDEST DAUGHTER. That is because we are not talking any more, grandfather.

THE GRANDFATHER. But why are you all silent?
THE UNCLE. What do you want us to talk about?—You are really very peculiar to-night.
THE GRANDFATHER. Is it very dark in this room?
THE UNCLE. There is not much light. [*Silence.*]
THE GRANDFATHER. I do not feel well, Ursula; open the window a little.
THE FATHER. Yes, child; open the window a little. I begin to feel the want of air myself. [*The girl opens the window.*]
THE UNCLE. I really believe we have stayed shut up too long.
THE GRANDFATHER. Is the window open?
THE DAUGHTER. Yes, grandfather; it is wide open.
THE GRANDFATHER. One would not have thought it was open; there is not a sound outside.
THE DAUGHTER. No, grandfather; there is not the slightest sound.
THE FATHER. The silence is extraordinary!
THE DAUGHTER. One could hear an angel tread!
THE UNCLE. That is why I do not like the country.
THE GRANDFATHER. I wish I could hear some sound. What o'clock is it, Ursula?
THE DAUGHTER. It will soon be midnight, grandfather.
[*Here* THE UNCLE *begins to pace up and down the room.*]
THE GRANDFATHER. Who is that walking round us like that?
THE UNCLE. Only I! only I! Do not be frightened! I want to walk about a little. [*Silence.*]—But I am going to sit down again;—I cannot see where I am going. [*Silence.*]
THE GRANDFATHER. I wish I were out of this place!
THE DAUGHTER. Where would you like to go, grandfather?
THE GRANDFATHER. I do not know where—into another room, no matter where! no matter where!
THE FATHER. Where could we go?
THE UNCLE. It is too late to go anywhere else. [*Silence. They are sitting, motionless, round the table.*]
THE GRANDFATHER. What is that I hear, Ursula?
THE DAUGHTER. Nothing, grandfather; it is the leaves falling.—Yes, it is the leaves falling on the terrace.

THE GRANDFATHER. Go and shut the window, Ursula.
THE DAUGHTER. Yes, grandfather. ·[*She shuts the window, comes back, and sits down.*]
THE GRANDFATHER. I am cold. [*Silence.* THE THREE SISTERS *kiss each other.*] What is that I hear now?
THE FATHER. It is the three sisters kissing each other.
THE UNCLE. It seems to me they are very pale this evening. [*Silence.*]
THE GRANDFATHER. What is that I hear now, Ursula?
THE DAUGHTER. Nothing, grandfather; it is the clasping of my hands. [*Silence.*]
THE GRANDFATHER. And that? . . .
THE DAUGHTER. I do not know, grandfather . . . perhaps my sisters are trembling a little? . . .
THE GRANDFATHER. I am afraid, too, my children. [*Here a ray of moonlight penetrates through a corner of the stained glass, and throws strange gleams here and there in the room. A clock strikes midnight; at the last stroke there is a very vague sound, as of someone rising in haste.*]
THE GRANDFATHER [*shuddering with peculiar horror*]. Who is that who got up?
THE UNCLE. No one got up!
THE FATHER. I did not get up!
THE THREE DAUGHTERS. Nor I!—Nor I!—Nor I!
THE GRANDFATHER. Someone got up from the table!
THE UNCLE. Light the lamp! . . . [*Cries of terror are suddenly heard from the child's room, on the right; these cries continue, with gradations of horror, until the end of the scene.*]
THE FATHER. Listen to the child!
THE UNCLE. He has never cried before!
THE FATHER. Let us go and see him!
THE UNCLE. The light! The light! [*At this moment, quick and heavy steps are heard in the room on the left.—Then a deathly silence.—They listen in mute terror, until the door of the room opens slowly, the light from it is cast into the room where they are sitting, and the Sister of Mercy appears on the threshold, in her black garments, and bows as she makes the sign of the cross, to announce the death of the wife. They understand, and, after a moment of hesitation and fright, silently enter the chamber of death, while* THE UNCLE *politely steps aside on the threshold to let the three girls pass. The*

blind man, left alone, gets up, agitated, and feels his way round the table in the darkness.]

THE GRANDFATHER. Where are you going?—Where are you going?—The girls have left me all alone!

[THE CURTAIN.]

FORTUNE AND MEN'S EYES
A DRAMA IN ONE ACT

By
JOSEPHINE PRESTON PEABODY

Josephine Preston Peabody (Mrs. Lionel S. Marks) was born in New York on May 30, 1874. She attended the Girls' Latin School in Boston and later went to Radcliffe College. From 1901 to 1903 she taught English literature at Wellesley College. Her verse, dramatic and lyric, has made her an outstanding figure in American letters.

Fortune and Men's Eyes (1900), the first of her published plays, is written in blank verse. *Marlowe,* likewise a study of a great Elizabethan, *The Wings,* the setting of which is early English, *The Piper,* a new version of the medieval legend made famous by Browning, and *The Wolf of Gubbio,* dominated by the lovely figure of St. Francis of Assisi, are also poetic dramas. Her best known play, *The Piper,* was awarded the first prize in 1910 in the Stratford-on-Avon competition in which there were three hundred and fifteen contestants. It was then produced at the Memorial Theatre at Stratford.

In recent years two playwrights have consulted Shakespeare's sonnets for dramatic themes; first, Josephine Preston Peabody found in them a motive for her poetic play, *Fortune and Men's Eyes,* and later George Bernard Shaw turned them to dramatic account, in his own fashion, in *The Dark Lady of the Sonnets.* The dramatic situation chosen for *Fortune and Men's Eyes* has been read by some Shakespearian scholars into the familiar dedication of the 1609 edition of the Sonnets, which runs: "To the only begetter of these ensuing sonnets Mr. W. H. all happiness and that eternity promised by our ever-living poet wisheth the well-wishing adventurer in setting forth T. T." The last initials stand for the name of the publisher, Thomas Thorpe. "Begetter" has been variously interpreted as inspirer of the Sonnets or as partner in the commercial enterprise of their publication. "Mr. W. H." has been more usually identified with William Herbert, earl of Pembroke, though some have thought that the initials were inverted and referred to Henry Wriothesly, earl of Southampton, to whom Shakespeare's other poems were dedicated. If W. H. does refer to the earl of Pembroke, it is usually held that the "dark lady" is in reality the blond Mistress Mary Fytton, whose name was coupled with Pembroke's. Whether the sonnets are in any sense at all autobiographical has also been endlessly debated. It was admittedly an age when every poet tried his hand at sonnet sequences and in all these sequences, not excepting Shakespeare's, there are to be found the same conventional conceits. But it is generally believed now that the sonnets of Spenser and Sidney refer to the personal experiences of their authors. It is quite possible, then, that Shakespeare, too, may have used a literary convention as a means of personal expression, though it seems impertinent in any case to question the feeling back of " When in disgrace with fortune and men's eyes." This brief reference to conflicting interpretations of the Sonnets shows how material of dramatic value may lurk even in the purlieus of textual criticism.

Josephine Preston Peabody herself says: " The play was written after long worship of the W. S. Sonnets, as a method of introspection, to satisfy my own curiosity concerning the truth of the sonnet theories. In spite of recurrent threats, by one actor after another, it has never yet been produced on the professional stage. But it has been read and recommended for reading, in various colleges, as a picture of Elizabethan times, and as an interpretation of the Pembroke-Fytton aspect of the sonnet story."

FORTUNE AND MEN'S EYES

" When in disgrace with Fortune and men's eyes " . . .
                                             Sonnet xxix.

CHARACTERS

WILLIAM HERBERT, *son of the Earl of Pembroke.*
SIMEON DYER, *a Puritan.*
TOBIAS, *host of " The Bear and The Angel."*
WAT BURROW, *a bear-ward.*
DICKON, *a little boy, son to* TOBIAS.
CHIFFIN, *a ballad-monger.*
A PRENTICE.

A PLAYER, *master W. S. of the Lord Chamberlain's Company.*

MISTRESS MARY FYTTON, *a maid-of-honor to Queen Elizabeth.*
MISTRESS ANNE HUGHES, *also of the Court.*
TAVERNERS AND PRENTICES.

Time represented: An afternoon in the autumn of the year 1599.

SCENE.—*Interior of " The Bear and the Angel," South London. At back, the center entrance gives on a short alley-walk which joins the street beyond at a right angle. To right and left of this doorway, casements. Down, on the right, a door opening upon the inn-garden; a second door on the right, up, leading to a tap-room. Opposite this, left, a door leading into a buttery. Opposite the garden-door, a large chimney-piece with a smoldering wood-fire. A few seats; a lantern (unlighted) in a corner. In the foreground, to the right, a long and narrow table with several mugs of ale upon it, also a lute.*

At one end of the table WAT BURROW *is finishing his ale and holding forth to the* PRENTICE *(who thrums the lute) and a group of taverners, some smoking. At the further end of the table* SIMEON DYER *observes all with grave curiosity.* TOBIAS *and* DICKON *draw near. General noise.*

PRENTICE [*singing*].
> *What do I give for the Pope and his riches!*
> *I's my ale and my Sunday breeches;*
> *I's an old master, I's a young lass,*
> *And we'll eat green goose, come Martinmas!*
> *Sing Rowdy Dowdy,*
> *Look ye don't crowd me:*
> *I's a good club,*
>   *—So let me pass!*

DICKON.
 Again! again!
PRENTICE.   *Sing Rowdy—*
WAT [*finishing his beer*]. Swallow it down.
 Sling all such froth and follow me to the Bear!
 They stay for me, lined up to see us pass
 From end to end o' the alley. Ho! You doubt?
 From Lambeth to the Bridge!
TAVERNERS. }   { 'Tis so; ay.
PRENTICES. }   { Come, follow! Come.
WAT.   Greg's stuck his ears
 With nosegays, and his chain is wound about
 Like any May-pole. What? I tell ye, boys,
 Ye have seen no such bear, a Bear o' Bears,
 Fit to bite off the prophet, in the show,
 With seventy such boys!
 [*Pulling* DICKON'S *ear*]. Bears, say you, bears?
 Why, Rursus Major, as your scholars tell,
 A royal bear, the greatest in his day,
 The sport of Alexander, unto Nick—
 Was a ewe-lamb, dyed black; no worse, no worse.
 To-morrow come and see him with the dogs;
 He'll not give way,—not he!
DICKON.   To-morrow's Thursday!
 To-morrow's Thursday!
PRENTICE.   Will ye lead by here?
TOBIAS.
 Ay, that would be a sight. Wat, man, this way!

WAT.
    Ho, would you squinch us? Why, there be a press
    O' gentry by this tide to measure Nick
    And lay their wagers, at a blink of him,
    Against to-morrow! Why, the stairs be full.
    To-morrow you shall see the Bridge a-creak,
    The river—dry with barges,—London gape,
    Gape! While the Borough buzzes like a hive
    With all their worships! Sirs, the fame o' Nick
    Has so pluckt out the gentry by the sleeve,
    'Tis said the Queen would see him.

TOBIAS. }   { Ay, 'tis grand.
DICKON. }   { O-oh, the Queen?

PRENTICE.
    How now? Thou art no man to lead a bear,
    Forgetting both his quality and hers!
    Drink all; come, drink to her.

TOBIAS.   Ay, now.

WAT.   To her!—
    And harkee, boy, this saying will serve you learn:
    "The Queen, her high and glorious majesty!"

SIMEON [*gravely*].
    Long live the Queen!

WAT.   Maker of golden laws
    For baitings! She that cherishes the Borough
    And shines upon our pastimes. By the mass!
    Thank her for the crowd to-morrow. But for her,
    We were a homesick handful of brave souls
    That love the royal sport. These mouthing players,
    These hookers, would 'a' spoiled us of our beer—

PRENTICE.
    Lying by to catch the gentry at the stairs,—
    All pressing to Bear Alley—

WAT.   Run 'em in
    At stage-plays and show-fooleries on the way.
    Stage-plays, with their tart nonsense and their flags,
    Their "Tamerlanes" and "Humors" and what not!
    My life on't, there was not a man of us
    But fared his Lent, by reason of their fatness,
    And on a holiday ate not at all!

TOBIAS [*solemnly*].
   'Tis so; 'tis so.
WAT.   But when she heard it told
   How lean the sport was grown, she damns stage-plays
   O' Thursday. So: Nick gets his turn to growl!
PRENTICE.
   As well as any player.
   [*With a dumb show of ranting among the* TAVERNERS.]
WAT.   Players?—Hang them!
   I know 'em, I. I've been with 'em. . . . I was
   As sweet a gentlewoman in my voice
   As any of your finches that sings small.
TOBIAS.   'Twas high.
   [*Enter* THE PLAYER, *followed by* CHIFFIN, *the ballad-
      monger. He is abstracted and weary.*]
WAT [*lingering at the table*].
   I say, I've played. . . . There's not one man
   Of all the gang—save one . . . Ay, there be one
   I grant you, now! . . . He used me in right sort;
   A man worth better trades.
            [*Seeing* THE PLAYER.]
                  —Lord love you, sir!
   Why, this is you indeed. 'Tis a long day, sir,
   Since I clapped eyes on you. But even now
   Your name was on my tongue as pat as ale!
   You see me off. We bait to-morrow, sir;
   Will you come see? Nick's fresh, and every soul
   As hot to see the fight as 'twere to be—
   Man Daniel, baited with the lions!
TOBIAS.   Sir,
   'Tis high . . . 'tis high.
WAT.   We show him in the street
   With dogs and all, ay, now, if you will see.
THE PLAYER.
   Why, so I will. A show and I not there?
   Bear it out bravely, Wat. High fortune, man!
   Commend me to thy bear.
         [*Drinks and passes him the cup.*]
WAT.   Lord love you, sir!
   'Twas ever so you gave a man godspeed. . . .

And yet your spirits flag; you look but palely.
I'll take your kindness, thank ye.
> [*Turning away.*]

                    In good time!
Come after me and Nick, now. Follow all;
Come boys, come, pack!
> [*Exit* WAT, *still descanting. Exeunt most of the* TAV-
> ERNERS, *with the* PRENTICE. SIMEON DYER *draws
> near* THE PLAYER, *regarding him gravely.* CHIFFIN
> *sells ballads to those who go out.* DICKON *is about to
> follow them, when* TOBIAS *stops him.*]

TOBIAS.
What? Not so fast, you there;
Who gave you holiday? Bide by the inn;
Tend on our gentry.
> [*Exit after the crowd.*]

CHIFFIN.   Ballads, gentlemen?
Ballads, new ballads?
SIMEON [*to* THE PLAYER.]
With your pardon, sir,
I am gratified to note your abstinence
From this deplorable fond merriment
Of baiting of a bear.
THE PLAYER.   Your friendship then
Takes pleasure in the heaviness of my legs.
But I am weary I would see the bear.
Nay, rest you happy; malt shall comfort us.
SIMEON.
You do mistake me. I am—
CHIFFIN.   Ballad, sir?
"How a Young Spark would Woo a Tanner's Wife,
And She Sings Sweet in Turn."
SIMEON [*indignantly*].
                    Abandoned poet!
CHIFFIN [*indignantly*].
I'm no such thing! An honest ballad, sir,
No poetry at all.
THE PLAYER.
Good, sell thy wares.

CHIFFIN.
"A Ballad of a Virtuous Country-Maid
Forswears the Follies of the Flaunting Town"—
And tends her geese all day, and weds a vicar.
SIMEON.
A godlier tale, in sooth. But speak, my man;
If she be virtuous, and the tale a true one,
Can she not do't in prose?
THE PLAYER.   Beseech her, man.
'Tis scandal she should use a measure so.
For no more sin than dealing out false measure
Was Dame Sapphira slain.
SIMEON.   You are with me, sir;
Although methinks you do mistake the sense
O' that you have read. . . . This jigging, jog-trot rime,
This ring-me-round, debaseth mind and matter,
To make the reason giddy—
CHIFFIN [*to* THE PLAYER].
                         Ballad, sir?
"Hear All!" A fine brave ballad of a Fish
Just caught off Dover; nay, a one-eyed fish,
With teeth in double rows.
THE PLAYER.   Nay, nay, go to.
CHIFFIN.
"My Fortune's Folly," then; or "The True Tale
Of an Angry Gull;" or "Cherries Like Me Best."
"Black Sheep, or How a Cut-Purse Robbed His Mother;"
"The Prentice and the Dell!" . . . "Plays Play not Fair,"
Or how a *gentlewoman's* heart was took
By a player that was king in a stage-play. . . .
"The Merry Salutation," "How a Spark
Would Woo a Tanner's Wife!" "The Direful Fish"—
Cock's passion, sir! not buy a cleanly ballad
Of the great fish, late ta'en off Dover coast,
Having two heads and teeth in double rows. . . .
Salt fish catched in fresh water? . . .
                                        'Od's my life!
What if or salt or fresh? A prodigy!
A ballad like "Hear All!" And me and mine,
Five children and a wife would bait the devil,
May lap the water out o' Lambeth Marsh

Before he'll buy a ballad. My poor wife,
That lies a-weeping for a tansy-cake!
Body o' me, shall I scent ale again?

THE PLAYER.
Why, here's persuasion; logic, arguments.
Nay, not the ballad. Read for thine own joy.
I doubt not but it stretches, honest length,
From Maid Lane to the Bridge and so across.
But for thy length of thirst—
    [*Giving him a coin.*]
                            That touches near.

CHIFFIN [*apart*].
A vagrom player, would not buy a tale
O' the Great Fish with the twy rows o' teeth!
Learn you to read! [*Exit.*]

SIMEON.
Thou seemest, sir, from that I have overheard,
A man, as one should grant, beyond thy calling. . . .
I would I might assure thee of the way,
To urge thee quit this painted infamy.
There may be time, seeing thou art still young,
To pluck thee from the burning. How are ye 'stroyed,
Ye foolish grasshoppers! Cut off, forgotten,
When moth and rust corrupt your flaunting shows,
The Earth shall have no memory of your name!

DICKON.
Pray you, what's yours?

SIMEON.   I am called Simeon Dyer.
    [*There is the sudden uproar of a crowd in the distance.
    It continues at intervals for some time.*]

PRENTICES. ⎱ Hey, lads?
          ⎰ Some noise beyond: Come, cudgels, come!
            Come on, come on, I'm for it.
    [*Exeunt all but* THE PLAYER, SIMEON, *and* DICKON.]

SIMEON.
Something untoward, without: or is it rather
The tumult of some uproar incident
To this . . . vicinity?

THE PLAYER.   It is an uproar
Most incident to bears.

DICKON.   I would I knew!

THE PLAYER [*holding him off at arm's length*].
    Hey, boy? We would have tidings of the bear:
    Go thou, I'll be thy surety. Mark him well.
    Omit no fact; I would have all of it:
    What manner o' bear he is,—how bears himself;
    Number and pattern of ears, and eyes what hue;
    His voice and fashion o' coat. Nay, come not back,
    Till thou hast all. Skip, sirrah!
              [*Exit* DICKON.]
SIMEON.   Think, fair sir.
    Take this new word of mine to be a seed
    Of thought in that neglected garden plot,
    Thy mind, thy worthier part. But think!
THE PLAYER.   Why, so;
    Thou hast some right, friend; now and then it serves.
    Sometimes I have thought, and even new sometimes,
    . . . I think.
SIMEON [*benevolently*]. Heaven ripen thought unto an harvest! [*Exit.*]
    [THE PLAYER *rises, stretches his arms, and paces the
                  floor, wearily.*]
THE PLAYER [*alone*].
    Some quiet now. . . . Why should I thirst for it
    As if my thoughts were noble company?
    Alone with the one man of all living men
    I have least cause to honor. . . .
                              I'm no lover,
    That seek to be alone! . . . She is too false—
    At last, to keep a spaniel's loyalty.
    I do believe it. And by my own soul,
    She shall not have me, what remains of me
    That may be beaten back into the ranks.
    I will not look upon her. . . . Bitter Sweet.
    This fever that torments me day by day—
    Call it not love—this servitude, this spell
    That haunts me like a sick man's fantasy,
    With pleading of her eyes, her voice, her eyes—
    It shall not have me. I am too much stained:
    But, God or no God, yet I do not live
    And have to bear my own soul company,

To have it stoop so low. She looks on Herbert.
Oh, I have seen. But he,—he must withstand.
He knows that I have suffered,—suffer still—
Although I love her not. Her ways, her ways—
It is her ways that eat into the heart
With beauty more than Beauty; and her voice
That silvers o'er the meaning of her speech
Like moonshine on black waters. Ah, uncoil! . . .
He's the sure morning after this dark dream;
Clear daylight and west wind of a lad's love;
With all his golden pride, for my dull hours,
Still climbing sunward! Sink all loves in him!
And cleanse me of this cursèd, fell distrust
That marks the pestilence. . . .
       '*Fair, kind, and true.*'
Lad, lad. How could I turn from friendliness
To worship such false gods?—
There cannot thrive a greater love than this,
'Fair, kind, and true.' And yet, if She were true
To me, though false to all things else;—one truth,
So one truth lived—. One truth! O beggared soul,
—Foul Lazarus, so starved it can make shift
To feed on crumbs of honor!—Am I this?
[*Enter* ANNE HUGHES. *She has been running in evident terror, and stands against the door looking about her.*]

ANNE.
  Are you the inn-keeper?
    [THE PLAYER *turns and bows courteously.*]
          Nay, sir, your pardon.
I saw you not . . . And yet your face, methinks,
But—yes, I'm sure. . . .
        But where's the inn-keeper?
I know not where I am, nor where to go.
THE PLAYER.
  Madam, it is my fortune that I may
  Procure you service. [*Going towards the door. The uproar sounds nearer.*]
ANNE.   Nay! what if the bear—
THE PLAYER.
  The bear?

ANNE.
>The door! The bear is broken loose.
>Did you not hear? I scarce could make my way
>Through that rank crowd, in search of some safe place.
>You smile, sir! But you had not seen the bear,—
>Nor I, this morning. Pray you, hear me out,—
>For surely you are gentler than the place.
>I came . . . I came by water . . . to the Garden,
>Alone, . . . from bravery, to see the show
>And tell of it hereafter at the Court!
>There's one of us makes count of all such 'scapes
>('Tis Mistress Fytton). She will ever tell
>The sport it is to see the people's games
>Among themselves,—to go *incognita*
>And take all as it is not for the Queen,
>Gallants and rabble! But by Banbury Cross,
>I am of tamer mettle!—All alone,
>Among ten thousand noisy watermen;
>And then the foul ways leading from the Stair;
>And then . . . no friends I knew, nay, not a face.
>And my dear nose beset, and my pomander
>Lost in the rout,—or else a cut-purse had it:
>And then the bear breaks loose! Oh, 'tis a day
>Full of vexations, nay, and dangers too.
>I would I had been slower to outdo
>The pranks of Mary Fytton. . . . You know her, sir?

THE PLAYER.
>If one of my plain calling may be said
>To know a maid-of-honor. [*More lightly.*] And yet more:
>My heart has cause to know the lady's face.

ANNE [*blankly*].
>Why, so it is. . . . Is't not a marvel, sir,
>The way she hath? Truly, her voice is good. . . .
>And yet,—but oh, she charms; I hear it said.
>A winsome gentlewoman, of a wit, too.
>We are great fellows; she tells me all she does;
>And, sooth, I listen till my ears be like
>To grow for wonder. Whence my 'scape, to-day!
>Oh, she hath daring for the pastimes here;
>I would—change looks with her, to have her spirit!
>Indeed, they say she charms Someone, by this.

THE PLAYER.
  Someone. . . .
ANNE.   Hast heard?
  Why sure my Lord of Herbert.
  Ay, Pembroke's son. But there I doubt,—I doubt.
  He is an eagle will not stoop for less
  Than kingly prey. No bird-lime takes him.
THE PLAYER.   Herbert. . . .
  He hath shown many favors to us players.
ANNE.
  Ah, now I have you!
THE PLAYER.   Surely, gracious madam;
  My duty; . . . what besides?
ANNE.   This face of yours.
  'Twas in some play, belike. [*Apart.*] . . . I took him for
  A man it should advantage me to know!
  And he's a proper man enough. . . . Ay me!
  [*When she speaks to him again it is with encouraging
        condescension.*]
  Surely you've been at Whitehall, Master Player?
THE PLAYER [*bowing*].
  So.
ANNE. And how oft? And when?
THE PLAYER.   Last Christmas tide;
  And Twelfth Day eve, perchance. Your memory
  Freshens a dusty past. . . . The hubbub's over.
  Shall I look forth and find some trusty boy
  To attend you to the river?
ANNE.   I thank you, sir.
  [*He goes to the door and steps out into the alley, looking
      up and down. The noise in the distance springs up
      again.*]
  [*Apart.*] 'Tis not past sufferance. Marry, I could stay
  Some moments longer, till the streets be safe.
  Sir, sir!
THE PLAYER [*returning*].
  Command me, madam.
ANNE.   I will wait
  A little longer, lest I meet once more
  That ruffian mob or any of the dogs.
  These sports are better seen from balconies.

THE PLAYER.
  Will you step hither? There's an arbored walk
  Sheltered and safe. Should they come by again,
  You may see all, an't like you, and be hid.
ANNE.
  A garden there? Come, you shall show it me.

[*They go out into the garden on the right, leaving the door shut. Immediately enter, in great haste,* MARY FYTTON *and* WILLIAM HERBERT, *followed by* DICKON, *who looks about and, seeing no one, goes to setting things in order.*]

MARY.
  Quick, quick! . . . She must have seen me. Those big eyes,
  How could they miss me, peering as she was
  For some familiar face? She would have known,
  Even before my mask was jostled off
  In that wild rabble . . . bears and bearish men.
HERBERT.
  Why would you have me bring you?
MARY.   Why? Ah, why!
  Sooth, once I had a reason: now 'tis lost,—
  Lost! Lost! Call out the bell-man.
DICKON [*seriously*].   Shall I so?
HERBERT.
  Nay, nay; that were a merriment indeed,
    To cry us through the streets! [*To* MARY.] You
      riddling charm.
MARY.
  A riddle, yet? You almost love me, then.
HERBERT.
  Almost?
MARY.
  Because you cannot understand.
  Alas, when all's unriddled, the charm goes.
HERBERT.
  Come, you're not melancholy?
MARY.   Nay, are you?
  But should Nan Hughes have seen us, and spoiled all—
HERBERT.
  How could she so?

MARY.   I know not . . . yet I know
    If she had met us, she could steal To-day,
    Golden To-day.
HERBERT.   A kiss; and so forget her.
MARY.
    Hush, hush,—the tavern-boy there.
    [*To* DICKON.]   Tell me, boy,—
    [*To* HERBERT.]   Some errand, now; a roc's egg!
    Strike thy wit.
HERBERT.
    What is't you miss? Why, so. The lady's lost
    A very curious reason, wrought about
    With diverse broidery.
MARY.   Nay, 'twas a mask.
HERBERT.
    A mask, arch-wit? Why will you mock yourself
    And all your fine deceits? Your mask, your reason,
    Your reason with a mask!
MARY.   You are too merry.
    [*To* DICKON.] A mask it is, and muffler finely wrought
    With little amber points all hung like bells.
    I lost it as I came, somewhere. . . .
HERBERT.   Somewhere
    Between the Paris Gardens and the Bridge.
MARY.
    Or below Bridge—or haply in the Thames!
HERBERT.
    No matter where, so you do bring it back.
    Fly, Mercury! Here's feathers for thy heels. [*Giving coin.*]
MARY [*aside*].
    Weights, weights! [*Exit* DICKON.]
    [HERBERT *looks about him, opens the door of the tap-
        room, grows troubled. She watches him with dis-
        satisfaction, seeming to warm her feet by the fire
        meanwhile.*]
HERBERT [*apart*].
    I know this place. We used to come
    Together, he and I . . .
MARY [*apart*].   Forgot again.
    O the capricious tides, the hateful calms,
    And the too eager ship that would be gone

Adventuring against uncertain winds,
For some new, utmost sight of Happy Isles!
Becalmed,—becalmed . . . But I will break this calm.
[*She sees the lute on the table, crosses and takes it up, running her fingers over the strings very softly. She sits.*]

HERBERT.
Ah, mermaid, is it you?

MARY.   Did you sail far?

HERBERT.
Not I; no, sooth. [*Crossing to her.*]
                         Mermaid, I would not think.
But you—

MARY.
I think not. I remember nothing.
There's nothing in the world but you and me;
All else is dust. Thou shalt not question me;
Or if,—but as a sphinx in woman-shape:
And when thou fail'st at answer, I shall turn,
And rend thy heart and cast thee from the cliff.
[*She leans her head back against him, and he kisses her.*]
So perish all who guess not what I am! . . .
Oh, but I know you: you are April-Days.
Nothing is sure, but all is beautiful!
[*She runs her fingers up the strings, one by one, and
   listens, speaking to the lute.*]
Is it not so? Come, answer. Is it true?
Speak, sweeting, since I love thee best of late,
And have forsook my virginals for thee.
All's beautiful indeed and all unsure?
"*Ay*" . . . (Did you hear?) *He's fair and faithless?*
"*Ay.*" [*Speaking with the lute.*]

HERBERT.
Poor oracle, with only one reply!—
Wherein 'tis unlike thee.

MARY.   *Can he love aught
So well as his own image in the brook,
Having once seen it?*

HERBERT.   Ay!

MARY.   The lute saith "*No.*" . . .
O dullard! Here were tidings, would you mark.
What said I? *Oracle, can he love aught*

So dear as his own image in the brook,
Having once looked? . . . No, truly.
[*With sudden abandon.*]   Nor can I!
HERBERT.
   O leave this game of words, you thousand-tongued.
Sing, sing to me. So shall I be all yours
Forever;—or at least till you be mute! . . .
I used to wonder he should be thy slave:
I wonder now no more. Your ways are wonders;
You have a charm to make a man forget
His past and yours, and everything but you.
MARY [*speaking*].
      "*When daisies pied and violets blue*
         And lady-smocks all silver-white"—
   How now?
HERBERT.
      "How now?" That song . . . thou wilt sing that?
MARY.
   Marry, what mars the song?
HERBERT.   Have you forgot
Who made it?
MARY.   Soft, what idleness! So fine?
So rude? And bid me sing! You get but silence;
Or, if I sing,—beshrew me, it shall be
A dole of song, a little starveling breath
As near to silence as a song can be.
[*She sings under-breath, fantastically.*]
         Say how many kisses be
         Lent and lost twixt you and me?
         '*Can I tell when they begun?*'
         Nay, but this were prodigal:
         Let us learn to count withal.
         Since no ending is to spending,
         Sum our riches, one by one.
         '*You shall keep the reckoning,*
         Count each kiss while I do sing.'
HERBERT.
   Oh, not these little wounds. You vex my heart;
Heal it again with singing,—come, sweet, come.
Into the garden! None shall trouble us.
This place has memories and conscience too:

Drown all, my mermaid. Wind them in your hair
And drown them, drown them all.
[*He swings open the garden-door for her. At the same moment* ANNE's *voice is heard approaching.*]
ANNE [*without*]. Some music there?
HERBERT.
Perdition! Quick,—behind me, love.
[*Swinging the door shut again, and looking through the crack.*]
MARY.
'Tis she—
Nan Hughes, 'tis she! How came she here? By heaven,
She crosses us to-day. Nan Hughes lights here
In a Bank tavern! Nay, I'll not be seen.
Sooner or later it must mean the wreck
Of both . . . should the Queen know.
HERBERT. The spite of chance!
She talks with someone in the arbor there
Whose face I see not. Come, here's doors at least.
[*They cross hastily.* MARY *opens the door on the left and looks within.*]
MARY.
Too thick. . . . I shall be penned. But guard you this
And tell me when they're gone. Stay, stay;—mend all.
If she have seen me,—swear it was not I.
Heaven speed her home, with her new body-guard!
[*Exit, closing door.* HERBERT *looks out into the garden.*]
HERBERT.
By all accursèd chances,—none but he!
[*Retires up to stand beside the door, looking out of casement. Re-enter from the garden,* ANNE, *followed by* THE PLAYER.]
ANNE.
No, 'twas some magic in my ears, I think.
There's no one here. [*Seeing* HERBERT.]
But yes, there's someone here:—
The inn-keeper. Are you—
Saint Catherine's bones!
My Lord of Herbert. Sir, you could not look
More opportune. But for this gentleman—

HERBERT [*bowing*].
     My friend, this long time since,—
ANNE.
     Marry, your friend?
THE PLAYER [*regarding* HERBERT *searchingly*].
     This long time since.
ANNE.   Nay, is it so, indeed?
     [*To* HERBERT.]   My day's fulfilled of blunders! O sweet sir,
     How can I tell you? But I'll tell you all
     If you'll but bear me escort from this place
     Where none of us belongs. Yours is the first
     Familiar face I've seen this afternoon!
HERBERT [*apart*].
     A sweet assurance.
     [*Aloud.*]   But you seek . . . you need
     Some rest—some cheer, some—Will you step within?
           [*Indicating tap-room.*]
     The tavern is deserted, but—
ANNE.   Not here!
     I've been here quite an hour. Come, citywards,
     To Whitehall! I have had enough of bears
     To quench my longing till next Whitsuntide.
     Down to the river, pray you.
HERBERT.   Sooth, at once?
ANNE.
     At once, at once.
     [*To* THE PLAYER.] I crave your pardon, sir,
     For sundering your friendships. I've heard say
     A woman always comes between two men
     To their confusion. You shall drink amends
     Some other day. I must be safely home.
THE PLAYER [*reassured by* HERBERT'S *reluctance to go.*]
     It joys me that your trials have found an end;
     And for the rest, I wish you prosperous voyage;
     Which needs not, with such halcyon weather toward.
HERBERT [*apart*].
     It cuts: and yet he knows not. Can it pass?
     [*To him.*] Let us meet soon. I have—I know not what
     To say—nay, no import; but chance has parted

Our several ways too long. To leave you thus,
Without a word—
ANNE.   You are in haste, my lord!
By the true faith, here are two friends indeed!
Two lovers crossed: and I,—'tis I that bar them.
Pray tarry, sir. I doubt not I may light
Upon some link-boy to attend me home
Or else a drunken prentice with a club,
Or that patched keeper strolling from the Garden
With all his dogs along; or failing them,
A pony with a monkey on his back,
Or, failing that, a bear! Some escort, sure,
Such as the Borough offers! I shall look
Part of a pageant from the Lady Fair,
And boast for three full moons, " Such sights I saw!"
Truly, 'tis new to me: but I doubt not
I shall trick out a mind for strange adventure,
As high as—Mistress Fytton!
HERBERT.   Say no more,
Dear lady! I entreat you pardon me
The lameness of my wit. I'm stark adream;
You lighted here so suddenly, unlooked for
Vision in Bankside. . . . Let me hasten you,
Now that I see I dream not. It grows late.
ANNE.
And can you grant me such a length of time?
HERBERT.
Length? Say Illusion! Time? Alas, 'twill be
Only a poor half-hour [*loudly*], a poor half-hour!
[*Apart.*]   Did she hear that, I wonder?
THE PLAYER [*bowing over* ANNE'S *hand*]. Not so, madam;
A little gold of largess, fallen to me
By chance.
HERBERT [*to him*].
A word with you—
[*Apart.*]   O, I am gagged!
ANNE [*to* THE PLAYER].
You go with us, sir?
  [*He moves towards door with them.*]
THE PLAYER.   No, I do but play
Your inn-keeper.

HERBERT [*apart, despairingly*].
  The eagle is gone blind.
  [*Exeunt, leaving doors open. They are seen to go down the walk together. At the street they pause,* THE PLAYER, *bowing slowly, then turning back towards the inn;* ANNE *holding* HERBERT'S *arm. Within, the door on the left opens slightly, then* MARY *appears.*]
MARY.
  'Tis true. My ears caught silence, if no more.
  They're gone. . . .
  [*She comes out of her hiding-place and opens the left-hand casement to see* ANNE *disappearing with* HERBERT.]
  She takes him with her! He'll return?
  Gone, gone, without a word; and I was caged,—
  And deaf as well. O, spite of everything!
  She's so unlike. . . . How long shall I be here
  To wait and wonder? He with her—with her!
  [THE PLAYER, *having come slowly back to the door, hears her voice.* MARY *darts towards the entrance to look after* HERBERT *and* ANNE. *She sees him and recoils. She falls back step by step, while he stands holding the door-posts with his hands, impassive.*]
  You! . . .
THE PLAYER.
  Yes. . . . [*After a pause.*] And you.
MARY.   Do you not ask me why
  I'm here?
THE PLAYER.
  I am not wont to shun the truth:
  But yet I think the reason you could give
  Were too uncomely.
MARY.   Nay;—
THE PLAYER.   If it were truth;
  If it were truth! Although that likelihood
  Scarce threatens.
MARY.   So. Condemned without a trial.
THE PLAYER.
  O, speak the lie now. Let there be no chance
  For my unsightly love, bound head and foot,
  Stark, full of wounds and horrible,—to find
  Escape from out its charnel-house; to rise

>   Unwelcome before eyes that had forgot,
>   And say it died not truly. It should die.
>   Play no imposture: leave it,—it is dead.
>   I have been weak in that I tried to pour
>   The wine through plague-struck veins. It came to life
>   Over and over, drew sharp breath again
>   In torture such as't may be to be born,
>   If a poor babe could tell. Over and over,
>   I tell you, it has suffered resurrection,
>   Cheating its pain with hope, only to die
>   Over and over;—die more deaths than men
>   The meanest, most forlorn, are made to die
>   By tyranny or nature. . . . Now I see all
>   Clear. And I say, it shall not rise again.
>   I am as safe from you as I were dead.
>   I know you.

MARY.   Herbert—
THE PLAYER.   Do not touch his name.
>   Leave that; I saw.

MARY.   You saw? Nay, what?
THE PLAYER.   The whole
>   Clear story. Not at first. While you were hid,
>   I took some comfort, drop by drop, and minute
>   By minute. (Dullard!) Yet there was a maze
>   Of circumstance that showed even then to me
>   Perplext and strange. You here unravel it.
>   All's clear: you are the clue. [*Turning away.*]

MARY [*going to the casement*].
>   [*Apart.*]   Caged, caged!
>   Does he know all? Why were those walls so dense?
>   [*To him.*] Nan Hughes hath seized the time to tune
>   your mind
>   To some light gossip. Say, how came she here?

THE PLAYER.
>   All emulation, thinking to match you
>   In high adventure:—liked it not, poor lady!
>   And is gone home, attended.

>   [*Re-enter* DICKON.]

DICKON [*to* MARY].   They be lost!—
>   Thy mask and muffler;—'tis no help to search.

Some hooker would 'a' swallowed 'em, be sure,
As the whale swallows Jonas, in the show.
MARY.
'Tis nought: I care not.
DICKON [*looking at the fire*].
Hey, it wants a log.
[*While he mends the fire, humming,* THE PLAYER *stands taking thought.* MARY *speaks apart, going to casement again to look out.*]
MARY [*apart*].
I will have what he knows. To cast me off:—
Not thus, not thus. Peace, I can blind him yet,
Or he'll despise me. Nay, I will not be
Thrust out at door like this. I will not go
But by mine own free will. There is no power
Can say what he might do to ruin us,
To win Will Herbert from me,—almost mine,
And I all his, all his—O April-Days!—
Well, friendship against love? I know who wins.
He is grown dread. . . . But yet he is a man.
  [*Exit* DICKON *into tap-room.*]
[*To* THE PLAYER, *suavely.*] Well, headsman?
  [*He does not turn.*]
            Mind your office: I am judged.
Guilty, was it not so? . . . What is to do,
Do quickly. . . . Do you wait for some reprieve?
Guilty, you said. Nay, do you turn your face
To give me some small leeway of escape?
And yet, I will not go . . .
  [*Coming down slowly.*]
            Well, headsman? . . .
You ask not why I came here, Clouded Brow,
Will you not ask me why I stay? No word?
O blind, come lead the blind! For I, I too
Lack sight and every sense to linger here
And make me an intruder where I once
Was welcome, oh most welcome, as I dreamed.
Look on me, then. I do confess, I have
Too often preened my feathers in the sun
And thought to rule a little, by my wit.
I have been spendthrift with men's offerings

To use them like a nosegay,—tear apart,
Petal by petal, leaf by leaf, until
I found the heart all bare, the curious heart
I longed to see for once, and cast away.
And so, at first, with you. . . . Ah, now I think
You're wise. There's nought so fair, so . . . curious,
So precious-rare to find as honesty.
'Twas all a child's play then, a counting-off
Of petals. Now I know. . . . But ask me why
I come unheralded, and in a mist
Of circumstance and strangeness. Listen, love;
Well then, dead love, if you will have it so.
I have been cunning, cruel,—what you will:
And yet the days of late have seemed too long
Even for summer! Something called me here.
And so I flung my pride away and came,
A very woman for my foolishness,
To say once more,—to say . . .

THE PLAYER.   Nay, I'll not ask.
What lacks? I need no more, you have done well.
'Tis rare. There is no man I ever saw
But you could school him. Women should be players.
You are sovran in the art: feigning and truth
Are so commingled in you. Sure, to you
Nature's a simpleton hath never seen
Her own face in the well. Is there aught else?
To ask of my poor calling?

MARY.   I deserved it
In other days. Hear how I can be meek.
I am come back, a foot-worn runaway,
Like any braggart boy. Let me sit down
And take Love's horn-book in my hands again
And learn from the beginning;—by the rod,
If you will scourge me, love. Come, come, forgive.
I am not wont to sue: and yet to-day
I am your suppliant, I am your servant,
Your link-boy, ay, your minstrel: ay,—wilt hear?
[*Takes up the lute, and gives a last look out of the casement.*]
The tumult in the streets is all apart
With the discordant past. The hour that is

Shall be the only thing in all the world.
[*Apart.*] I will be safe. He'll not win Herbert from me!
[*Crossing to him.*]
Will you have music, good my lord?
THE PLAYER [*catching the lute from her.*] Not that.
Not that! By heaven, you shall not. . . . Nevermore.
MARY.
So . . . But you speak at last. You are, forsooth,
A man: and you shall use me as my due;—
A woman, not the wind about your ears;
A woman whom you loved.
THE PLAYER [*half-apart, still holding the lute*].
        Why were you not
That beauty that you seemed? . . . But had you been,
'Tis true, you would have had no word for me,—
No looks of love!
MARY.   The man reproaches me?
THE PLAYER.
Not I—not I. . . . Will Herbert, what am I
To lay this broken trust to you,—to you,
Young, free, and tempted: April on his way,
Whom all hands reach for, and this woman here
Had set her heart upon!
MARY.   What fantasy!
Surely he must have been from town of late,
To see the gude-folks! And how fare they, sir?
Reverend yeoman, say, how thrive the sheep?
What did the harvest yield you?—Did you count
The cabbage heads? and find how like . . . nay, nay!
But our gude-wife, did she bid in the neighbors
To prove them that her husband was no myth?
Some Puritan preacher, nay, some journeyman,
To make you sup the sweeter with long prayers?
This were a rare conversion, by my soul!
From sonnets unto sermons:—eminent!
THE PLAYER.
Oh, yes, your scorn bites truly: sermons next.
There is so much to say. But it must be learned,
And I require hard schooling, dream too much
On what I would men were,—but women most.
I need the cudgel of the task-master

To make me con the truth. Yes, blind, you called me,
And 'tis my shame I bandaged mine own eyes
And held them dark. Now, by the grace of God,
Or haply because the devil tries too far,
I tear the blindfold off, and I see all.
I see you as you are; and in your heart
The secret love sprung up for one I loved,
A reckless boy who has trodden on my soul—
But that's a thing apart, concerns not you.
I know that you will stake your heaven and earth
To fool me,—fool us both.

MARY [*with idle interest*].
                  Why were you not
So stern a long time since? You're not so wise
As I have heard them say.

THE PLAYER [*standing by the chimney*].
    Wise? Oh, not I.
Who was so witless as to call me wise?
Sure he had never bade me a good-day
And seen me take the cheer. . . .
                              I was your fool
Too long. . . . I am no longer anything.
Speak: what are you?

MARY [*after a pause*].
    The foolishest of women:
A heart that should have been adventurer
On the high seas; a seeker in new lands,
To dare all and to lose. But I was made
A woman.
             Oh, you see!—could you see all.
What if I say . . . the truth is not so far,
             [*Watching him.*]
Yet farther than you dream. If I confess . . .
He charmed my fancy . . . for the moment,—ay
The shine of his fortunes too, the very name
Of Pembroke? . . . Dear my judge,—ay, clouded brow
And darkened fortune, be not black to me!
I'd try for my escape; the window's wide,
No one forbids, and yet I stay—I stay.

    .   .   .   .

Oh, I was niggard, once, unkind—I know,

Untrusty: loved, unloved you, day by day:
A little and a little,—why, I knew not,
And more, and wondered why;—then not at all:
Drank up the dew from out your very heart,
Like the extortionate sun, to leave you parched
Till, with as little grace, I flung all back
In gusts of angry rain! I have been cruel.
But the spell works; yea, love, the spell, the spell
Fed by your fasting, by your subtlety
Past all men's knowledge. . . . There is something rare
About you that I long to flee and cannot:—
Some mastery . . . that's more my will than I.
[*She laughs softly. He listens, looking straight ahead,
not at her, immobile, but suffering evidently. She
watches his face and speaks with greater intensity.
Here she crosses nearer and falls on her knees.*]
Ah, look: you shall believe, you shall believe.
Will you put by your Music? Was I that?
Your Music,—very Music? . . . Listen, then,
Turn not so blank a face. Thou hast my love.
I'll tell thee so till thought itself shall tire
And fall a-dreaming like a weary child, . . .
Only to dream of you, and in its sleep
To murmur You. . . . Ah, look at me, love, lord . . .
Whom queens would honor. Read these eyes you praised,
That pitied, once,—that sue for pity now.
But look! You shall not turn from me—
THE PLAYER.   Eyes, eyes!—
  The darkness hides so much.
MARY.   He'll not believe. . . .
What can I do? What more,—what more, you . . . man?
I bruise my heart here, at an iron gate. . . .
  [*She regards him half gloomily without rising.*]
Yet there is one thing more. . . . You'll take me, now?—
My meaning. . . . You were right. For once I say it.
There is a glory of discovery [*ironically*]
To the black heart . . . because it may be known
But once,—but once. . . .
                            I wonder men will hide
Their motives all so close. If they could guess,—
It is so new to feel the open day

Look in on all one's hidings, at the end.
So. . . . You were right. The first was all a lie:
A lie, and for a purpose . . . . . .
Now,—[*she rises and stands off, regarding him abruptly*],
And why, I know not,—but 'tis true, at last,
I do believe . . . I love you.
                                Look at me!
[*He stands by the fireside against the chimney-piece. She crosses to him with passionate appeal, holding out her arms. He turns his eyes and looks at her with a rigid scrutiny. She endures it for a second, then wavers; makes an effort, unable to look away, to lift her arms towards his neck; they falter and fall at her side. The two stand spellbound by mutual recognition. Then she speaks in a low voice.*]

MARY.
Oh, let me go!
[*She turns her head with an effort,—gathers her cloak about her, then hastens out as if from some terror.*]
[THE PLAYER *is alone beside the chimney-piece. The street outside is darkening with twilight through the casements and upper door. There is a sound of rough-throated singing that comes by and is softened with distance. It breaks the spell.*]

THE PLAYER.
So; it is over . . . now. [*He looks into the fire.*]

. . . .
"Fair, kind, and true." And true! . . . My golden
    Friend.
Those two . . . together. . . . He was ill at ease.
But that he should betray me with a kiss!
. . . .
By this preposterous world . . . I am in need.
Shall there be no faith left? Nothing but names?
Then he's a fool who steers his life by such.
Why not the body-comfort of this herd
Of creatures huddled here to keep them warm?—
Trying to drown out with enforcèd laughter
The query of the winds . . . unanswered winds
That vex the soul with a perpetual doubt.
What holds me? . . . Bah, that were a Cause, indeed!

To prove your soul one truth, by being it,—
Against the foul dishonor of the world!
How else prove aught? . . .
                    I talk into the air.
And at my feet, my honor full of wounds.
Honor? Whose honor? For I knew my sin,
And she . . . had none. There's nothing to avenge.
[*He speaks with more and more passion, too distraught to
notice interruptions. Enter* DICKON, *with a tallow-
dip. He regards* THE PLAYER *with half-open mouth
from the corner; then stands by the casement, leaning
up against it and yawning now and then.*]
I had no right: that I could call her mine
So none should steal her from me, and die for't.
There's nothing to avenge . . . Brave beggary!
How fit to lodge me in this home of Shows,
With all the ruffian life, the empty mirth,
The gross imposture of humanity,
Strutting in virtues it knows not to wear,
Knave in a stolen garment—all the same—
Until it grows enamored of a life
It was not born to,—falls a-dream, poor cheat,
In the midst of its native shams,—the thieves and bears
And ballad-mongers all! . . . Of such am I.
[*Re-enter* TOBIAS *and one or two* TAVERNERS. TOBIAS *re-
gards* THE PLAYER, *who does not notice anyone,—
then leads off* DICKON *by the ear. Exeunt into tap-
room.* THE PLAYER *goes to the casement, pushes it
wide open, and gazes out at the sky.*]
Is there naught else? . . . I could make shift to bind
My heart up and put on my mail again,
To cheat myself and death with one fight more,
If I could think there were some worldly use
For bitter wisdom.
                But I'm no general,
That my own hand-to-hand with evil days
Should cheer my doubting thousands . . .
                                    I'm no more
Than one man lost among a multitude;
And in the end dust swallows them—and me,

And the good sweat that won our victories.
Who sees? Or seeing, cares? Who follows on?
Then why should my dishonor trouble me,
Or broken faith in him? *What is it suffers?
And why?* Now that the moon is turned to blood.
[*He turns towards the door with involuntary longing, and seems to listen.*]
No . . . no, he will not come. Well, I have naught
To do but pluck from me my bitter heart,
And live without it.
[*Re-enter* DICKON *with a tankard and a cup. He sets them down on a small table; this he pushes towards* THE PLAYER, *who turns at the noise.*]
                So . . .? Is it for me?

DICKON.
Ay, on the score! I had good sight o' the bear.
Look, here's a sprig was stuck on him with pitch;—
    [*Rubbing the sprig on his sleeve.*]
I caught it up,—from Lambeth marsh, belike.
Such grow there, and I've seen thee cherish such.

THE PLAYER.
Give us thy posy.
  [*He comes back to the fire and sits in the chair near by.* DICKON *gets out the iron lantern from the corner.*]

DICKON.   Hey! It wants a light.
[THE PLAYER *seems to listen once more, his face turned towards the door. He lifts his hand as if to hush* DICKON, *lets it fall, and looks back at the fire.* DICKON *regards him with shy curiosity and draws nearer.*]

DICKON.
Thou wilt be always minding of the fire . . .
Wilt thou not?

THE PLAYER.   Ay.

DICKON.   It likes me, too.

THE PLAYER.   So?

DICKON.   Ay. . . .
I would I knew what thou art thinking on
When thou dost mind the fire. . . .

THE PLAYER.   Wouldst thou?

DICKON. Ay.
  [*Sound of footsteps outside. A group approaches the door.*]
  Oh, here he is, come back!
THE PLAYER [*rising with passionate eagerness*].
                              Brave lad—brave lad!
DICKON [*singing*].
  Hang out your lanthorns, trim your lights
  To save your days from knavish nights!
  [*He plunges, with his lantern, through the doorway,
    stumbling against* WAT BURROW, *who enters, a sorry
    figure, the worse for wear.*]
WAT [*sourly*].
  Be the times soft, that you must try to cleave
  Way through my ribs as tho' I was the moon?—
  And you the man-wi-'the-lanthorn, or his dog?—
  You bean! . . .
  [*Exit* DICKON. WAT *shambles in and sees* THE PLAYER.]
                What, you sir, here?
THE PLAYER.
  Ay, here, good Wat.
  [*While* WAT *crosses to the table and gets himself a chair,*
    THE PLAYER *looks at him as if with a new conscious-
    ness of the surroundings. After a time he sits as
    before. Re-enter* DICKON *and curls up on the floor,
    at his feet.*]
WAT.
  O give me comfort, sir. This cursèd day,—
  A wry, damned . . . noisome. . . . Ay, poor Nick,
    poor Nick!
  He's all to mend—Poor Nick! He's sorely maimed,
  More than we'd baited him with forty dogs.
  'Od's body! Said I not, sir, he would fight?
  Never before had he, in leading-chain,
  Walked out to take the air and show his parts. . . .
  'Went to his noddle like some greenest gull's
  That's new come up to town. . . . The prentices
  Squeaking along like Bedlam, he breaks loose
  And prances me a hey,—I dancing counter!
  Then such a cawing 'mongst the women! Next,
  The chain did clatter and enrage him more;—
  You would 'a' sworn a bear grew on each link,

And after each a prentice with a cudgel,—
Leaving him scarce an eye! So, howling all,
We run a pretty pace . . . and Nick, poor Nick,
He catches on a useless, stumbling fry
That needed not be born,—and bites into him.
And then . . . the Constable . . . And now, no show!
THE PLAYER.
Poor Wat! . . . Thou wentest scattering misadventure
Like comfits from thy horn of plenty, Wat.
WAT.
Ay, thank your worship. You be best to comfort.
[*He pours a mug of ale.*]
No show to-morrow! Minnow Constable. . . .
I'm a jack-rabbit strung up by my heels
For every knave to pinch as he goes by!
Alas, poor Nick, bear Nick . . . oh, think on Nick.
THE PLAYER.
With all his fortunes darkened for a day,—
And the eye o' his reason, sweet intelligencer,
Under a beggarly patch. . . . I pledge thee, Nick.
WAT.
Oh, you have seen hard times, sir, with us all.
Your eyes lack luster, too, this day. What say you?
No jesting. . . . What? I've heard of marvels there
In the New Country. There would be a knop-hole
For thee and me. There be few Constables
And such unhallowed fry. . . . An thou wouldst lay
Thy wit to mine—what is't we could not do?
Wilt turn't about?
[*Leans towards him in cordial confidence.*]
Nay, you there, sirrah boy,
Leave us together; as 'tis said in the play,
'Come, leave us, Boy!'
[DICKON *does not move. He gives a sigh and leans his head against* THE PLAYER'S *knee, his arms around his legs. He sleeps.* THE PLAYER *gazes sternly into the fire, while* WAT *rambles on, growing drowsy.*]
WAT.
The cub there snores good counsel. When all's done,
What a bubble is ambition! . . . When all's done . . .
What's yet to do? . . . Why, sleep. . . . Yet even now

I was on fire to see myself and you
Off for the Colony with Raleigh's men.
I've been beholden to 'ee. . . . Why, for thee
I could make shift to suffer plays o' Thursday.
Thou'rt the best man among them, o' my word.
There's other trades and crafts and qualities
Could serve . . . an thou wouldst lay thy wit to mine.
Us two! . . . us two! . . .

THE PLAYER [*apart, to the fire*].
" Fair, kind, and true." . . .

WAT.   . . . Poor Nick!
[*He nods over his ale. There is muffled noise in the tap-
    room. Someone opens the door a second, letting in a
    stave of a song, then slams the door shut.* THE
    PLAYER, *who has turned, gloomily, starts to rise.*
    DICKON *moves in his sleep, sighs heavily, and settles
    his cheek against* THE PLAYER'S *shoes.* THE PLAYER
    *looks down for a moment. Then he sits again, look-
    ing now at the fire, now at the boy, whose hair he
    touches.*]

THE PLAYER.
So, heavy-head. You bid me think my thought
Twice over; keep me by, a heavy heart,
As ballast for thy dream. Well, I will watch . . .
Like slandered Providence. Nay, I'll not be
The prop to fail thy trust untenderly,
After a troubled day. . . .
                          Nay, rest you here.

[THE CURTAIN.]

THE LITTLE MAN

By
JOHN GALSWORTHY

"Close by the Greek temples at Paestum there are violets that seem redder, and sweeter, than any ever seen—as though they have sprung up out of the footprints of some old pagan goddess; but under the April sun, in a Devonshire lane, the little blue scentless violets capture every bit as much of the spring." Affection for the West country that was the home of John Galsworthy's ancestors heightens the glamour of this enchanting bit of writing from one of his essays. As he himself has said, the Galsworthys have been in Devonshire as far back as records go—"since the flood of Saxons at all events." He was born, though, at Coombe in Surrey in 1867. From 1881 to 1886, he was at Harrow where he did well at work and games. He was graduated with an honor degree in law from New College, Oxford, in 1889. Following his father's example, he took up the law and was called to the bar (Lincoln's Inn) in 1890. "I read," he says, "in various chambers, practised almost not at all, and disliked my profession thoroughly."

For nearly two years thereafter, Galsworthy traveled, visiting among other places, Russia, Canada, Australia, New Zealand, the Fiji Islands, and South Africa. On a sailing-ship plying between Adelaide and the Cape he met and made a friend of the novelist, Joseph Conrad, then still a sailor. Galsworthy was soon to become a writer himself, publishing his first novel in 1899. Since that date he has written novels, plays, essays, and verse that have made him famous.[1] Through his writings he has become a great social force. In this respect his influence resembles that of Charles Dickens. He has made people who read his books or see his plays acted think about the justice or injustice of institutions commonly accepted without a question. The presentation of his play *Justice* (1909), moved the Home Secretary of the day, Winston Churchill, to put into effect several important reforms affecting the English prison system.

[1] For a short bibliography, see Sheila Kaye-Smith, *John Galsworthy*, London, 1916.

THE LITTLE MAN

The Little Man, no less a socializing agency in its way, was produced in New York at Maxine Elliott's Theatre in February, 1917, as a curtain raiser to G. K. Chesterton's play, *Magic.* The part of the Little Man himself was taken by O. P. Heggie, one of the most intelligent and distinguished actors on the English-speaking stage. J. Ranken Towse, reviewing the performance for the Saturday Magazine of the *New York Evening Post,* on February 17, 1917, wrote: " Another entertainment of notable excellence is that provided by the double bill at Maxine Elliott's Theatre, consisting of Galsworthy's *The Little Man* and Chesterton's *Magic.* Here are two plays of diverse character and superior quality, in which some highly intelligent and artistic acting is done by Mr. O. P. Heggie. Some sensitive reviewers have found cause of offense in Mr. Galsworthy's somewhat fanciful American, but the dramatist has been equally disrespectful in his handling of Germans, Dutch, and English. The value and significance of the piece, of course, are to be looked for, not in its broad humors—which are largely conventional—but in the ethical and moral lesson and profound social philosophy which they suggest and illustrate." It is hard to sympathize with the " sensitive reviewers," though to the native ear, to be sure, the utterances of the American lack verisimilitude. The author of *The Little Man* has even been humorously reproached with using the speech of Deadwood Dick for his model.

The play was also given quite recently, during the season of 1920-21, as part of the repertory at the Everyman Theatre in London. On the programs invariably appears the note which is prefixed also to this as to every printed version. It explains carefully that this play was written before the days of the Great War. This note bespeaks the playwright's perfect detachment which is, as has been said, " an artistic device, not a matter of divine indifference." Yet the satire does seem to be directed, incidentally at least, against certain familiar national characteristics, for it is the humanity of the Little Man, whose mixed ancestry is described by the American as being " a bit streaky," that puts to shame the various types of human arrogance and indifference with which he is surrounded.

THE LITTLE MAN *

SCENE I.—*Afternoon, on the departure platform of an Austrian railway station. At several little tables outside the buffet persons are taking refreshment, served by a pale young waiter. On a seat against the wall of the buffet a woman of lowly station is sitting beside two large bundles, on one of which she has placed her baby, swathed in a black shawl.*

WAITER [*approaching a table whereat sit an English traveler and his wife*]. Zwei Kaffee?
ENGLISHMAN [*paying*]. Thanks. [*To his wife, in an Oxford voice.*] Sugar?
ENGLISHWOMAN [*in a Cambridge voice*]. One.
AMERICAN TRAVELER [*with field-glasses and a pocket camera—from another table*]. Waiter, I'd like to have you get my eggs. I've been sitting here quite a while.
WAITER. Yes, sare.
GERMAN TRAVELER. Kellner, bezahlen! [*His voice is, like his mustache, stiff and brushed up at the ends. His figure also is stiff and his hair a little gray; clearly once, if not now, a colonel.*]
WAITER. Komm' gleich! [*The baby on the bundle wails. The mother takes it up to soothe it. A young, red-cheeked Dutchman at the fourth table stops eating and laughs.*]
AMERICAN. My eggs! Get a wiggle on you!
WAITER. Yes, sare. [*He rapidly recedes. A* LITTLE MAN *in a soft hat is seen to the right of the tables. He stands a moment looking after the hurrying waiter, then seats himself at the fifth table.*]
ENGLISHMAN [*looking at his watch*]. Ten minutes more.

* AUTHOR'S NOTE

Since it is just possible that someone may think *The Little Man* has a deep, dark reference to the war, it may be as well to state that this whimsey was written in October, 1913.

ENGLISHWOMAN. Bother!
AMERICAN [*addressing them*]. 'Pears as if they'd a prejudice against eggs here, anyway. [*The English look at him, but do not speak.*]
GERMAN [*in creditable English*]. In these places man can get nothing. [*The* WAITER *comes flying back with a compote for the* DUTCH YOUTH, *who pays.*]
GERMAN. Kellner, bezahlen!
WAITER. Eine Krone sechzig. [*The* GERMAN *pays.*]
AMERICAN [*rising, and taking out his watch—blandly*]. See here! If I don't get my eggs before this watch ticks twenty, there'll be another waiter in heaven.
WAITER [*flying*]. Komm' gleich!
AMERICAN [*seeking sympathy*]. I'm gettin' kind of mad! [*The* ENGLISHMAN *halves his newspaper and hands the advertisement half to his wife. The* BABY *wails. The* MOTHER *rocks it. The* DUTCH YOUTH *stops eating and laughs. The* GERMAN *lights a cigarette. The* LITTLE MAN *sits motionless, nursing his hat. The* WAITER *comes flying back with the eggs and places them before the* AMERICAN.]
AMERICAN [*putting away his watch*]. Good! I don't like trouble. How much? [*He pays and eats. The* WAITER *stands a moment at the edge of the platform and passes his hand across his brow. The* LITTLE MAN *eyes him and speaks gently.*]
LITTLE MAN. Herr Ober! [*The* WAITER *turns.*] Might I have a glass of beer?
WAITER. Yes, sare.
LITTLE MAN. Thank you very much. [*The* WAITER *goes.*]
AMERICAN [*pausing in the deglutition of his eggs—affably*]. Pardon me, sir; I'd like to have you tell me why you called that little bit of a feller " Herr Ober." Reckon you would know what that means? Mr. Head Waiter.
LITTLE MAN. Yes, yes.
AMERICAN. I smile.
LITTLE MAN. Oughtn't I to call him that?
GERMAN [*abruptly*]. Nein—Kellner.
AMERICAN. Why, yes! Just " waiter." [*The* ENGLISHWOMAN *looks round her paper for a second. The* DUTCH YOUTH *stops eating and laughs. The* LITTLE MAN *gazes from face to face and nurses his hat.*]

LITTLE MAN. I didn't want to hurt his feelings.
GERMAN. Gott!
AMERICAN. In my country we're vurry democratic—but that's quite a proposition.
ENGLISHMAN [*handling coffee-pot, to his wife*]. More?
ENGLISHWOMAN. No, thanks.
GERMAN [*abruptly*]. These fellows—if you treat them in this manner, at once they take liberties. You see, you will not get your beer. [*As he speaks the* WAITER *returns, bringing the* LITTLE MAN'S *beer, then retires.*]
AMERICAN. That 'pears to be one up to democracy. [*To the* LITTLE MAN.] I judge you go in for brotherhood?
LITTLE MAN [*startled*]. Oh, no! I never—
AMERICAN. I take considerable stock in Leo Tolstoi myself. Grand man—grand-souled apparatus. But I guess you've got to pinch those waiters some to make 'em skip. [*To the* ENGLISH, *who have carelessly looked his way for a moment.*] You'll appreciate that, the way he acted about my eggs. [*The* ENGLISH *make faint motions with their chins, and avert their eyes. To the* WAITER, *who is standing at the door of the buffet.*] Waiter! Flash of beer—jump, now!
WAITER. Komm' gleich!
GERMAN. Cigarren!
WAITER. Schön. [*He disappears.*]
AMERICAN [*affably—to the* LITTLE MAN]. Now, if I don't get that flash of beer quicker'n you got yours, I shall admire.
GERMAN [*abruptly*]. Tolstoi is nothing—nichts! No good! Ha?
AMERICAN [*relishing the approach of argument*]. Well, that is a matter of tempérament. Now, I'm all for equality. See that poor woman there—vurry humble woman—there she sits among us with her baby. Perhaps you'd like to locate her somewhere else?
GERMAN [*shrugging*]. Tolstoi is sentimentalisch. Nietzsche is the true philosopher, the only one.
AMERICAN. Well, that's quite in the prospectus—vurry stimulating party—old Nietzsch—virgin mind. But give me Leo! [*He turns to the red-cheeked youth.*] What do you opine, sir? I guess by your labels, you'll be Dutch. Do they read Tolstoi in your country? [*The* DUTCH YOUTH *laughs.*]

AMERICAN. That is a vurry luminous answer.
GERMAN. Tolstoi is nothing. Man should himself express. He must push—he must be strong.
AMERICAN. That is so. In Amurrica we believe in virility; we like a man to expand—to cultivate his soul. But we believe in brotherhood too; we're vurry democratic. We draw the line at niggers; but we aspire, we're vurry high-souled. Social barriers and distinctions we've not much use for.
ENGLISHMAN. Do you feel a draught?
ENGLISHWOMAN [*with a shiver of her shoulder toward the* AMERICAN]. I do—rather.
GERMAN. Wait! You are a young people.
AMERICAN. That is so; there are no flies on us. [*To the* LITTLE MAN, *who has been gazing eagerly from face to face.*] Say! I'd like to have you give us your sentiments in relation to the duty of man. [*The* LITTLE MAN *fidgets, and is about to open his mouth.*]
AMERICAN. For example—is it your opinion that we should kill off the weak and diseased, and all that can't jump around?
GERMAN [*nodding*]. Ja, ja! That is coming.
LITTLE MAN [*looking from face to face*]. They might be me. [*The* DUTCH YOUTH *laughs.*]
AMERICAN [*reproving him with a look*]. That's true humility. 'Tisn't grammar. Now, here's a proposition that brings it nearer the bone: Would you step out of your way to help them when it was liable to bring you trouble?
GERMAN. Nein, nein! That is stupid.
LITTLE MAN [*eager but wistful*]. I'm afraid not. Of course one wants to—
GERMAN. Nein, nein! That is stupid! What is the duty?
LITTLE MAN. There was St. Francis d'Assisi and St. Julien l'Hospitalier, and—
AMERICAN. Vurry lofty dispositions. Guess they died of them. [*He rises.*] Shake hands, sir—my name is— [*He hands a card.*] I am an ice-machine maker. [*He shakes the* LITTLE MAN'S *hand.*] I like your sentiments—I feel kind of brotherly. [*Catching sight of the* WAITER *appearing in the doorway.*] Waiter, where to h—ll is that flash of beer?
GERMAN. Cigarren!
WAITER. Komm' gleich! [*He vanishes.*]
ENGLISHMAN [*consulting watch*]. Train's late.

ENGLISHWOMAN. Really! Nuisance! [*A station* POLICE-MAN, *very square and uniformed, passes and repasses.*]

AMERICAN [*resuming his seat—to the* GERMAN]. Now, we don't have so much of that in Amurrica. Guess we feel more to trust in human nature.

GERMAN. Ah! ha! you will bresently find there is nothing in him but self.

LITTLE MAN [*wistfully*]. Don't you believe in human nature?

AMERICAN. Vurry stimulating question. That invites remark. [*He looks round for opinions. The* DUTCH YOUTH *laughs.*]

ENGLISHMAN [*holding out his half of the paper to his wife*]. Swap! [*His wife swaps.*]

GERMAN. In human nature I believe so far as I can see him—no more.

AMERICAN. Now that 'pears to me kind o' blasphemy. I'm vurry idealistic; I believe in heroism. I opine there's not one of us settin' around here that's not a hero—give him the occasion.

LITTLE MAN. Oh! Do you believe that?

AMERICAN. Well! I judge a hero is just a person that'll help another at the expense of himself. That's a vurry simple definition. Take that poor woman there. Well, now, she's a heroine, I guess. She would die for her baby any old time.

GERMAN. Animals will die for their babies. That is nothing.

AMERICAN. Vurry true. I carry it further. I postulate we would all die for that baby if a locomotive was to trundle up right here and try to handle it. I'm an idealist. [*To the* GERMAN.] I guess *you* don't know how good you are. [*As the* GERMAN *is twisting up the ends of his mustache—to the* ENGLISHWOMAN.] I should like to have you express an opinion, ma'am. This is a high subject.

ENGLISHWOMAN. I beg your pardon.

AMERICAN. The English are vurry humanitarian; they have a vurry high sense of duty. So have the Germans, so have the Amurricans. [*To the* DUTCH YOUTH.] I judge even in your little country they have that. This is a vurry civilized epoch. It is an epoch of equality and high-toned ideals. [*To the* LITTLE MAN.] What is *your* nationality, sir?

LITTLE MAN. I'm afraid I'm nothing particular. My father was half-English and half-American, and my mother half-German and half-Dutch.
AMERICAN. My! That's a bit streaky, any old way. [*The* POLICEMAN *passes again.*] Now, I don't believe we've much use any more for those gentlemen in buttons, not amongst the civilized peoples. We've grown kind of mild—we don't think of self as we used to do. [*The* WAITER *has appeared in the doorway.*]
GERMAN [*in a voice of thunder*]. Cigarren! Donnerwetter!
AMERICAN [*shaking his fist at the vanishing* WAITER]. That flash of beer!
WAITER. Komm' gleich!
AMERICAN. A little more, and he will join George Washington! I was about to remark when he intruded: The kingdom of Christ nowadays is quite a going concern. The Press is vurry enlightened. We are mighty near to universal brotherhood. The colonel here [*he indicates the* GERMAN], he doesn't know what a lot of stock he holds in that proposition. He is a man of blood and iron, but give him an opportunity to be magnanimous, and he'll be right there. Oh, sir! yes. [*The* GERMAN, *with a profound mixture of pleasure and cynicism, brushes up the ends of his mustache.*]
LITTLE MAN. I wonder. One wants to, but somehow— [*He shakes his head.*]
AMERICAN. You seem kind of skeery about that. You've had experience maybe. The flesh is weak. I'm an optimist— I think we're bound to make the devil hum in the near future. I opine we shall occasion a good deal of trouble to that old party. There's about to be a holocaust of selfish interests. We're out for high sacrificial business. The colonel there with old-man Nietzsch—he won't know himself. There's going to be a vurry sacred opportunity. [*As he speaks, the voice of a* RAILWAY OFFICIAL *is heard in the distance calling out in German. It approaches, and the words become audible.*]
GERMAN [*startled*]. Der Teufel! [*He gets up, and seizes the bag beside him. The* STATION OFFICIAL *has appeared, he stands for a moment casting his commands at the seated group. The* DUTCH YOUTH *also rises, and takes his coat and hat. The* OFFICIAL *turns on his heel and retires, still issuing directions.*]

ENGLISHMAN. What does he say?
GERMAN. Our drain has come in, de oder platform; only one minute we haf. [*All have risen in a fluster.*]
AMERICAN. Now, that's vurry provoking. I won't get that flash of beer. [*There is a general scurry to gather coats and hats and wraps, during which the lowly woman is seen making desperate attempts to deal with her baby and the two large bundles. Quite defeated, she suddenly puts all down, wrings her hands, and cries out: " Herr Jesu! Hilfe!" The flying procession turn their heads at that strange cry.*]
AMERICAN. What's that? Help? [*He continues to run. The* LITTLE MAN *spins round, rushes back, picks up baby and bundle on which it was seated.*]
LITTLE MAN. Come along, good woman, come along! [*The woman picks up the other bundle and they run. The* WAITER, *appearing in the doorway with the bottle of beer, watches with his tired smile.*]

SCENE II.—*A second-class compartment of a corridor carriage, in motion. In it are seated the* ENGLISHMAN *and his wife, opposite each other at the corridor end, she with her face to the engine, he with his back. Both are somewhat protected from the rest of the travelers by newspapers. Next to her sits the* GERMAN, *and opposite him sits the* AMERICAN; *next the* AMERICAN *in one window corner is seated the* DUTCH YOUTH; *the other window corner is taken by the* GERMAN'S *bag. The silence is only broken by the slight rushing noise of the train's progression and the crackling of the English newspapers.*

AMERICAN [*turning to the* DUTCH YOUTH]. Guess I'd like that winder raised; it's kind of chilly after that old run they gave us. [*The* DUTCH YOUTH *laughs, and goes through the motions of raising the window. The* ENGLISH *regard the operation with uneasy irritation. The* GERMAN *opens his bag, which reposes on the corner seat next him, and takes out a book.*]
AMERICAN. The Germans are great readers. Vurry stimulating practice. I read most anything myself! [*The* GERMAN *holds up the book so that the title may be read.*] " Don Quixote "—fine book. We Amurricans take considerable stock

in old man Quixote. Bit of a wild-cat—but we don't laugh at him.

GERMAN. He is dead. Dead as a sheep. A good thing, too.

AMERICAN. In Amurrica we have still quite an amount of chivalry.

GERMAN. Chivalry is nothing—sentimentalisch. In modern days—no good. A man must push, he must pull.

AMERICAN. So you say. But I judge your form of chivalry is sacrifice to the state. We allow more freedom to the individual soul. Where there's something little and weak, we feel it kind of noble to give up to it. That way we feel elevated. [*As he speaks there is seen in the corridor doorway the* LITTLE MAN, *with the* WOMAN'S BABY *still on his arm and the bundle held in the other hand. He peers in anxiously. The* ENGLISH, *acutely conscious, try to dissociate themselves from his presence with their papers. The* DUTCH YOUTH *laughs.*]

GERMAN. Ach! So!

AMERICAN. Dear me!

LITTLE MAN. Is there room? I can't find a seat.

AMERICAN. Why, yes! There's a seat for one.

LITTLE MAN [*depositing bundle outside, and heaving* BABY]. May I?

AMERICAN. Come right in! [*The* GERMAN *sulkily moves his bag. The* LITTLE MAN *comes in and seats himself gingerly.*]

AMERICAN. Where's the mother?

LITTLE MAN [*ruefully*]. Afraid she got left behind. [*The* DUTCH YOUTH *laughs. The* ENGLISH *unconsciously emerge from their newspapers.*]

AMERICAN. My! That would appear to be quite a domestic incident. [*The* ENGLISHMAN *suddenly utters a profound* "Ha, Ha!" *and disappears behind his paper. And that paper and the one opposite are seen to shake, and little squirls and squeaks emerge.*]

GERMAN. And you haf got her bundle, and her baby. Ha! [*He cackles dryly.*]

AMERICAN [*gravely*]. I smile. I guess Providence has played it pretty low down on you. I judge it's acted real mean. [*The* BABY *wails, and the* LITTLE MAN *jigs it with a sort of gentle desperation, looking apologetically from face to face. His wistful glance renews the fire of merriment wherever it alights.*

The AMERICAN *alone preserves a gravity which seems incapable of being broken.*]

AMERICAN. Maybe you'd better get off right smart and restore that baby. There's nothing can act madder than a mother.

LITTLE MAN. Poor thing; yes! What she must be suffering! [*A gale of laughter shakes the carriage. The* ENGLISH *for a moment drop their papers, the better to indulge. The* LITTLE MAN *smiles a wintry smile.*]

AMERICAN [*in a lull*]. How did it eventuate?

LITTLE MAN. We got there just as the train was going to start; and I jumped, thinking I could help her up. But it moved too quickly, and—and—left her. [*The gale of laughter blows up again.*]

AMERICAN. Guess I'd have thrown the baby out.

LITTLE MAN. I was afraid the poor little thing might break. [*The* BABY *wails; the* LITTLE MAN *heaves it; the gale of laughter blows.*]

AMERICAN [*gravely*]. It's highly entertaining—not for the baby. What kind of an old baby is it, anyway? [*He sniffs.*] I judge it's a bit—niffy.

LITTLE MAN. Afraid I've hardly looked at it yet.

AMERICAN. Which end up is it?

LITTLE MAN. Oh! I think the right end. Yes, yes, it is.

AMERICAN. Well, that's something. Guess I should hold it out of winder a bit. Vurry excitable things, babies!

ENGLISHWOMAN [*galvanized*]. No, no!

ENGLISHMAN [*touching her knee*]. My dear!

AMERICAN. You are right, ma'am. I opine there's a draught out there. This baby is precious. We've all of us got stock in this baby in a manner of speaking. This is a little bit of universal brotherhood. Is it a woman baby?

LITTLE MAN. I—I can only see the top of its head.

AMERICAN. You can't always tell from that. It looks kind of over-wrapped-up. Maybe it had better be unbound.

GERMAN. Nein, nein, nein!

AMERICAN. I think you are vurry likely right, colonel. It might be a pity to unbind that baby. I guess the lady should be consulted in this matter.

ENGLISHWOMAN. Yes, yes, of course—I—

ENGLISHMAN [*touching her*]. Let it be! Little beggar seems all right.

AMERICAN. That would seem only known to Providence at this moment. I judge it might be due to humanity to look at its face.

LITTLE MAN [*gladly*]. It's sucking my finger. There, there—nice little thing—there!

AMERICAN. I would surmise you have created babies in your leisure moments, sir?

LITTLE MAN. Oh! no—indeed, no.

AMERICAN. Dear me! That is a loss. [*Addressing himself to the carriage at large.*] I think we may esteem ourselves fortunate to have this little stranger right here with us; throws a vurry tender and beautiful light on human nature. Demónstrates what a hold the little and weak have upon us nowadays. The colonel here—a man of blood and iron—there he sits quite ca'm next door to it. [*He sniffs.*] Now, this baby is rather chastening—that is a sign of grace, in the colonel—that is true heroism.

LITTLE MAN [*faintly*]. I—I can see its face a little now. [*All bend forward.*]

AMERICAN. What sort of a physiognomy has it, anyway?

LITTLE MAN [*still faintly*]. I don't see anything but—but spots.

GERMAN. Oh! Ha! Pfui! [*The* DUTCH YOUTH *laughs.*]

AMERICAN. I am told that is not uncommon amongst babies. Perhaps we could have you inform us, ma'am.

ENGLISHWOMAN. Yes, of course—only—what sort of—

LITTLE MAN. They seem all over its— [*At the slight recoil of everyone.*] I feel sure it's—it's quite a good baby underneath.

AMERICAN. That will be rather difficult to come at. I'm just a bit sensitive. I've vurry little use for affections of the epidermis.

GERMAN. Pfui! [*He has edged away as far as he can get, and is lighting a big cigar. The* DUTCH YOUTH *draws his legs back.*]

AMERICAN [*also taking out a cigar*]. I guess it would be well to fumigate this carriage. Does it suffer, do you think?

LITTLE MAN [*peering*]. Really, I don't—I'm not sure—

THE LITTLE MAN

I know so little about babies. I think it would have a nice expression—if—if it showed.
AMERICAN. Is it kind of boiled-looking?
LITTLE MAN. Yes—yes, it is.
AMERICAN [*looking gravely round*]. I judge this baby has the measles. [*The* GERMAN *screws himself spasmodically against the arm of the* ENGLISHWOMAN'S *seat.*]
ENGLISHWOMAN. Poor little thing! Shall I—? [*She half-rises.*]
ENGLISHMAN [*touching her*]. No, no— Dash it!
AMERICAN. I honor your emotion, ma'am. It does credit to us all. But I sympathize with your husband too. The measles is a vurry important pestilence in connection with a grown woman.
LITTLE MAN. It likes my finger awfully. Really, it's rather a sweet baby.
AMERICAN [*sniffing*]. Well, that would appear to be quite a question. About them spots, now? Are they rosy?
LITTLE MAN. No—o; they're dark, almost black.
GERMAN. Gott! Typhus! [*He bounds up onto the arm of the* ENGLISHWOMAN'S *seat.*]
AMERICAN. Typhus! That's quite an indisposition! [*The* DUTCH YOUTH *rises suddenly, and bolts out into the corridor. He is followed by the* GERMAN, *puffing clouds of smoke. The* ENGLISH *and* AMERICAN *sit a moment longer without speaking. The* ENGLISHWOMAN'S *face is turned with a curious expression—half-pity, half-fear—toward the* LITTLE MAN. *Then the* ENGLISHMAN *gets up.*]
ENGLISHMAN. Bit stuffy for you here, dear, isn't it? [*He puts his arm through hers, raises her, and almost pushes her through the doorway. She goes, still looking back.*]
AMERICAN [*gravely*]. There's nothing I admire more'n courage. Guess I'll go and smoke in the corridor. [*As he goes out the* LITTLE MAN *looks very wistfully after him. Screwing up his mouth and nose, he holds the* BABY *away from him and wavers; then rising, he puts it on the seat opposite and goes through the motions of letting down the window. Having done so he looks at the* BABY, *who has begun to wail. Suddenly he raises his hands and clasps them, like a child praying. Since, however, the* BABY *does not stop wailing, he hovers over it in indecision; then, picking it up, sits down again to dandle it,*

with his face turned toward the open window. Finding that it still wails, he begins to sing to it in a cracked little voice. It is charmed at once. While he is singing, the AMERICAN *appears in the corridor. Letting down the passage window, he stands there in the doorway with the draught blowing his hair and the smoke of his cigar all about him. The* LITTLE MAN *stops singing and shifts the shawl higher, to protect the* BABY'S *head from the draught.*]

AMERICAN [*gravely*]. This is the most sublime spectacle I have ever envisaged. There ought to be a récord of this. [*The* LITTLE MAN *looks at him, wondering.*] We have here a most stimulating epitome of our marvelous advance toward universal brotherhood. You are typical, sir, of the sentiments of modern Christianity. You illústrate the deepest feelings in the heart of every man. [*The* LITTLE MAN *rises with the* BABY *and a movement of approach.*] Guess I'm wanted in the dining-car. [*He vanishes.*] *The* LITTLE MAN *sits down again, but back to the engine, away from the draught, and looks out of the window, patiently jogging the* BABY *on his knee.*]

SCENE III.—*An arrival platform. The* LITTLE MAN, *with the* BABY *and the bundle, is standing disconsolate, while travelers pass and luggage is being carried by. A* STATION OFFICIAL, *accompanied by a* POLICEMAN, *appears from a doorway, behind him.*

OFFICIAL [*consulting telegram in his hand*]. Das ist der Herr. [*They advance to the* LITTLE MAN.]
OFFICIAL. Sie haben einen Buben gestohlen?
LITTLE MAN. I only speak English and American.
OFFICIAL. Dies ist nicht Ihr Bube? [*He touches the* BABY.]
LITTLE MAN [*shaking his head*]. Take care—it's ill. [*The man does not understand.*] Ill—the baby—
OFFICIAL [*shaking his head*]. Verstehe nicht. Dis is nod your baby? No?
LITTLE MAN [*shaking his head violently*]. No, it is not. No.
OFFICIAL [*tapping the telegram*]. Gut! You are 'rested. [*He signs to the* POLICEMAN, *who takes the* LITTLE MAN'S *arm.*]
LITTLE MAN. Why? I don't want the poor baby.

OFFICIAL [*lifting the bundle*]. Dies ist nicht Ihr Gepäck —pag?
LITTLE MAN. No.
OFFICIAL. Gut. You are 'rested.
LITTLE MAN. I only took it for the poor woman. I'm not a thief—I'm—I'm—
OFFICIAL [*shaking head*]. Verstehe nicht. [*The* LITTLE MAN *tries to tear his hair. The disturbed* BABY *wails.*]
LITTLE MAN [*dandling it as best he can*]. There, there— poor, poor!
OFFICIAL. Halt still! You are 'rested. It is all right.
LITTLE MAN. Where is the mother?
OFFICIAL. She comm by next drain. Das telegram say: Halt einen Herrn mit schwarzem Buben und schwarzem Gepäck. 'Rest gentleman mit black baby und black—pag. [*The* LITTLE MAN *turns up his eyes to heaven.*]
OFFICIAL. Komm mit us. [*They take the* LITTLE MAN *toward the door from which they have come. A voice stops them.*]
AMERICAN [*speaking from as far away as may be*]. Just a moment! [*The* OFFICIAL *stops; the* LITTLE MAN *also stops and sits down on a bench against the wall. The* POLICEMAN *stands stolidly beside him. The* AMERICAN *approaches a step or two, beckoning; the* OFFICIAL *goes up to him.*]
AMERICAN. Guess you've got an angel from heaven there! What's the gentleman in buttons for?
OFFICIAL. Was ist das?
AMERICAN. Is there anybody here that can understand Amurrican?
OFFICIAL. Verstehe nicht.
AMERICAN. Well, just watch my gestures. I was saying [*he points to the* LITTLE MAN, *then makes gestures of flying*], you have an angel from heaven there. You have there a man in whom Gawd [*he points upward*] takes quite an amount of stock. This is a vurry precious man. You have no call to arrest him [*he makes the gesture of arrest*]. No, sir. Providence has acted pretty mean, loading off that baby on him [*he makes the motion of dandling*]. The little man has a heart of gold. [*He points to his heart, and takes out a gold coin.*]
OFFICIAL [*thinking he is about to be bribed*]. Aber, das ist zu viel!

AMERICAN. Now, don't rattle me! [*Pointing to the* LITTLE MAN.] Man [*pointing to his heart*] Herz [*pointing to the coin*] von Gold. This is a flower of the field—he don't want no gentleman in buttons to pluck him up. [*A little crowd is gathering, including the two* ENGLISH, *the* GERMAN, *and the* DUTCH YOUTH.]

OFFICIAL. Verstehe absolut nichts. [*He taps the telegram.*] Ich muss mein duty do.

AMERICAN. But I'm telling you. This is a good man. This is probably the best man on Gawd's airth.

OFFICIAL. Das macht nichts—gut or no gut, I muss mein duty do. [*He turns to go toward the* LITTLE MAN.]

AMERICAN. Oh! Vurry well, arrest him; do your duty. This baby has typhus. [*At the word "typhus" the* OFFICIAL *stops.*]

AMERICAN [*making gestures*]. First-class typhus, black typhus, schwarzen typhus. Now you have it. I'm kind o' sorry for you and the gentleman in buttons. Do your duty!

OFFICIAL. Typhus? Der Bub'—die baby hat typhus?

AMERICAN. I'm telling you.

OFFICIAL. Gott im Himmel!

AMERICAN [*spotting the* GERMAN *in the little throng*]. Here's a gentleman will corroborate me.

OFFICIAL [*much disturbed, and signing to the* POLICEMAN *to stand clear*]. Typhus! Aber das ist grässlich!

AMERICAN. I kind o' thought you'd feel like that.

OFFICIAL. Die Sanitätsmachine! Gleich! [*A* PORTER *goes to get it. From either side the broken half-moon of persons stand gazing at the* LITTLE MAN, *who sits unhappily dandling the* BABY *in the center.*]

OFFICIAL [*raising his hands*]. Was zu thun?

AMERICAN. Guess you'd better isolate the baby. [*A silence, during which the* LITTLE MAN *is heard faintly whistling and clucking to the* BABY.]

OFFICIAL [*referring once more to his telegram*]. 'Rest gentleman mit black baby. [*Shaking his head.*] Wir must de gentleman hold. [*To the* GERMAN.] Bitte, mein Herr, sagen Sie ihm, den Buben zu niedersetzen. [*He makes the gesture of deposit.*]

GERMAN [*to the* LITTLE MAN]. He say: Put down the

baby. [*The* LITTLE MAN *shakes his head, and continues to dandle the* BABY.]
OFFICIAL. Sie müssen—you must. [*The* LITTLE MAN *glowers, in silence.*]
ENGLISHMAN [*in background—muttering*]. Good man!
GERMAN. His spirit ever denies; er will nicht.
OFFICIAL [*again making his gesture*]. Aber er muss! [*The* LITTLE MAN *makes a face at him.*] Sag' ihm: Instantly put down baby, and komm' mit us. [*The* BABY *wails.*]
LITTLE MAN. Leave the poor ill baby here alone? Be-be-be- d—d first!
AMERICAN [*jumping onto a trunk—with enthusiasm*]. Bully! [*The* ENGLISH *clap their hands; the* DUTCH YOUTH *laughs. The* OFFICIAL *is muttering, greatly incensed.*]
AMERICAN. What does that body-snatcher say?
GERMAN. He say this man use the baby to save himself from arrest. Very smart—he say.
AMERICAN. I judge you do him an injustice. [*Showing off the* LITTLE MAN *with a sweep of his arm.*] This is a vurry white man. He's got a black baby, and he won't leave it in the lurch. Guess we would all act noble, that way, give us the chance. [*The* LITTLE MAN *rises, holding out the* BABY, *and advances a step or two. The half-moon at once gives, increasing its size; the* AMERICAN *climbs onto a higher trunk. The* LITTLE MAN *retires and again sits down.*]
AMERICAN [*addressing the* OFFICIAL]. Guess you'd better go out of business and wait for the mother.
OFFICIAL [*stamping his foot*]. Die Mutter sall 'rested be for taking out baby mit typhus. Ha! [*To the* LITTLE MAN.] Put ze baby down! [*The* LITTLE MAN *smiles.*] Do you 'ear?
AMERICAN [*addressing the* OFFICIAL]. Now, see here. 'Pears to me you don't suspicion just how beautiful this is. Here we have a man giving his life for that old baby that's got no claim on him. This is not a baby of his own making. No, sir, this a vurry Christ-like proposition in the gentleman.
OFFICIAL. Put ze baby down, or ich will gommand someone it to do.
AMERICAN. That will be vurry interesting to watch.
OFFICIAL [*to* POLICEMAN]. Nehmen Sie den Buben. Dake it vrom him. [*The* POLICEMAN *mutters, but does not.*]

AMERICAN [*to the* GERMAN]. Guess I lost that.
GERMAN. He say he is not his officer.
AMERICAN. That just tickles me to death.
OFFICIAL [*looking round*]. Vill nobody dake ze Bub'?
ENGLISHWOMAN [*moving a step—faintly*]. Yes—I—
ENGLISHMAN [*grasping her arm*]. By Jove! Will you!
OFFICIAL [*gathering himself for a great effort to take the* BABY, *and advancing two steps*]. Zen I gommand you— [*He stops and his voice dies away.*] Zit dere!
AMERICAN. My! That's wonderful. What a man this is! What a sublime sense of duty! [*The* DUTCH YOUTH *laughs. The* OFFICIAL *turns on him, but as he does so the* MOTHER *of the* BABY *is seen hurrying.*]
MOTHER. Ach! Ach! Mei' Bubi! [*Her face is illumined; she is about to rush to the* LITTLE MAN.]
OFFICIAL [*to the* POLICEMAN]. Nimm die Frau! [*The* POLICEMAN *catches hold of the* WOMAN.]
OFFICIAL [*to the frightened* WOMAN]. Warum haben Sie einen Buben mit Typhus mit ausgebracht?
AMERICAN [*eagerly, from his perch*]. What was that? I don't want to miss any.
GERMAN. He say: Why did you a baby with typhus with you bring out?
AMERICAN. Well, that's quite a question. [*He takes out the field-glasses slung around him and adjusts them on the* BABY.]
MOTHER [*bewildered*]. Mei' Bubi—Typhus—aber Typhus? [*She shakes her head violently.*] Nein, nein, nein! Typhus!
OFFICIAL. Er hat Typhus.
MOTHER [*shaking her head*]. Nein, nein, nein!
AMERICAN [*looking through his glasses*]. Guess she's kind of right! I judge the typhus is where the baby's slobbered on the shawl, and it's come off on him. [*The* DUTCH YOUTH *laughs.*]
OFFICIAL [*turning on him furiously*]. Er hat Typhus.
AMERICAN. Now, that's where you slop over. Come right here. [*The* OFFICIAL *mounts, and looks through the glasses.*]
AMERICAN [*to the* LITTLE MAN]. Skin out the baby's leg. If we don't locate spots on that, it'll be good enough for me. [*The* LITTLE MAN *fumbles out the* BABY'S *little white foot.*]
MOTHER. Mei' Bubi! [*She tries to break away.*]

AMERICAN. White as a banana. [*To the* OFFICIAL—*affably.*] Guess you've made kind of a fool of us with your old typhus.

OFFICIAL. Lass die Frau! [*The* POLICEMAN *lets her go, and she rushes to her* BABY.]

MOTHER. Mei' Bubi! [*The* BABY, *exchanging the warmth of the* LITTLE MAN *for the momentary chill of its* MOTHER, *wails.*]

OFFICIAL [*descending and beckoning to the* POLICEMAN]. Sie wollen den Herrn accusiren? [*The* POLICEMAN *takes the* LITTLE MAN'S *arm.*]

AMERICAN. What's that? They goin' to pinch him after all? [*The* MOTHER, *still hugging her* BABY, *who has stopped crying, gazes at the* LITTLE MAN, *who sits dazedly looking up. Suddenly she drops on her knees, and with her free hand lifts his booted foot and kisses it.*]

AMERICAN [*waving his hat*]. 'Ra! 'Ra! [*He descends swiftly, goes up to the* LITTLE MAN, *whose arm the* POLICEMAN *has dropped, and takes his hand.*] Brother, I am proud to know you. This is one of the greatest moments I have ever experienced. [*Displaying the* LITTLE MAN *to the assembled company.*] I think I sense the situation when I say that we all esteem it an honor to breathe the rather inferior atmosphere of this station here along with our little friend. I guess we shall all go home and treasure the memory of his face as the whitest thing in our museum of recollections. And perhaps this good woman will also go home and wash the face of our little brother here. I am inspired with a new faith in mankind. We can all be proud of this mutual experience; we have our share in it; we can kind of feel noble. Ladies and gentlemen, I wish to present to you a sure-enough saint—only wants a halo, to be transfigured. [*To the* LITTLE MAN.] Stand right up. [*The* LITTLE MAN *stands up bewildered. They come about him. The* OFFICIAL *bows to him, the* POLICEMAN *salutes him. The* DUTCH YOUTH *shakes his head and laughs. The* GERMAN *draws himself up very straight, and bows quickly twice. The* ENGLISHMAN *and his wife approach at least two steps, then, thinking better of it, turn to each other and recede. The* MOTHER *kisses his hand. The* PORTER *returning with the* Sanitätsmachine, *turns it on from behind, and its pinkish shower, goldened by a ray of sunlight, falls around the* LITTLE

MAN'S *head, transfiguring it as he stands with eyes upraised to see whence the portent comes.*]

AMERICAN [*rushing forward and dropping on his knees*]. Hold on just a minute! Guess I'll take a snap-shot of the miracle. [*He adjusts his pocket camera.*] This ought to look bully!

[THE CURTAIN.]

www.ingramcontent.com/pod-product-compliance
Lightning Source LLC
Chambersburg PA
CBHW022056150426
43195CB00008B/163